AFTER THE FUTURE

Contemporary Studies in Philosophy and Literature 2
Hugh J. Silverman, Editor

GENERAL EDITOR

Hugh J. Silverman, Executive Director
International Association for Philosophy and Literature

ADVISORY BOARD

After the Future

Postmodern Times and Places

Edited by
Gary Shapiro

STATE UNIVERSITY OF NEW YORK PRESS

Published by
State University of New York Press, Albany

For information, address State University of New York
Press, State University Plaza, Albany, NY 12246
Library of Congress Cataloging-in-Publication Data

After the Future: Postmodern times & places / edited by Gary
Shapiro.
p. ■■ cm.—(Contemporary studies in philosophy and literature; 2)
Bibliography: p.
Includes index.
ISBN 0–7914–0209–6. —ISBN 0–7914–0210–X (pbk.)
1. Criticism. 2. Postmodernism (Literature) 3. Literature,
Modern—20th century—History and criticism. 4. Postmodernism.
5. Philosophy, Modern—20th century. 6. Politics and literature.
I. Shapiro, Gary, 1941–   . II. Series.
PN98.P64P68 1990
801'.95'0904—dc20
89-4628
CIP

10 9 8 7 6 5 4 3 2 1

Contents

VII. QUESTIONS OF LANGUAGE

Acknowledgments

This book was constituted with the help of many people. The University of Kansas provided various forms of assistance, including the invaluable typing and secretarial skills of Janice Doores, Cindi Hodges, Pam LeRow and Beth Ridenour. Bill Martin worked tirelessly on the early stages of this project. Ted Mehl provided help in proofreading and indexing the manuscript. Lynne Margolies Shapiro reminded me at crucial points that this collection was worth assembling and that the postmodern could be fun. The "Postpositivism Group" at the University of Kansas helped in ways that they probably did not realize by demonstrating that there was a genuine desire for contemporary social and cultural thinking that transcends conventional disciplinary and professional boundaries.

Illustrations are reproduced with the generous permission of the Mary Boone Gallery and the Anselm Kiefer Studio.

Introduction

Gary Shapiro

For better or for worse, the term "postmodernism" has entered the general language of our culture. A generation or so ago, newspapers and popular magazines gestured toward the intellectual movement of the day by speaking of "existentialism" and a raft of associated concepts. One might suspect that every new tendency in thought or the arts must suffer the fate of degradation through journalism in a world where mass media provide the most fundamental social bond. But this time is different for several reasons. At least within the anglophone world, the elapsed time between the theoretical elaboration of an idea or the flowering of a cultural movement and its popularization and dissemination has been dramatically compressed. And the popular extension of postmodernism has rapidly gone beyond the arts and literary pages and into the advertising that supports them. The ads speak of "postmodern fashions"; while there may have once been an existential style—black slacks and turtle neck—there were no obvious efforts to market it as such. The plays of Beckett and Sartre were taken to be the latest word on freedom, anxiety, or the absurd, but they were also seen implicitly as high culture, demanding at least as awed and respectful an audience in the theater as Shakespeare or Ibsen. "Postmodern MTV" has effortlessly established itself as one of the many alternatives available to a mass audience that can happily co-exist with meals, love-making or financial discussions. And while other television programs—one thinks of the defunct "Max Headroom" or the fabulously popular "Moonlighting"—may not title themselves postmodern, the adjective has been frequently deployed in discussing them, not only by critics of popular culture, writing in their esoteric journals, but by the media's own analysts.

Because it is generally agreed that one of the principal tendencies of the postmodern is to relax the rigid separations that modernism insisted upon between high and popular culture (think of T. S.

Eliot's criticism or the priestcraft of the New Critics, for example), it is not surprising that it may be difficult to disentangle or even distinguish the theory and practice of postmodernism from its reception and popularization. One mark of this situation is the fact that it is with regard to architecture, an art that compels attention both by its structuring of the environment and its requirement of massive investment of resources, that postmodernism forced itself upon the public attention. Yet just as one could argue that postmodernism's straddling of the elite and popular lanes of the cultural highway is in keeping with its deepest tendencies, so one could add that these same tendencies will necessarily lead to postmodernism's becoming a kind of schizophrenic interchange, like the hyperreal traffic spaces of southern California, in which anything (and nothing) goes.

The 1987 conference on postmodernism held by the International Association for Philosophy and Literature at the University of Kansas was intended to serve not so much as a vehicle for mastering this actual and possible snarl but as a preliminary effort to chart the patterns of movement. Included in this collection are nineteen essays that explore various aspects of the postmodern situation and the discourses that it generated. In terms of subject matter the papers presented at the conference ranged diachronically from new views of the Greeks to the most recent films; in terms of topics they touched, among other things, on feminist ethics, deconstructive architecture, body art, and the question of narrativity. The essays assembled here may perhaps serve as a way of delineating some of the main directions in the traffic flow.

Certainly one of the major questions that a discourse on postmodernism must address is that of periodization. Is postmodernism to be construed as the name of an era or epoch, the successor of modernism in a lineage that goes back to the ancient and the medieval? This is perhaps the most general way of understanding the concept, and it may function both as pop *Geistesgeschichte,* as in ads for postmodern clothes, and in a very subtle neo-Marxist attempt at periodization, as in the powerful and influential analyses of Fredric Jameson. But one might also suspect that the very project of periodization itself is a distinctively modern enterprise, one that finds its paradigms in the enlightenment's story of the progress of reason and freedom, in Hegel's dialectical and spiritual version of that narrative, or in Marx's materialistic retelling of Hegel. In Jean-François Lyotard's account of *The Postmodern Condition,* the definitive characteristic of the postmodern is taken to be the rejection of such all-encompassing metanarratives. Even if a periodizing metanarrative should remain open in some respects by leaving room for epochs that would follow the postmodern, it is ineluctably modern in style. Postmodernism is engaged in a difficult and ambitious struggle with the project of periodization. It might be more aptly if barbarously named postperiodization. Such a term, a deliberate oxymoron, would have the virtue of suggesting that what is at issue are alternatives to the sequential, developmental, and unitary emplotments of modern consciousness. In various ways the essays in this collection examine some of these alternatives, exploring the possibilities of a genealogical or archeological perspective (as in Michel Foucault) or articulating the critique of teleological thought implicit in the "always already" of Martin Heidegger and Jacques Derrida.

Searching questions concerning the attempt to restore anything like a Hegelian unity of history and reason are raised in Anthony J. Cascardi's essay, which looks at Hans Blumenberg's attempt to defend the legitimacy of the modern. Cascardi considers the sort of objections that Foucault would make to even such a subtle and nuanced defense of the moral and epistemological claims of modernity in its attempt to establish itself as a normative position from which to assess all history. While not endorsing Foucault—in fact he finds that program more indebted to the modernist project than Foucault could acknowledge—Cascardi also finds Blumenberg's narrative not fully adequate to the conflicts within the presumed founding era of modernity. Mary Bittner Wiseman investigates the conflicts that arise when critics, cultural institutions, and all of us for that matter, construct narratives that will demonstrate our place with respect to the primitive. She elaborates Roland Barthes's suggestion that photography can open up a sense of an absolute past and a nondialectical sense of history. At the same time she demonstrates how such a postmodern substitution of the index for the continuous growth of meaning posited by the modern can lead to our rethinking the nature of representation, ultimately allowing us to be invaded and wounded by the past. These are not (as Hegel said) the wounds of the spirit that heal without leaving a scar, but those marks of experience without which we cannot really be said to have encountered the other.

What place will there be for the subject in the stories that might be told after renouncing the privileges of the omniscient narrator who recounts the story of history as freedom or who guides us effortlessly through the museum without walls? Carol Bernstein and Antony Easthope ask such a question in rereading some of the canonical moments of nineteenth- and twentieth-century poetry in English. In Keats's *Hyperion*, Bernstein finds that Apollo, the god of poetry, is already situated at the uncanny intersection of the modern and the postmodern. Easthope traces the decline of the transcendental subject of poetry from John Donne's *Elegies* to T. S. Eliot's *Wasteland* and finally to Ezra Pound's *Pisan Cantos*. Like Bernstein he gives us a way of seeing poems claimed by the modernist canon that frees them from the unitary, lyrical voice of the tradition, and can accordingly construe dispersal, fragmentation, and conflict in terms other than those of the pathology that modernism all too facilely invokes when it senses the faltering or failure of the transcendental subject. John Johnston offers a guide to the theory of the postmodern subject that enables such readings. Like Bernstein and Easthope he rejects the view of "vulgar postmodernism" (easily ridiculed by its critics) that there are no more subjects. But subjects are situated and contextualized; they may also be seen, as in the analysis of Deleuze and Guattari, as "desiring machines," schizophrenically living out the manifold pulses of desire, inscribing themselves in jagged territories rather than constrained by an ideological assignment to patriarchal social space.

Will traditional humanistic disciplines such as philosophy still have something to say in a context where the transcendental subject has been dislodged? The problem for philosophy would seem to be particularly acute, for it has always sought the absolute, the certain, and the universal. Alan Schrift explores the paradoxes that would be involved in philosophy now declaring itself to *be* postmodern—that is, to have attained a new set of postmodern categories of understanding and methods of analysis. The alternative, he suggests, is that, implicit in Nietzsche and explicit in Derrida, philosophy can be seen as the process or activity of challenging the figure of authority (and not merely a particular series of traditional authorities) and the deconstruction of binary oppositions. By volatilizing itself, philosophy would seem to escape the fate of prematurely declaring itself to be the final step in transcendental reflection. But the problem of philosophy living on after the surrender of its absolutistic aspirations is not limited to thought within the continental tradition. Richard Shusterman claims that Ludwig Wittgenstein became the greatest postmodern philosopher in his later work after having formulated the principle that "ethics and aesthetics are one." Richard Rorty is a contemporary heir of Wittgenstein who has attempted to think through the consequences of the collapse of foundationalism (what the continental tradition would see as a transcendental ground) and therefore has surrendered the assurance that an unassailable foundation would offer to ethics. Shusterman explores the possibility that Rorty has retained a modernist conception of organic unity in his amalgamation of the aesthetic and the ethical; and he offers some reasons for thinking that such a norm cannot be attained as easily in a world of fragmented quasi-selves "constituted by alternative, constantly changing, and often incommensurable narratives and vocabularies."

Timothy Gould further pursues the difficulties besetting the proposed marriage of philosophy and postmodernism by explicitly comparing some continental and analytical forms of this uncertain union. Gould's subject is precisely philosophy's traditional quest for purity, a quest that requires it to practice a logic of exclusion, banning otherness and difference from its privileged realm. He finds that while Richard Rorty describes the exclusionary tactics of philosophy in terms that might apply to any political or personal practice, Stanley Cavell and Jacques Derrida have attempted to articulate a more specific sense of what it is that philosophy excludes or represses; for Cavell this is "reading" and for Derrida it is "writing." These terms each convey something that Gould characterizes variously as the passive, or the feminine, which traditional philosophy would exclude in favor of a presumptive, masculine form of activity. Perhaps the becoming postmodern of philosophy is to be construed as a constant interrogation of these temptations toward exclusionary claims.

If postmodern philosophy's questioning of the division between inside and outside depends on a metaphorical sense of these prepositions, it is in contemporary architectural theory and practice that this interrogation has its most obvious, material, and public manifestations. As Edward Casey suggests, there is a far-reaching convergence between the architectonic metaphors of a foundationalist (for example, Kantian) philosophy and modernism's aim at a self-enclosed and self-sufficient structure; the rigorous interrogation of the barrier between inside and outside, foundation and ground, associated with a philosopher like Derrida finds its architectural analogue in postmodern architecture in which the relation between edifice and environing terrain is destabilized. The very construction of a Derridean text, Casey shows, with its parallel columns and insertions can be read in a way not unlike our "reading" of a postmodern architectural structure with its refusal of a centered space and a dominant style to which all details would be subordinated.

Roger Bell offers an account of one exemplary postmodern architect, Frank Gehry, who produces structures that vary the assumed interconnections of home, neighborhood, and city, which have—at least since Aristotle's *Economics* and *Politics*—formed the horizon of Western thinking about building, dwelling, and thinking. As an architectural critic and historian, Diane Ghirardo takes issue with what she sees as the inflationary claims of postmodernism. As the title of her essay, "The Deceit of Postmodern Architecture," suggests, she is attempting to renew the spirit of the modernist theory and practice that values above all authenticity and honesty in the constructions by which we shape our environments. Ghirardo's critique (like Shusterman's of Rorty) asks in effect whether anyone could really live in a postmodern construction, and she points to the fact that much "deconstructive architecture" exists only in plans and drawings, not in concrete. The answer may take some time to emerge, although it is important to note that works like those of Frank Gehry and Charles Moore (commented on by Bell and Casey) continue to have an impact.

In any case, some version of the language of postmodernism seems inevitable in accounting for contemporary art. Ever since Hegel announced that art on its highest side is a thing of the past, art has struggled to come to terms with its own history and its historicity. Postmodernism in art, Stephen Melville suggests, is to be understood as the acceptance of its own belatedness, and the rejection of any nostalgia for restoring the cultural supremacy it seemed to have in fifth-century Athens or fifteenth-century Florence. Such an art will explore the modes of rejecting or countering the assumptions of originality and creativity that dominate modern aesthetics; it will be unashamedly repetitive of the past, assimilating and appropriating the art of modernism.

If grandeur and heroism are possible in postmodern art, they may perhaps be found in a confrontation with the very power that has colonized art through the mass media or has apparently rendered it irrelevant: technology. This is the possibility that John Gilmour articulates in his attempt to situate the art of Anselm Kiefer. Kiefer, in his juxtaposition of contemporary industrial wasteland with archaic myth and of the enframing universal powers of technology with alchemy and magic, is not so much nostalgic for an earlier age as questioning the periodization that would fix art within the narrow confines of a present, in the latest room of the last wing of the museum without walls.

Vito Acconci is an artist who has often made use of technology (especially video) in order to question representation and traditional representation's most constant subject, the human body. Philip Auslander shows how Acconci's performance art in which the transformations and representations of his own body become the subject helps to expose the ideological constructions of gender and of the allegedly whole or integral body which, as critics like John Berger have shown, govern the traditions of painting as well as the general circulation of images (by advertising, journalism, and propaganda) in society.

All the artists and artistic movements just discussed are political insofar as they are postmodern and postmodern insofar as they are political; they are all engaged in questioning authorities, traditions, ideologies, and representations that are not limited to the art world. Their interrogations, however, suggest that whatever the claims of that world to be grounded in universal values, it has always been a site of strategic and political contestation. Similarly, it is possible to regard the entire postmodern intervention as a series of political gestures (so long as we do not qualify those gestures as "merely" political). Stephen David Ross, developing some thoughts of Heidegger and Foucault, presents the case that these gestures find an exemplary field in technology. This is because technology as we know it now is disruptive of the temporal continuity of past, present, and future implicitly supposed in political praxis that aims at furthering or constructing the totalistic subject of a metanarrative (this would include political thought within the Hegelian tradition, such as that of Marx and Sartre).

While asserting a claim to order and regularity unlike any previous claim, technology in practice propels us into disjoint, unpredictable futures. Jean-François Lyotard has argued that the appropriate response is to surrender the totalistic ambitions of modern politics for an indefinitely pluralistic agonistics in which partial, regional activities take the place of the absolutist aspirations of the revolutionary subject. In his critical essay Steve Fuller responds to such a position—with respect to the politics of knowledge and research—with a question, "Does it Pay to Go Postmodern If Your Neighbors do Not?" He gathers together some reasons for thinking that we have not yet fully worked out the logic of such a pluralistic model of knowledge; what is called for is a study of the deep structure of various models of pluralism analogous to those reconstructions of convergent scientific inquiry offered by philosophers like Charles Peirce and Jürgen Habermas. But how far can such pluralism go? Richard Rorty has argued that just because we can find no foundation for common values any deeper than tradition and pragmatic efficacy, that is no reason to surrender such values and the communities they serve.

Some of the most acute analysts of postmodernism, as John O'Neill points out in his essay on Daniel Bell and Fredric Jameson, have suggested that a renewal of the religious bond, or something very much like it, is necessary to halt our dangerous slide into a fragmented and incoherent social condition. In these and a number of other theorists O'Neill detects a Durkheimian nostalgia for a lost sense of community, which cuts across their more obvious and explicit identification of the conventional left and right poles of the political spectrum. Yet just as the "post" in postmodern art means that art must live on after its classical consummations without nostalgia, it would seem that postmodern culture would be generally defined as living in the long shadow of God's death without attempting to revive God.

Nietzsche not only announced the death of God; he also detected analogues of the transcendental powers and central place that God occupies in religious thought in the quest for many forms of certainty. He anticipated a poststructuralist view of language with the remark "I fear that we have not gotten rid of God, because we still believe in grammar." Language can come to play the same foundational role that the ontotheological tradition assigns to the Platonic ideas, God, the Cartesian cogito, or absolute spirit. Philosophical and artistic modernism are alike in concentrating much of their efforts on the project of articulating a pure language whose constructions would have an unquestionable force and coherence. At the same time, whether in Wittgenstein, Hofmannsthal, or Mallarmé, this quest has confronted the motivated silence or void that must be the context out of which such privileged speech or inscriptions emerge. The postmodern linguistic turn consists in challenging and interrogating this duality of the articulate and the inarticulate. Gerald Bruns details Heidegger's move in this direction by tracing his attempts to show just how uncanny—that is, how ungrammatical and unformalizable—language can be. If there were to be a final or ultimate Heideggerian word, Bruns suggests, it would not be a foundation, but a provocation to perpetual risk, like "an endless pun whose changes could never be terminated."

Focusing not on the ultimacy of language, but on the very attempt to articulate the distinction between the articulate and the inarticulate, Virgil Lokke investigates the many ways in which postmodern thinkers have understood the hinge, virgule, or slash that both links separates and marks language and its other. What Lokke's analysis does is to clarify the very multiplicity of postmodern discourses on language, risking the pun (virgule/Virgil) while exemplifying the power of naming.

Language has turned on us. It is no longer assumed to be the instrument by which we construct representations and correspondences; rather it places us in question. Postmodernism, as I suggested above, ought not to be construed as the name of the latest period of history or culture in which we could situate ourselves and confirm an achieved (if novel) identity. As in these meditations on language, it is precisely the tendency to unsettle such facile identifications by excavating the deepest structures of narrative, art, and utterance.

Part I

Postperiodization

1

History, Theory, (Post)Modernity

Anthony J. Cascardi

> "There are no witnesses to changes
> of historical epoch."
>
> **Blumenberg, *The Legitimacy of the
> Modern Age*, p. 469**

> "One can certainly wager that man
> would be erased, like a face drawn
> in sand at the edge of the sea."
>
> **Foucault, *The Order of Things*,
> p. 387**

The following pages on history and theory are meant as a contribution to the larger debate concerning the relationship between modernity and postmodernism, as it has recently been focused in the writings of Jürgen Habermas, Jean-François Lyotard, Richard Rorty, and others.[1] While these discussions have been sharpened by the increasingly apparent contradictions of the "postmodern" age, it must at the outset be said that the "problem of modernity" is now nearly two centuries old, and dates at least from Hegel's critique of "modern philosophy" as the philosophy of subjective self-consciousness that found its culminating expression in Kant. Hegel's critique of subjectivity as the basis of modernity is combined, in the *Phenomenology* and elsewhere, with a series of insights into the religious, social, and economic transformations of history, which took decisive roles in the development of the modern world: the Reformation, which claimed a part in liberating consciousness from mystification; commodity capitalism, which confirmed the "desacralization" of nature accomplished elsewhere by rational means; and the French revolution, which attempted to secure a realm of ethical freedom and thereby render concrete the notion of abstract right.

1

In Hegel's thought, modernity may properly be regarded as a realm of freedom, yet at the same time his judgment is that modernity failed to establish a legitimate social order, in part because it remained unable to reconcile its social and historical ambitions with the modes of rationality available to it. The dichotomy of history and theory is symptomatic of this failure, and it would not be too much to propose that the Hegelian dialectic was conceived in order to resolve the antinomic relationship of these terms. The French revolution remained the decisive event of modernity for Hegel, but he ultimately viewed it as a threat to the ground of philosophy itself. Thus, as Habermas incisively observed, "in order not to sacrifice philosophy to the challenge posed by the revolution, Hegel elevated revolution to the primary principle of his philosophy."[2] In this respect—and notwithstanding the fact that thinkers from Nietzsche and Heidegger to Derrida have seen in Hegel the very culmination of the philosophy of subjectivity representative of the modern age[3]—Hegel attempts to distance himself from the modern paradigm in order to reconcile its antithetical terms.

We shall in conclusion see that Hegel's critique of modernity is possible only by virtue of a "double movement," in which the totality is seen as divided into History and Reason, which are then recuperated into a self-surpassing Spiritual whole. This recuperative movement is necessary, for if philosophy is on the one hand identified with the activity of Reason, then it would seem incapable of acknowledging any world other than itself; and if on the other hand philosophy recognizes the contingent and fragmented world of human nature and history, it would seem unable to take that world as an essential manifestation of Reason. As one Hegel scholar wrote of these conflicting goals, "from the outset and throughout, the Hegelian system seems faced with the choice between saving the claims of an absolute and therefore all-comprehensive philosophic thought, but at the price of loss of any actual world besides it, and saving the contingent world of human experience at the price of reducing philosophic thought itself to finiteness."[4] To say that Hegel resolves this dilemma by recourse to "Spirit" is also to say that Hegel sacralizes human history, in effect subsuming the historical emergence of every new form of consciousness, including the self-assertion of subjective "reason," into a pattern that repeats the spiritual cycles of the Christian faith; as we shall also see, he thereby also sacrifices the historical autonomy of the modern age.

To begin, however, I want to locate the antinomy of history and theory and the philosophical "founding" of modernity in the historical emergence of reason in the philosophy of Descartes; from there we may proceed to assess the postmodern and historicist critiques of reason in the work of Hans Blumenberg and Michel Foucault.[5] Descartes identified reason as the ordering of structures and quantities, and fashioned his philosophical method along these lines, yet he also claimed that his project was radically new and marked an unprecedented achievement on the historical plane. Thus the Cartesian conception of reason may be taken as a defining characteristic of the modern age, but modernism is not reducible to it. Indeed, the "postmodern" challenge, brought sharply into focus in the work of critics such as Blumenberg and Foucault, has been to construct a vision of modernity that is not at the same time subordinate to the notion of a rationally centered whole. This is to say that any description of modernity must continue to make reference to culture as a totality, but therefore also to those elements within culture which Cartesian reason remained from the start unable to control (cf. Hegel: "what Enlightenment declares to be an error and a fiction is the very same thing as Enlightenment itself is"[6]).

Modernism so conceived is marked not only by the emergence of the "subject" and the mathematical ground that lends it support, but also by the consolidation of the powers of the absolutist state, by a redistribution of the authority of faith and science, by an increased mobility of the psyche, and by a reconception of the nature of the "literary" work of art. Together, these changes become visible in the period roughly contemporary with Descartes in the works of Cervantes, Hobbes, Pascal, and in various versions of the myth of Don Juan. And while each establishes a domain within a total cultural field that is at this moment in history constituted anew, the truth of modernist culture is revealed only in their differentiation from within. For while modernism may initially be described in speculative terms as a socio-cultural whole, the meaning of its various elements can be grasped only as the relationship of mutually antithetical terms. The founding of epistemology as "first philosophy" by Descartes, for instance, depends on the containment of "literature" or "fiction" outside the realm of truth. Similarly, the Hobbesian conception of reason, which is closely linked to that of Descartes,[7] is by itself unable to account for the founding of the modern state, which Hobbes regards as motivated by fear and dread. History and theory, in their part, remain sharply divided realms: as the example of the French revolution would later bear out, historical events resist complete determination by the philosophy of subjectivity, just as Cartesian reason, which claimed unique applicability to motions in the sublunary world, remained unable to account for its own genesis on a historical plane.

Modernism in this and many other ways constitutes a "de-totalized" whole, and is marked by what Max Weber described as the segmentation of culture into a series of separate value- or interest-spheres. Habermas sees in modernism the development of the "inner logic" of each of these spheres,[8] and regards it both substantively and historically as coextensive with the Enlightenment (namely, as the period in which reason came to manifest itself as the natural human destiny). On these grounds he attempts a reconstruction of modernism from within its own "centered" point of view, and regards this as necessary for the preservation of its rational goals. By contrast, I take "modernism" as an already decentered cultural whole, which is to say as a totality no more than one facet of which may be held clearly in view at a time. The story that is told about the Cartesian conception of reason, including the history of corrections and historic replies it receives, may with equal legitimacy be narrated from the perspective of the mobile psyche of modernist desire. It may be told from the vantage point of the structures of terror and authority at work in the modern state. Or it may viewed in terms of the shifting and unequal balance of faith and science. Each provides a provisional center and is but a means for grasping the whole.

These preliminary facts are further confirmed when modernism is regarded as a transhistorical phenomenon and considered from a postmodern point of view. Habermas has consistently taken postmodernism at its face value and sees it as the rejection of modernism; but I would argue that postmodernism deepens, rather than resolves, the contradictions of the modernist past. Indeed, the two most important postmodern critiques—those of history and of metaphysics—begin as responses to subjectivity and to the vision of history that subjectivity founds. Yet they conclude either in the loss of history as a potential value ground, or in the historically indiscriminate critique of "Western metaphysics" as a whole. Moreover, these critiques are incompatible among themselves;[9] they are intelligible only against the background of a prior disjunction of reason and history, which in turn reveals their common inheritance from the modernist past.

Modernism thus conceived is not coextensive with the Enlightenment, as Habermas has claimed, but rather is the field of a series of contradictions of which the dichotomy of history and theory is but one. This dichotomy is central to any effort to describe modernism, yet it remains unacknowledged by such thinkers as Hans Blumenberg and Michel Foucault. My critique of their work remains in important ways indebted to the Hegelian perspectives sketched above, yet it differs from Hegel in significant ways. For whereas Hegel conceived the problem of modernity as solvable only through the recovery by the philosophy of Spirit of the religious consciousness that modernity lost, I begin with the provisional acceptance of Blumenberg's assumption that the secular and historical character of modernity cannot be treated as the "loss of substance" of the sacred or ancient worlds. As a spokesman for modernity in a decidedly "postmodern" age, Blumenberg recognizes the contradictions of modernism and acknowledges their potentially damaging effects. His theses on the specific origins of modernity seem to me to need serious revision, yet his notion of the historical "reoccupation" of cultural positions offers a powerful alternative to the dominant trend in postmodern historiography—that is, the "archeology" and "geneal-ogy" of Michel Foucault.

Consider, then, the critique of modernity put forward by Foucault. In the opening chapters of *The Order of Things* and in the theoretical discussion surrounding that work, Foucault described the eclipse of the late medieval and Renaissance world by what I have termed the modern age as exemplary of the phenomenon of historical discontinuity of which his "archeological" method was designed to give account. If the historicist model of explanation took discontinuity as the sign of a temporal dislocation, which it was historians' task to explain and remove, as the given of their analysis but also as that which was inassimilable by it ("the raw material of history, which presented itself in the form of dispersed events . . . which, through analysis, had to be rearranged, reduced, effaced") archeology was by contrast conceived as an enterprise in which all preexisting forms of continuity could be held in suspense.[10] Insofar as the notion of con-tinuity was presupposed by historicist explanation in its "classical" (i.e., nineteenth-century) form, the process of its interrogation by suspension or *epochē* may be regarded as the means by which history so-called transcends and finally cancels itself. Archeology is posthistory, and is followed by Foucault's version of "genealogy." This is not an account or *logos* of the genesis and transformation of historical paradigms, as Hegel had proposed to give, but something closer to Nietzsche's ideal of a history of absolute difference. As such, archeology was forced to reject those images of the whole on which history so-called customarily relied. Foucault wrote in "Nietzsche, Genealogy, History":

Nietzsche's criticism, beginning with the second of the *Untimely Meditations*, always questioned the form of history that re-introduces (and always assumes) a suprahistorical perspective: a history whose function is to compose the finally reduced diversity of time into a totality fully closed upon itself; a history that always encourages subjective recognitions and attributes a form of reconciliation to all the displacements of the past; a history whose perspective on all that precedes it implies the end of time, a completed development.[11]

Yet even within the limits of such concepts as "regularity," "order," "law," and "rule," which Foucault's archeology genially accepted, there was an effort to internalize difference as the element that classical history necessarily had to elide: "[Archeology] establishes that we are difference, that our reason is the difference of discourses, our history the difference of times, our selves the difference of masks. That difference, far from being the forgotten and recovered origin, is this dispersion that we are and make" (*Archaeology of Knowledge*, p. 131).

The transition from "resemblance" or "similitude" to "representation" and "order," marking the rise to dominance of the modern age, is exemplary of a variety of functions that, while contiguous in some chronological space, are from the vantage point of the new order of things seen as discontinuous with the past. As the concept of fixed essences comes under pressure, there is no longer a "nature" to secure the relationship of sign and signified. A system based on the comparison of structures and quantities comes to replace a hierarchy of intricate analogies and detailed correspondences; the network of similitudes, in principle infinite or bounded only by a transcendent plenitude, yields to an order of orders—a mathesis—in which it would be possible to give a complete analysis or enumeration of the whole. The theory and practice of mimesis shifts from imitation to representation, with a corresponding change in the focus of attention from human action (which, as an index of character, was considered to be imitation's proper object) to the concept of world, which as the object of representation was a creation of the seventeenth-century philosophy of mind. These changes correspond to the creation of philosophy as a science in the writings of Descartes, and to the differentiation of philosophical, historical, and aesthetic discourse. They are consolidated in the position of the subject, which Heidegger rightly saw as underlying the modern age.[12]

The point of Foucault's analysis is that there is no rational process or movement that will account for the transformation of any one of these functions or moments into the next, or perhaps more accurately still, that it is based only on the presupposition of some underlying substance or ground (e.g., "history," "reason," "man") that such functions could be conceived as continuous among themselves.

So seen, the purpose of *The Order of Things* is not simply to account for the phenomenon that historians of science have come to identify as a "paradigm shift," but to do so without reference to the notions of self-conception and purpose in terms of which discontinuities there have been understood. This is in part the reason why historical orders are seen by Foucault mysteriously to rise and then suddenly to disappear. I cite from the Preface to *The Order of Things,* which typifies this vision of abrupt and arbitrary historical change: "It is this [Classical] configuration that, from the nineteenth century onwards, *changes entirely;* the theory of representation *disappears* as the universal foundation of all possible orders; language as the spontaneous *tabula . . . is eclipsed* in its turn; a profound historicity *penetrates* into the heart of things."[13]

We see here evidence of the quality that Richard Rorty described as the peculiar "dryness" of Foucault's style, the systematic exclusion of any appeal to a self-interpreting community or, as Rorty puts it, the absence of any "we."[14] It may additionally be said that this "dryness" is symptomatic of an inability to theorize the relationship between knowledge and power, and suggests Foucault's deep-seated fear of power as well. Moreover, the dryness of Foucault's style points toward the eventual disintegration of his "archeological" stance, for it indicates, somewhat paradoxically, the *absence* of history as a ground on which to claim a stance (Foucault: "my discourse, far from determining the locus in which it speaks, is avoiding the ground on which it could find support," *Archaeology of Knowledge,* p. 205). Phrased in slightly different terms, it could be said that the archeologist's "dryness" results from the effort to speak difference itself, a project that when severed from the concept of a rational or social whole can only result in the disarticulation of a stance.[15]

Following Nietzsche's remarks in *The Will to Power*—"there is no 'totality;' . . . no evaluations of human existence, of human aims, can be made in regard to something that does not exist"[16]—terms such as "discontinuity" and "difference" are often invoked in postmodern discourse in order to shatter the notion of a (rational, social, historical) whole. Yet the whole is not thereby altogether elided. Foucault substitutes for the whole the notion of the archive, which as a fully historicized positivity represents a lawlike formation demarcating all that can validly be said:

> To describe a group of statements not as the closed, plethoric totality of a meaning, but as an incomplete, fragmented figure; to describe a group of statements not with reference to the interiority of an intention, a thought, or a subject, but in accordance

with the dispersion of an exteriority; to describe a group of statements, in order to rediscover not the moment or the trace of their origin, but the specific forms of an accumulation, is certainly not to uncover an interpretation, to discover a foundation, or to free constituent acts; nor is it to decide on a rationality, or to embrace a teleology. It is to establish what I am quite willing to call a positivity. [*Archaeology of Knowledge*, p. 125]

The concept of mathesis, which Descartes invoked against Aristotelian teleology at the beginning of the modern age, remains powerfully operative in Foucault's appeal to regularity and rule, and it remains likewise severed from the concepts of purpose and end. In this light one may well understand Foucault's need to speak of historical change as originating in a space that lies *outside* that of existing thought. ("Discontinuity—the fact that within the space of a few years a culture sometimes ceases to think as it had been thinking up till then and begins to think things in a new way—probably begins with an *erosion from outside*, from the space which is, for thought, *on the other side*" [*The Order of Things*, p. 50; emphasis added].) Yet it is unclear just how the notion of history as a series of epistemes, insulated from one other, could provide for such change; for the episteme is a finite totality, and must be presumed to represent a given moment of history, fully present to itself. *The Order of Things* begins with an allegorical account of the incommensurability of epistemes through a reference to one of Borges's tales, and it concludes with the indication of a possible "future thought."

"These [historical analyses] are not affirmations," Foucault writes; "they are at most questions to which it is not possible to reply; they must be left in suspense, where they pose themselves, only with the knowledge that the possibility of posing them may well open the way to a future thought" (p. 386). Yet Foucault proves unable to formulate the language in which such a thought might be expressed. Moreover, he rejects the possibility that theory could comprehend, much less help project, the transformations involved.[17]

Only in a later interview does Foucault confront the question of what it might mean to conceive a world that we might not yet be able to inhabit:

I am well aware that I have never written anything but fictions. I do not mean to say, however, that truth is therefore absent. It seems to me that the possibility exists for fictions to function in truth, for a fictional discourse to induce effects of truth, and for bringing it about that a true discourse engenders or "manufactures" something that does not as yet exist, that is, "fictions" it. One "fictions" history on the basis of a political reality that makes it true, one "fictions" a politics not yet in existence on the basis of a historical truth.[18]

Yet in the majority of his work, the conception of history not simply as a succession of events but as a value ground—that is, as a drama of exemplary deeds and the repository of cultural models—is eclipsed by the positivist conception already noted, and history in this guise remains the master of theory. History controls language (discourse) and the projective powers of imagination as well. This mastery is evident in the inscrutable transformations described above, and also in the alliance of cognition and power implicit in the very terms "discourse" and "episteme." Yet the collapse of all forms of consciousness into manifestations of power implies the impossibility of a critique of history in view of any transhistorical goals, and explains why Habermas and other neo-Marxists have found it necessary to draw sharp boundaries between their work and Foucault's.[19] At the very least it reveals the fact that Foucault embraces a stance toward history that is conditioned by conflicting demands.

Foucault inherits from the modernist culture, which he follows, the will to revise all existing institutions and ideas; yet he seeks to reject modernist forms of discourse and the modes of consciousness they imply. These contradictory orientations are regarded as somehow overcome in the abandonment of the ideal that reason might provide the ground of a historical critique, and ultimately in the *dépassement* of the ground of history itself. History may thus be thought of as prior to theory, but it is for Foucault little more than a refuge for endangered subjective thought. ("If the history of thought could remain the locus of uninterrupted continuities, if it could endlessly forge connexions that no analysis could undo without abstraction, if it could weave, around everything that men say and do, obscure synthesis that anticipate for him, prepare him, and lead him endlessly towards his future, it would provide a privileged shelter for the sovereignty of consciousness" [*Archaeology of Knowledge*, p. 12].)

The relationship between history and theory in Foucault, which may be taken as indicative of their interrelationship in postmodernism more generally, is nonetheless intelligible as a transformation of the modernist project, which superficially it rejects. As we shall see in relation to the work of Blumenberg, Foucault's alliance of knowledge and power gives expression, in postmodern guise, to one of the latent truths of the modern world. For although postmodernism openly declares a break with its modernist past, it would be more accurate to say that the reversal of history in its relationship to theory, which might conceivably serve for its transformative critique, is possible only because history and theory are themselves unreconciled in modernist thought. From its beginnings in the seventeenth century, modernism combined the project of a critique of all existing forms of consciousness and ideas with the notion that mathematics supplies the contextfree "language of nature" and constitutes the natural language of thought.

In the *Meditations*, the *Discourse on Method*, and the *Rules for the Direction of the Mind*, Descartes carried out a revisionary program calling for a critique of historical experience and the wisdom inherited from the past in favor of those truths that could be validated in solitude by the methods of the mathematical mind. Descartes clearly placed the claims of theory over against those of history, but rather than say that history was thus eliminated from modernism, it would be more accurate to say that Descartes construes history as open to the possibility of radical revision by speculative thought.

At the same time, the modernist project envisioned in the Cartesian texts was meant to provide the groundwork for a positive program of self-revision. To be sure, Descartes established the absolute certainty of mathematics as exemplary of rational activity and conceived his philosophical method as modeled on it ("I applied [the method] to certain other problems which I could put into something like mathematical form by detaching them from all the principles of the other sciences, which I did not find sufficiently secure"[20]); but he never lost sight of the fact that the end of reason lies in praxis, or that the basis of action is human freedom, which knowledge is meant to secure.

The work of reason in Descartes is directed toward what Habermas has called "emancipatory" interests, which operate through the transformation of nature, history, society, and the self. Yet the exercise of freedom with regard to history begins for Descartes with the prior abandonment of the encumbrances of the past: "regarding the opinions to which I had hitherto given credence, I thought that I could not do better than undertake to get rid of them, all at one go, in order to replace them afterwards with better ones, or with the same ones once I had squared them with the standards of reason" (*Discourse on Method*, p. 117). As Descartes sets himself the task of a rational historical critique, he invokes a division of history and reason ("science") of which reason is unable to give account: "even though we have read all the arguments of Plato and Aristotle, we shall never become philosophers if we are unable to make a sound judgment on matters which come up for discussion; in this case what we would seem to have learnt would not be science but history."[21]

The self-grounding nature of the reason that Descartes describes is conceived in terms of a mathematical substance that virtually insures that the moment of its own founding cannot be comprehended by it. The cogito, as "founding" act of thought, is thus not wholly ahistorical, but creates the impression within history of a radical discontinuity or gap. Hence the modernist desire to seek the absolute foundations of knowledge indicates a crisis in the relationship between reason and history that here manifests itself in the desire to begin entirely from oneself; the latter impulse, it might be added, is tantamount to the will to begin from nothing at all. As a result, the freedom expressed as what Hans Blumenberg would call modernist "self-assertion" becomes a manifestation of the phenomenon that Nietzsche would describe in terms of the "will to power" over the past. In this sense, it could be said that the subjective ground of Cartesian reason is not "foundational" at all but groundless; it rests on foundations that can be secured only by the will.

In contrast to Foucault's postmodern critique of history, Blumenberg accepts the self-description of modernity as that age in which reason manifested itself within history as one's natural vocation and definitively prevailed.[22] Yet he also points to the paradoxical timelessness of Descartes's intention to make an absolute beginning in time, and to the antinomic vision of the shape of history that results therefrom:

> Reason's interpretation of itself as the faculty of an absolute beginning excludes the possibility that there could appear even so much as indications of a situation that calls for reason's application now, no sooner and no later. Reason, as the ultimate authority, has no need of a legitimation for setting itself in motion; but it also denies itself any reply to the question why it was ever out of operation and in need of a beginning. What God did before the Creation and why He decided on it—where reason was before Descartes and what made it prefer this medium and this point in time—these are questions that cannot be asked in the context of the system constituted by their basic concepts. [*Legitimacy of the Modern Age*, p. 145]

As Blumenberg goes on to say, modernism depends for its identity on a sharply dualistic conception of its relationship to every former age; that which precedes modernity is imagined as the province of superstition, mythical thinking, or animistic beliefs. Yet any "corrective" to the self-conception of modernity that would propose to assimilate the prior history of reason to some unified historical plan would only threaten the legitimacy of modernism as a historical epoch. Attempts to bridge the gap between the Middle Ages and the modern world by the invocation of an unbroken continuum of rational activity, for instance, can be understood as attempts to rationalize what was originally irrational in modernism's understanding of itself; such attempts threaten modernism's epochal self-conception and jeopardize its claims to have brought about a "final phase of self-possession and self-realization" (*Legitimacy of the Modern Age*, p. 378).

Blumenberg's notion of historical method as the discovery of "reoccupied positions" may fruitfully be juxtaposed to Foucault's "archeology," and its later, Nietzschean variant, "genealogy," on a number of points. The invocation of cultural functions or positions allows Blumenberg to conceive of meaning and purpose in history without recourse to a thesis about the telos of history as a whole. Moreover, Blumenberg conceives no substance (no "reason" or "spirit") through which history is transformed; instead he regards history as the repository of solutions to a series of problems that we continue to confront. Accordingly, judgments about the "legitimacy" of modernism must be based upon its ability to produce new and historically effective ideas.

As for the category of "progress" and its crucial place in modern thought, it is worthwhile to recall that Blumenberg began his project as a response to the arguments of Karl Löwith, who in *Meaning and History* proposed that "progress" was modernity's reappropriation of the eschatological pictures of history of the Jewish and Christian faith. It was hence a sign of the fundamental inauthenticity of the modern project, and of modernity's misinterpretation of the purpose of reason in the world. These facts about modernity were confirmed for Löwith in the Hegelian synthesis of reason and history, which relied on the recovery, by philosophy, of a religious substance that had been carried forward into modernity but remained nonetheless suppressed:

> Hegel himself did not feel the profound ambiguity in his great attempt to translate theology into philosophy and to realize the Kingdom of God in terms of the world's real history. He felt no difficulty in identifying the "idea of freedom," the realization of which is the ultimate meaning of history, with the "will of God"; for, as a "priest of the Absolute," "damned by God to be a philosopher," he knew this will and the plan of history. He did not know it as a prophet predicting future catastrophe but as a prophet in reverse, surveying and justifying the ways of the Spirit by its successive successes.[23]

We shall, in conclusion, briefly return to Hegel's attempt to reconcile reason and history on spiritual grounds. But it must first be said that Blumenberg's critique of Löwith in his defense of the "legitimacy" of the modern age raises a series of questions about the origins and rationality of the category of the new as a defining feature of the modern world. We have seen that for Foucault, the sources of the new remain unfathomable by reason. For Blumenberg, the legitimacy of the modern age is a function of its ability to articulate novel solutions to questions that may themselves be inherited from the past. For despite modernism's legitimate claims to historical autonomy, it can be seen that if modernity did not spring into existence from "outside" history (which is also to say that if the philosophy of subjectivity, though "transcendentally" grounded, remains nonetheless a *historical* event), it must be traceable to preexisting ideas.

Blumenberg seeks to resolve this paradox of history and theory by combining the consciousness of a historical inheritance with an appeal to the powers of speculative thought. These methodological innovations remain valid despite the fact that Blumenberg's thesis regarding the specific origins of modernity in the second overcoming of gnosticism is largely inconsistent with the proximity of such early modern writers as Descartes, Cervantes, Hobbes, and Pascal, to the already secularized culture of the high Renaissance. Moreover, Blumenberg seriously misinterprets the *querelle des anciens et des modernes* as an instance in which the moderns succeeded in freeing themselves from the "encumbrances" of the past. In both cases, Blumenberg ignores the prior attempts to reconcile history and reason on the grounds of a provisional and contingent totality, the *communitas*, in the civic humanism of the Renaissance. Indeed, as late as Montaigne, the past still constitutes a sphere of exemplary behavior and a scene of virtual action relevant to present purposes, rather than the store of potential errors as it had become for Descartes.

These arguments are not meant to suggest that what Descartes calls "reason," and what may more generally be referred to as a conjunction of modernist practices and beliefs, can only be understood in terms of the predecessor culture they negate. Examples drawn from premodern times offer no immediate alternatives to the problem of modernity, if only because they deny modernist notions of reason their principal historical force—namely, that of something radically new, of the unprecedented achievement of reason on the historical plane. What Blumenberg proposes to explain through his thesis of reoccupied positions, however, is not just the novelty of modernity, but also its transformative effects on the questions it inherits from the past. Thus the idea that "progress" lends meaning to the shape of history as a whole did not, in his view, become possible as a consequence of some prior theological eschatology; rather, originally modest notions of spiritual progress and salvation were extended to embrace the "philosophy of history" as a whole, at the same time presenting modernism with teleological questions it had no framework to answer.

Here again the contrast with Hegelian historiography is germane, for Hegel sought to resolve the contradictions of modernism by answering the question of the meaning of the totality of history. While Hegel may thus have succeeded in balancing the demands of history and theory, the origins and novelty of the modernist project nevertheless remain for him mysterious, objects that suddenly present themselves before consciousness as both necessary and yet wholly new ("it is just this necessity itself, or the *origination* of the new object, that presents itself to consciousness without its understanding how this happens, which proceeds for us, as it were, behind the back of consciousness" [*Phenomenology of Spirit*, p. 56, sec. 87]).

In contrast to the modernist gestures of Descartes, who spoke of razing the existing structures of knowledge to the ground in order to build from new foundations, Hegel proposed to stand on a ground that was not just foundational, or new, but was totalizing, or absolute. The emergence of reason on a historical plane as the manifestation of that which was both necessary and new is thus concealed within a circle "that returns into itself, the circle that presupposes its beginning and reaches it only at the end" (*Phenomenology of Spirit*, p. 488, sec. 802). This is why Adorno's critique of Hegel, which was far more radical than Blumenberg's, had to reject both the dialectical totality and the modernist philosophy of origins that the dialectic was meant to correct: "The first and the absolutely new are complementary, and dialectical thought had to dispose of both of them. . . . Dialectics is the quest to see the new in the old instead of just the old in the new. As it mediates the new, so also it preserves the old as the mediated."[24] In the dialectic, modernist "progress" becomes the movement through which reason is carried forward and also raised up; its medium and its validation are to be found in the long procession of historical cultures and individuals, in what Hegel calls "actual history." Hegel said that history is the court of the world's judgment, which suggests that it is both secular and rational. Yet Hegel's concept of history remained a sacred and sacrificial affair, one in which reason mimes a plan of spiritual death and redemption, sloughing off, but also recollecting, the prior stages of its existence as it moves ahead: "the two together," he wrote, "form alike the inwardizing [recollection] and the Calvary [sacrifice] of absolute Spirit" (*Phenomenology of Spirit*, p. 493, sec. 808).

Notes

1. See Jürgen Habermas, *The Philosophical Discourse of Modernity* (Cambridge: MIT Press, 1987); Jean-François Lyotard, *The Postmodern Condition: A Report on Knowledge* (Minneapolis: University of Minnesota Press, 1984); and the essays gathered in *Habermas and Modernity*, ed. Richard J. Bernstein (Cambridge: MIT Press, 1985).

2. Habermas, "Hegel's Critique of the French Revolution," in *Theory and Practice* (Boston: Beacon, 1974), p. 121.

3. This is a hotly contested point. See Heidegger, *Hegel's Concept of Experience* (New York: Harper and Row, 1970); Hans-Georg Gadamer, "Hegel and Heidegger," in *Hegel's Dialectic: Five Hermeneutical Studies* (New Haven: Yale University Press, 1976); Gilles Deleuze, *Nietzsche and Philosophy* (New York: Columbia University Press, 1983), esp. pp. 147–94; and David Kolb, *The Critique of Pure Modernity: Hegel, Heidegger, and After* (Chicago: University of Chicago Press, 1986). Following Heidegger, Derrida reads Hegel as absolutizing, or infinitizing, the philosophy of subjectivity. For example, in *Of Grammatology:* "On the one hand [Hegel] undoubtedly summed up the entire philosophy of the logos. He determined ontology as absolute logic; he assembled all the determinations of philosophy as presence; he assigned to presence the eschatology of parousia, of the self-proximity of infinite subjectivity" (Baltimore: Johns Hopkins University Press, 1976, p. 24).

4. Emil Fackenheim, *The Religious Dimension in Hegel's Thought* (1967; repr. Chicago: University of Chicago Press, 1982), p. 76.

5. These aims are supported at a number of points by issues raised in a parallel study; see A. J. Cascardi, "Genealogies of Modernism," *Philosophy and Literature*, 11 (1987): 207–25.

6. Hegel, *Phenomenology of Spirit* (New York: Oxford University Press, 1977), p. 334, sec. 549.

7. Hobbes's relationship to Descartes has been a subject of some debate, not least because of Hobbes's own written "Objections." Yet on such crucial questions as the mathematical nature of reason, the two are in fundamental agreement.

8. See, for instance, Habermas, *Reason and the Rationalization of Society*, vol. 1 of *The Theory of Communicative Action* (Boston: Beacon, 1981).

9. The dispute between Foucault and Derrida (including Derrida's response to Foucault's *Histoire de la folie*), "*Cogito* and the History of Madness," in *Writing and Difference* (Chicago: University of Chicago Press, 1978), pp. 31–63, is symptomatic in this regard.

10. *The Archaeology of Knowledge* (New York: Harper and Row, 1972), p. 8.

11. Foucault, "Nietzsche, Genealogy, History," in *Language, Counter-Memory, Practice* (Ithaca: Cornell University Press, 1977), p. 153.

12. See Heidegger's "The Age of the World Picture," in *The Question Concerning Technology and Other Essays* (New York: Harper and Row, 1977).

13. Foucault, *The Order of Things* (New York: Random House, 1970), p. xxiii, italics added.

14. Rorty, "Habermas and Lyotard on Postmodernity," in *Habermas and Modernity*, pp. 161–75.

15. This difficulty is shared by Derrida, whose work brings it into sharpest relief. He writes that "difference is articulation" (*Of Grammatology*, p. 66); yet, as Gillian Rose has pointed out in *Dialectic of Nihilism: Post-Structuralism and Law* (Oxford: Blackwell, 1984), if this is so, then it follows that "the *articulans* cannot itself be articulated, nor can it be articulate" (p. 139). Implicit is the rejection of Hegel's claim to have achieved a complete (i.e., wholly articulate) discourse.

16. Nietzsche, *The Will to Power* (New York: Random House, 1967), p. 378, sec. 711.

17. This is, to be sure, a difficult point. In work nearly contemporaneous with *The Order of Things*, Foucault seems to indicate that thought, as opposed to sight and speech, has the capacity to direct itself toward an "outside"—that is, to relations of powers that have not yet been stratified. See Foucault's "La pensée du dehors," *Critique*, 229 (juin 1966): 523–46. The gap between a thought that directs itself to the "outside," and visible or legible signs, nonetheless remains. Gilles Deleuze provides some discussion of this point in his *Foucault* (Paris: Minuit, 1986), pp. 92–93.

18. Foucault, *Power/Knowledge*, ed. Colin Gordon (New York: Random House, 1980), p. 193.

19. See Habermas on Foucault in *The Philosophical Discourse of Modernity*, pp. 238–93, and also Perry Anderson's critique of structuralism and poststructuralism, *In the Tracks of Historical Materialism* (London: Verso, 1983).

20. Descartes, *Discourse on Method*, in *The Philosophical Writings of Descartes* (Cambridge: Cambridge University Press, 1984), 1:125.

21. Descartes, *Rules for the Direction of the Mind*, in *The Philosophical Writings of Descartes*, 1:13.

22. See Blumenberg, *The Legitimacy of the Modern Age* (Cambridge: MIT Press, 1983), p. 377.

23. Löwith, *Meaning in History* (Chicago: University of Chicago Press, 1949), p. 58.

24. Adorno, *Against Epistemology* (Cambridge: MIT Press, 1983), p. 38.

2

Photographs: Primitive and Postmodern

Mary Bittner Wiseman

Inscribed in Roland Barthes's *Camera Lucida: Reflections on Photography* (1981) are notions of a genetic identity as sprawling as the ancestral tree whose lines it draws and a specular identity as short-lived as the click of the camera. Temporal and conceptual boundaries of the subject self split and shift: they go wild. What *Camera Lucida* goes wild about is the photograph, and what it says about the photograph's wildness is that it may be tamed, and this in one of two ways: by being made into art or by being banalized, generalized, made familiar and everyday. But the photograph need not be tamed and when it is not, it can bring madness. For it is a trace of the past real, whereas the system of intelligibility within which we understand the world is one in which what is present is real and what is past or future is not.

The two ways of taming the photograph are exemplified by the two sides of a debate about how to interpret the irruption of primitivism into the field of early modern art, the difference between the sides beginning with their definitions of "primitivism." One defines it as interest in tribal works as objects of aesthetic appreciation; the other as interest in their function within the tribal culture. *Camera Lucida* bears the fruit born by the juxtaposition of what may be called the aesthetic and the functional conceptions—namely, a third conception: primitivism is interest in *artifacts that embody, incorporate, or bear traces of some real thing,* where any artifact, whether or not from the hand of a member of a tribal culture, is primitive when it is the direct or immediate presentation of the real. Photographs, then, are primitive. The contradiction between the aesthetic and the functional conceptions of primitivism "yields in his eyes by the discovery of a third term, which is not a synthesis but a *translation:* everything comes back, but it comes back as Fiction i.e., at another turn of the spiral."[1] What is translated is the contradiction between the belief in a transhistorical and transcultural human nature implied by the aesthetic conception and the belief that all natures are context-dependent implied by the functional. The translation consists in the experimental imagination of the conjunction of the incompatible elements in the humanist and contextualist conceptions of primitivism, together with the generation of a new conception out of the revision of the familiar conceptual scheme required by the hithertofore impossible conjunction.

The new conception of primitivism transposes the scene of the difference between the aesthetic and the functional to the scene of the difference between the Peircean symbol (or Saussurean sign) and the index, the difference descried along another axis between Western writing and tribal carving. The conflict between the first two conceptions ceases to be pertinent when tribal objects are regarded as indices of the real, where the real is what is not conventionally coded. If "real" means what it meant before the linguistic turns of this century and if the turns have simply turned everything around, then *Camera Lucida* founds a neorealism and the real "comes back as Fiction, i.e., at another turn of the spiral." But if something may be faintly heard murmuring off stage, what may be made out of the murmurs is the beginning of a reconception of the real in the barely sounded name of what is embodied, incorporated, or traced in certain objects. What is to be made out is a writing by genes, by light, by electronic impulses, a writing done by no one in no time, a writing that is an encoding by nature or machine. *Camera Lucida* is the hieroglyph in which may be deciphered what has so far barely been heard, barely been seen. Its final reflection on photography, what finally it says about the wild madness of the photograph, is this:

> Mad or tame? Photography can be one or the other: tame if its realism remains relative, tempered by aesthetic or empirical habits (to leaf through a magazine at the hairdresser's, the dentist's); mad if this realism is absolute and, so to speak, original, obliging the loving and terrified consciousness to return to the very letter of Time: a strictly revulsive movement which reverses the course of the thing, and which I shall call, in conclusion, the photographic *ecstasy*.
>
> Such are the two ways of the photograph. The choice is mine: to subject its spectacle to the civilized code of perfect illusions, or to confront in it the wakening of intractable reality.[2]

The conceptions of primitivism map onto three ways of fronting photography—namely, making it into an art, generalizing it by making it part of everyday experience, and confronting in it "the wakening of intractable reality." Because what it is about the photographic image that makes it different from every other kind of image is what makes it like a tribal carving—its madness, its magic, its immediate presentation of the power of the nonpresent real, I will characterize the way of seeing demanded by the photograph's transparence to the past by way of the debate inspired by "'Primitivism' in Twentieth-Century Art: Affinity of the Tribal and the Modern" (1984) at the Museum of Modern Art in New York. The new way of seeing is preeminently a new way of seeing relations between a so-called present and its past, and photograph and postmodern work alike embody a past, unraveling the skein of history as they do.

Out of Place and Out of Date

The Art Deco elements in the contemporary Humana building in Louisville, Kentucky, are *out of date* in more or less the same way as the Kwakiutl split mask is *out of place* in the Museum of Modern Art. This suggests that place and date share the same logic, where place is cultural place with its intimations of propriety. When the notions of the out of place and out of date are made to resonate with those of the *in place* and *up to date,* the privilege usually accorded present place and present time seems not to be deserved; for the present and only the present is supposed to be the immediate, the unmediated. The conjunction of the culturally or historically disparate, the recontextualization of the mask and the Art Deco elements, is an argument rather than an accident. The curators, William Rubin and Kurt Varnadoe, and the architect, Michael Graves, intentionally conjoined them, in the one case to revise the history of modernism and in the other to give the lie to certain of modernism's presuppositions. I want to focus on the referents of our talk about the building and the show rather than on the art historical intentions with which the combinations were made, however.[3] What the examples show is an incorporation of the past and the culturally other into our present culture that fractures the unity of the style, shape, plan, pattern, form of the present time and present culture even as it plays havoc with beliefs about the absence of the past and the presence of the present.

Inasmuch as the examples indicate that the *postmodern* involves styles that are out of date and the *primitive* involves the out of place, where the place is Western culture, demonstration of the structural exchangeability of date and place suggests a formal relation between postmodern and primitive that is of interest insofar as it argues a formal relation between present in time and present in space. Postmodernism may be characterized informally as the repudiation of

modernism's commitment to a historicism two of whose tenets are
that a work reflects its time and there is an irreversible order in history. Talk of works of art or science, say, reflecting their time supposes
that there is "a time" related primarily and necessarily either to past
or to contemporary theories and art works. Hegel told the story of the
spirit of the world's development over time and made of time the
womb in which is born whatever is determined to realize itself.[4]
Foucault tells a different story, a story of structure, and goes down,
not forward or back, down to an archeological bedrock in which are
fossilized the conditions that determine what can be thought and
said, made and done, the conditions that shape the world, its theories, and its arts.[5]

Hegel's diachronic and Foucault's synchronic relations are necessary: each carve out "a time." What it usually means to say that a
work reflects its time is that it expresses the time in which it was
made; vacuity threatens, however, when a work cannot fail to express its birth time. Since Art Deco, for example, neither grows out of
late modernism nor shares an underlying structure with earth works
or performance art, it does not reflect "our time" understood either as
a stage in a development or the manifestation of a latent
configuration.

The tenets imply norms. A work is *authentic* only if reflects the
time at which it presents itself on the world stage, and a work that
contains temporally distinct styles is *coherent* only if they are sequent
in time: history's coherence is precisely the fixed order of its stages.
The picture drawn is that of a rigidly designated present that fixes
segments of the past with respect to their distance from the present
and therefore to each other. Because time brings changes and does
not repeat itself, every product is marked by its time and what is
produced at a given time is essentially different from, although continuous with, what went before.

Michael Graves violates both norms. For the Humana building
is not a hymn to the present; if it reflects anything, it is the times that
gave birth to Art Deco and the Italian renaissance, not the time of its
being built. Moreover, if the most important thing about the past is its
temporal relation to the present, then past times that stand in markedly different temporal relations to the present are markedly out of
joint with each other. Graves undermines the supposition that this is
the most important thing about the past by using temporally discontinuous, disjoint, styles. The building, therefore, is inauthentic and
incoherent. Or it is a celebration of freedom from the myth of the
present and the corollary right to cruise the no longer protected past.

It has been objected to this that the Humana building is *"very much* a 'hymn to the present' insofar as Graves is consumed with a desire to be the leading exponent and definer of a new style of the present; and with . . . an entirely Modernist notion of history (Styles, Zeitgeists, Avant-gardes) he elevates and flaunts the 'right to cruise the no longer protected past' merely as the *latest version of* (not freedom from) the 'myth of the present.' "[6] In being an amalgam of historically discontinuous styles, the building signals both the end of the conception of history as a succession of (present) styles and the end of style as a unifying principle. To call the uniqueness and the unity of the present and the succession of presents myths is to claim that a look at this succession through another lens than modernism's would reveal quite another conceptual geometry. The objection supposes that there is no other geometry, however: the juxtaposition of historically disjunct styles is just another *style;* in demonstrating against the new, Graves presumes to be the voice of the *present.* The culture conserves the conceptual schemes it has ordained by refusing to hear what speaks against it. It is the impossibility of criticism.

Peoples are called "primitive" when, having no writing, they have no written histories and there is nothing in which their language or their past is inscribed. Their language is action, and their past, present, and future embedded in ritual and myth. When "primitivism" refers to interest in or theories about the practices of primitive peoples, it may be characterized informally as the theory of what is outside the practices and the systems of intelligibility of peoples with writing, and when it refers to the practice or the desire of someone from the West, as the repudiation of Western culture's languages of power, which, in the West, is all the languages there are. Because these languages are written, their power to dictate what can be said and what can be true transcends the limited power of any speaker. There is in primitive worlds no alphabetic writing, no writing that records speech, but there are registers, records, inscriptions of a power different from languages' power to say what can be said: they are masks, totems, tribal carvings. They invite comparison with written documents, for the written and the carved are both significant even though related to their objects in different ways. Linguistic signs are Peircean symbols and carved signs indices, the one conventionally, the other causally, related to its object. An examination of how tribal masks function, coupled with the experimental imagination of a utopia of language in which language is adequate to the real, may begin to unscramble what has so far been perceived only as noise.

Masks and tribal carvings abound in cultures without writing, however, and their installation in the Museum of Modern Art might not be thought to silence the question: What violence is done to works of art that inhabit a world encoded in writing, a written world, when they are claimed to have affinities with primitive works, denizens of worlds without writing? The answer, of course, depends on what the affinity is supposed to be: Is it merely *formal*, and if so does it comprise the objects' forms or their makers' effective desire to create form, or does the affinity reside in the works' *"magical force*, in the sense of the irrational . . . the magical roots of image making?"[7] The answer depends not only on deciding how most felicitously to characterize the affinities but also on what to conclude from their existence, and this in turn depends on one's answer to the question of our relation to the past, in particular, on our attitude toward the claims implicit in modernism about its relation to the past. For the Humana building is inauthentic and incoherent by modernism's critical lights and an expression of the end of the tyranny of the present over the past by postmodernism's. But the question of whether and how the works of high modernism, the works of tribal craftsmanship, the relation between modernism and primitivism, or the history of modernism must be reconceived and reevaluated is not so ready of answer, for the reason that primitivism has not yet been formulated as a theory, has not been theorized, not been analyzed. If it is argued that there is a deeper connection than had been realized between modernism and the primitive, and if to this it is objected that the alleged connection is really a bastardization of the primitive and a real connection with the primitive would constitute a renunciation of the claims of modernism and the inauguration of a postmodernism, one has to analyze the concepts of "the primitive" at work in order to speak to the question. These are the conceptions of the primitive and primitivism that have emerged in the critical debate surrounding the show at the Museum of Modern Art.

Primitive and Out of Place

The involvement with primitive art has something to do with a sense of crisis, and also with a sense of a broad need to renew the tradition. If there is a radical break within the history of modernism, it takes place in the last fifteen years, when you shift into earth works and other kinds of things that don't belong to the same history that links Monet and, let us say, Pollock. Wherever you have a break like that, there is always a searching for new roots, and inevitably you look backwards as well as forwards.

People look back now in the same way that they did in the

turn-of-the-century break that led to the "Demoiselles d'Avignon"; in the primitivism of that work, Picasso was looking backwards and forwards at the same time. I think that for the last fifteen years we have been in—and are in now—one of those periods of break and transition. That is why the current exhibition is so apposite.[8]

Are the changes that have occurred in the past fifteen years redirections of the history of modern art, that is, changes of the sort that Picasso effected in 1906, or the end of the history of modern art?[9] In the name of postmodernism McEvilley accuses the curators of mounting the show in order to keep a dying modernism alive by showing its universality and consequent indestructibility: "modernism must speak to something universal in the human heart or mind since even the primitives are modernists." Is there an account of the primitive that is both intuitively plausible and such that the primitive and the modern share a conceptual space and, if there is, will the account so change our conception of the modern as to affect theories of the postmodern?

The thesis of "'Primitivism' in Twentieth-Century Art": is that tribal art was able to influence modern art only when changes within modern art itself made tribal art pertinent to European art—only when, that is to say, there was already an *affinity* between the two. "Primitive objects had less to do with redirecting the history of modern painting than with reinforcing and sanctioning developments already under way."[10] The affinity between them appeared when around 1906 avant-garde art moved from styles based on perception to those based on conceptualization. Ideas, not resemblances to things in nature, are what governed the production of avant-garde art early in the twentieth century and, it is conjectured, of tribal objects also. "Primitivism" applies to the beliefs and attitudes of early modern artists toward certain objects from tribal cultures: it describes the primitive as seen through Western eyes. The term is unabashedly ethnocentric. McEvilley objects to the show at the Museum of Modern Art that, taking artifacts out of the setting of ritual and myth for which they were intended so falsifies them as to render nonsensical any talk of affinities between tribal and modern. Careless of the real significance of the tribal objects, McEvilley avers, Rubin simply misreads them as works of fine art, classifying them in modernism's terms of the properties for which works of art are prized: originally, inventiveness, expressivity. Rubin is well aware of the virtual inevitability of misreading tribal objects, however, citing as examples the interpretation of certain features of works as expressions of psychic states, reading them as works of European expressionism, and the appreciation of tribal objects for their plastic beauty alone, thereby detaching them "from the symbolic and thaumaturgic role central to their place in the matrix of Primitive culture."[11]

The issue between them is how to assess the misreading that accompanies the objects' recontextualization. The one argues that any reading done from a place in Western culture violates the integrity of the objects and were better not done, for its doing makes of the reader a nineteenth-century person guilty of the nineteenth-century sin of imperialism, while the other, mindful of the fact that Westerners have been touched by the objects under whatever descriptions they have confronted them, allows that the objects may without compromising the integrity of the viewer be regarded *as if* they expressed psychic states or *as if* their significance lay only in their form. McEvilley celebrates the truth of the object, Rubin the truth of the viewers' response. The latter would acknowledge that one would be wrong to infer that tribal craftsmen intended to express certain psychological states in their carving, but this is just because one would be wrong to infer anything about the intentions of tribesmen, unless the inference were qualified as an inference to a "perceived intention" in deference to the irreducible and distorting contribution of the Western perspective. We are, at bottom, talking more about our perceptions than about their intentions: the reasons given for any perception, no matter how deeply embedded in no matter how wide a knowledge of the tribal world, are themselves ethnocentric.

More fundamental than Rubin's holding that ethnocentrism is inevitable and McEvilley that it is immoral is the latter's claiming what the former would deny—namely, that it is now possible "to look at tribal objects from the point of view of their own culture and to realize that, whatever they are, they fall in between the categories of our grid."[12] Were every aspect of the tribal object context relative, then since we cannot by Rubin's lights leave our own context behind, everything read off the tribal object would be a reading of ourselves and the affinities between tribal and modern would just be the reinscription within the history of modernism of the distinction between tribal and modern. This reinscription would seem to change our conception of the modern and, indeed, of ourselves, but the question McEvilley forces is whether what the conventional marker "tribal" marks can properly be said to be a tribal object or whether precisely by virtue of being inscribed within modernism it does not cease to be tribal and become just another modernist text. Were the tribal to lose its difference from the modern in being inscribed within the latter's history, then its inscription would not change our conception of the modern and the primitivism show would not, contrary to its curators' claim, revise the history of modernism.

The Museum of Modern Art's answer is that shared by the tribal objects in their cultural contexts and by the "Demoiselles d'Avignon" is a common denominator, something that escapes parochial conceptual schemes and is therefore what it is independent of its being observed by eye or mind. Intuition and instinct are what are contextfree, their trace to be made out in tribal and modern works alike: they are transcultural capacities of human beings that provide the basis for the affinities between the tribal and the modern. It might be objected, however, that the shift in the history of modern art that made modernist tribalism possible is said to be a shift from an art of perception to one of conceptualization, where the process of conceptualizing is what is common to tribal and modern; but surely this is not free from the system of beliefs and values that is the cultural context. The claim that it is contextfree opposes conceptualizing to illusionistically imitating what is seen, however. The conceptualized forms are not copies of seen forms but are *a fortiori* signs of the artist's choice of forms, of inventiveness in choosing among the crafted forms the artist has inherited and in choosing how to render them. Conceptualizing is not thinking but making, relative not to language and culture but to intuition and instinct, pressed into the service of negotiating inherited forms. Tribal craftsmen routinely invent their forms; when the modern artist, seeking to cut through layers of conventions governing illusionism, began to do so likewise, they came to have an affinity with the tribesmen.

Rubin holds that ethnocentrism is inevitable with respect to what is caught within the classificatory net of language and systems of concepts but that an "aesthetic impulse" toward conceptual form eludes the net. McEvilley holds that nothing falls outside some net or other, but, even so, ethnocentrism is not inevitable if it is taken to imply that we cannot escape our own ethos. For we can cruise the field of ethnocenters and look at tribal objects from the point of view of their own culture. The curator counters that what would be discovered from whatever points we viewed the field of human productions are, however, certain language independent impulses toward art:

> Ethnologists might argue that . . . the tribal sculptor creating ritual objects had no consciousness whatever of aesthetic solutions. . . . Even if this could be proven true, however, it would not contradict my contention insofar as the finding of artistic solutions is ultimately an *intuitive* rather than an intellectual

activity. . . . The "art-ness" of the best tribal objects alone demonstrates that great artists were at work and that a variety of
aesthetic solutions were arrived at, however little the artists
themselves might have agreed with our description of the process.[13] The solutions of genius in the plastic arts are all essentially *instinctual*, regardless of such intellectual superstructures
as might be built around them after the fact by the artists themselves, other artists, or critics and art historians. [italics added][14]

The evidence for this is the response of a kind of ideal observer,
one knowledgeable about art by virtue of an immediate involvement
with its works and whose response to its plastic and tactile values is
informed by this involvement. Such an observer is Picasso, the hero
of the retelling of the story of the effect that objects from Africa and
Oceania had on the turn-of-the-century break that led to the "Demoiselles d'Avignon." The curator's gloss on the artist's words characterizes both the alleged affinity between Picasso and African carvings
and the aesthetic conception of primitivism; for it is Picasso's and the
other early modernists' ideas about tribal objects that pertain to the
history of modern art:

> Tribal art . . . was eminently accessible to Picasso, who sym-
> pathized with its direct, simple, and reductive solutions. Picas-
> so . . . saw how these . . . could help him build a modern art
> that would share the quintessential and universal quality he
> recognized in tribal sculpture. The "elementalism" of the "De-
> moiselles" . . . required cutting back through layers of inherited
> conventions to a set of plastic rudiments—an endeavor that
> Picasso associated with tribal art. But the "Demoiselles" implied
> more than just a return to basic formal building blocks, as we
> shall see. Picasso associated the return to fundamentals with *the
> rediscovery of that direct magical affectiveness he knew to be the inher-
> ent power of the visual arts, an affectiveness with which the Western
> tradition had somehow lost contact*. The revelation of this magic had
> come to him on his first visit to the Musée d'Ethnographie du
> Trocadero. [italics added][15]

The difference between tribal and modern is breached as they
are reinscribed within a larger common field: tribal carvings and certain modernist works alike are expressions of an impulse to create
form, the more inventive or original the form, the more expressive it
is of its maker's creative power. The cultural context of neither tribal
nor modern maker is left behind: the modern artist has refused an

inheritance, the tribesman has not, and this is a difference between them. But in refusing, modernists have sought to express in the work of their hands something unmediated by conventions governing the representation of the seen world—namely, "the quintessential and universal quality [to be] recognized in tribal sculpture" and so far as he succeeds, he has, in leaving behind its conventions, left his context behind. Is this quality formal or affective? Picasso associated the return to fundamentals of form with the "direct magical affectiveness he knew to be the inherent power of the visual arts." Whence "magical"? The word gets lost in the exchange between the Museum of Modern Art and *Artforum* but is to be found in *Camera Lucida*, whose photographs are to Barthes what African carvings were to Picasso.

Marcel Mauss's *A General Theory of Magic* (1902) folds into Barthes's account of the effect that certain photographs have on him. The account conjoins the Museum of Modern Art's aestheticizing (photographs are works of art) with *Artforum*'s contextualizing (photographs are symptoms of our cultural condition) and disjoins both with his incorporating the out of place and out of date, precisely *as* out of place and date, into contemporary culture (photographs are mad). The experimental and imaginative use of the notion of magic whose milieu is beyond the pale of the grand metaphysical concepts of the Western world to characterize an inhabitant of that world, indifferently the photograph or its spectator, is neither intuitively plausible nor descriptive of a space that can contain primitive and modern conceptions of identity and temporal continuity. In putting this primitive concept into a Western context, Barthes takes no side in the life-and-death struggle of the modern but gently leaves the stage on which the battle rages and listens instead to voices murmuring offstage, speaking another language: foreign, exotic, primitive, naive, without the culture from whose place they are heard.

In *Writing Degree Zero* Barthes describes the modern writer's predicament as tragic because writers refuse to inherit tradition's conventions and therefore must choose the form of their writing but have no basis on which to choose one form rather than another. Modern artists, under Rubin's description, are not tragic, because they are not party to the writer's necessity to choose forms arbitrarily. Beyond the reach of inherited conventions lies the "set of plastic rudiments," "basic formal building blocks," from which artists who refuse to inherit the past may choose. Their choice, guided by intuition and instinct, is neither arbitrary nor in thrall to the tradition they refuse: it approaches the primitive. "Primitive" in its aesthetic sense names what lies beneath the layers of conventions deposited over time and beyond the differences of cultures: always there and often invisible, it is the will to art. Lying "beneath" conventions it is, then, "beneath" writing. Primitivism, in turn, attracts early modern artists' interest in the objects crafted by peoples with no writing, no written records of the past, no rules for reproducing the look of the surface of the world.

"Primitivism" in its functional sense names Western artists' interest in, say, African carving, where what African carvings really are is what they are in the original context in which they were made and used. Perhaps the validity of the concept of tribal carvings should not be adjudged by comparing it with the function the carvings have in their original context, however. For even though they cannot fulfill their original end when they are recontextualized, to claim that tribal carvings are significant only in their original context is to fall sway to the myth of origins and to blind oneself to the fact that they do touch, pierce, puncture, wound their viewers. A tribal carving may function as a *punctum*, leaping out of the *studium* that is Western culture; the blood need not be on the ritual objects for them to leap out at us: it is sufficient that they be different from what our culture has encoded for them to irrupt within the field of culturally coded. African carvings may be said to be a function of all the different things they are in all the contexts in which they do or can appear.

This is, for two connected reasons, two difficulties encountered, preferable to fixing them in their original contexts. The first is that one must be prepared uniquely to specify the original context, to say what really it is. The problem is not so much that one has then got too much (for to say what is the original context one must know what it is in its original context, and so on to the whole of the world), but rather that it is hard to know what one has got. It is hard to find nonarbitrary reasons for drawing the boundary around "the original context" here rather than there, or somewhere else that has not even been imagined. The second reason is that even if one is satisfied that one has more or less got the original context, one has further to suppose some inaugurating, initiating, authorizing acts of mind, some meaning-conferring intention, to which the objects under the concept "African carving" owe their lives.

The picture behind *Artforum*'s objections to the Museum of Modern Art is that of *objects* inextricably wedded to their contexts and divorced from any instinct, impulse, intuition, or intention of their makers and of *people* who must move within the conceptual context of some culture or other but who can move freely in imagination from one to another. Objects are falsified by being recontextualized, while people are not made false, do not play false, by looking at tribal objects from the point of view of tribal culture. Cultural artifacts are context-bound, people are context-free. The Museum's picture reverses *Artforum*'s: objects can be recontextualized, but cannot see through the lens of a culture whose history is not theirs. There are, however, other pictures. In each of those just drawn human beings are seen to stand in a relation to their contexts opposite to the one in which objects stand to theirs: people are independent of their cultural contexts if and only if objects are not. Suppose that the relations among human beings, objects, and contexts were thought anew. Suppose further that instead of looking inside the tribal and modern masters of their crafts for either their world composing sets of beliefs or their deep lying instinct for form, one were to look inside the objects they make. Suppose finally that one were to look at the master maker as a machine or a purely natural object. The picture that reveals itself under these suppositions is one drawn by light, the pencil of nature. The picture is a photograph.

Photographed and Out of Date

Contexts

The writerly reader figured in *S/Z* and eroticized in *The Pleasure of the Text* reads in the way demanded by the avant-garde text, the text that makes no sense when read from the point of view of the received beliefs about the border relations among the concepts of language, literature, and life, and permitted by the classic text. The writerly reader subverts the assignments of value made by the culture, subsets of whose predicates comprise her particular identity just as its conception of what the human being is makes her the kind of thing she is and in so doing she subverts the claims to truth or to any kind of felicity made by the familiar conceptions of the self by which she can identify herself, specific "her" and generic "self" alike. Does she thereby read through other than her culture's eyes, adopt the points of view of cultures other than her own? Yes and no.

Yes, for the reader might make the assignments of meaning that one from a different culture would naturally make: she would make them only to unmake them, however; she would try them out, would not insist on their rightly or truly yielding up the meaning of what is read. The writerly readers would not read the Xwexwe mask-in-the-context-of-Kwakiutl-ritual in which it is used as really being what takes the place of noxious prehistoric monsters of which the Xwexwe is the last avatar, nor would she read the mask-in-the-primitivism-show as telling the truth about the mask as really being the product of the impulse to form shared by tribal and modern master. For the writerly reader plays the text she reads, follows the signifying chains, the paths out of the text, makes substitutions and combinations only to see the more that can be made. To express a text is to take its signs out of their familiar contexts, contextualize them anew, and recontextualize them yet again along the lines sighted from the first new context. Another *culture* is just one kind of new context, one new universe of discourse; a second kind is the framework specified by another *theory*, and a third is simply another *syntagm*, a different string of signs from the string in which the sign appears in the text being read. Any proper part of what is being read may be put into the context of another culture (another theory, another syntagm): it does not take up residence there but only passes through it as part of the intertext, part of what is most available when the keeper of culture, the censor, sleeps. Writerly reading begins with the reader's doing what is parallel to the psychoanalytic patient's noticing and reporting whatever comes into one's head and not being misled, for instance, into suppressing an idea because it strikes one as unimportant or irrelevant or because it seems meaningless. One must adopt a completely impartial attitude to what occurs, for it is precisely one's critical attitude that is responsible for one's being unable, in the ordinary course of things, to achieve the desired unraveling of one's dream or obsessional idea or whatever it may be.[16]

No, the writerly reader does not read through other than Western eyes or adopt the points of view of cultures other than her own, since her reading undoes the fixity, the self-containment, the integrity of any culture's point of view. Reading that is productive, writerly, is so precisely by virtue of its changing the lenses through which and the positions from which the reader is accustomed to look and adopting, seriatim, indefinitely many other starting points (of view): the more points at which the reader enter the text, the more plural her reading.

One result is that the supposition that there is something properly to be called Western or tribal eyes, Japanese or Mayan eyes, is called into question. A culture itself constitutes a text whose reading in the readerly way consists in accepting its systematic assignment of values and whose reading in the writerly way consists in making the reassignments of the system's signs, the substitutions and combinations, licensed by the possibilities of language. To see a Kwakiutl mask through tribal eyes, then, is to see it embedded in the particular sets of relations valorized by the tribe: it is to read the tribal culture in light of its received interpretations of itself and the mask in light of its place in that culture. To read the *mask* in a writerly way is to break it into units that are then severally and ceaselessly put into various contexts of which the tribal culture under its received interpretations is but one; to read the *tribal culture* in a writerly way is, in precisely the same manner, to divide it into units and ceaselessly to recontextualize them.

The question of when what such a reading produces can no longer properly be called "the Kwakiutl culture" is of a piece with the question of how much anything can change and still be the same thing. Both are instances of the puzzle that led to the Greek's supposition of the existence of substance, to the Enlightenment's transportation of substance into the nominal essences that are concepts, to the nineteenth century's temporalization of essences enduring in world or mind into ordered and inevitable change, and to the contemporary suspicion that what drives change is randomness ruled by the contrary forces of repetition, life's version of the law of conservation, and the will to activity exemplified by instincts. This is a puzzle, of course, just in case things *can* change, and one contemporary response to the identity questions the puzzle generates is to cast doubt on this possibility, mindful of the consequence that if nothing can change, then there can be nothing new unless the new itself springs from nothing. Something can be said to have changed only if it was some one bounded thing, self-same, ready of capture by thought: only so can *it* be said to have changed, and only if not all its properties are essential to it can it be said to have *changed* rather than to have ceased to exist. Things change when what is essential about them persists and only the accidents change. For this to be intelligible, however, it is necessary to be able to distinguish essence from accident, to make sense of a property's belonging to a thing albeit incidently, and to distinguish accident from context, figure from ground, sculpture from surrounding space, foreground from background, mask from tribal ritual.

Because of problems met in making the last distinction, it is tempting to argue with *Artforum* that because there may be no nonarbitrary way to mark the difference between mask and context, to recontextualize an object is to risk leaving behind something essential to its being what it is—tempting, that is, to argue that things are context-dependent in the strong sense of being falsified in being taken out of their contexts. The notions of what is essential to an object and its own proper context are, however, themselves rife with problems of the sort this move was designed to avoid and, more important, Barthes's conception of writerly reading has the effect of exploding the presumed proprieties of any contexts and any objects. The issue, then, becomes not whether tribal masks may or may not be taken out of their ritual contexts without ceasing to be tribal masks but, rather, how to read. For a readerly reading accepts the official description of any context at its face value, while a writerly reading reveals what the face hides, showing the face to be a kind of mask, a false face.

What such a reading reveals is that, for example, Japan, Barthes's empire of signs, Mayan civilization, written in stone, African, Oceanic, and Amerindian tribal cultures are intelligible only in light of what they do not say, what they exclude, what they deny, and what is excluded, hidden, concealed is in turn intelligible only in terms of what *it* does not say, and on without end. The conjunction of what cultures do and do not say, of what they sow and what they hide, of surface and depth, of what stands on each side of cultures' borders, absent the distinguishing mark that makes only one of the opposing elements worthy of being named by the culture, displaces the text that is, say, Japan or the Kwakiutl culture. If a thing is what it is by virtue of its place in a system, then the conjunction of unmarked opposites—one within, the other without, the system—destroys what it displaces.

Objects

Artforum's preoccupation with looking through eyes not one's own gives way to *Camera Lucida*'s preoccupation with looking at objects of a time not one's own, with looking at the past immobilized in photographs, and the former's specification of a class of objects that *share the intentionality proper to* primitive objects gives way to the latter's specification of a class of objects that *embody traces of some real thing*. The class of objects that share the world-constituting set of beliefs, desires, and intentions constitutive of a culture governed by shamanism includes artifacts made by both tribal craftsmen and contemporary Western artists who have succeeded in forgetting the values of Western civilization. The class of objects that embody traces of real things includes both the ritual objects made by tribal craftsmen and photographs.

Because photographs are not only indexical, as primitive works are, but also index the past as postmodern works do, they stand at a place where the primitive and the postmodern intersect. Postmodern works incorporate past styles, ritual objects incorporate the power of ancester or god, and photographs incorporate light-formed traces of the physical object that stood before the camera. When light rays are bent and imprinted upon chemically treated plates, it is because there is an object before the plate. And when power resides in a primitive mask, it is because there is a being whose power may be summoned by wearing the mask. Material object and powerful being alike are independent of the artifacts to which they are causally related: neither the object's materiality nor the being's power is exhausted by the photograph or the mask. The photographed object may be out of date, indeed, it may no longer exist, but the imprint of the light rays it shaped is present in the photograph. The ancestor or god may be in a place different from the place of the mask—in nature or a nether world—but its power inhabits the mask. The space between past and present, and between nature or nether worlds and social worlds, is bridged by the artifacts themselves. By a carnal skin is the first space said to be bridged:

> A sort of umbilical cord links the body of the photographed thing to my gaze: light, though impalpable, is here a carnal medium, a skin I share with anyone who has been photographed. . . . And if Photography belonged to a world with some *residual sensitivity to myth*, we should exult over the richness of the symbol: the loved body is immortalized by the mediation of a precious metal, silver (monument and luxury); to which we might add the notion that this metal, like all the metals of Alchemy, is alive. [italics added][17]

Science and magic are names for what spans the divide between nature (or nether world) and society, where the society that negotiates nature by science is civilized, the one that negotiates by magic primitive. The ritual object by magic incorporates the power of ancestor or god or natural force, the photograph by light incorporates its object.

By what power does the postmodern trace or embody the past? What is the medium that links them, what the umbilical cord? Is the relation between postmodern buildings and past styles, for example, in any way like the relation between photographs and their objects? How can the postmodern building be said to index the past by incorporating designs from the past into its design? Peirce's characterization of the index suggests how a postmodern work indexes the past it includes:

> An *index* is a sign which would, at once, lose the character which makes it a sign if its object were removed, but would not lose that character if there were no interpretant. Such, for instance, is a piece of mould with a bullet-hole in it as a sign of a shot; for without the shot there would have been no hole, but there is a hole there, whether anybody has the sense to attribute it to a shot or not.[18]

The Humana building would lose the character that makes elements in it a sign of the outdated Art Deco style had there not been such a style, and the elements are tokens of the style whether anyone recognizes them as such or not. Parts of the building *index* the outdated style. Yet the example of the bullet hole indexing the shot that caused it seems to raise a problem. For an index is said to be a sign that refers to its object *by virtue of being really affected by* that object, where what makes it a sign is not the quality it has in common with the object by which it is affected but the *actual modification of it* by the object. This supposes sign and object to be distinct, the sign having been causally affected by the object. Inasmuch as a building and its style are not causally related, how can the Humana building be an index of the Art Deco style?

It is precisely the Humana building's being an amalgam of different moments from the past that challenges both the conception of an artifact as an expression of the spirit, the life, the style of the time in which it was built and the value of unity. Moreover, a part whose style is not that of other parts and of the whole is like a quotation in not being integral to the discourse within which it appears. Not integral to the unity of the building whose elements they are, the Art Deco elements in the Humana building are relics of another time, as quotations in a discourse are relics of the speech of another person: their presence signals or *indexes* the other time and the other speech. The quoted elements may be said *actually to modify* the building by disrupting its unity as a univocal expression of any one time. For in so doing they change what the building is: they turn it into a collage of fragments from the past.

What links the past style and its incorporation in the postmodern building? Where light is "a sort of umbilical cord that links the body of the photographed thing to my gaze," *similarity of configuration* of line and plane is what links past styles to postmodern artifacts. Lines and planes, not the maker's intention to design in a certain style, are what determine whether or not a work is in a particular style. The similarity of configuration is geometrical, formal, not causal, as is the relation between a photograph and its object, but the configural similarity of lines and planes and the light-carried shape of the photographed object are alike in *not being intentional*. The style quoted in the postmodern building and the body apparent in the photograph are alike in *being past*. Finally, neither is postmodernism simply one style among others nor is the photographic image simply one image among others.

The elements of a postmodern building, for example, are not original and the building itself is not self-contained because each quotation is a path out of the building to the past whose style is quoted, and the photographic image is not a copy:

> The realists, of whom I am one and of whom I was already one when I asserted that the Photograph was an image without a code—even if, obviously, certain codes do inflect our reading of it—the realists do not take the photograph for a "copy" of reality, but for an emanation of *past reality:* a *magic,* not an art.[19]

This emanation is a mutant, "neither image nor reality; a new being, really: a reality one can no longer touch."[20] Here lies a difference between photographs and postmodern works that is all in all: the photographic image is a reality, albeit one that cannot be touched, a public sense datum, whereas the past style embodied in the postmodern object is configural, not real, mathematical, not material. True, the past reality proved by the photograph, the material something that fronted the camera, has been dissolved by the camera into light, and this dissolution of mass into light, the destabilizing of the object, mimes what Einstein discovered—namely, that when objects move at a speed approaching the speed of light, their mass increases to infinity.

The relativity of the real to having been caught by the camera and, hence, its conversion to light, its reduction to the moment the camera clicks, suggests that not matter but light and the air through which it travels, measuring time and space as it goes, are what are real. Neither past style nor photographic image is material and both are configured, but where style is a configuration of *lines* not determined by the matter it configures, the image is a configuration of rays of *light* determined by the matter that configures it. The photograph is a *new* form of hallucination, a *new* being, neither image nor reality; it affords a *new* experience, a *new* order of proof, an immediate experience of the past. Barthes calls the photograph the advent of the new: its coming divides the history of the world because for the first time the past can be reached unmediated by memory, by witnesses' words, or by monuments that declare time's passage. The photograph, like the fossil, stops the play of the world, and so too do we when we are touched by the stillness and the pastness of the still past world, more touched by photograph than fossil, for while the fossil speaks the death, the photograph speaks the life of its own dead object.

New to a people with writing and written histories in which their language and their past are inscribed, the photograph, foreign to language and to history, is not new to a people who can write neither their speech nor their past, a people we call primitive. Photography is not new to primitive peoples in that a photograph's ahistorical and unmediated presentation of the light-configuring real is akin to a tribal carving's ahistorical and unmediated presentation of its originating power, its mana:

> The idea of mana is one of those troublesome notions which we had thought to have discarded; we therefore experience difficulty in grasping it. It is obscure and vague, yet the use to which it is put is curiously definite. It is abstract and general, yet quite concrete. Its primitive nature—that is, its complexity and confusion—resists any attempt at a logical analysis, and we must remain content to describe the phenomenon. . . .
>
> The idea of mana consists of a series of fluid notions which merge into each other. At different times it may be a quality, a substance or an activity. . . . Mana is a force, more especially the force of spirit beings, that is to say, the souls of ancestors and nature spirits.[21]

Photograph and tribal carving avoid the system of representation regnant in Western culture and achieve their end, the emanation of a power to configure light or to intervene in nature's course, not by the intentional action of an agent: photographer and tribal artesan are handmaiden to the referent from which neither photograph nor tribal carving can be distinguished.

Barthes says of himself that in being affected as he is by particular photographs, he is a primitive without (Western) culture. In this he may seem to be like *Artforum*'s Western primitivist artist who has forgotten the values of the West and adopted the point of view of one from a tribal culture. He is not, however, for two reasons. The first is that *Artforum* supposes that there is something properly to be called, say, the Kwakiutl culture, while Barthes holds that whatever is significant can be read in a writerly way, where it properly is what is made out of it in the act of reading. For McEvilley the significance of a tribal carving is a function of its cultural horizon, the *studium,* the field of culturally coded information on which it appears, whereas for Barthes this significance is secondary to the carving's *punctum:* "the direct magical affectiveness [Picasso] knew to be the inherent power of the visual arts, an affectiveness with which the Western tradition had somehow lost contact."[22] The power in question is a power that inheres in the visual art objects themselves, not in maker, not in her impulses, instincts, intentions. To recognize the *studium* is, Barthes says, to encounter the maker's intentions, but to be wounded, pricked, pierced, marked, punctuated, stung by the *punctum* is to be affected by an accident, a detail, a partial thing that does not attest to the maker's art or to his intention to make an object of a certain kind.

Photographs are postmodern under Barthes's description; they index the past real as postmodern buildings index past styles. They index *forces*, the power to figure light, to obliterate the distance between past and present, to carry the spectator who is touched by them back to the time of their taking. The buildings index *figures*, lines and planes related in a characteristic way. When matter is seen to increase without limit at a certain speed and the absolute fixity of material things is undone, then forces and figures become the extreme terms of the opposition between matter and form that generated the conceptual scheme drawn in classical Greece and replaced by the one conceived in classical France, one whose founding opposition is between subject and object. A different music sounds here from that heard in the Museum of Modern Art's hymn to viewers' responses and *Artforum*'s hymn to objects' original contexts, a music written in Athens, written in a scale different from that of Descartes's triumph. Postmodern in being a present index of the past real, photographs are postmodern too in being mad *and* tame, in being instruments on which are played the songs written in New York *and* the song Barthes's writes in Paris, a lament, an ode to joy, a sad song, but above all else a love song to his mother, whose photograph as a little girl in a winter garden showed him the magic of photographs as African masks showed Picasso their magic.

Notes

1. Roland Barthes, *Roland Barthes by Roland Barthes* (New York: Hill and Wang, 1977), p. 69.

2. Roland Barthes, *Camera Lucida* (London: Jonathan Cape, 1982), p. 119.

3. The referents may be types or tokens (individual examples of types). Historic preservations and art and ethnographic museums are devoted to the preservation and display of tokens from the past and other cultures. Postmodernist architecture uses styles, types, from the past, and certain Western twentieth-century works of art are said to be "primitivist"; not themselves tokens of primitive works, they are nonetheless of the same type as the primitive works.

4. G. W. F. Hegel, *The Phenomenology of Mind* (New York: Harper and Row, 1967).

5. Michel Foucault, *The Order of Things* (New York: Pantheon, 1971) and *The Archaeology of Knowledge* (New York: Pantheon, 1972).

6. John E. Hancock, professor of architecture, College of Design, Architecture, Art, and Planning, University of Cincinnati. Private correspondence.

7. Reference by William Rubin to conversations with Picasso in Douglas C. McGill, "What does Modern Art Owe to the Primitives?," *The New York Times*, sec. 2, Sept. 23, 1984, p. 16.

8. William Rubin's words to Barbara Rose as reported by her in "The Man from MOMA," *Vogue*, August 1984, p. 416.

9. This is the question on which the critical exchange between the Museum of Modern Art and *Artforum* turns. Thomas McEvilley, "Doctor Lawyer Indian Chief: '"Primitivism" in Twentieth-Century Art' at the Museum of Modern Art in 1984," *Artforum*, November 1984. Exchange between William Rubin, Kurt Varnadoe, and Thomas McEvilley, *Artforum*, February 1985. Further response by Rubin and reply by McEvilley, *Artforum*, May 1985. Also, Kurt Varnadoe, "On the Claims and Critics of the 'Primitivism' Show," *Art in America*, May 1985. Janet Malcolm, "Profiles: A Girl of the Zeitgeist—II," *The New Yorker*, October 27, 1986.

10. William Rubin, "Modernist Primitivism," *"Primitivism" in Twentieth-Century Art*, ed. William Rubin (New York: Museum of Modern Art, 1984), 1:55. Subsequent references to Rubin are from this article.

11. Ibid., p. 38.

12. McEvilley, *Artforum*, February 1985, p. 51.

13. Rubin, *"Primitivism,"* p. 28.

14. Ibid., p. 78.

15. Ibid., pp. 53, 55.

16. Sigmund Freud, *The Interpretation of Dreams* (New York: Avon Books, 1965) pp. 133–34.

17. *Camera Lucida*, p. 81.

18. Justus Buchler, *Philosophical Writings of Peirce* (New York: Dover Books, 1955), pp. 101ff.

19. *Camera Lucida*, p. 88.

20. Ibid., p. 87.

21. Marcel Mauss, *A General Theory of Magic* (New York: Norton, 1975), pp. 108–9.

22. Rubin, *"Primitivism,"* p. 55.

Part II

Subjects and Stories

3

Subjectivity as Critique and the Critique of Subjectivity in Keats's *Hyperion*

Carol L. Bernstein

One of the problems of postmodernist literary criticism has been that of aligning it with other cultural objects of modernity and of postmodernity itself. Like Twemlow in Dickens's *Our Mutual Friend*, who faces the bottomless abyss of deciding whether he is Veneering's oldest or his newest friend, criticism faces the abyssal decision of where to situate its primary—or its ultimate—affiliations. It would seem to be a contradiction in terms for poststructuralist criticism to defend only the new, although a defense of the old would put its very qualities at risk.

We have seen the results of complicity between criticism and its object before: a poem may be read as a failed epic or as evidence of a struggle for authorial identity, depending on one's critical approach. Add to this the labyrinthine relations of the modern and the postmodern, and the decision regarding affiliation, no matter how critical, does seem to be an impossible one to make. One way out, however, appears in Andreas Huyssen's suggestion that poststructuralism's critical stance, its "retrospective reading" of modernity, locates poststructuralism liminally in the territories of both the modern and the postmodern.[1]

In a similar vein, Lyotard argues that a work of art "can become modern only if it is first postmodern. Postmodernism thus understood is not modernism at its end but in the nascent state,"[2] for modernism comes into being in the conceptualizations that succeed it. Yet the question of "what follows" abhors linearity; a more fitting image might be Coleridge's new moon, which holds the old moon in its arms.[3] Let us look at that part of the modernist scenario that foregrounds subjectivity or self-reflexivity: whether it be figured as the progress of reason or the inquiry into the human heart, the theme of a coming to consciousness (which unfolds from or is folded into the unconscious) grounds or reappears in an array of modernist projects or texts.

Poststructuralist theory, as we know, tends to undermine the primacy of subjectivity. Yet ironically, the postmodern questioning of the subject, especially insofar as it is understood to be unitary and conscious, assumes a certain self-consciousness in the act of questioning itself. In effect, self or self-consciousness is separated from its cultural origin, but only in order to return to it by way of a critical gaze, by way of speculation or specularity. It seems as if postmodernism is engaged in a salvage operation at the same time that it is prepared to jettison the very premises of modernism; the "death" of the subject gets played out by way of repression and displacement, for subjectivity reappears in order to constitute a mode of critique. Thus a postmodern stance would want to have it both ways, placing thoughtful man "under erasure" at the same time that its critique incorporates fragments of subjectivity: those fragments are now both part of the mind's machinery and the relics upon which that machinery focuses. Bricoleurs, it seems, would have a field day.

One way of construing this structure appears in Foucault's conception of the double, which "presents itself to reflection as the blurred projection of what man is in his truth, but that also plays the role of a preliminary ground upon which man must collect himself and recall himself in order to attain his truth."[4] For Foucault, what man thinks about himself, what he knows about himself, and what he conceives of as his origin are played out against the background of the Other, of what is alien to or historically independent of mankind. It would be a contradiction in terms to speak of the alien or the Other except in relation to man: the separation depends upon a specular or perspectival relation, here repressed as a function or culture. Just as thought is definable only in relation to the unthought—a move that suspends all certainties about being—so speech is dependent upon prior conceptions of language:

> [When man] attempts to define his essence as a speaking subject, prior to any effectively constituted language, all he ever finds is the previously unfolded possibility of language, and not the stumbling sound, the first word upon the basis of which all languages and even language itself became possible. It is always against a background of the already begun that man is able to reflect on what may serve for him as origin. [*The Order of Things*, p. 330]

The double in its various manifestations then represents both man and his truth, "projected" or "thrown forward," in which man is nevertheless inseparable from his alien origins; "blurred" yet distinct from his grounds, almost from himself. ("Grounding," we may observe, is the metaphor that allows the progress of reason or the inquiry into the human heart to appear as a figure. Yet inasmuch as suspicion of the ground is a salient feature of poststructuralist criticism, to call the ground into question would also make indeterminate the status of the figure.) Preliminary ground and projection, origin and end, then form a structure comprised of two dependent parts. Reflection upon oneself, or self-reflection, is inevitably implicated with the not-self. "Man" is himself diacritical, prone to the self-division of the double but also to an imaginary reconstitution in the mirror of theoretical reflection. Such a scenario is replicated in the cultural narrative of modernism, in which the status of man and his subjectivity is so central.

In this dyadic relation, the modern generates the postmodern, but the modern is nevertheless inconceivable without the prior knowledge and critical understanding of the postmodern. The latter thus appears as a critical double moment in the continuing narrative of modernism. Both Huyssen and Foucault, then, project figurative structures for cultural history, which are at once linear and folded, continuous and ruptured. Although they are somewhat abstract, these figures are necessarily diacritical, products of the very structures they cast on to their subjects. The rhetoric of doubling and projection, of otherness and specularity, of finiteness and indeterminacy, of progression and rupture, and of an innocent afterlife or a more sinister belatedness, inhabits contemporary theorizing about modernity and postmodernity. But while the debate tends to favor an either/or form, a both/and form seems more promising. If the link is repressed, if it is represented only in the bar between the terms, that bar may signal that the death of the subject generates an afterlife, a return of the repressed.

I

Ironically, another analogous situation appears in Keats's *Hyperion*, in which the fall of the Titans and the succession of the Olympian gods is limned. While the poem transposes a Miltonic transposition of biblical myth, it also represents the birth of the modern poet in the figure of Apollo. But the violent emergence of the poet figure in the fragmentary third book challenges one myth of the second book, in which world history appears to be represented, in Oceanus's speech, as a succession of gradual and progressive events. While one might be justifiably wary of granting pride of place to Oceanus, many readers have been prone to do just that, and to associate his grand narrative of progress with the Enlightenment. This has been identified as one of Keats's projects: Oceanus then prophesies the modernity that is to be incarnated in Apollo. Yet Apollo's "modernity" comes as no easy birth: rather it is represented as an agonized dying into life, which breaks off abruptly. The effective collapse of the Enlightenment perspective with the gesture toward the unrepresentable, toward a sublime cancellation or supersession of history, might then be identified with postmodernity. Oceanus's reading of divine succession as a continuing process in which the more beautiful must be the more powerful, appears in a more violent register in Apollo, who incorporates almost literally the "Knowledge enormous" of the past, but whose brain is filled with "Creations and destroyings" that belie the conception of gentle progress. I do not mean to shift the historical frames of modernity and postmodernity, but rather to suggest that the poem "reads" those cultural moments by offering an allegory of their relation. Both are revolutionary, but each moment marks a turn upon the other's revolutionary premise.

In construing the agonistic meeting ground, *Hyperion* represents a symbiotic or reversible structure in which each perspective casts light upon the other. Thrown into the abyss of temporality and mortality, the Titans attempt nevertheless to control the future by narrative projection. To the bellicose Saturn, Oceanus proffers a narrative of progress that will convert the "pain of truth" into a "balm."[5] In counterpoint, the emergence of Apollo, whose brain is filled with texts of past events, or with "knowledge enormous" of the events themselves, signifies an attempt to control the past. Both instances, of projection on the one hand and of introjection on the other, involve repetition, but repetition in translation, as it were. There is an implicit conversion of feeling tone. Although both are gestures of narrative reaching out, the Titans look back upon a catastrophic recent past while the Olympian moves forward by facing the past, propelled, like Klee's angel in Benjamin's account, into the future by his retrospective stance.[6]

Hyperion's "reading" of modernity and postmodernity, then, casts them into the form of a doublet in which each plays the role of ground for the other. Three of the major problematic areas of the doublet are represented in the poem: the death of the subject and its textual reconstitution; the grand march of history with its recasting into a form of narrative representation; the critique of representation as a power play in which "A power more strong in beauty, born of us / And fated to excel us, as we pass in glory that old darkness" (II, 213–15) turns and re-turns. Oceanus identifies repetition grounded in excess, where "glory" surpasses darkness and beauty then "excels" glory, although is account masks conflict in the transfer of power: "doth the dull soil / Quarrel with the proud forests it hath fed"? (II, 217–18). The poem figures the uncanny in local ways, but it also figures uncannily the advent of modernism-postmodernism as both structure and problematic.

To view the poem in this light, in a figurative reading of its own figural role, would be to appropriate and revise Huyssen's remark that poststructuralism is a discourse of and about modernism. Now Romanticism plays an analogous role for the poet of Enlightenment, who sees himself as the modern poet compelled to create a new and appropriate discourse for poetic mythology. Huyssen goes on to say that French poststructuralist theory "provides us . . . with an *archeology of modernity,* a theory of modernism at the stage of its exhaustion" (*After the Great Divide*, p. 209). One might say the same of Keats, insofar as the gesture of Romantic modernism places the Enlightenment idea of progress in the ambiguous light of Apollo's agonies, of a succession without distinct beginning or end, *archē* or *telos.* (The Egyptian imagery, incidentally, not only runs counter to the Enlightenment Hellenism in a political sense,[7] but it evokes that very archeological setting which, with its indecipherable hieroglyphics and indeterminate Memnonic sounds, mystifies reading and memory—or Mnemosyne.)

Apollo, moreover, is not just passively filled with "knowledge enormous": his agony reads that history of the past by evoking the strife-filled elision that marks Oceanus's account as well as that of Keats, whose account of a benign Coelus represses the strife of Giants and Titans. Not only do Keats's Apollo and Hyperion anticipate Nietzsche's reading of an Apollinian in tension with its dark underside,[8] but they offer a reading of the ambiguities of historical mythologizing.

II

My point here is not to dislocate our sense of cultural periods—although Keats's poem raises radical questions about the length of the period needed to identify them—but to suggest that reading on the cultural scale can be a two-way process. One mediating conception is that of translation, in which the centered self or narrative or text is decentered, and in which the translation bears—to borrow

Benjamin's image—a tangential relation to the original. There is in fact a double transformation: "For just as the tenor and the significance of the great works of literature undergo a complete transformation over the centuries, the mother tongue of the translator is transformed as well."[9]

Translation, as Benjamin suggests, is situated in some pivotal space where it gathers up the "afterlife" of the old original language as well as the "suffering" of the new. The oxymoronic construction, linking the afterlife of the old with the suffering of the new, allows *Hyperion* to prefigure the modernity-postmodernity doublet. (We may note here too that "afterlife" is only a step away from the *Nachtraglichkeit* or belatedness that infects the very term "poststructuralism.") The selfhood of language, or the language of the self, cannot be unitary. The more promising side of this double play is the implication that text and subject are enfolded in one another, and that the domain of subjectivity is not less but more extensive than a determinate modernism might have allowed

Hyperion thus stages a scene of translation, of the Miltonic into the modern; of Titans into Olympians; of the "mother tongue" into the language of Keats—the Other tongue; of a mourning malady (the Titans' "mourning words," the "aspen malady" of Saturn's "palsied tongue") into a morning melody (the "melodious throat" of Apollo, the sun god).[10] But within this narrative of divine displacement and linguistic change there is also resistance, for translation, Benjamin remarks, focuses upon a "life" that can be known only by indirection, by some form of figuration. Yet Benjamin is enigmatic: Does the life reside in the textual relationships themselves? It would seem so, for the birth of Apollo in book 3 is prefigured by the myth of progress and the virtually inarticulate cries of Clymene in book 2. The subject, the product of a combined articulation and disarticulation, is already written, and Apollo's awareness of those "Creations and destroyings" is his vocal repetition of that earlier writing. Inasmuch as undoing is part of the process—and a violent one at that—translation cannot be a linear move. Apollo's cry—"Knowledge enormous makes a god of me"(III,113)—proclaims his subjectivity at the same time that it makes it other than himself, some ground, which we may call Foucaultean, upon which his self or "truth" may be articulated. One may also suspect that sublimation is at work here, with its conspiratorial ally, repression. If Apollo is the modern poet, he is born into modernity at the same time that he is borne past it by dying into life. Earlier, Saturn, the fallen Titan, laments his self-division: "I am gone / Away from my own bosom; I have left / My strong identity, my real self. . . ."(I,112–14).

The space of *Hyperion* is liminal: while the Olympian Apollo has no identity other than earlier texts (which is not quite the same as having no identity at all), the Titans are separated from their strong identities. Saturn has left his "somewhere between the throne and where I sit / Here on this spot of earth"(I,115–16). Although Saturn speaks as if identity or selfhood were locatable in a distinct place, "throne" and "spot" are metaphors for plenitude and deprivation. By this logic, however, Saturn's loss of identity ought to restore him to the place he has lost, if Apollo is indeed part of the new race who have no identities at all.

The birth of Apollo does recuperate the loss of the Titans, but not by substitution. It is not merely a case of the beautiful being replaced by the more beautiful, nor even one in which the loss of identity is heralded and then confirmed. Rather, transition is a rough business, inhabited by creations and destroyings that may be retrieved later as knowledge, but that preclude direct communication. One logic would link creation with the beautiful, and destroyings with the more beautiful: surely this hints at a suppression of the sublime, or a sublime repression. If we project these divine disturbances onto the modernity-poststructuralism doublet with which we started, then the one cannot be the simple continuation of the other in some figurative afterlife. (Afterlife itself has a double meaning: it is not just survival, but life after a violent rupture.) The knowledge that confers divinity is restorative, but it comes obliquely.

It would seem, then, as if the role of poststructuralism vis-à-vis modernity is recuperative only upon the understanding that repetition can never be the same. Even "rewriting" seems to be too tame a category. Thus Huyssen writes that the "postmoderns . . . counter the modernist litany of the death of the subject by working toward new theories and practices of speaking, writing, and acting subjects. The question of how codes, texts, images, and other cultural artifacts constitute subjectivity is increasingly being raised as an always already historical question" (*After the Great Divide*, p. 213). His brain filled with texts, Apollo seems to represent the recuperated postmodern subject. Yet those very textual fragments mark the death of the poem, the fragmenting of the text, which ends at that point with Apollo's agonized cry.

We seem to have gone from the work to a text that is relentlessly indeterminate, neither singular nor plural. What is most determinate is that Apollo undergoes a vertiginous expansion of consciousness: this is what deifies him. Elevation is coupled with an excess that casts a curious backward glance upon Oceanus's idealizing speech in book 2. Surely Apollo is not acting out the measured progress that Oceanus prophesies. No more is his sublime—but not sublimated—elevation identical with Saturn's descent into pathos or subjectivity: the one dies into life as the other falls into mortality. The cultural model, like that of any doubling, conjoins sameness with difference.

III

Let us return to postmodernist criticism's Twemlovian dilemma concerning its relation to earlier literature. In its simplest forms, it offers new ways of reading old texts: those old texts appear as more or less neutral moments in the poststructuralist project. In those instances, the texts are neither transformed nor recuperated: rather, they attest to the power of new interpretive strategies. That puts them into a passive situation where their period contexts are more or less irrelevant. Archeology, which on the contrary might privilege those period contexts, is equally irrelevant, for it entails no transformative procedures but rather tips the balance the other way. One of the premises of poststructuralist theory, however, is that such an imbalance must be ruled out in the name of intertextuality: the literary text assumes a posture of equality in the face of theory. Huyssen's conception presents an additional dilemma, moreover, for it is difficult to locate the point at which poststructuralism separates itself from modernity in the saga of the subject. Nevertheless, Keats's poem offers a viable critical frame at these points:

First, the myth of the war in heaven, of the overthrow of the old regime of gods by the new regime, claims to be a totalizing myth not only because it accounts for progress or enlightenment, but precisely because it claims to align biblical with classical myths. Whatever the local version, all myths are in fact versions of the one true myth. But the "grand narrative" of myth is not always identical with that of history. The relation between myth and history is likely to be one of difference, especially since myth's "progress" is frequently figured as diminution. The fallen Thea speaks to Saturn "In solemn tenour and deep organ tone / Some mourning words," which, translated into "our feeble tongue" are "frail" compared with "that large utterance of the early Gods!"(I, 48–49, 50–51). Hers is the language of belatedness, a form of diminishment, in which frailty appears as woman who is ironically separated from the mother tongue.

Second, Apollo's dying into life in the third book of *Hyperion* presents a point of rupture that is also a moment of sublimity. Apollo, who overwhelms his predecessors, is engulfed by the very textual traces of the Titans that should empower him. This is what overturns the myth of progress, and what argues that history itself proceeds by radical breaks. Not reason, not the "more beautiful," but the sublime marks the succession of history. But the sublime itself involves a communion with the unthinkable, the unconditioned, the unrepresentable: thus the project of the future is always to seek out what is impossible or what was always unthought before. Here we may return to an analogue in Foucault's doubles. If the narrative rhetoric of book 2 represents the thought, it is shadowed and eventually eclipsed by the unthought of book 3.

Third, the fall of Hyperion signifies a fall into temporality, thus providing the conditions for the grand narrative in which myth itself is subject to historical movement. The third book, however, interrupts that temporality and reverses the movement. In effect, it thematizes the birth of the postmodern, which appears in that oxymoronic phrase as "Creations and destroyings." The postmodern is then subject to the same evasions and ruptures as any construction of mythic narrative. However covertly, myth here is ideologically weighted, as if, subject to history, it undergoes diminution.

Fourth, by way of a conclusion we may return to the beginning of *Hyperion* where Saturn, newly fallen, mourns his absence from himself. The remarkable closure of the sound patterns figures a verbal narcissism, which is repeated in the image of "fallen divinity" shading and deadening the stream by which he sits. This is indeed an oxymoronic still life or *nature morte*. His footsteps marked in the "margin-sand," his right hand "nerveless" on the sodden ground, this mourning Saturn is the very figure of *disjecta membra*—an image made all the more powerful if we remember that this is not just a fragmentary reminiscence of Milton rewritten in Keats, but one of Wordsworth as well, for surely Saturn sitting stonelike near his lair recalls the familiar image of the leech-gatherer as both stone and sea-beast.[11] If this pairing questions authorial resolution and independence, it also makes of the self a poetic archive of sorts.

Further, Saturn's listening to the Earth, his ancient mother, evokes uncannily the passage in *The Prelude,* which Keats could not have seen, where the young Wordsworth listens to the ghostly language of the ancient earth.[12] Poetic nurture, made "ghostly" or external, grounds the subject outside himself.[13] Here is a fantasy of dismemberment, of some prearticulate time in which language reveals its own independence of the speaker. Here too the fall into humanity, onto "margin-sand," moves dangerously close to what Foucault characterizes as "the erasure of man, like a face drawn in sand on the edge of the sea" (*The Order of Things,* p. 387). Keats's poem situates fallen divinity in some marginal area where mortality lies adjacent to what Foucault calls "sandy stretches of non-thought" (ibid., 323).

Yet such a reading, even though it reveals the indissoluble links between the modern and the postmodern subjects, the latter indeed appearing like some return of the repressed, might seem to be too neatly allegorical. All those figures, from the various doubles to the Titanic figure on the sandy ground, tell us as much about the way in which we are prone to construe cultural relations as about those relations themselves. We should remember, however, not only the importance of the fragment in both Keats's poems and poststructuralist texts, but also the importance of the Egyptian images in *Hyperion*, images that bespeak a romantic poetics of the lost and the incomprehensible or indecipherable.[14] These images, like Saturn lying nerveless or "sans sense,"[15] evoke the problematic of translation, which unseats such a straightforward reading and suggests that an understanding of the contemporary moment requires a third term to invoke the figurative, the mediated, or the deferred. Theorists of translation remind us of its violent, nonlinear nature, whether in the myth of the tower of Babel or the image of amphora.[16]

While translation seems to double the available text, the very process is divisive. The images of voice and tongue dispersed throughout *Hyperion*, moreover, are concerned not only with the material but with adequation, with the subject's *mode* of subjectivity, with utterance as a sublime act: with translation. The very materiality of voice, the tongue of fallenness, of postdivinity, is, belatedly, unable to evoke the newly sublime. The inadequation that inheres in the sublime moment is at its most ironic here. Nevertheless, if the sublime encounter often acts as a check to self-reflection, it may foster an inner awareness of feeling. Not only is sorrow, bafflement, or terror aroused in Saturn, Apollo, or Hyperion, but an awareness of oneself experiencing those powerful emotions. While they may halt narrative, they do so in the name of a consciousness of self far more powerful than what is available to self-reflection. In this respect, the sublime interfaces with the fragment or aphorism: both bespeak intensity as well as loss.

In this scheme, Keats's modern poet, like his newly emergent Apollo, cannot simply follow the course of the sun, for he is too much in the place of the son. Even in his fallen state, golden-haired Hyperion appears as a "shape majestic, a vast shade / In midst of his own brightness" (II, 372–73). If Hyperion appears like some Nietzschean sunspot, Apollo reverses the image, appearing masklike as some "luminous" [spot] to cure eyes damaged by gruesome night."[17] Even as a curative figure, however, Apollo cannot be independent. His immortality emerges as the afterlife of old texts, as the creation of divine and poetic catastrophe. For it is a revolutionary sublime that halts the progress of the allegorical, deferring—if deference is possible at such a time—to a detour into translation. Yet if Apollo is subject to old texts or Titanic narratives, never was the consciousness of subjectivity more intense. We might remember that, if we assume that postmodernism and modernism are in collusion to ensure the death of the subject: for subjectivity may be at its most intense at its most catastrophic moment.

Notes

1. See Andreas Huyssen, *After the Great Divide: Modernism, Mass Culture, Postmodernism* (Bloomington and Indianapolis: Indiana University Press, 1986). Huyssen's "Mapping the Postmodern" foregrounds some of the complexities that must be encountered in identifying the domain of modernism or postmodernism. Thus the very use of the quasi-historical "postmodernism" seems problematic when history and narrative themselves are called into question. In this essay, I try to limit the term "poststructuralism" to critical discourse, and to treat modernism and postmodernism as abstract cultural moments.

2. Jean-François Lyotard, *The Postmodern Condition: A Report on Knowledge* (Minneapolis: University of Minnesota Press, 1984), p. 79.

3. See S. T. Coleridge, "Dejection: An Ode," stanza 1.

4. Michel Foucault, *The Order of Things: An Archaeology of the Human Sciences* (New York: Random House, 1973), p. 327.

5. John Keats, *Hyperion, A Fragment. The Poems of John Keats,* ed. Miriam Allott (New York: Norton, 1970), 2:202, 243. All quotations are from this edition.

6. See Walter Benjamin, "Theses on the Philosophy of History," in *Illuminations* (New York: Schocken Books, 1979), pp. 257–58.

7. For an account of the political import of Keats's Egyptian images, see Alan J. Bewell, "The Political Implications of Keats's Classicist Aesthetics," *Studies in Romanticism,* 25 (Summer 1986): 220–29.

8. See Tilottama Rajan, *Dark Interpreter: The Discourse of Romanticism* (Ithaca and London: Cornell University Press, 1980), pp. 167–70. Rajan, however, locates the recognition in Keats's later poem, *The Fall of Hyperion.*

9. "The Task of the Translator," in *Illuminations,* p. 73.

10. *Hyperion,* I, 49–51, 92–94; III, 81.

11. See William Wordsworth, "Resolution and Independence," stanza 9.

12. See *The Prelude*, II, 302–11.

13. See Geoffrey H. Hartman, "Spectral Symbolism and Authorial Self in Keats's *Hyperion*," in *The Fate of Reading* (Chicago: University of Chicago Press, 1975), pp. 57–73.

14. See, e.g., *Hyperion*, I, 31–33, 275–80; II, 372–77.

15. See Cynthia Chase's commentary on Derrida's use of *sans* in "Paragon, Parergon: Baudelaire Translates Rousseau," in *Difference in Translation*, ed. Joseph F. Graham (Ithaca and London: Cornell University Press, 1985), p. 74.

16. See Jacques Derrida, "Des Tours de Babel," trans. Joseph F. Graham, in *Difference in Translation*, pp. 165–207, and Walter Benjamin, "The Task of the Translator."

17. See Friedrich Nietzsche, *The Birth of Tragedy* (New York: Random House, 1967), sec. 9, p. 67.

4

Eliot, Pound, and the Subject of Postmodernism

Antony Easthope

> "There's no more nature"
>
> **Beckett,** *Endgame*

We should now be especially wary of homologies. The concept of postmodernism promises to help us in the crucial endeavor of thinking the present but it does so at the risk of assuming, for example, that recent innovations in architecture, *Miami Vice* on television, problems in philosophy (the crisis of epistemology), and developments in communication technology all derive from a common center. This form of conceptualization, seeing the social formation as unified and homogeneous, an "expressive totality," is precisely that against which the work of Althusser intervenes, notably in asserting the necessity to decenter our conception of time.

Naming the dominant concept of linear and chronological time as burgeois time, affirming the specific effects of each level and mode of practice operating according to its internal necessities, Althusser argues that "we have to assign to each level a *peculiar time*, relatively autonomous and hence relatively independent."[1] This argument, set out in 1968, precedes and helps to make possible Lyotard's conceptualization of postmodernism and may have a touch of novelty for American readers (who have so far remained relatively impervious to the work of Althusser). But it should be no surprise that it is a view underwritten by Jacques Derrida, who, citing Althusser, remarks, "I have always subscribed to this."[2]

Nevertheless, in confronting the present, an idea of postmodernism, and especially that outlined in Lyotard's *The Postmodern Condition*, can be drawn on if the argument confines itself to a single "time," to the autonomy and specific effectivity of a particular level in the social formation. Here I shall consider three instances of a specific and relatively homogeneous historical discourse—the

English poetic tradition—to test how appropriately analysis of the three texts may be framed in the concepts of classicism, modernism, and postmodernism. The poems are Donne's "Elegy 19," Eliot's *The Waste Land,* Pound's *Pisan Cantos.*

One further unavoidable preliminary. Each text will be discussed within a perspective that may be named as British poststructuralism—that is, the analysis of aesthetic texts in terms of the position they offer to the reader.[3] We no longer think of the text apart from the reader or subject of that text; analysis, therefore, must take on board the possibility of subjectivity as historically constituted and historically varied. At the same time the concept of the subject necessarily opens onto the question of gender, as we shall see.

Donne: The Classical Subject

Donne's "Elegy 19," "To his Mistris Going to Bed," an imitation of Ovid's *Amores 1.5,* is, I hope, too well known to need full citation. It begins with an imperative ("Come, Madam, come"), continues with a performative description of his touching her ("Licence my roaving hands . . ."), and then shifts dramatically into the simple present: "Full nakedness! All joyes are due to thee." In the first paragraph the man's look passes across her clothes item by item in a fetishistic metonomy. Her clothes stop the eyes of "busy fooles" but not his privileged gaze before which she "reveals" her beauty. In the second stanza vision gives way to touch but the metaphors trade not between two empirically perceivable objects but exchange the body for a something always more abstract—America, Newfoundland, an empire, "mystick books," an angel, "A heaven like Mahomets Paradise." The substitutions cohere in a single meaning: intercourse with the woman's body acquires transcendental significance as a "far fairer world," Eden before the fall, the American utopia, heaven after the resurrection of the body—though the act itself is kept off-stage, outside the text. Described it would discover its inadequacy as objective correlative for the desire that outruns it.

The poem is an instance of what Foucault has invited us to consider as confessional discourse, the speaker presenting himself as the interrogator to whom the woman should reveal the inwardly concealed truth about her sexuality, a truth of course veiled in her but to which he presumes immediate and transparent access. His (would-be) transcendental position is that of a bearer of knowledge, a coherent point for the intersection of a range of discourses (geographical, medical, theological, mythical). The speaker is thus a mastering subject for whom his mistress is a corresponding and complementary object.

There cannot be a signified without a signifier, a represented without representation. Yet the rhetorical strategy of "Elegy 19" is precisely to contain the process of representation, to disavow it by promoting in its place a coherent represented. On the one hand the speaker's diegetic reality is substantiated. His knowledge moves forward from clothed "appearance" to the "naked truth" behind it, which is claimed as a final reality, an object reciprocally constituting the speaker as a fully present subject. On the other hand the linguistic process of the text, phonetic and semantic, is effaced by the vivid dramatization of speaker in a particularized situation, a scenario so persuasively and fluently scripted that we are led to forget it is scripted at all. The reader is interpellated into identification with a represented speaker who is a full subject and the bearer of knowledge. The text thus secures a position for the classical humanist subject.

Eliot and the Subject of Modernism

While the classical subject presumes a foundation in the transparency of discourse, Eliot's *The Waste Land* subverts any such foundation by foregrounding its own textuality. Fissured with isolated quotations, broken phrases, citations, interjections, truncated dialogue, uncompleted scenes, with disruptions and lacunae of all kinds, the text releases its writing from any determinate context, surrounds it with space on the page, and leaves it to attract a swarm of suggestions, overtones, connotations, resonances.

The Waste Land admits its own derivation from a structuring of the signifier. Yet it may be defined as modernist, as distinct from postmodernist (so it will be argued), in that even on this basis *The Waste Land* nevertheless continues to be an *expressive* text, seeking to recuperate its own textuality. For it dramatizes a psychologically consistent state of mind in a single unnamed speaker provided for the reader's identification. Like the hero of Tennyson's *Maud* or Beckett's *The Unnameable*, he (for it is a he) has no name; like Prufrock he assumes different roles and the voices of others in the course of the poem—Iachimo in Imogen's bedroom, Phlebas the Phoenician, the mask of Tiresias put on while the speaker is voyeuristic witness to the sexual encounter of typist and young man.

The first person singular—"I" twenty-nine times, "me" twice—is used throughout *The Waste Land* to identify a single voice and a single subject, albeit one in a state of mind poised close to the edges between madness and sanity, hallucination and perception. One way to interpret this psychological consistency would be to refer to the following distinction Eliot makes in his essay on Baudelaire:

Baudelaire has perceived that what distinguishes the relations of man and woman from the copulation of beasts is the knowledge of Good and Evil. . . . Having an imperfect, vague romantic conception of Good, he was at least able to understand that the sexual act as evil is more dignified, less boring than as the natural, "life-giving," cheery automatism of the modern world.[4]

In the absence of a supposedly transcendental spiritual dimension, absolute Good and Evil, the world is seen to be mechanical and meaningless. But when the source of this absence is located in sexuality, another reading presses itself forward, one in terms of what Freud called psychical impotence. Thus, through the asymmetry of the oedipal transition, men are more likely to overvalue and retain the first sexual object (the mother) so that any love for other women risks recalling that forbidden image (an argument I have pursued in more detail elsewhere[5]). In consequence there is a tendency to regard "the sexual act basically as something degrading," this generating a profound separation between love sacred and profane, between a "vague romantic conception of Good" in spiritual love and "the copulation of beasts."[6]

After the introductory paragraph of the poem the speaker dons the mantle of Ezekiel ("son of man") to announce a final truth, a scene in which he will demonstrate "fear in a handful of dust." The passage begins with a woman recalling a moment of love in the hyacinth garden. But what matters to the speaker is what he saw about the act of love afterward, when they came back:

> . . . I could not
> Speak, and my eyes failed, I was neither
> Living nor dead, and I knew nothing,
> Looking into the heart of light, the silence.

[lines 38–41]

Looking into what should have been "the heart of light," a paradise, the speaker found a brilliant and silent void, waste and empty, an experience of transcendent *horror*. Expecting ideal love, he discovered in sexual intercourse only "copulation." His eyes turned to Pearl and for the rest of the poem he sees sexuality as death. He may have seduced the hyacinth girl "a year ago" (line 35) and certainly for him she is like the corpse "planted last year" (line 71); the woman "undone" (sexually betrayed) is like one "undone" by death (lines 63, 292, 294); "White bodies naked on the low damp ground" (line 193) may be making love or they may be rotting. In the final section, as Hugh Kenner points out, the heart "beating obedient / To controlling hands" (lines 421–22) may be that of a woman made love to or, like Desdemona, being strangled.[7]

Desiring (in the hyacinth garden) a traditional sexual and spiritual fulfillment, the speaker finds only the apparently absolute negation of his absolute expectations ("I knew nothing"). Through a version of negative theology the *absence* of a transcendental truth is able to function as a structuring center for the poem. The vision of horror counts as a vision nevertheless. The speaker's drive for scopophilic domination is continually denied by his sense of blindness, yet the poem remains predicated upon this "I" that "knew," even though what he knew was "nothing." Even the presentation of gender is recuperated within the same traditional structuring exemplified in Donne's "Elegy." As the famous note says to line 218, "all the women are one woman." Thus, although they are rendered more as objects of horror rather than desire, the women are abstracted into the idea of The Woman, which is then located exclusively as the site of a sexuality whose inward truth is to be mastered.

If, as Nietzsche proposes, "God is dead," this does not dispose altogether with the concept of the deity, but rather preserves it as a positively felt absence, a loss, a God-shaped hole. In *The Waste Land* shock at what is perceived as absence is used to recuperate that absence. The speaker's loss of vision and mastery performs as a knowledge of truth nevertheless. His disintegrating self measures and registers the implied possibility of a unified self. His state of mind puts down dark tentacular roots, which are able to make good even the most remote turns of the poem's textuality by giving them an expressive connotation as part of his diffused incoherence. Denial of the transcendent thus functions to provide the text's reader with a position approximating that of the transcendental subject. And this negative strategy permits us to characterize *The Waste Land* as modernist against what is arguably the postmodernism of Pound.

The Cantos

We cannot yet begin to understand Pound's *Cantos* any more than we can yet understand Pynchon's *Gravity Rainbow*, another text set in "The Zone." What follow are no more than notes on a text whose decentering may well be inseparable from mere inconsistency and bad writing. Nevertheless a contrast with *The Waste Land* can be brought out in various ways.

The poem foregrounds the work/play of the signifier in a mode that is both pleasurable and promises to deny a position to the ego as transcendental because it makes plain the dependence of its represented speaker or narrator on the discourse by which he is constructed as an effect, as indeed "ego scriptor."[8] The text thus refuses to provide the reader with anything more than a temporarily and provisionally coherent position as subject relative to the process of signifier.[9]

"Most people," writes Lyotard in *The Postmodern Condition*, "have lost the nostalgia for the lost narrative."[10] Not the Pound of the *Cantos*, one might say. Yet in seeking as it does to unfold a grand narrative encompassing the whole of human history and ambition, to lead the reader through a Dantean pilgrimage from despair, across the purgatory of human error, to a newfound secular paradise, the text manifestly deconstructs the possibility of any such metanarrative, shows de facto if not de jure that, to cite Lyotard again, "the grand narrative has lost its credibility."[11]

But though the *Cantos* certainly wish for a metanarrative, they entirely step aside from any traditional metaphysical center that could underpin consecutive narrative linearity. Thematically they do seek to integrate history, the just economy, the hierarchy of civil society, the state, the individual, relations of gender, art, and knowledge. Although the poem seeks truth, it is able to uphold only localized and contradictory truths in the necessarily diverse fields of history, political economy, gender, and aesthetics. The poem does not assume meaning as an absolute point of origin; nor for that matter (and here the contrast with *The Waste Land* is strongest) does it admit, through negation, the positive absence of such a center. In Pound's paganism the God of Christianity is simply not in question. The commitment of the *Cantos* is to a material rather than transcendental utopia, to finding meaning in history and political economy or not at all. The city of Dioce is envisaged not as a city of God but an earthly paradise, political, secular, erotic.

No transcendental subject of the text; a failed or perhaps botched transcendence in the place of the grand narrative; the possibility of a metaphysical anchoring point not envisaged at all: the *Cantos* are grounded in a decentered immanence. Their outlook is thoroughly, if waywardly, historical and social, and this radically affects the rendering of subjectivity and of gender. The individual, though often solitary, whether presented as a hero (the represented speaker himself, Mussolini) or villain (Roosevelt), takes on value in relation to other people and society. Though the self is shown both suffering and enduring, it is not apparently threatened with dissolution, because it does not claim an origin for itself in a transcendent unity. This shows itself most clearly in relation to love.

Though the vision of sexuality in the *Cantos* is undeniably para-
noic and phallocentric, nevertheless it can claim no foundation in the
subject as bearer of truth and mastery. Correspondingly, in the images of Aphrodite and Circe, the "three ladies," Cunizza da Romano
and Botticelli's La Nascita, sexuality as a version of inward truth
vested in the idealized figure of woman gives way to a celebration of
the body and its pleasures:

> bel seno (in rimas escarsas, vide sopra)
> 2 mountains with the Arno, I suppose, flowing between them
> so kissed the earth after sleeping on concrete
>
> bel seno   copulatrix
>   thy furrow[12]

Beautifully figured but also profoundly phallocentric (as is argued
both by Maud Ellman and Alan Durant), this sexual fantasy resists
intention and velleity, halting instead at a vivid rendition of the surfaces of the body.[13] Its portrayal of a diffuse corporeality, tactile and
synesthetic, does not construct sexuality as a version of spiritual
truth. Masculine mastery, though not finally unseated, no longer lays
claim to transcendental sanction.

Modernism and Postmodernism in Poetry

Lyotard's distinction between scientific and narrative knowledge, and his resolute claim that it is "impossible to judge the existence or validity of narrative knowledge on the basis of scientific
knowledge and vice versa" is questionable.[14] In any case his epistemological arguments are much less interesting and have, rightly,
gained far less currency than the accounts he offers (somewhat in the
margins) of the contemporary cultural situation (the book is entitled
The Postmodern Condition). Following through the view that cultural
and discursive forms generally are based in and derive their force
from narrative, Lyotard proposes that the classical period, roughly
from the Enlightenment to the close of the nineteenth century, was
presided over by two metanarratives, that of the emancipation of the
people and that of the triumph of speculative reason or pure knowledge. Now, in the postwar period after the great upheaval of modernism, a postmodern condition has emerged in which all metanarratives
have lost their credibility. Hierarchization as legitimation of scientific
knowledge has given way to a "'flat' network of areas of inquiry" to
"islands of determinism," local areas of maneuver judged by their

capacity to come up with new moves in a system that Lyotard terms
"paralogy" (thus replacing the notion of an overarching logos with
that of nonexclusive parallelism).[15] It is his willingness to acknowledge this avowedly new situation (nonhierarchic, decentered,
postmodern) and its cultural consequences as "an increase of . . . ju-
bilation" that has attracted most controversy.[16]

In *The Political Unconscious* Fredric Jameson had already underwritten Lyotard's account of the foundation of human culture in narrative, but developed it crucially in two directions, first by making the
poststructuralist assertion that such narrativization was constituted
as a necessary epistemological occlusion of a historical reality that
works always behind our backs, and then by affirming that Marxism
survived ineluctably as the one great narrative through its ability to
comprehend and make sense of all the others. In a long essay,
"Postmodernism, or the Cultural Logic of Late Capitalism" (1984),
Jameson was able to follow through and validate his previous account
in a cultural analysis of postmodernism.

This study inspects a whole range of high and popular cultural
forms, including Hollywood film along with Godard, architecture,
painting, advertising, as well as a contemporary poem, "China" by
Bob Perelman. Admitting that these do not exhibit entire homogeneity, it is argued nevertheless that they conform to the cultural dominant of postmodernism. This, consistent with Lyotard's description
of paralogy and illustrated by a contrast between Van Gogh's "Peasant Shoes" and the postmodernism of Warhol's "Diamond Dust
Shoes," is characterized as "a new kind of flatness or depthlessness,"
mere stylistic collocation, one that denies the reader or viewer any
critical distance or awareness in relation to the presented text.[17]
Whereas, so it is implied, the modernist text works to shock or alien-
ate its reader (often with politically progressive intentions), the
postmodern text does not.

In consequence, postmodernism differs from modernism in that
"the alienation of the subject is displaced by the fragmentation of the
subject," a fragmentation that is arguably schizoid; in postmodern
culture "there is no longer a self to do the feeling."[18] In consequence
again, our critical sense of the historical and of alternatives to a her-
metically closed present is eroded if not made altogether impossible.
For an explanation of the postmodern condition Jameson is prepared
with a master narrative: late capitalism, as analyzed by Earnest Mandel, seeks to extend commodification into every area: "what has happened is that aesthetic production today has become integrated into
commodity production generally."[19] In the world space of multinational capital, traditional forms of criticism and resistance are blocked

as the subject is transformed into an adjunct of localized consumption.

Jameson's argument advances an evaluation of postmodernism entirely opposite to that of Lyotard, yet both are liable to a common objection. Each, though to a different degree, works through a form of totalizing argument, making the assumption that all the different levels and effects of contemporary culture express a single origin or cause, for Lyotard the postmodern condition resulting from the end of metanarrative, for Jameson late capitalism. This presumption is particularly manifest in their willingness to enter judgment for or against postmodernism as though it were a homogeneous unity. If, however, analysis proceeds on another basis altogether, one that accords a specific effectivity to each mode and recognizes the social formation as a decentered structure in which each social and discursive practice acts within its own time, then such overall assessments become much harder to make. Architecture, film (whether Godard or Hollywood), literature—and within literature, poetry—must be considered in terms of that particularity. In Jameson this difficulty is compounded by the fact that his argument can be viewed as functionalist, not least in its failure to explain at all the mechanisms by which late capitalism comes to effect and operates through the diverse cultural forms discussed (this kind of objection to certain forms of Marxist argument is now most closely associated with the writing of Jon Elster).[20]

Yet in spite of this, a contrast between modernism and postmodernism can be constructively deployed if it is restricted to a specific discursive form—in this case poetry, especially the poetry of Eliot and Pound—and if it is drawn on as a means to focus attention to the question of the subject. Jameson argues that postmodern culture entails "the disappearance of the individual subject" and his account of a contrast between the modernist and postmodernist subject has been well developed elsewhere.[21] Terry Eagleton has distinguished between modernism and postmodernism modernism in terms of the presence and absence of the subject. With modernism there is a subject indeed, though a subject alienated from itself; with postmodernism alienation vanishes, for "there is no longer any subject to be alienated."[22] On this basis Eagleton has discriminated and defended modernism as a preferred alternative:

> Old-fashioned modernism . . . is still agonizedly caught up in metaphysical depth and wretchedness, still able to experience psychic fragmentation and social alienation as spiritually wounding, and so embarrassingly enmortgaged to the very

bourgeois humanism it otherwise seeks to subject. Postmodernism, confidently post-metaphysical, has outlived all that fantasy of interiority.[23]

This supports the previous account of *The Waste Land* in two rather different ways. First, it points acutely to the close continuity between the traditional dramatization in poetry of the transcendental, would-be autonomous subject for which the speaker of "Elegy 19" has been taken as a representative instance. This subject—the classical subject—is not superseded but rather reproduced with a difference in modernist poetry, at least as exemplified by *The Waste Land*. The modernist subject alienated from its own plenitude is perfectly imaged in Eliot's text with its portrayal of a subject whose absolute transcendence, according to the poem's negative theology, is predicated on a sense of absolute loss.

Second, Eagleton's account corresponds well with the distinctions indicated here between texts of Eliot and Pound, between a modernist and postmodernist subject. If the modernist subject of *The Waste Land* is "agonisedly caught up in metaphysical depth," the subject of *The Cantos* is postmodernist, one whose nonaccession to spirituality, transcendence, and interior dimension is matched by the realization of its potential across a more concrete and material exteriority, historical, social, aesthetic, and a corporeal sexuality rendered closely in terms of the body.

Attending to the specificities of poetry, and particularly those specificities represented by the two texts contrasted here, a qualified endorsement of postmodernism can be entered. Fears for a postmodernist loss of the individual subject seem to be much exaggerated, and in fact to arise from the posing of a doubtful either/or: either the full subject or no subject at all; that is, either the modernist subject, whose plenitude is expressed negatively in its alienation and source of absolute loss or the postmodernist subject, fragmented and psychotic, deprived of all coherent interiority.

In an essay of 1938, "A Category of the Human Mind: The Nature of Person, the Notion of 'Self,'" the anthropologist Marcel Mauss notes that there has never been a language in which "the word 'je—moi' . . . did not exist" and that "there has never been a human being without the sense not only of . . . body, but also . . . simultaneously mental and physical individuality."[24] The entire disappearance of the individual subject seems unlikely, especially if the subject (to shift the terms) is in fact always present as an ego, as what Lacan terms the imaginary. The classical subject, apparently self-made, would-be effect only of its ultimately concealed depth and inwardness, the bourgeois subject in other words, is historically determined and does not represent the only form the ego can take or the only way individuals can make choices. Pound's presentation of the postmodern subject is one possible version of a relative stability of an I that claims no transcendence.

At the same time, if the modernist crisis of the classical subject and its postmodernist fading imply that there will be no more (bourgeois) nature, the evidence of these three texts is that this may well be a good thing. In the continuity of the tradition exemplified in Donne's "Elegy 19" the emergence and persistence of the classical subject has come to be understood as in every respect aggressive and exploitive: assuming itself to be as self-originating as God, it is constituted in the need to appropriate everything other than itself to its own avowed self-sufficiency as origin of power and knowledge. This feature has been strongly marked in the field of sexuality.

The effect is not accidental but functional. For the "I" must maintain itself against its other, both diachronically by persisting as a continuous identity and synchronically by defining itself against what it is not, what operates to constitute it. A would-be transcendental ego, like that of the represented speaker in Donne, seeks to establish itself *absolutely* in a position "outside and looking on" (like the eye of God in traditional Masonic symbolism). But subject and object come into existence together and so this dominant subject can hold itself in place only in relation to an equally dominated object. As soon as sexuality is drawn into this schema—as inevitably it is through the interaction of narcissism and sexuality—these positions become charged in relation to masculine and feminine. Masculine/feminine is assigned to the places of subject and object, as they are so vividly in Donne's text; the mastering gaze is confirmed as its own point of origin insofar as the feminine object appears to be entirely an object. Within a patriarchal culture the transcendental ego reveals itself therefore as a *masculine* ego, an assertion that can be supported by a second line of analysis.

The "I" that would be self-sufficient must substantiate itself in entire homogeneity; it cannot admit difference, either in the temporal dimension in which it must assert "I am that I am and that I will be," or in the spatial dimension in which it must appear to itself sincere and undivided. Sexual difference threatens especially the second axis of the ego's self-consistency by introducing the possibility of a radical self-division, a view unmistakably put forward in Freud's repeated assertion that the human subject never abandons its "constitutional bisexuality."[25] The would-be absolute integrity and homogeneity of the "I" is therefore subverted by the enemy within, one against whom the masculine "I" seeks to defend itself by trying to be masculine and only masculine. Once again, the more absolute, the more (impossible) monosexual; and the more absolute, the more aggressively it seeks to be present to itself in the face of its other.

So the classical subject constantly strives to maintain its dominance by equating masculinity with knowledge, activity, looking, and mastery, and femininity with sexuality, passivity, and being looked at. In sum, the "I" of this subject depends on the idea of The Woman as its subordinate Other. Postmodern culture, at least on the contradictory evidence of Pound's *Cantos*, envisages an end to socially instituted phantasies structured around male scopophilic narcissism.

In the domain of sexuality, but also in terms of the constitution of the subject itself, the concept of postmodernism and a reading of Pound's poetry in relation to it begins to indicate a positive aspect, an assessment that may be further substantiated if *The Pisan Cantos* are examined more generally as a form of phantasy. For if the ego is constituted by a split in the subject between conscious and unconscious, and if neither the transcendent ego nor its modernist inversion as loss are at issue in the text, then it may be read as pointing to new possibilities for the psychoanalytic subject. Thus, while phantasy structures are put to work in and around the speaker of *The Cantos*, they defy analysis in terms of a *consistent* mechanism or related set of mechanisms, whether the oedipal transition, psychical impotence, paranoia, or megalomania (though there are phantasy effects corresponding to each of these). Within psychoanalysis this loosening or dispersal may be referred to the complex notion of defense, a process in which the ego is both stake and agent, both what is to be defended and what does the defending. An ego aiming to function transcendentally will in defence of itself construe as pathological psychic operations it might count as less of a threat if it did not try to defend itself absolutely. It may be that if less is claimed in and for the ego, less needs to be expelled in order to give it room.

Hence follows a conclusion to be made with some hesitancy and hedged round with more than the usual number of "ifs." If the categories of neurosis and psychosis do not fully apply to *The Pisan Cantos*, there is a respect in which they may be considered post-Freudian. If the text does not assume a point of transcendence, it is because it does not work via a dramatization of the ego as transcendent. And without this, the lines between sanity and madness, conscious and unconscious, truth and phantasy, some pathological, are offered to the reader in a dispersal across the poem, but there may be no unified development corresponding to the inherited idea of the individual. This poetic text may anticipate a possible redrawing of the boundaries of consciousness and repression in and across the subject.

By directing attention at the present, the concept of postmodernism opens a discussion that in an unprecedented way calls for a revised reading of the historical past and forms for a possible future. For undeniably the tendency of Lyotard, Jameson, and Eagleton together has been to install the concept of postmodernism within the context of a deeply historical perspective. Thus, the very concept of postmodernism, while explicitly denying this in its own constitution, necessarily and contradictorily presumes a historical metanarrative: a classical temporality opposed to postmodernism in Lyotard, a modernist versus postmodern period in Jameson and Eagleton. But if we live in a postmodern culture as it is described, we would no longer know how to say so. Postmodernism would be as invisible to us as water to the fish who breathes it. In this way the very concept of postmodernism and discussion of it becomes a site for criticism and resistance.

Notes

1. Louis Althusser and Etienne Balibar, *Reading Capital* (London: New Left Books, 1970), p. 99.

2. Jacques Derrida, *Positions* (London: Athlone, 1981), p. 58.

3. See Colin MacCabe, *James Joyce and the Revolution of the Word* (London: Macmillan, 1978); Catherine Belsey, *Critical Practice* (London: Methuen, 1980), Antony Easthope, *Poetry as Discourse* (London: Methuen, 1983) and *British Poststructuralism* (London: Croom Helm, 1988).

4. T. S. Eliot, *Selected Essays* (London: Faber, 1961), pp. 428–29.

5. See Antony Easthope, *The Masculine Myth in Popular Culture* (London: Paladin, 1986), pp. 102–41.

6. Sigmund Freud, "On the Universal Tendency to Debasement in the Sphere of Love," *Standard Edition of the Complete Psychological Works* (London: Hogarth Press, 1957), 11:186.

7. Hugh Kenner, *The Invisible Poet: T. S. Eliot* (New York: Citadel, 1964), p. 162.

8. Ezra Pound, *The Cantos* (revised collected edition) (London: Faber, 1975), p. 458.

9. See Antony Easthope, *Poetry as Discourse,* pp. 138–59.

10. Jean-François Lyotard, *The Postmodern Condition: A Report on Knowledge* (Manchester: Manchester University Press, 1984), p. 41.

11. Ibid., p. 37.

12. Pound, *Cantos* pp. 469–70.

13. See Maud Ellman, "Floating the Pound: The Circulation of the Subject of 'The Cantos,'" *Oxford Literary Review*, 3/3, pp. 116–27; and Alan Durant, *Ezra Pound: Identity in Crisis* (Brighton: Harvester, 1981).

14. Lyotard, *Postmodern Condition*, p. 26.

15. Ibid., p. 39, 59.

16. Ibid., p. 81.

17. Fredric Jameson, "Postmodernism, or The Cultural Logic of Late Capitalism," *New Left Review*, 146 (July/August 1984): 60.

18. Ibid., p. 63.

19. Ibid., p. 56.

20. See Jon Elster, *Making Sense of Marx* (Cambridge: Cambridge University Press, 1985).

21. Jameson, "Postmodernism," p. 64.

22. Terry Eagleton, *Against the Grain* (London: Verso, 1986), p. 132.

23. Ibid., p. 143.

24. See Marcel Mauss, "A Category of the Human Mind: the Nature of Person, the Notion of 'Self,'" in *Sociology and Psychology* (London: Routledge Kegan Paul, 1970), p. 61.

25. Freud, *Standard Edition*, 19:31.

5

Ideology, Representation, Schizophrenia: Toward a Theory of the Postmodern Subject

John Johnston

I

In an interview published in 1977 Michel Foucault gave three reasons why the notion of ideology was "difficult to make use of."[1] First, it always stands in opposition to something else that is supposed to count as the truth, whereas for Foucault the problem is to see historically how "effects of truth are produced within discourses which in themselves are neither true nor false." Secondly, the concept of ideology refers necessarily to some kind of subject, whereas for Foucault the constitution of the subject within a historical framework is precisely what must be accounted for. And thirdly, ideology is always conceived as standing in a secondary position to something that functions as its infrastructure, or as its material, economic determinant, whereas for Foucault discourse does not "reflect" or derive from the relations of production and distribution, but is a constitutive power in its own right.

Foucault's refusal of the concept of ideology is typical of the body of thought loosely designated as poststructuralist, and has met with both strong criticism from Marxists and uncritical assent from many of the so-called postpolitical partisans of postmodernism. In their variously styled advocacy of "structures of difference," poststructuralists like Foucault, Jacques Derrida, Gilles Deleuze, Félix Guattari, Jean-François Lyotard, Julia Kristeva, and Jean Baudrillard reject forms of dialectical thinking, Marx's labor theory of value and the importance he accords to the mode of production, as well as the key Marxist concepts of class struggle, ideology, and totality. For many contemporaries this raises the question of how their conceptual frameworks and new methodologies should be seen in relation to the European tradition of critical, oppositional thought, especially Marxism and critical theory: Are they to be understood as symptomatic by-products of the further breakdown of that tradition, as their detractors claim, or do they indeed offer something new and useful in the analysis of social, historical, and cultural phenomena?

Needless to say, I cannot attempt to answer such a question here, especially given the many differences that distinguish the individual poststructuralists listed above. Instead, I shall simply focus on a single point of contention and controversy, the current status of the subject, or more specifically, of the new "postmodern subject" in the present historical juncture. This new subject has been described by the Marxist literary theorist Terry Eagleton as a "dispersed, decentered network of libidinal attachments, emptied of ethical substance and psychical interiority, the ephemeral function of this or that act of consumption, media experience, sexual relationship, trend or fashion."[2] What disturbs Eagleton, evidently, is that the postmodern subject cannot be viewed as a responsible moral agent, to whom a coherent consciousness and intentionality can be attributed. Such a subject, his description implies, must be seen as an almost purely ideological construct, without any identifiable human center of resistance or capacity for self-reflection and critical analysis. Thus, at bottom, Eagleton's postmodern subject appears to be the infantilized subject constructed by and for our mass-media consumer society, a subject whose lack of autonomy and self-determination renders him or her incapable of appealing to any values other than those of the empirical status quo.

Now of course this subject is not exactly a new actor on the scene of Western history. From their early studies of the authoritarian personality to their analyses of the manipulations of the "culture industry," theorists of the Frankfurt School were centrally concerned with this subject of ideological construction whose presence they discerned in Germany in the 1930s and in America after the Second World War. In contemporary America itself we can find a comparable anxiety about this new "subject" in Christopher Lasch's *The Culture of Narcissism* (1979) and *The Minimal Self* (1984). However, Lasch's psychologized and popularizing jeremiad around the loss of the individual subject or bourgeois humanist ego—which for the Frankfurt School became the object of a philosophically grounded critique—may also be viewed symptomatically, as an instance of the culture industry's offering up its own antidote (or placebo) to the very crisis it precipitates, and thus as yet another symptom to be accounted for.

What Marxists like Eagleton find so objectionable about poststructuralism is not the ineffectiveness of its critique, as could be said of Lasch. It is, rather, that poststructuralism seems to provide no critique at all; rather than articulating new points of resistance around which a critical subject could possibly emerge—somewhere on the Left, it goes without saying—poststructuralism dissolves the subject even more completely in the endless aporias of textuality and libidinal politics (with May 1968 in France serving as the example par excellence), and celebrates this dissolution in a gesture of transgressive, Nietzschean laughter and haughty disdain. So it should come as no surprise to hear that Marxists and liberal humanists alike have stigmatized poststructuralism as the "ideology" of postmodernism, taking ideology in the older sense of an articulated body of beliefs that give coherence and meaning to a set of behaviors and attitudes. But before turning to consider several examples of this reputedly irresponsible "ideology," several preliminary clarifications are in order.

First of all, within Eagleton's remarks, as within those of Fredric Jameson, another Marxist theoretician who has similarly described the postmodern subject, one can easily detect a vacillation between two incompatible positions.[3] One is the older, historicist position, which argues that a once existing centered subject—the autonomous, self-directed bourgeois ego associated with the period of classical capitalism and the nuclear family—has dissolved in the almost complete interweaving of the social fabric with organized bureaucracy, corporate capitalism, and "the soft sell" messages of a postindustrial service economy. The newer, updated position, based primarily on the theories of Jacques Lacan and Louis Althusser and sometimes blending with poststructuralism, argues that such a subject never existed in the first place but amounted to something like an ideological mirage, although certainly accompanied by real effects, inasmuch as it obviously functioned socially and provided a workable sense of reality for numerous and diverse groups. The first position is an essentially humanist one grounded in Kantian anthropology. It assumes that there is a core of humanity or human essence that always remains partially impervious to ideological manipulation and penetration, and against which we can measure the deleterious effects of, in this case, postmodernism. The second is a stringently antihumanist position, insofar as it denies the existence of any such human nature or essence, and sees the human as an ever-varying matrix of biological, social, and cultural determinants. Furthermore, the two positions entail a different function for ideology. For the first, ideology is a matter of "false consciousness" and functions to insure that a worker or member of the proletariat (to take the obvious example) believes that she is acting in her own best interests when in fact she is serving the interests of the ruling class. For the second, ideology is a matter of "subject construction," the net effect produced by the set of images and discourses that give the subject a sense of coherent identity. Ideology thus functions to mask those contradictions that might question the legitimacy and desirability of accepting existing subject positions as binding definitions of human reality or of one's identity.

Now the Marxist "slide" between these two positions is especially evident when the question of postmodernism is foregrounded. When Eagleton denounces the postmodern or "schizophrenic subject," as it is often called, he assumes the unstated norm to be the coherent, autonomous, self-intentional subject fostered by bourgeois, humanist culture, and implicitly bemoans its loss. On the other hand, Eagleton can also write the following:

> Discourse, sign-systems and signifying practices of all kinds, from film and television to fiction and the languages of natural science, produce effects, shape forms of consciousness and unconsciousness, which are closely related to the maintenance or transformation of our existing systems of power. They are thus closely related to what it means to be a person. Indeed "ideology" can be taken to indicate no more than this connection—the link or nexus between discourses and power.[4]

Here Eagleton simply reformulates Louis Althusser's now classic definition of ideology as "a representation of the Imaginary relationship of individuals to their real conditions of existence."[5] But what allows Eagleton to slide between these two very different positions is an unexamined reliance upon two, different understandings of representation. Putting it somewhat crudely, in the first or "humanist" understanding of ideology, representation is seen to work externally, by orienting the subject toward a set of external actions, whereas in the second (Althusserian) understanding it insures that subjects will conceive of themselves in a specific way. Thus the second version assumes a more thorough internalization, so that we are no longer talking about a set of attitudes but about identity itself, or the subject position *from which* attitudes are formed. Thus what is really at stake is self-representation.

Finally, what can be heard in both Eagleton's and Jameson's negative characterizations of postmodernism is a worry about the loss or collapse of this representational dimension. That is, both conceive the postmodern subject as somehow being without true or authentic representation, and therefore incapable of self-representation, because deprived of those necessary mediations provided by specific images and discourses that make self-reflection and meaningful intentionality possible. In this regard the postmodern subject seems "beyond ideology," not in Daniel Bell's earlier (and vacuous) sense as an inevitability of postindustrial capitalism, but rather in the poststructuralist sense of being beyond representation. As we shall see, this "nonrepresentable subject," which emerges specifically in the work of Foucault, Deleuze, and Guattari, is not a utopian subject but the outcome of a series of strategic positionings in relation to power and desire. These strategic positions are never totalized in any transcendent or unified way such as Marxism provides (and demands). Thus, to reverse Eagleton's view, the postmodern subject must be seen as refusing such totalizations in a necessary attempt to slide through different representations in order to avoid "capture" by those images and discourses that only reproduce an already defined subjectivity, and thereby make the subject available for other uses beyond or along side his or her conscious intentions. In this escape from the various mechanisms by which modern Western culture "subjectivizes" through representation, postmodern subjectivity thus exhibits a critical side impossible to grasp in Eagleton's terms. If representation creates an ideological subject that is at once centered (albeit in an illusionary way) and invisibly integrated into a totalizing system, then the postmodern escape cannot be crystalized in a counterideological subject, for every subject qua subject is defined by a specific set of representations that can never be ideologically neutral.

Eagleton's postmodern subject bears a close enough resemblance to the Nietzschean "subject-as-multiplicity" advocated by Foucault and Deleuze so that Eagleton can reasonably refer to poststructuralism as the ideology of postmodernism. But this position can be maintained only by ignoring the poststructuralist critique of representation and the implications of that critique for any analysis of "ideology." As a Marxist, Eagleton oddly fails to examine with any particularity the contemporary historical context of his claims, although our consumerist, mass-media society is explicitly evoked. This context can be described as one in which the postmodern subject passes through two related forms of subjection: one consists in a form of individuation shaped by the demands of power, the other in a fixing of each individual with a known, stable identity, well determined once and for all, through a channeling of desire. In response to these two forms of subjection, postmodern subjectivity—since there is no self-identical "postmodern subject" per se—presents itself as the right to difference, to variation, and to metamorphosis. In the work of Foucault, Deleuze, and Guattari, this claim for an authentic subjectivity is not at all the dialectical obverse of the pathetic subjectivity of consumerist ideology denounced by Eagleton, but the logical and strategic outcome of a new conceptualization of the social and cultural field.

II

In *The Order of Things* Michel Foucault argues that the humanist subject "man" is the product of a specific historical "episteme," the appearance of which required the disintegration of a classical discourse and of the representation it subtended. "Before the end of the eighteenth century," he writes, "*man* did not exist, any more than the potency of life, the fecundity of labour, or the historical density of language."[6] Foucault further argues that if indeed the appearance of the *sciences humaines* gave birth to humanist "man" as both the subject and object of study, modern developments in psychoanalysis, ethnology, and linguistics are dissolving "man" into unconscious structures that no longer support any of the anthropocentric claims made on "his" behalf. Although Foucault's final chapter concludes with the often-cited "wager" that if the discourses which secured "man" were to disappear, "that man would be erased, like a face drawn in sand at the edge of the sea," the book itself demonstrates that modern thought has already paved the way for the emergence of posthumanist conceptions of life and new configurations of the human with(in) the nonhuman.[7]

Yet Foucault does not dispense altogether with the notion of the subject. In "What is an Author?," published three years later, he suggests how one specifically defined subject—the author of written texts—should be grasped as a discursive function:

> The subject should not be entirely abandoned. It should be reconsidered, not to restore the theme of an originating subject, but to seize its functions, its interventions in discourse, and its system of dependencies. . . . We should ask: under what conditions and through what forms can an entity like the subject appear in the order of discourse; what position does it occupy; what functions does it exhibit; and what rules does it follow in each type of discourse? In short, the subject (and its substitutes) must be stripped of its creative role and analyzed as a complex and variable function of discourse.[8]

Foucault adamantly rejects any notion of the subject—whether transcendental as in Kant or phenomenological as in Husserl—that would make it foundational or constitutive, and therefore the center or origin of an intentional act and consequently of a praxis. For Foucault there is no transcendent or universal subject that assumes concrete form at particular historical moments and whose dialectical unfolding traces the evolution of human liberty, but only various configurations of the human in the conjunction of discursive and nondiscursive practices that form and dissolve in Nietzschean eternal recurrence. Indeed, much of Foucault's work can be understood as an elaboration of Nietzsche's assertion that there is no subject behind or underneath human activity: "there is no 'being' behind doing, effecting, becoming: the 'doer' is merely a fiction added to the deed—the deed is everything."[9]

In conceiving of the subject in relation to specific discursive functions, Foucault clearly participates in the structuralist decentering of the subject in and through language and social sign systems. In this general sense his work runs parallel to the psychoanalytic theory of subject formation as elaborated by Jacques Lacan and parallel to Louis Althusser's theory of subject formation as a process of interpellation ("hailing") by the ideological apparatuses of church, school, and state. Common to both Lacan's and Althusser's theories is the idea that the subject achieves identity through a "misrecognition" of his or her own imaginary construction of the real, and that psychoanalysis and Marxism respectively provide corrective and foundational "truths" having scientific validity. Foucault, though once Althusser's student and a regular auditor of Lacan's early seminars, was never interested in such generally formed subjects, but rather in specific subject positions made available historically by particular discourses and the institutional practices that give those discourses validity and authority.

In *The Archaeology of Knowledge* Foucault defines a number of "enunciative modalities," speaking situations and positions within which and from which the individual subject can speak authoritatively (i.e., "truthfully") in relation to specific institutions and object domains. In contrast to Lacan, who theorizes the subject as irremediably "split" by the unconscious, and forever unable to coincide with himself, Foucault's subject is "dispersed":

> To the various statuses, the various sites, the various positions that he can occupy or be given when making a discourse. To the discontinuity of the planes from which he speaks. And if these planes are linked by a system of relations, this system is not established by the synthetic activity of a consciousness identical with itself, dumb and anterior to all speech, but by the specificity of a discursive practice. . . . Thus conceived, discourse is not

the majestically unfolding manifestation of a thinking, knowing, speaking subject, but, on the contrary, a totality,in which the dispersion of the subject and his discontinuity with himself may be determined. It is a space of exteriority in which a network of distinct sites is deployed."[10]

Curiously, Marxists like Michel Pêcheux, less bothered by this dispersion of the subject than by Foucault's refusal to take into account the existence of class struggle in (ideological) discourse, accused him of "regressing into a sociology of institutions and roles."[11] But Foucault's point was not to deny the ideological conflict within discourse, only to show that institutional discourses created their own objects, and not as distorted reflections of political struggles that were somehow outside them, but rather according to concepts like "science" or "rationality" that were in turn the result of a whole grid or way of ordering things pervading the culture at a particular time. The truth claims that Lacan or Althusser made about their own discourses were dependent on the whole modern "episteme," which was exactly what Foucault wanted to distance himself from critically and to axiomatize. Just as in his early books Foucault had wanted to demonstrate once and for all that "medicine," "disease," "madness," "life," and "history" were radically contingent concepts, so in *The Order of Things* and *The Archaeology of Knowledge* he shows that the epistemological subject was a contingent position within a particular discursive formation that had already undergone several mutations and reconfigurations since the Renaissance. As in the case of Derridean deconstruction, the political implications of such a project were highly contextual and unavoidably ambiguous.

Foucault's next book, *Discipline and Punish*, responded less to Pêcheux's kind of criticism than to his own new sense of how power operates in modern society. Foucault said that he was writing a history of the present, and two passages from a contemporary American novel, Don Delillo's *Running Dog* (1978), catch what could be said to be Foucault's point of departure:

"You can't escape investigation [one character says to another]. The facts about you and your whole existence have been collected or are being collected. Banks, insurance companies, credit organizations, tax examiners, passport offices, reporting services, police agencies, intelligence gatherers. It's a little like what I was saying before. Devices make us pliant. If *they* issue a printout saying we're guilty, then we're guilty."

Later a similar exchange takes place between two other characters:

> "Go into a bank, you're filmed," he said. "Go into a department store, you're filmed. Increasingly we see this. Try on a dress in the changing room, someone's watching through a one-way glass. Not only customers, mind you. Employees are watched too, spied on with hidden cameras. Drive your car anywhere. Radar, computer traffic scans. They're looking into the uterus, taking pictures. Everywhere. What circles the earth constantly? Spy satellites, weather balloons, U-2 aircraft. What are they doing? Taking pictures. Putting the whole world on film."
>
> "The camera's everywhere."[12]

How could this pervasive, anonymous, all-seeing surveillance, increasingly a function of modern technology, come into being? And what kind of subject appears in the field of its cross-illuminating gaze? To answer these questions Foucault turned from a narrow focus on discourse to a consideration of the disciplinary technologies that produce forms of power immanent to the field of application, and not, as in feudal or monarchical regimes, emanating from a source that could be said to possess power. Furthermore, *Discipline and Punish* demonstrates that the specific power relations in modern society cannot be deduced from the mode of production, but, inversely, that the development of specifically capitalist productive forces presupposes a form of disciplinary power; that is, the disciplinary organization of the workshop and the disciplining of the workforce were necessarily prior conditions for the existence of capitalist production. In short, discipline was required to convert workers into labor power.[13]

Foucault's concept of "discipline" stems from his attempt to write a Nietzschean genealogy of a particular modern institution, the penal system, and of the "scientifico-legal complex from which the power to punish derives."[14] In *Discipline and Punish*, subtitled *The Birth of the Prison*, Foucault focuses on the watershed changes in penal practice that occurred in France in the eighteenth century when punishment was a bloody and archaic spectacle exercised by the king's representatives on the body of the condemned. His purpose is to show how the efforts of humanist reformers to substitute a more just, efficient, and humane punishment far exceeded their intentions and gave birth to a whole new disciplinary technology whose application quickly transcended the limited context of the prison. The full story involves profound changes—in the individual's relation to the law, in the very nature of power and its application—but for Foucault a key element was the adaptation of Jeremy Bentham's model of the panopticon to the structure and organization of the prison. Bentham's plan called for a tower at the center of a circular building divided into levels and cells, with a window in each cell opening onto the inner courtyard and through which the prisoner's every act could be surveyed. Thus the prisoner is put into a position of permanent visibility, and objectified by a total, unending, all-seeing gaze.

Though Bentham's panopticon was not always deployed in the construction of the new "model" prisons in the early nineteenth century, Foucault shows how it precipitated a whole new set of administrative attitudes and practices, mainly because it served a multipurpose function and could be applied in diverse contexts. Within the prison, it served as an efficient and completely anonymous means of observation, segregation, and control. And because the prisoner never knew when the guard was watching, it also fostered a kind of self-surveillance and internalized self-regulation. Moreover, because it was also an adaptable and "neutral" technology for the ordering and individuating of groups, it could be applied, in its assumptions and principles, to other contexts where humans would be subjected to administration and control: to schools, hospitals, army barracks, workshops, and factories. Thus the panopticon finally made possible a new kind of power: depersonalized, diffused, relational, and anonymous, which could be extended over more and more dimensions of social life. Foucault emphasizes, however, that this new kind of power does not operate primarily by constraint and restriction, but positively by producing new subjects and new knowledges about them. Essentially the prison (as well as other institutions where the principles of the panopticon were applied) became a laboratory for the constitution of not only new subjects but also new objects of knowledge, like criminality and delinquency. The modern individual produced by this system is at once subject and object, a position in the discourse of knowledge, and also a docile and regulated body. But what is perhaps most diabolic about this form of human management is that "power is not entrusted to someone who would exercise it alone, over others, in absolute fashion; rather this machine is one in which everyone is caught, those who exercise this power as well as those who are subjected to it."[15]

This "abstract machine" operates under the supposedly neutral mask of "normalization." The production of normalized individuals does not occur through ideological brainwashing, as Marxist accounts would have it. For Foucault normalized individuals are not the dupes of false consciousness who think they are acting in their own interest while in reality they are acting in the interests of the ruling powers. Instead, the individual is the product of interlocking and overlapping institutions, which have no overall unified plan or purpose. Indeed, it is "the disciplinary" itself that traverses all our institutions and ideological apparatuses, linking them together, extending them, making them converge, and it is the combination of "power-knowledge" that the disciplinary makes possible, with its structures and hierarchies, its inspections, exercises, and methods of training and conditioning, that gives a consistency to the social field. For the aim of the new discipline was not so much to punish wrongdoers as to prevent even the possibility of wrongdoing by immersing people in a field of total visibility where the opinion, observation, and discourse of others would restrain them from "abnormal" acts. And because the new disciplinary technologies were not identified with any specific form of government, they were not subject to "take-over" and modification as in the Leninist model for revolution. No matter who was governing, disciplinary power would only increase with the growth of modern institutions and technologies. In sum, Foucault shows that the modern individual subject, far from being the result of progressive liberations, as in the Enlightenment view, is produced by a complex of overlapping disciplinary technologies.

Although there seems to be no avenue of escape from this "carceral society," which has been compared with Max Weber's vision of modern life as an "iron cage," Foucault in fact advocated and practiced strategies of resistance. These strategies, which Foucault expressed in summary or directive form in a Preface to the English edition of Gilles Deleuze and Felix Guattari's *Anti-Oedipus,* indicate very clearly the kind of subject Foucault can be said to espouse:

> Develop action, thought, and desires by proliferation, juxtaposition, and disjunction, and not by subdivision and pyramidal hierarchization.
>
> Withdraw allegiance from the old categories of the Negative (law, limit, castration, lack, lacuna), which Western thought has so long held sacred as a form of power and an access to reality. Prefer what is positive and multiple, differences over uniformity, flows over unities, mobile arrangements over systems. Believe that what is productive is not sedentary but nomadic. . . .
>
> Do not demand of politics that it restore the "rights" of the individual, as philosophy defined them. The individual is the product of power. What is needed is to "de-individualize" by means of multiplication and displacement, diverse combina-

tions. The group must not be the organic bond uniting hier-
archized individuals, but a constant generator of de-individuali-
zation.[16]

In Foucault's call for a deindividualized subject, and for mobile,
multiple, nontotalized and nontotalizing investments in the social
field, we can hear a recognizable echo of Eagleton's postmodern subject. But what for Eagleton is an empty cipher and site of consumerist
manipulation, for Foucault becomes a strategy of resistance against
normalization. The difference is not one of intentionality, but lies in
how action is conceived. As a militant intellectual Foucault refused to
speak for—that is, to represent—oppressed groups, but worked instead to create conditions in which they could act and speak according to their own needs and desires.[17] Theory in such a context becomes not only an "intensifier of thought" but "a relay from one
practice to another," and a means of forming networks among diverse practices. And here again, the subject is neither the place nor
the means of integration, but a site of dispersion into networks of
political resistances that are and should remain local, specific, and
even transitory.

III

The question of how power is related to desire lies at the heart of
Foucault's relationship with Gilles Deleuze. In the dialogue with Deleuze cited above, Foucault agreed that a Marxist analysis of interests,
especially class interests, could not deal adequately with the more
diffuse problem of power: a people whose interests are not being
served by the existing power structure may still support it, not because of false consciousness, but because of their conscious and unconscious investments of desire. President Reagan's great popularity,
despite his manifest incompetence and obvious support of "special
interests," was a case in point. During certain historical periods,
many people may even desire fascism, and not necessarily because it
serves their interests or those of the ruling class. What must be investigated in any social or historical conjuncture, therefore, is the production and investment of desire in the social field, and how subjects
are formed as a result.

This general argument underlies Deleuze's collaboration with
Félix Guattari. *Anti-Oedipus*, the first fruit of this collaboration, com-
mences with the most spectacular version heretofore of the
postmodern subject:

It [*ça*] is at work everywhere, functioning smoothly at times, at other times in fits and starts. It breathes, it heats, it eats. It shits and fucks. What a mistake to have ever said *the* id. Everywhere *it* is machines, machines being driven by other machines—real ones, not figurative ones: machines driving other machines, machines being driven by other machines, with all the necessary coupling and connections. An organ-machine is plugged into an energy-source-machine: the one produces a flow that the other interrupts. The breast is a machine that produces milk, and the mouth a machine coupled to it. The mouth of the anorexic wavers between several functions: its possessor is uncertain as to whether it is an eating-machine, an anal machine, a talking machine, or a breathing machine (asthma attacks). Hence we are all handymen; each with his little machines. For every organ-machine, an energy-machine: all the time, flows and interruptions. Judge Schreber has sunbeams in his ass. *A solar anus.* And rest assured it works: Judge Schreber feels something, and is capable of explaining the process theoretically. Something is produced: the effects of a machine, not mere metaphors. [pp. 1–2].

The point of view is jarringly unfamiliar: "desiring-machines" formed by the coupling of parts, human and nonhuman, with no distinction drawn between them, the introduction of the schizophrenic as a model of "desiring production," not to mention the antiacademic presentation and sheer heterogeneity of materials considered. Yet it all signals an auspicious beginning: the subject is not only decentered but no longer even recognizably anthropocentric; and theory itself is conducted as a dispersion and collaging of diverse knowledges. Indeed, *Anti-Oedipus* mixes history, social, and psychoanalytic theory, psychiatric case study, literary example, anthropological lore, reflections on the body and molecular biology in a delirious erudition reminiscent of Robert Burton's great obsessive compendium of Renaissance learning, *The Anatomy of Melancholy*, which set down everything known about the great affliction of that age. And although *Anti-Oedipus* does something similar with schizophrenia, it would be wrong to treat the book as a mere curiosity or as only the "carnivalizing" of philosophy in the euphoric aftermath of the May 1968 student revolts. For Deleuze and Guattari provide not only a fully contemporary, postmodern theory of the subject, but also a theory of social formations and their corresponding sign systems or "semiotic regimes." This double contribution must be stressed, because it is in terms of the latter that the former is to be defined and ultimately situated.

Deleuze and Guattari are primarily concerned with the way desire is produced, coded, and invested in the social field within different types of social organization. On one level, therefore, *Anti-Oedipus* may be described as a semiotic updating of Henry G. Morgan's older classification of cultures into the triad of the savage, the barbarian, and the civilized. Greatly simplified, their theory proposes that the primordial flux of desire is always coded in relation to both a semiotic regime and a territory. In primitive regimes this primary coding is inscribed in multiple and nonhierarchical forms on the body, in dance, ritual, and myth, and takes as its ultimate referential territory the body of the earth. In barbaric regimes, in contrast, signs undergo a paranoid reorganization and are "overcoded" through constant (re)interpretation by a priest class as certain signifiers are centered and become privileged over others, and the ultimate territory becomes the body of the despot or monarch. Finally, in civilized or capitalist society these traditional and archaic codings are progressively undone or "decoded" in a process of release and abstraction in which all values are redefined in relation to capital.

Compared to the previous regimes, then, capitalism is both more cynical (or nihilistic) and paradoxically more productive. Capitalism decodes and deterritorializes all previous traditional value systems, recognizing, as Marx has shown in great detail, only those values that can be made equivalent to its own (re)production. In the capitalist regime, in fact, there is no longer any corresponding territory except for the deterritorialized body of capital itself on which the flux of desire is inscribed. Moreover, in its decoding and deterritorializing, in its axiomatizing of all values in the exchange process, capitalism releases new physical and social energies and expands productive capacity beyond all former limits. However, in order to control and regulate this energy and productive potential, capitalism must defer and displace its own limits and reinscribe them in repressive channels, structures, and inhibitions. In short, capitalism not only destroys traditional values, identities, and social structures, but also has to reinstall and shore them up in "artificial reterritorializations" in order to function.

This reterritorialization is effected primarily through the introjection and inscription of what Deleuze and Guattari simply call "Oedipus" within the historically altered position of the family. Here again the explanation involves a double process. On the one hand Freud's discovery of the unconscious and the centrality of desire made possible a radically new understanding of human behavior. But Freud short-circuits the implications of his theory in relation to the social field where desire is always invested. Instead of envisaging the unconscious as a "factory" or site where desire operates through a conjunction with forces and materials "outside," Freud encloses desire in a theater and subjects it to a representational model. His own decipherings of the rebuslike logic of the dream and neurotic behavior disorders notwithstanding, Freud construes the workings of the unconscious as unfolding on "another scene." Even more fatal theoretically, Freud submits desire to the reductive constraints of the "oedipal triangulation": Daddy-Mommy-Me. The result is a privatized individual whose desire is mistakenly assumed to be a personal matter.

The peculiar status of the private person as a "simulacrum or second-order image of the social individual" derives ultimately from a historical reversal of the family's location within the social field under capitalism. In the primitive and despotic regimes the family is "an open praxis, a strategy that is coextensive with the social field [and] the relations of filiation and alliance are determinant," whereas in the capitalist regime the family is removed from the social field so that the forces of social and capitalist reproduction can be *applied* to it from without: "The alliances and filiations no longer pass through people but through money; so the family becomes a microcosm, suited to expressing what it no longer dominates." Thus the position of the family in relation to the economic, political, and cultural field is radically altered: "instead of constituting and developing the dominant factors of social reproduction, [the family] is content to apply and envelope these factors in its own mode of reproduction." Father, mother, and child in turn become simulacral images of capital: "Mister Capital, Madame Earth, and their child the Worker" (p. 264).

Though Deleuze and Guattari's formulation is comic, the argument is complex and compelling. Under capitalism desire is never territorialized, but only invested on the deterritorialized flux of money and labor exchange. If not blocked and channeled, it tends toward "schizophrenia," or an absolute limit in which libidinal flows travel in a free, unbound state on a completely desocialized body. For capitalism's inherent dynamic carries it toward a threshold limit of decoding that will destroy its abstract and quantifying axiomatic by unleashing desires it cannot rechannel and recode. To prevent this from happening, a "counteractive tendency" recodes and reterritorializes desire within the family by means of the "oedipal triangulation." That is, through the inscription of Oedipus the desire that extends throughout the social field is rechanneled and recontained in the family, which now functions only as a (biological and ideological) reproductive unit. Thus the oedipus complex, whether defined as a social taboo or psychic structure, is less a universal than a figure of "desiring-production under determinate conditions," or a specific way of producing, coding, and channeling the flux of desire. In precapitalist societies Oedipus exists only as a potentiality or unfilled space because the determinate conditions do not exist. But when those conditions are fulfilled under capitalism, Oedipus migrates to the heart of the representational system and comes to occupy the primary position as representative of desire.

But if the "schizophrenic" subject functions heuristically as the absolute limit and semiotic model of capitalist decoding and deterritorialization, how are we to understand the specifically clinical and literary incarnations that pervade *Anti-Oedipus?* While Deleuze and Guattari have much to say about the "breakdowns" of the literal schizophrenic, more essential is their redefinition of the familiar typology of neurotic, pervert, and schizophrenic:

> The neurotic is trapped within the residual or artificial territorialities of our society, and reduces all of them to Oedipus as the ultimate territoriality—as constructed in the analyst's office and projected upon the full body of the psychoanalyst (yes, my boss is my father, and so is the Chief of State, and so are you Doctor). The pervert is someone who takes the artifice seriously and plays the game to the hilt: if you want them, you can have them—territorialities infinitely more artificial than the ones that society offers us, totally artificial new societies, secret lunar societies. As for the schizo, continually wandering about, migrating here, there, and everywhere as best he can, he plunges further and further into the realm of deterritorialization, reaching the furtherest limits of the decomposition of the socius on the surface of his own body without organs. [p. 35]

By defining each type of "illness" as a sign system or manner of inscribing desire on a particular territory, Deleuze and Guattari transform psychological determinants into socio-political ones and extend Foucault's argument (in *Madness and Civilization*) that forms of "mental illness" are always determined historically and reveal the unspoken limits of a given social system. To be sure, schizophrenics occupy a privileged position, for their deterritorialized wanderings and scrambling of all codes reveal the normally hidden relationship between desire and social production, which capitalism, more than any other system, attempts to keep separate. In contrast to the pervert and the neurotic, who operate within the circumscribed limits of desiring production under capitalism, the schizophrenic cannot be recoded or reterritorialized but passes to the limits of the system along a "line of flight." A clinical schizophrenic, then, is one for

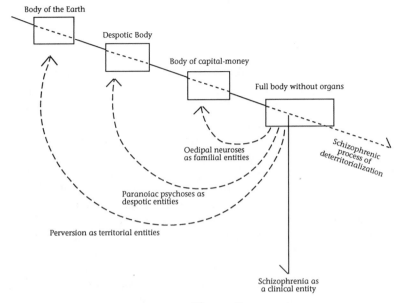

Figure 1

whom this line has been broken and the process blocked. These relations are schematized in Figure 1.

According to their method of "schizo-analysis," Deleuze and Guattari assume, following Nietzsche, that the individual subject is a multiplicity constituted by many overlapping (and contradictory) investments of desire. But where (on what body or territory) is desire inscribed, and along what lines does desire flow for the subject? Deleuze and Guattari find that desire is invested in two opposing ways: in paranoid investments, wherein desire inscribes itself on large "molar," statistical aggregates that are unifying or totalizing, and in schizophrenic investments where the flux of desire remains "molecular." The former allow something like the ego to assume palpable form, whereas the latter are recognized by the "lines of flight" along which desire flows and the "subject" is carried away in a process of "becoming" and the self-identical ego dissolves (or no longer exists). Yet it is usually not a question of one or the other but of both processes occurring simultaneously. Thus the subject is always in a state of conflictual tension between "molar" desires that center and stabilize (but which are also "fascist") and "molecular" desires that pull centrifugally toward an outside along "lines of flight."

What makes Deleuze and Guattari's picture of the subject so unusual is that the subject's "desiring machines" and not the ego occupy the center position. A "desiring machine" is any arrangement of heterogeneous parts by which the flow of energy is produced, cut into, recorded, and consumed. In contrast to a mechanical system, the parts of a "desiring machine" may be connected, disjointed, or conjoined in a variety of ways, as long as desire or energy (libido) is made to flow, inscribed on a surface, and siphoned off to be consumed for pleasure. And unlike a mechanical system, desiring machines work best by "breaking down," for in fact they are constituted as a system *of* interruptions and breaks. In Beckett's fiction Molloy's sucking stones or the elaborate arrangements by which the dogs are fed in *Watt* are examples of desiring machines precisely because they both involve flows that are cut into and constantly redistributed, without ever being successfully *organized*. For a desiring machine (or the tendency within it toward organization) is always opposed by a "body without organs," a term Deleuze and Guattari take from Antonin Artaud to designate the slick or smooth opaque surface of "the unproductive, the sterile, the unengendered, the unconsumable"— in short, whatever inhibits the links and connections of desiring production. At the same time, the body without organs makes possible as its material a full body that functions as a *socius*, whether it be the body of the earth, that of the despot, or of capital, where all desires can be inscribed. In fact, it is on this recording surface or socius that the "subject" can be discerned:

> It is a stange subject, however, with no fixed identity, wandering about over the body without organs, but always remaining peripheral to the desiring-machines, being defined by the share of the product it takes for itself, garnering here, there, and everywhere a reward in the form of a becoming or an avatar, being born of the states that it consumes and being reborn with each new state. "It's me, and so it's mine." [p. 16[

The subject thus comes into being as a mere residuum of pleasure alongside the desiring machines. Even suffering, Deleuze and Guattari add, quoting Marx, is a form of self-enjoyment, although here the authors remain closer to Freud. As an "appendix" or "spare part adjacent to the machine," the subject passes through various states or zones of intensity marked by circles of disjunction (sites where desire is inscribed), which converge on the desiring machine that makes them possible. And here we can distinguish between the formation of a "normal" and a schizophrenic subject. For the former, these zones become organized into a hierarchy of distinctions as the ego emerges through oedipalization, much in the manner described by Freud. In the process, the desiring machines undergo an illusionary displacement and repression. In the case of the schizophrenic, on the other hand, the desiring machine remains at the center, leaving the subject to wander on the periphery, with no fixed identity, forever decentered, and defined only by the states through which it passes. In schizophrenic delirium these states of intensity are described and given names, having first been "miraculated" and inscribed via "celibate machines." In fact, no small part of *Anti-Oedipus*'s appeal lies in its showing that schizophrenics like Judge Schreber, Artaud, and Beckett provide precise and richly differentiated accounts of their desires and bodily experiences. Drawing on Pierre Klossowski's study of the relationship between Nietzsche's intensely physical existence and his efforts to think in a new way, Deleuze and Guattari present Nietzsche himself as one such example of the schizophrenic subject:

> There is no Nietzsche-the-self, professor of philology, who suddenly loses his mind and supposedly identifies with all sorts of strange people; rather, there is the Nietzschean subject who passes through a series of states, and who identifies these states with the names of history: "every name in history is I. . . . " The subject spreads itself out along the entire circumference of the circle, the center of which has been abandoned by the ego. At the center is the desiring-machine, the celibate machine of the eternal return. A residual subject of the machine, Nietzsche-as-subject garners a euphoric reward (Voluptas) from everything that this machine turns out, a product that the reader had thought to be no more than the fragmented *oeuvre* by Nietzsche. [p. 21]

By totally reversing the anthropocentric perspective, Deleuze and Guattari intend to peal away the systems of repression that foster and support the illusion of an individual subject and the possibility of personal or individual expression. However, it is not until *A Thousand Plateaus*, the second volume of *Capitalism and Schizophrenia*, that they make good on this ambition. Dropping the concept of the desiring-machine, they now argue that representation and expression of every kind are *agencé* (produced and arranged) by what they call "collective assemblages of enunciation," which always work in conjunction with a corresponding "machinic assemblage" of bodies, actions, and passions. Together these two functions articulate the horizontal axis of a total "assemblage," while its two "sides"—the territorial or territorialized sides, which stabilize it, and the cutting edges of deterritorialization, which decompose it along a line of flight—define its vertical axis. The assemblage thus requires a tetravalent analysis:

Taking the feudal assemblage as an example, we would have to consider the interminglings of bodies defining feudalism: the body of the earth and the social body; the body of the overlord, vassal, and serf; the body of the knight and the horse and their new relation to the stirrup; the weapons and tools assuring a symbiosis of bodies—a whole machinic assemblage. We would also have to consider statements, expressions, the juridical regime of heraldry, all of the incorporeal transformations, in particular oaths and their variables (the oath of obedience, but also the oath of love, etc.): the collective assemblage of enunciation. On the other axis, we would have to consider the feudal territorialities and territorializations, and at the same time the line of deterritorialization that carries away both the knight and his mount, statements and acts. We would have to consider how all this combines in the Crusades.[18]

The theory of the "assemblage" presented in *A Thousand Plateaus* may well be the fullest single elaboration of what postmodernism is all about, for it allows Deleuze and Guattari to analyze a whole range of cultural phenomena as so many diverse conjunctions of different "semiotic regimes" with various material arrangements, all while avoiding recourse to any transcendent unity or expressive function that would stand outside the historical, material field. Every transcendent view (or set of statements) will now be seen to have its basis in a particular cultural assemblage; even claims for universal laws or values function as parts of an assemblage that requires culture-specific conditions in order to work. In fact, universalist claims, whether philosophic or scientific, always function as part of a state apparatus of power by conveying a certain "image of thought" and specific notions about the nature of truth.[19]

As the title itself suggests, an essential strategy of *A Thousand Plateaus* is to displace the hierarchical and dichotomous logic of the tree with the laterally proliferating logic of the rhizome. Above all this entails a rejection of language as a primary condition and autonomous object of study. In an extended critique of the four basic postulates of modern linguistics, Deleuze and Guattari offer a radically pragmatist view of language based on the assumption that every semiotic system is doubly articulated into both forms of content and forms of expression.[20] What can be meaningfully said (and effected through speech) at any given cultural conjuncture is reciprocally determined by a particular disposition of bodies and their possible combinations. This imbrication of the corporal and incorporal enables the different "regimes of signs" to account for the way bodies are incorporeally transformed by statements (as when the accused at a trial becomes the condemned), how the human face functions as a site where signs are always reterritorialized (thus *visageité* or "faceness" as a semiotic variable), and the many different "becomings" that deterritorialization sets in motion.

Modern subjectivity is now analyzed as the product of a "postsignifying regime" in which the subject is split into a double: the subject of enunciation and the subject of the statement. But as Deleuze and Guattari show, the linguistic formulation hides the manner in which the individual subject emerges in relation to a double set of reference points: the points of subjectivization along which the subject articulates his or her desire, and a machine of interpretation (like psychoanalysis or even pop psychology), which insures the redundancy and resonance of signs necessary for the unity and coherence of a point of view. In this regime, however, the individual subject's "line of subjectification" is still segmentary (cut up according to highly coded oppositions like male/female, young/old, white/ethnic), and only relatively or negatively deterritorialized as compared to the absolute deterritorializations that define a "becoming." In the latter, metamorphoses of identity occur through alliances and relays that tear the subject away from self-identity and launch him or her in a process of becoming-other: becoming-woman, becoming-animal, and becoming-imperceptible are the basic forms, but the possibilities are endless.

In contrast to imitation or emulation, the process of becoming-other involves at least two unlike beings allied in a reciprocal relay in which both pass along a line of flight toward unknown, experimental states. It is an escape, but only from dominant significations and means of control, never into fantasy or the unreal. For any given social and historical conjuncture the assemblage is what constructs the real, hence each mode of individuation effected by the assemblage must be measured in relation to the deterritorializations and reterritorializations that it makes possible. The most radically deindividualized subjects, those in a process of becoming, will always appear along the edges of the assemblage at its points of greatest deterritorialization.

The assemblage can also be considered in relation to two opposing "planes." The first, or plane of transcendence, is what insures the development of forms and the formation of subjects, both in a structural and genetic sense. It is never directly visible or given in itself, but must be inferred or induced on the basis of what it organizes. The plane of consistency, on the other hand, is immanent to the continuums of intensity, the blocs of becoming, the combinations of flux, and the emissions of particles that traverse it:

> A thing, an animal, a person are now only definable by movements and rests, speeds and slownesses (longitude) and by affects, intensities (latitude). There are no more forms but cinematic relations between unformed elements; there are no more subjects by dynamic individuations without subjects, which constitute collective assemblages. Nothing develops, but things arrive late or in advance, and enter into some assemblage according to their compositions of speed. Nothing becomes subjective but hecceities take shape according to the compositions of non-subjective powers and effects.[21]

If the plane of transcendence defines a mode of individuation in which subjects and objects are formed, develop, and combine in harmonious relations, the plane of immanence defines one in which singularities cluster and intensities propagate, as in fogs, plagues, sudden jumps or immobilizations. It is what accounts for the consistency of Brontë's "wind," Woolf's "waves" (or Mrs. Dalloway's stroll through London), Hardy's "heath," or Schumann's music: an individuation without a subject, packets of sensation in the raw (as Deleuze describes Hardy's characters). But if these artistic becomings are not fully intended or occur as side effects in works of romantic and modernist art, to reach the plane of consistency becomes a deliberate program in the work of Deleuze and Guattari.

Consequently, if the postmodern is to be understood as a culture of difference, immanence, and multiplicity (terms that modernism could conceive only in relation to the negative, the dialectical, or the transcendent), then surely they are its most far-reaching theoreticians. In their conceptualization, forms of postmodern subjectivity emerge not only as strategies of resistance to power as in Foucault, but also as "becomings" situated along the edges of greatest deterritorialization in contemporary assemblages.[22]

IV

In the various debates provoked by poststructuralism, Marxists like Eagleton and Jameson have not been alone in rejecting or refusing the postmodern subject as extrapolated here from the work of Foucault, Deleuze, and Guattari. Fred R. Dallmayr, acknowledging "the powerful appeal" of contemporary antihumanism, warns that the casualties are likely to be self-reflection and moral responsibility, and, on the cognitive-epistemological level, a proclivity toward "objectivism."[23] Emphasis on preconscious or extrahuman structures will obscure the "dimension of human autonomy and responsibility," and curtail the "reflective capacity needed for the critique of knowledge claims." Peter Dews argues that the contradictions of Nietzschean pluralism, which lie at the heart of poststructuralism, made its (assumed) demise (at the end of the 1970s) inevitable.[24] Hence its (assumed) displacement by claims like those of the *nouveaux philosophes* that a *right* to difference can be upheld only by universal principles. Similar objections have also been raised by German thinkers like Jürgen Habermas and Manfred Frank, who stress the logical necessity and political importance of the communicative dimension missing in poststructuralist thinking.[25]

These differences are not likely to be soon resolved to everyone's satisfaction. One postmodern retort to the above is simply that values such as "personal autonomy," "moral responsibility," and "communication" assume and depend upon a privileged, white, male, high-salaried point of view; that is, these values are real only for certain subjects in certain positions. They may be desirable in themselves, but all too often they mask patterns of domination and fierce competitiveness necessary for the working of (a still patriarchal) capitalism. "Speak to us responsibly, in our language—which, it goes without saying, is philosophically grounded in universals—and we shall integrate you into the system where we can discuss these things in a civilized manner." On these occasions the postmodern "schiz," as Deleuze and Guattari would say, hears Oedipus talking. And sometimes, if in the mood, the "schiz" can also speak that language.[26]

But rather than respond in the paranoid and bureaucratic languages of interpretation that reduce him or her to a solitary subjectivity, the "schiz" would simply prefer to continue his or her experimental way along the proliferating lines of flight within an increasingly energetic postmodern culture. H/she (the "schiz" finds such typographic arrangements still too dichotomizing, but preferable to the old sexist ones) acknowledges that defining postmodernism remains difficult, almost as difficult as avoiding its special dangers, the black holes and suicidal vectors. Some of its forms are even carefully disguised among the pallid and academic modernisms espoused by "yuppie" and neoconservative purists. Nevertheless, the sensibility is easily recognizable: a radical eclecticism based on the juxtaposition and collage of materials and values perceived by modernists as antithetical. Thus the "schiz" finds certain oppositions of limited interest: high art versus popular culture, universal versus historical (or "nominalist") values and meanings, defining the purity of the art medium versus mixing representational modes, iconic versus serial structures, figures of high definition versus fields of singularity and intensity, and so on. Of course some oppositions are utterly boring: mind/body, subject/object, public/private, space/time, and worst of all signifier/signified (the "schiz" knows that all semiotic systems are doubly articulated into forms of content and forms of expression, words and things, with neither being reducible to the other).

Although the "schiz" proclivity for discontinuous inscription and a textuality of surfaces problematizes the formation of typical themes, he or she will admit to a continuing fascination with the logic of the simulacrum, with networks and circuitry, both informational and physical (as in the highway as semiotic system), with the body as site or screen, with space, sights, and sounds (not the modernist place), with speed-ups and slow-downs (not modernist simultaneity), with dispersions, dispossessions, becomings (not modernist archetypal recurrences and recenterings). Furthermore, the "schiz" has remarked that others find his or her behavior a source of fascination, especially the looping and syncoped states of consciousness, the Lacanian "fadings" and, above all, affects in extremis: either flat and toneless, or hallucinatory and delirious. (To these observers, neurotic styles of behavior now appear "campy" and humorous.)

But what the "schiz" finds especially pleasing, given a propensity for hanging out in zones of near invisibility, is that whereas before one could only be rigorously modern, and systematically opposed to the tastes and intellectual habits of the stolid bourgeois citizenry, now many different people participate in postmodern culture on many levels in music, film, and video (academics will add literature and philosophy), without necessarily feeling "postmodern." This sense of multiple and partial participations and investments some perceive as symptomatic of a wallowing in the entropic, Alexandrian mix of Western culture at its low ebb of decadence. But the "schiz" knows that this is not postmodernism, but a paranoid fantasy projected on the historical field out of which postmodernism emerges.

If we are to have any hope of disengaging the postmodern as a field of articulations visible against such a background, then the postmodern "schiz" or "schiz-function" must replace the modernist author-function. First, because the author-function forces questions upon us that are irrelevant and ill-suited to the nature of postmodern art. Questions like "What does it mean?" or "What does the author intend?" must be replaced by questions like "What does it work in conjunction with?" and "What new intensities does it produce?" If the author-function once proved viable, it was because modern art essentially corresponds to the "postsignifying regimes" that individuate subjects along lines of subjectification. Postmodern art, by contrast, is about "becomings." Moreover, modernist art is essentially an art of the *symbol,* which corresponds to a relative or negative deterritorialization, one that allows a "recoding" in any of the various "private languages" that we have all now learned to read.[27] Postmodern art, in contrast, is an art of the *diagram,* tracing and conjoining lines of deterritorialization already operating within aesthetic materials.

In a first moment (sometimes barely distinguishable from modernism), an intense awareness of the materiality and textuality of cultural production leads postmodernist art to discover various means of releasing materials of their signifying capacity (significance) in order to construct new asignifying semiotic regimes and assemblages. The most obvious examples of such art—Pollock's paintings, Duchamp's constructions, Tinguely's machines, Varèse's or Morton Feldman's sound machines, the music of Berio and Stockhausen, the "novels" of Raymond Roussel—simply take to a limit the logic of deterritorialization already at work within modernism by going all the way, setting the material at hand into a state of rhythmic agitation, and refusing the artificial personalizations of such reterritorializations as the symbol.

In a second postmodernist moment, roughly that of the present conjuncture, a mixing of different semiotic regimes becomes the strategy for deterritorializing representation itself. As a consequence, the postmodern or schizophrenic subject emerges as a central figure. In Thomas Pynchon's *Gravity's Rainbow,* which mixes oedipal, paranoid, and schizoid regimes of signs in an archeological probe into recent history, the main character escapes structures of power and significance in a "becoming-imperceptible." In William Gaddis's *JR* the English language is radically deterritorialized in a becoming-delirious, as flows of stock at Wall Street investment firms and flows of consumer objects to schools and apartments accelerate beyond control. But it is perhaps in film and video, in both popular and elitist manifestations, that the mixing of different semiotic regimes and the exploration of various "becomings" is most strikingly noticeable.

However, to suppose that films like *Bladerunner, Videodrome, Alien*(s), and *The Fly* are "double-coded" for both a modernist and popular audience, which is Charles Jencks's formula for postmodernism, is precisely to miss the significance of the postmodernist mixing of different semiotic regimes.[28] Mixing semiotic regimes, moreover, is quite different from mixing "styles" in a "decentered culture without significant cultural orchestration," as another theorist of the postmodern has put it.[29] For the notion of "style" derives from a "postsignifying regime," implies a distinctive mode of subjectification in relation to a national language, and usually corresponds to a set of themes dealing with an emergent bourgeois cultural order. Of course many films with a "postmodern look" also bear traces of oedipal and familial reterritorialization. In *Bladerunner* the human/replicant opposition is effectively dissolved, while conventional gender roles are reaffirmed (in Deleuze and Guattari's terms, Decker's flight is *not* a becoming-replicant). Yet the most striking figure of the film remains Roy, the replicant who has seen all manner of things with eyes made by others and who will destroy the eyes of his oedipal father. (The latter's corporation, which constructs the slave replicants, clearly constitutes a despotic regime, as the pyramid-shaped architecture of its building signals early on.) Feminists have been right to critique the undercurrent sexism in films like *Videodrome*, where the main character's dissolution into a televisual network (*the* desiring machine in contemporary culture) entails a becoming-woman (a "schiz" told me the film was about a "TV man who couldn't keep a VCR tape out of his vagina"), or *Aliens*, where "the mother alien is blasted by that Rambo bitch" (as another "schiz" reported it).

But the important point is that despite these archaisms and reversions (i.e., reterritorializations), such films suggest the emergence of something new, a larger postmodern culture in which desire is always explicitly machinic (it only functions as part of an assemblage), and is expressed most authentically in figures of "becoming-other" through strange alliances and unholy couplings. (Hence the symptomatic importance of films like Cronenberg's remake of *The Fly*.)[30] These artistic productions comprise "collective assemblages of enunciation," and assume that all languages, whether natural or artistic, can only re-present already uttered discourses, in a patchwork or mosaic of references, allusions, and quotations. The "individual subject" does not speak, *it* speaks, an unconscious machine, individual in its ordering but collective in its origin and the materials out of which it is made. What does *it* say? It speaks the new desires of a postmodern subjectivity.

Notes

1. Michel Foucault, "Truth and Power," in *Power/Knowledge: Selected Interviews 1972–1977*, ed. Colin Gordon (New York: Pantheon, 1980), p. 118.

2. Terry Eagleton, "Capitalism, Modernism and Postmodernism," *New Left Review*, 152 (July/August 1985): 71.

3. Fredric Jameson acknowledges this vacillation in his essay "Postmodernism," or The Cultural Logic of Late Capitalism," *New Left Review*, 146 (July/August 1984): 63.

4. Terry Eagleton, *Literary Theory: An Introduction* (Minneapolis: University of Minnesota Press, 1983), p. 210.

5. Louis Althusser, "Ideology and Ideological State Apparatuses," in *Lenin and Philosophy* (London: Monthly Review Press, 1971), p. 165.

6. Michel Foucault, *The Order of Things* (New York: Vintage Books, 1970), p. 308.

7. Ibid., p. 387.

8. Michel Foucault, "What Is an Author?" in *Language, Counter-memory, Practice*, ed. and trans. Donald F. Bouchard (Ithica: Cornell University Press, 1977), pp. 137–38.

9. Friedrich Nietzsche, *Genealogy of Morals* (New York: Vintage Books, 1967), p. 45.

10. Michel Foucault, *The Archaeology of Knowledge* (New York: Pantheon, 1972), pp. 54–55.

11. Michel Pêcheux, *Language, Semantics and Ideology* (1975; New York: St. Martin's Press, 1982), p. 181.

12. Don DeLillo, *Running Dog* (New York: Vintage Books, 1978), pp. 93 and 149–50, respectively.

13. Frank Lentricchia rightly emphasizes this point in his two-part essay *Discipline and Punish*. However, Lentricchia does not find Foucault essentially antagonistic to Marx: "both [are] necessary components within a fully articulated theory of historical materialism" ("Reading Foucault [Punishment, Labor, Resistance]," *Raritan*, 1:4 [Spring 1982]: 13).

14. Michel Foucault, *Discipline and Punish* (New York: Vintage Books, 1979), p. 23.

15. Michel Foucault, "The Eye of Power," in *Power/Knowledge*, p. 156.

16. Michel Foucault, Preface to *Anti-Oedipus: Capitalism and Schizophrenia* by Gilles Deleuze and Félix Guattari (New York: Viking Press, 1977),

pp. xiii-xiv. Page numbers for subsequent quoted passages will be inserted into the text.

17. Foucault: "A theorizing intellectual, for us, is no longer a subject, a representing or representative consciousness. Those who act and struggle are no longer represented, either by a group or a union that appropriates the right to stand as their conscience. Who speaks and acts? It is always a multiplicity, even within the person who speaks and acts. All of us are 'groupuscules.' Representation no longer exists; there is only action - theoretical action and practical action which serve as relays and form networks" (Foucault and Gilles Deleuze, "Intellectuals and Power," in *Language, Counter-Memory, Practice*, pp. 206–7).

18. Deleuze and Guattari, *A Thousand Plateaus* (Minneapolis: University of Minnesota Press, 1987), p. 89. Their most extended analysis of a single assemblage, however, is is found in *Kafka: Toward a Minor Literature*. Kafka's writings are especially apt because there the Oedipus complex can be shown to be not a projection outward from the family (especially the father) onto figures of social authority but the reverse: the crystalization and internalization of figures representing forces and blockages of desire in the social field. Moreover, a reversal and dissolution of the oedipal configuration also entails a different or functionalist view of writing, which is no longer seen as the personal expression of an author but a mapping of desire, a diagraming of the historico-social assemblage, and a "becoming-minor" of the dominant German language. See my essay, "Postmodern Theory/Postmodern Fiction" in *Clio*, 16:2 (Winter 1987), for a discussion of this reversal of the oedipal, symbolic reading of Kafka's work and of Kafka's "writing machine" considered as an "assemblage of collective enunciation."

19. This is a recurrent theme in Deleuze's philosophy. For an early and extended exposition, see his *Nietzsche and Philosophy* (1964; New York: Columbia University Press, 1985), esp.pp. 103–10.

20. The four postulates are: language is informative and communicative; language is an autonomous object; there are linguistic constants and universals that enable us to study it as a homogenous system; a language can be studied scientifically only in relation to its standard form, as opposed to dialects and idolects. See *A Thousand Plateaus*, pp. 75–110.

21. Gilles Deleuze and Claire Parnet, *Dialogues* (1977; New York: Columbia University Press, 1987), p. 93.

22. In *A Thousand Plateaus* Deleuze and Guattari summarize their differences with Foucault as follows: "(1) to us the assemblages seem fundamentally to be assemblages not of power but of desire (desire is always assembled), and power seems to be a stratified dimension of the assemblage; (2) the diagram and abstract machine [here they are referring specifically to Foucault's notion of the "disciplinary" in *Discipline and Punish* and "biopower" in *The History of Sexuality*, vol. 1] have lines of flight that are primary,

which are not phenomena of resistance or counterattack in an assemblage, but cutting edges of creation and deterritorialization" (p. 531).

23. Fred R. Dallmayr, *Twilight of Subjectivity* (Amherst: University of Massachusetts Press, 1981), pp. 29–30.

24. Peter Dews, *Logics of Disintegration* (London and New York: Verso, 1987).

25. See Habermas's *The Philosophical Discourse of Modernity* (Cambridge: MIT Press, 1987), and Frank's *Was ist Neostructuralismus?* (Frankfurt: Suhrkamp, 1983).

26. This is obviously one area where postmodern and feminist concerns overlap. Many feminists have been extremely wary of the postmodern or poststructuralist decentered subject, and see in such theorizations a potential subversion of their attempts to define or reclaim an authentic and autonomous female subject. Alice Jardine usefully explores some of these problems in her book *Gynesis* (Ithaca: Cornell University Press, 1987). However, to argue as she does that Deleuze and Guattari's subversive notion of "becoming-woman" limits the struggle for new identities to men and makes women into mere catalysts of male transformation is somewhat unfair, for Deleuze and Guattari make it clear that this is the case precisely because the white male is the current cultural norm.

27. In the terms of traditional, art-historical periodization, premodern art is comprised of *icons*, which pertain directly to religious reterritorialization, whereas primitive art is comprised of *indexes*, which are simply territorial signs. See Fredric Jameson, "Beyond the Cave: Modernism and the Modes of Production," in *The Horizon of Literature*, ed. Paul Hernadi (Lincoln: University of Nebraska Press, 1982) for further discussion of how modernist works constitute a "recoding."

28. See Charles Jencks, *What is Post-Modernism?* (New York: St. Martin's Press, Academy Editions, 1986), pp. 14–19.

29. James Collins, "Postmodernism and Cultural Practice: Redefining the Parameters," in *Postmodern Screen*, 28:4 (Fall 1987): 12.

30. For a Deleuzian reading of the film, see Brian Massumi, "Realer than Real: The Simulacrum According to Deleuze and Guattari," in *Copyright*, 1 (Fall 1987).

Part III

Postmodern Philosophies

6

The Becoming-Postmodern
of Philosophy

Alan D. Schrift

What is it that we reflect upon when we speak about "postmodern philosophy"? I am not sure whether what is called "postmodern" in other fields, in literature or art history, for example, is all that clear. Certainly, what is to be called "postmodern" in philosophy is not clear. When graduate students enter the job market, they discover (if they did not already know this) that "modern philosophy" names the period in the history of philosophy that runs roughly from Descartes through Hume or Kant, depending on who has written the job announcement or who is doing the hiring. Philosophers, for whom time and history have always been problems, thus consider modernity to have ended by the beginning of the nineteenth century. Now, I take it that questions concerning "postmodern philosophy" are not interested in a recounting of the history of post-Kantian philosophy. Instead, I would like to address some remarks to the role that postmodern thinking is to play in the future of the history of philosophy in an effort to show that *becoming*-postmodern *is* the future of the history of philosophy.

What I mean by the "becoming-postmodern of philosophy" has something to do with one of the central motifs in postmodern thought: refusing to appropriate the traditional vocabulary, concepts, and categories of ontology. What I mean also has something to do with the place of Nietzsche in the contemporary intellectual landscape. It is Nietzsche, we must recall, who affirms *"becoming,* along with the radical repudiation of the very concept of *'being,'"*[1] who criticizes the history of philosophy (with Heraclitus as the lone exception) for refusing to recognize that everything becomes and that nothing *is*. This affirmation of becoming and refusal of the category "being" announces the fall of metaphysics from its hegemonic position within the philosophical tradition and, in so doing, it initiates the *becoming*-postmodern of philosophy. When Nietzsche writes, in the notebooks that were to become part of *The Will to Power*, that "The question 'what is that?' is an imposition of meaning from some other viewpoint,"[2] he indicates that this question will not elicit the sort of substantialist-metaphysical answer desired by the questioner. Nietzsche has other desires, nonsubstantive desires. With his affirmation of becoming and change, Nietzsche planted seeds that have sprouted rhizomatically through the twentieth century.[3]

To follow through on this image, the food that nourished these seeds was provided by Heidegger. Not the Heidegger of *Being and Time*, but the Heidegger who returned from the project of phenomenological/fundamental ontology—announcing the erasure of *Sein* and proclaiming the *Ereignis*. The "meaning" of this proclamation is still controversial, but what I will take it to indicate, in the context of the becoming-post-modern of philosophy, can be expressed quite simply: the substantialist ontology of Being, the ontology that has guided the history of metaphysics since Socrates, gives way to an ontology of processes, events, and becomings. What unites those thinkers categorized under labels like postmodernists, poststructuralists, deconstructionists, and the like, is a suspicious response to *stasis*, to all ontologically static things, concepts, and categories. The ways of thinking that they offer in place of the static, logocentrist metaphysics differ considerably, but a unifying thread is found in the *dynamic* and nonexclusionary quality of the suggested alternatives. And a second unifying thread in the discourses of postmodern philosophizing is the appeal to Nietzsche, as the various representatives of postmodernity seek in most cases to align themselves rather explicitly with the Nietzschean legacy. I hope to show just how intertwined these two threads are.

I begin with a brief "story" on the relation of the modern and the postmodern, the point of which is to situate the postmodern historically as a coming to terms with the modernist critique of authority executed by Nietzsche, Freud, and Marx. In other words, modernism names the period in Western history during which the position of authority itself came under suspicion. In the work of Nietzsche, Freud, and Marx, we find a critique not of particular authority-figures (*the* pope, *my* father, King Leopold I); rather, we find a thoroughgoing critique of the figure of authority itself for exercising a mastery over others that is unwarranted and unjustified. We find in these three suspicious critics of modernity a renunciation of the accepted discourse of legitimation. Thus, behind the workings of morality and religion, Nietzsche locates the forces of decadence; behind the stability of the family, Freud locates a psychodrama of neurotic desire; and behind the functions of the state, Marx locates strategies of economic domination.

I would like to suggest, at this point, that there is a sense in which the Marxist and Freudian critiques remain modern, while the Nietzschean critique opens onto the terrain of the postmodern. I mean by this the following: Lyotard has defined modernity and postmodernity in a useful way. Speaking of the obligation of science to legitimate the rules of its own game by producing a discourse of legitimation with respect to its own status, Lyotard uses "the term *modern* to designate any science that legitimates itself with reference to a metadiscourse of this kind making an explicit appeal to some grand narrative, such as the dialectics of Spirit, the hermeneutics of meaning, the emancipation of the rational or working subject, or the creation of wealth."[4] "Postmodern" then becomes simply an incredulity toward metanarratives.[5]

Returning to Nietzsche, Freud, and Marx, it appears to me that Freud and Marx are not sufficiently incredulous about the possibility of a legitimating metanarrative. Instead, they replace one metanarrative with another, thereby replacing one authority with another. This is most clear in Freud, whose desire to facilitate a transference blinds him to the transference *internal to* and *inherent in* the psychoanalytic encounter as the authority of the father is transferred to the analyst.[6] Marx presents similar problems. Perhaps it would be more accurate to say that while Marx's critique, insofar as it advocates a communal/collective form of nonauthoritarian rule, is *post*modern in the sense that I am using the term, most Marxists are not postmodern insofar as they advocate transferring the authority of the state to the party (what we might call naive Leninism, and what appears all-too-frequently to be the empirical consequence of Marxist revolutions) or the authority of the owners to the workers without recasting the nature of authoritarian relations themselves.

Nietzsche, on the other hand, from his earliest philological reflections to the published writings and unpublished notes of his final years, remains consistent in his rejection of authority. Whether he is dismantling the authority of the moral-theological tradition, deconstructing the authority of God, or excising the hidden metaphysical authority within language, Nietzsche's refusal to legitimate any figure of authority remains constant. This holds for his own authority as a writer,[7] the authority of his "prophet" Zarathustra, and the authority of the *Übermensch*. As he remarks apropos moral authority:

> In the presence of morality, as in the face of any authority, one is not *allowed* to think, far less to express an opinion: here one has to *obey!* As long as the world has existed no authority has yet been willing to let itself become the object of critique.[8]

Because authority demands obedience, a philosophy of the future will necessitate a critique of authority. If values are to be transvalued, obedience to the previous values must be undermined. The whole Nietzschean project of genealogy is directed toward deconstructing the foundations of the dominant values of modernity, which is to say that Nietzsche's project of a transvaluation of values presupposes a delegitimation of the existing (moral) authority.

It seems to me profoundly mistaken to read Nietzsche as a philosopher of the Superman or as someone who seeks to exalt humankind as that being who will serve as God's replacement in terms of some new anthropo-theology following the death of God. The *Übermensch* is not a being who will either exercise authority or be appealed to as an authority. "*Übermensch*" is, rather, the name given to a certain idealized conglomeration of forces. Nietzsche does not provide a philosophy for *Übermenschen;* he provides instead suggestions for steps to take in order to become-*Übermensch*. And coping with the nonplace of authority is an essential moment in becoming-*Übermensch*. We can only speak of the becoming-*Übermensch* of human beings, of the process of accumulating strength and exerting mastery outside the limits of external authoritarian impositions. Nietzsche calls this process of becoming-*Übermensch* "life-enhancement," and he indicates by this a process of self-overcoming and increasing of will to power rather than an ideal form of humanity.[9] In other words, Nietzsche sketches an *übermenschliche* Ethos, an attitude that will promote a transvaluation toward postmodern values, not a centered super-subject called "Overman."

In the remainder of my paper, I should like to highlight some of the themes running through the discourses of postmodern philosophizing that also promote this transvaluation. I begin with a fairly detailed discussion of the first theme to show how tracking the postmodern returns us to Nietzsche, and I will close by outlining several other postmodern themes and the Nietzschean traces that I locate within them.

Jean-François Lyotard has written that "oppositional thinking . . . is out of step with the most vital modes of postmodern knowledge,"[10] and perhaps the most obvious link among those writers whose work is considered postmodern is the refusal to sanction the hierarchical relations among certain privileged conceptual oppositions that have been transmitted by the Western tradition. Nowhere is this refusal more clear than in the writings of Derrida, who reads the history of philosophy as a history of certain classical philosophical oppositions: intelligible/sensible, truth/error, speech/writing, literal/figurative, presence/absence, and the like. What he finds is that these oppositions do not peacefully coexist. Rather, one side of each binary opposition has been privileged and the other side has been devalued. That is to say, a "violent hierarchy" and "order of subordination" has been established within these oppositions, and truth has come to be valued over error, presence has come to be valued over absence, and so forth. Derrida takes as his task the dismantling or deconstruction of these binary positions. In *Positions* we find the following disclosure of his critical strategy:

> I try to keep myself at the *limit* of philosophical discourse . . . the limit on the basis of which philosophy became possible, defined itself as the *episteme*, functioning within a system of fundamental constraints, conceptual oppositions outside of which philosophy becomes impracticable. . . . To "deconstruct" philosophy, thus, would be to think—in the most faithful, interior way—the structured genealogy of philosophy's concepts, but at the same time to determine—from a certain exterior that is unqualifiable or unnameable by philosophy—what this history has been able to dissimulate or forbid, making itself into a history by means of this somewhere motivated repression.[11]

In practice, the deconstruction of these oppositions involves a biphasic movement that Derrida has called "double writing" or "double science." The first phase initiates an overturning of the hierarchy. A certain reading of Derrida that focuses only on this phase finds him valorizing those poles traditionally subordinated by the history of philosophy. Derrida's text is thus read as privileging, for example, writing over speech, signifier over signified, or the figurative over the literal. Such a reading appears to me to be oversimplistic; Derrida, like Heidegger before him, realizes that in overturning a metaphysical hierarchy, care must be taken to avoid reappropriating the same hierarchical structure.[12] It is the hierarchical oppositional structure itself that is metaphysical, and to remain within the binary logic of metaphysical thinking is to reestablish and confirm the closed field of these oppositions.

To rest at the view of deconstruction as a simple inversion of these classical philosophical oppositions omits the second phase of deconstruction's "double writing": "we must also mark the interval between inversion, which brings low what was high, and the irruptive emergence of a new 'concept,' a concept that can no longer be, and never could be, included in the previous regime."[13] These new "concepts" are the Derridean "undecidables" (e.g., *differánce*, "trace," *pharmakon*, "supplement," "spacing," "hymen"): marks that in one way or another resist the formal structure imposed by the binary logic of philosophical opposition and expose the optional character of the choice that has been traditionally privileged as dominant. Much of Derrida's early work involves elucidating the play of these undecidables: the play of the trace, which is both present and absent; the play of the *pharmakon*, which is both poison and cure; the play of the supplement, which is both surplus and lack.

When marking the interval between philosophy's classical hierarchical oppositions and the undecidables, Derrida marks the limits of the binary logic that guides the history of metaphysics. In so doing, he displays another sort of logic that he calls the "logic of supplementarity."[14] This "other" logic has been repressed and excluded by the history of philosophy. Whereas binary logic operates within the limits of an exclusive disjunction ("either . . . or . . . "), Derrida's undecidable logic of supplementarity is a logic of "both . . . and . . . " that resists and disorganizes classical binary thinking. The fundamental laws of binary logic are the principles of identity ($A = A$) and noncontradiction (not [A and not-A]). The movement of the undecidables exhibits a different principle: the nonexclusive conjunction *both* A *and* not-A.

The *pharmakon*, for example, "acts as both remedy and poison. . . . [It] can be—alternatively or simultaneously—beneficent or maleficent."[15] *Pharmakon* plays between the poles of remedy and poison, and to render it as either "remedy" or "poison," as the binary thinking of the history of metaphysics is prone to do, cancels out the resources of signification reserved in that sign. Thus, when Socrates drinks the *pharmakon* at the conclusion of the *Phaedo*, the metaphysical tradition is quick to translate this *pharmakon* as "poison." In so doing, the tradition must repress Socrates' final speech in the *Apology*, where he claims we have reason to hope that death is a good that a virtuous person man need not fear, and it forces us to interpret as *ironic* his last words, concerning the debt his death will incur with Asclepius. This overdetermination of the meaning of *pharmakon* (= poison) is, for Derrida, paradigmatic, and his focus on the movement of the *pharmakon* exposes the limits of metaphysical thinking: because *pharmakon* is *both* remedy *and* poison, both a remedial poison and a poisonous remedy, its movement cannot be thought in the binary fashion that characterizes metaphysics. Derrida refuses to determine a univocal meaning for the *pharmakon* or the other undecidables; instead he emphasizes the tension and oscillating play that guides their use. His point, it must be stressed, is not to reify these terms or to privilege them as foundational. Instead, he seeks both to expose the foundational choices of the philosophical tradition and to bring into view that which the tradition has repressed, excluded, or, in Derridean terminology, marginalized. The strategy of marginal, double writing thus permits the deconstructive critique to circumvent the border between what is within the philosophical tradition and what is external to that tradition. By seizing concepts within the tradition and marking a movement of these concepts that the tradition both authorizes and excludes, deconstruction succeeds in inhabiting the closed field of metaphysics' binary oppositions without at the same time confirming that field. In so doing, it displays those choices, neither made explicit nor explicitly made, by means of which the tradition constitutes and legitimates itself *as* a tradition.

An example may be helpful here, and we can return to the use Derrida makes of the *pharmakon*, this time in terms of the remark in the *Phaedrus* that writing is a *pharmakon* (229d, 274e-275a). Again the polysemy of *pharmakon* (writing as a remedy for the weakness of memory and as a poison infecting the purity of speech) is overdetermined, as the tradition affirms Socrates' condemnation of writing as inferior to and derivative of speech. Derrida highlights this overdetermination to show how the privileging of the spoken word over the written word follows from the determination of metaphysics as the metaphysics of presence. The immediate presence of meaning in the spoken word is the ideal of Western metaphysics, which must then devalue the written word as a secondary, derivative *re*-presentation of speech. By engaging in the strategy of double writing, Derrida first uses the *pharmakon* to question the privileging of speech over writing, and then proceeds to question the assumptions of the metaphysics of presence, which make the binary opposition of speech/writing possible.

In other words, after Derrida shows that the primacy of speech over writing is itself grounded on the oppositions of presence over absence and immediacy over representation, he can demonstrate that the spoken word, which is itself a phonic signifier of a mental signified, is no more immediate a presentation of meaning than the written word. This demonstration makes possible his substitution of the notion of the "trace," always differing and deferring, for the concept of the sign, and it is a typical example of Derrida's strategy of using the binary concepts of the metaphysical tradition in order to intervene in and deconstruct that tradition.[16]

The method of critique utilized by Derrida in his resistance to traditional metaphysical thinking appears also in the writings of Nietzsche. It takes the form in Nietzsche's text, as in Derrida's, of a rejection of the binary logic of classical philosophy. The "typical prejudice" and "fundamental faith" that gives away the metaphysicians of all ages, he writes, "is *the faith in opposite values.*"[17] Throughout his critique of morality, philosophy, and religion, Nietzsche attempts to deconstruct such oppositional hierarchies as good/evil, truth/error, being/becoming. And in this deconstruction, we can locate instances of the same biphasic movement that animates Derridean double writing. For example, regarding the genealogy of the will to truth, we find Nietzsche overturning the traditional hierarchy of truth over falsity. Investigating the origin of the positive valuation of truth, Nietzsche finds it simply a moral prejudice to affirm truth over error.[18] To this, he suggests that error might be *more* valuable than truth, that error might be a necessary condition of life. His analysis does not stop here, however, as Heidegger assumed when he accused Nietzsche of "completing" the history of metaphysics through a "mere inversion" of Platonism. By adopting a perspectival attitude, Nietzsche displaces the truth/falsity opposition altogether.

A prime example of this displacement appears in the famous chapter of *Twilight of the Idols* where Nietzsche traces the history of the belief in the "true world," as he moves quickly from the overturning of the true/apparent world hierarchy to a deconstruction of the oppositional structure itself:

> The true world we have abolished: what world then remains? The apparent one perhaps? . . . But no! *with the true world we also abolished the apparent one!*[19]

We have abolished the apparent world because it has come to be defined as "apparent" only in terms of its opposition to the "true" world. Without the "true world" to serve as a standard, the designation as "apparent" is rendered meaningless. That is to say, the traditional (de)valuation of "appearance" is wholly dependent on its being the negation of that which the tradition has affirmed as "truth." In deciphering one pole of the binary opposition (the "true world") as an illusion, the opposition itself loses its critical force.

Nietzsche, like Derrida, discovers a certain faith in binary thinking at the center of philosophical discourse. Whereas Derrida highlights the oscillation between undecidable opposites, Nietzsche shows the way these opposites merge into one another. That is to say, he genealogically uncovers the will to power whose imposition of a certain value gives rise to the two poles of that opposition. And in bringing to light this original imposition of value, genealogy obviates the force the opposition is believed to have.

The clearest example of this strategy is his deconstruction of the good-evil opposition. Nietzsche moves *beyond* good and evil precisely by showing that both "good" and "evil" owe their meaning to a certain type of will to power—the slavish, reactive will to power of herd morality. To simply invert the values of slave morality, making "good" what the slave judges to be "evil," is no less reactive than the original imposition of value by the slave, who judges all that is different from himself to be "evil" and defines the good in reactionary opposition to what is other than himself. A reading of Nietzsche as an "immoralist" or "nihilist" remains at this level of mere inversion.

Such a reading fails to recognize Nietzsche's postmodern insight that by conforming to the oppositional structure, one inevitably confirms its validity and its repressive, hierarchizing power.[20] But a reading of Nietzsche as the "transvaluer of values" locates a second movement in the Nietzschean critique of morality. This second movement flows from the *active* imposition of new values arising from a healthy will to power that has displaced the hierarchy of good/evil altogether. In rejecting the binary structure of moral evaluation, Nietzsche's transvaluation calls forth a playful experimentation with values and multiplication of perspectives that he labels "active interpretation."[21] The affirmation of perspectival multiplicity thus emerges as the life-enhancing alternative for those with a will to power sufficient to go beyond the reactive decadence of binary morality.

It is important to note that in resorting to the language of life-affirmation and life-negation or healthy and decadent will to power, Nietzsche appears himself to be offering another privileged binary opposition. I would suggest, however, that this appearance is due to Nietzsche's remaining to some extent caught in the metaphysical snares of grammar and the oppositional structures inherent in language. Regarding the origin of both our moral and epistemological values, Nietzsche writes:

> *Language*, here as elsewhere, will not get over its awkwardness and will continue to talk of opposites where there are only degrees and many subtleties of gradation.[22]

The basic presuppositions of the metaphysics of language involve us in a "rude fetishism" that tends to dichotomize our world into truths and appearances, causes and effects, subjects and objects:

> The separation of the "deed" from the "doer," of the event from someone who produces events, of the process from a something that is not process but enduring, substance, thing, body, soul,

etc.—the attempt to comprehend an event as a sort of shifting and place-changing on the part of a "being," of something constant: this ancient mythology established the belief in "cause and effect" after it had found a firm form in the functions of language and grammar.[23]

Although Nietzsche may not have been able to follow completely his own call "to free ourselves from the seduction of words,"[24] his analysis does suggest a way to avoid these binary structures. That is to say, an interpretation of healthy and decadent will to power in a nonoppositional sense is possible in terms of viewing "health and disease" or "affirmation and negation" as two poles of a single continuum that is will to power.[25] Such an interpretation does not posit two mutually exclusive alternatives that call for some choice, as is the case with the classical binary oppositions. Instead, the affirmation and negation of life are the normative limits of an open-ended continuum of will to power that admits only of "degrees of gradation." This continuum is to be appraised in terms of the degree to which an *active* imposition of creative force is manifested. Nietzsche indicates such an interpretation when he speaks of the will to power as the procreative force that *is* life. This will to power can be increased or decreased, but there is no binary opposition involved: there is only will to power.

This way of reading Nietzsche previews a second postmodern strategy closely connected to the rejection of binary, oppositional thinking: framing one's project in terms of a monism that is also a pluralism. We can locate examples of this strategy in Derrida's discussion of "writing" (set between the limits of speech and "writing in the narrow sense"), Deleuze's discussion of "desire" (between the limits of repression and production), Cixous's discussion of "bisexuality" (between the limits of the masculine and the feminine), Bourdieu's discussion of "doxa" (between/outside the limits of orthodoxy and heterodoxy), and Foucault's discussion of "power" (between the limits of domination and subordination). Each of these thinkers recasts the forced choice or exclusive disjunction between binary opposites in terms of something akin to a "monistic" continuum: for Foucault, a continuum of power/knowledge; for Deleuze, of desiring production; for Bourdieu, of *doxa* and *habitus*; for Cixous, of bisexuality as the nonexclusivity of sexual difference; and for Derrida, of writing and difference.

I think Nietzsche attempted something similar with his introduction of the will to power, recasting all substantive differences in kind in terms of differences in degree of will to power. This recasting serves as a model for postmodern thinking and it should not be taken as reductive, any more than Foucault's discussion of power or Deleuze's discussion of desire is reductive. Instead, the monistic framework serves three positive functions: first, it suggests the interconnectedness of things while suggesting also the complexity of organization and the radically contextualized and optional nature of making what appear to be even simple determinations and distinctions; second, it directs our attention away from questions of substance and toward questions of value; and third, it promotes change by acknowledging the fluidity/contingency of judgments (what Deleuze and Guattari speak of as cuts in the flow).[26]

Before closing, I would like to mention three additional themes characteristic of postmodern thinking and traceable to Nietzsche, which deserve to be examined in some detail, although I can only touch on them briefly. First, the postmodern emphasis on dynamics rather than ontology, process rather than entities, becoming rather than Being. I find this affirmation most explicit in Heidegger's later philosophy, in Deleuze and Guattari's talk of flows and cuts, rhizomes, becomings, and assemblages, and in Derrida's *différance*. And not surprisingly, I find this also a central component in Nietzsche's philosophy of the will to power and his emphasis on becoming.

Second, we find postmodern discourses instantiating the values of performance in addition to or in lieu of the values of competence. Recognition of this escapes many philosophers, whose disciplinary prejudices limit their appreciation of linguistic use in philosophy to the goals of competence and representational accuracy. For this reason, philosophers are often frustrated, angered, and even outraged at the "excesses" of some of Derrida's or Deleuze's more eccentric/exorbitant writings, and they have great difficulty accepting, for example, Deleuze and Guattari's call for "an asignifying *intensive utilization* of language."[27] These philosophers have similar problems with Nietzsche, whose aphorisms ("hard nuts to crack") are "lightning bolts"[28] that desire not so much to express a truth or be understood as to have an effect.

The third and final theme is the strategy of aporia over *Aufhebung*—that is, allowing for the nonresolution of oppositions, the affirming of differences and contradictions, rather than demanding that consensus or synthesis be attained. This strategy appears most clearly in the Derridean focus on the impossibility of choice that he calls undecidability, the affirmation of nomadic "lines of escape" advocated by Deleuze and Guattari, and Lyotard's call for legitimation by paralogy. But it appears as well in all those writers who can be located under the banner of the postmodern insofar as nonresolution, the affirmation of differences, and the acceptability of multiple and discordant voices is the inevitable consequence of refusing to sanction the move to a metanarrative, as Nietzsche articulated so well when he acknowledged that the absence of truth left open the possibility of infinite interpretations.[29]

And to return to the discussion of authority and its legitimation with which I began, we can perhaps locate an aporia at the very center of postmodern thinking: the problem of devising legitimating criteria for even the provisional exercising of authority. This problem, which is at the center of Nietzsche's philosophizing, is the central question animating the work of Foucault, and it is central also to the works of Derrida, Lyotard, Deleuze, and others. As yet, this problem is unsolved and perhaps there is no solution. In fact, perhaps this is the essence, if we can still use such a word, of philosophy's becoming-postmodern: we are always on the way to a solution—to a becoming-solved of the problem—but we never arrive; the problem always recedes, the solution is always deferred. This provides the clearest indication that the becoming-postmodern of thought is a process that must be ongoing. We must resist philosophy's being hypostatized into postmodern*ism* by the guiding metaphysical question "what is . . . ?" Instead we must locate the future of philosophy in its continued becoming-postmodern, its continued refusal to rest; we must admit and affirm the radically contextualized character of all judgment while refusing to accept the primacy of any grand, legitimating metanarrative.[30]

Notes

1. Friedrich Nietzsche, *Ecce Homo*, BT3. While I have made use of all the existing translations of Nietzsche's texts, the responsibility for the translations appearing here is my own.

2. Friedrich Nietzsche, *The Will to Power*, sec. 556.

3. This image, developed at length by Gilles Deleuze and Félix Guattari in *Rhizome* and *Mille Plateaux* (see, for example, "Rhizome," translated by Paul Patton in *I&C*, 8 [Spring 1981]: 52–62), is suggested by Nietzsche in *The Gay Science* (371): "we ourselves keep growing, keep changing, we shed our old bark, we shed our skins every spring, we keep becoming younger, fuller of future, taller, stronger, we push our roots ever more powerfully into the depths—into evil—while at the same time we embrace the heavens ever more lovingly, more broadly, imbibing their light ever more thirstily with all our twigs and leaves. Like trees we grow—this is hard to understand, as is all of life—not in one place only, but everywhere, not in one direction but

equally upward and outward and inward and downward; our energy is at work simultaneously in the trunk, branches, and roots; we are no longer free to do only one particular thing, to *be* one particular thing." For a discussion of Nietzsche's *arbre fantastique* in contrast to Descartes's firmly rooted tree of philosophical knowledge (cf. the Preface to *Principles of Philosophy*), see Sarah Kofman, *Nietzsche et la métaphore* (Paris: Payot, 1972), pp. 158–63.

4. Jean-François Lyotard, *The Postmodern Condition* (Minneapolis: University of Minnesota Press, 1983), p. xxiii.

5. Lyotard, *Postmodern Condition*, p. xxiv. Derrida makes a similar point when he claims that there is nothing outside the text. See *Of Grammatology* (Baltimore: Johns Hopkins University Press, 1974), p. 158; also *Positions* (Chicago: University of Chicago Press, 1981), p. 111.

6. This problem is perhaps most obvious in the Dora Case. See, for example, the essays collected in *In Dora's Case: Freud–Hysteria—Feminism*, eds. Charles Bernheimer and Claire Kahane (New York: Columbia University Press, 1984).

7. I have discussed Nietzsche's views on literary authority elsewhere; see my "Reading, Writing, Text: Nietzsche's Deconstruction of Author-ity," *International Studies in Philosophy*, 17/2 (1985): 55–64.

8. Friedrich Nietzsche, *Daybreak*, preface 3.

9. Bernd Magnus makes a similar distinction when he contrasts the interpretations of the *Übermensch* as an ideal of human perfectibility and as a representation of a particular attitude toward life. See Bernd Magnus, "Perfectibility and Attitude in Nietzsche's *Übermensch*," *The Review of Metaphysics*, 36/3 (March 1983): 633–60.

10. Lyotard, *Postmodern Condition*, p. 14.

11. Derrida, *Positions*, p. 6.

12. See, e.g., Heidegger's discussion of Nietzsche's inversion of Platonism in *Nietzsche. The Will to Power as Art* (San Francisco: Harper and Row, 1978), pp. 200–220.

13. Derrida, *Positions*, p. 42; see also *Margins of Philosophy* (Chicago: University of Chicago Press, 1982), p. 329.

14. Derrida, *Of Grammatology*, pp. 179, 215.

15. Derrida, *Dissemination* (Chicago: University of Chicago Press, 1981), p. 70.

16. As Derrida notes, deconstruction cannot "proceed immediately to a neutralization: it must, by means of a double gesture, a double science, a double writing, practice an *overturning* of the classical opposition *and* a gener-

al *displacement* of the system. It is only on this condition that deconstruction will provide itself the means with which to *intervene* in the field of oppositions that it criticizes" (*Margins of Philosophy*, p. 329).

17. Nietzsche, *Beyond Good and Evil*, sec. 2.

18. Ibid., sec. 34.

19. Nietzsche, *Twilight of the Idols*, "How the 'True World' Finally Became a Fable."

20. Avoiding this confirmation is one of the problems of enacting revolutionary change, and the difficulties faced in trying to solve this problem have been acknowledged by a number of postmodern thinkers including, among others, Derrida, Deleuze, and Lyotard.

21. See Nietzsche, *The Will to Power*, sec. 600, 604, 605. Derrida has also used the term "active interpretation" to distinguish deconstructionist reading from the textual doubling of commentary. See *Of Grammatology*, p. 157–64.

22. Nietzsche, *Beyond Good and Evil*, sec. 24.

23. Nietzsche, *The Will to Power*, sec. 631; see also *Genealogy of Morals*, Second Essay, sec. 13.

24. Nietzsche, *Beyond Good and Evil*, sec. 16.

25. See, e.g., Nietzsche's remark in *The Gay Science* (sec. 112) where he offers the idea of a "continuum of which we isolate a couple of pieces" as an alternative to the "duality" of "cause and effect." This remark, incidently, precedes by eight sections Nietzsche's discussion of the "Health of the Soul" in which he comments that "there is no health in itself [*Gesundheit an sich*]."

26. Lyotard takes note of a number of these positive functions in discussing the will to power in the context of explaining "paganism" and his conception of the ability to judge without criteria. See Lyotard and Jean-Loup Thebaud, *Just Gaming* (Minneapolis: University of Minnesota Press, 1985), pp. 15–18.

27. Gilles Deleuze and Félix Guattari, *Kafka: Toward a Minor Literature* (Minneapolis: University of Minnesota Press, 1986), p. 22.

28. Friedrich Nietzsche, *Ecce Homo*, UM3. Nietzsche discusses the explosive, stimulating character of his writing in several places; see *Ecce Homo*, IV 1; *Schopenhauer as Educator*, 8; Colli and Montinari, *Kritische Gesamtausgabe*, IV, 3: 47[7] and V, 1: 6[88].

29. See Nietzsche, *The Gay Science*, sec. 374.

30. Part of the research for this paper was supported by a grant from the American Council of Learned Societies, to whom I wish to express my gratitude. Sections of my discussion of Derrida's and Nietzsche's critiques of

binary thinking are modified from an earlier paper in which I undertake a more detailed examination of this theme. See "Genealogy and/as Deconstruction: Nietzsche, Derrida, and Foucault on Philosophy as Critique," in *Postmodernism and Continental Philosophy*, eds. Hugh Silverman and Donn Welton (Albany: State University of New York Press, 1988), pp. 193–213.

7

"Ethics and Aesthetics are One": Postmodernism's Ethics of Taste

Richard Shusterman

I

Wittgenstein, who became our greatest postmodernist philosopher after having authored the most exquisite masterpiece of modernist philosophy, asserted in his *Tractatus* that "ethics and aesthetics are one."[1] The message appears as cryptic as it is bold; it is pronounced parenthetically with no further clarification or justification, in that austere economy of pregnant minimalist expression so characteristic of the modernist style. What the young Wittgenstein meant can best be surmised by looking not only at the tractarian context but at his earlier *Notebooks*,[2] where the dictum originally appeared along with some sketchy subsequent elucidation. Apparently, he wished to convey the idea that ethics and aesthetics were fundamentally unified or identical in at least three significant aspects.

First, both involve seeing things *sub specie aeternitatis*—that is, transcendentally "from outside," in "such a way [that] they have the whole world as background." In aesthetics, "the work of art is the object seen *sub specie aeternitatis*; . . . [while in ethics] the good life is the world seen *sub specie aeternitatis*. This is the connection between art and ethics" (*Notebooks*, 83). Secondly, both ethics and aesthetics concern the realm of "the mystical," not only because their statements (being neither empirical nor logical propositions) belong to the unsayable, but because both employ that transcendental holistic perspective he associates with the mystical and with "absolute value."[3] Thirdly, both are essentially concerned with happiness: "the artistic way of looking at things . . . looks at them with a happy eye," "art is cheerful." And with respect to ethics, "I am either happy or unhappy; that is all. One can say: there is no good or evil: (*Notebooks*, 86).

These connections, whatever sense and cogency we see in them, hardly establish the utter unity of ethics and aesthetics. Moreover, though the doctrine is not repudiated (as so many tractarian

115

doctrines are) in Wittgenstein's later philosophy, neither is it explicitly affirmed or developed. Indeed, it is quite plausible to assume that his later decentered, nontranscendental, and pluralistic philosophy of language games, which Lyotard rightly claims as a major source and prototype of postmodernist thought,[4] would be hostile to any radical unification of the ethical and aesthetic domains. For these domains surely appear to involve different (and often not even parallel) language games.[5] On the other hand, the substantial underlying connection and ineluctable overlap of ethics and aesthetics is implicit in Wittgenstein's later account of aesthetic appreciation as something irreducible to isolated, formulizable critical rules and expressions of approval, but rather something firmly and necessarily situated in a complex cultural background, entwined in ways of living that cannot but include an ethical dimension.[6] Wittgenstein's ultimate position on this matter was probably the sensible if uninspiring view that ethics and aesthetics are neither fully united nor completely distinct.

Let us now leave Wittgenstein aside, having paid what I hope will be sufficient exegetical dues for appropriating his language, and turn to why his parenthetical phrase is today so meaningful. The answer, I believe, is that the dictum "ethics and aesthetics are one" gives pointed expression to important insights and problems of both aesthetic and ethical theorizing in our postmodern age. It denies modernism's aesthetic ideology of artistic purism, common to the literary modernism of the early Eliot and his ilk, as well as to the formalist and abstract movements in plastic art. Instead it implies that such isolationist ideology, probably a vestige of the fin de siècle defensive strategy of "art for art's sake," is no longer viable in our age, which has seen the traditional compartmentalization of knowledge disintegrate into manifold forms of interdisciplinary inquiry. In its wake, there is not only room but need for a criticism of art that is morally and socially motivated. (Eliot himself was quick to recognize this, which explains his significant and often lamented postmodernist turn from a rigorously aesthetic and technical criticism to a concentration on the "relationship of poetry to the spiritual and social life.")[7]

I shall say no more of the moral metamorphosis in aesthetic theory, but shall devote the rest of my paper to its no less significant converse, the aestheticization of the ethical. The idea here, to adumbrate its more salient aspects in a phrase, is that aesthetic considerations are or should be crucial and ultimately perhaps paramount in determining how we choose to lead or shape our lives, and how we assess what a good life is. It fleshes out Wittgenstein's ambiguous dictum that ethics and aesthetics are one by erecting the aesthetic as the proper ethical ideal, the preferred model and criterion of assessment for the good life. Such aestheticization is understandably directed primarily to what might be called the private ethical realm, the question of how individuals should shape their life to fulfill themselves as persons.[8] But it can be very naturally extended to the public realm, to questions of what a good society should be like, at the very least so as to insure the possibility, if not the productive fostering, of the good life for its constituent individuals. Moreover, it has been quite common and still remains tempting to characterize good societies themselves by aesthetic standards, conceiving them as organic unities with an optimal balance of unity in variety—that classic and still potent definition of the beautiful.

If, as I believe, the aestheticization of the ethical is a dominant (though hardly unprecedented)[9] current in our postmodernist age, it is perhaps more evident in our everyday lives and the popular imagination of our culture than in academic philosophy. It is evidenced by our culture's preoccupation with glamor and gratification, with personal appearance and enrichment. The celebrated figures of our time are not men of valor or women of virtue but those significantly called the "beautiful people." We are less inclined to the imitation of Christ than to imitating the cosmetics and fashion of Princess Diana; no one today reads the lives of the saints for edification and example, but the biographices of film stars and the success stories of corporate millionaires are perennial best-sellers.

However, the postmodernist ethics of taste is not without philosophical apologists. Several philosophers seem to support the position by implication, perhaps unknowingly or even unwillingly. But, as usual, the most outspoken and outrageous philosophical exponent of America's popular imagination is Richard Rorty, who explicitly advocates "the aesthetic life" as the ethically good life. For Rorty, "this aesthetic life" is a life motivated by the "desire to enlarge oneself," "the desire to embrace more and more possibilities" (R, 25), which is expressed in "the aesthetic search for novel experiences and novel language" (R, 35). In other words, aesthetic self-enrichment and gratification is sought not only through actual experiments in living but through the more timid option of employing "new vocabularies of moral reflection" so as to characterize our actions and self-image in a more freshly appealing and richer way. Rorty's case for the aesthetic life will occupy much of this paper, as his avid and tireless advocacy of postmodernism makes such concentration appropriate. But I should proleptically note that there are other visions of and arguments for the aesthetic life that deserve and will claim our attention.

II

How are we to explain or justify postmodernism's aestheticization of the ethical? The rise of the ethics of taste can be largely explained as the result of the fall of more traditional models of the ethical. Just as once born we have to live our lives in some fashion, once we start reflecting ethically on how to live we must reflect in some fashion. Erosion of faith in traditional ethical theories left an ethical *horror vacui* that the ethics of taste naturally rushes to fill. Rorty seems close to saying this when he argues that after Galileo, Darwin, and Freud "neither the religious nor the secular and liberal morality seems possible, and no third alternative has emerged," except for the aesthetic one he subsequently advocates.[10] The most powerful reasons impelling contemporary philosophers to reject traditional ethics would seem to derive from two general philosophical attitudes. The first is historicist and contingently pluralist antiessentialism as to human nature; the second expresses a perception of severe limitations in morality, which make it clearly inadequate for a full-blown satisfying ethic. We might describe this second view as the underdetermination of ethics by morality. Each of these attitudes involves a number of aspects or levels that merit attention.

1. Traditionally, ethical theories have sought to justify not only themselves but the whole ethical enterprise from what Bernard Williams has called "an Archimedean point," "something to which even the amoralist or skeptic is committed but which, properly thought through, will show us that he is irrational, or unreasonable, or at any rate mistaken."[11] Typically, such foundationalist theories base themselves on general theories of human nature, trying to derive what life is essentially good for humankind from what is essential to or essential in human kind, and recognizing that any ethical "ought" depends on some nonethical "can." The desire for pleasure or happiness and the capacity for and exercise of rational thought and action have been the most familiar and compelling candidates for such essential features. In synthesizing them both, as well as in giving a much more concrete and substantial picture of what constitutes the good life for man (though not for women and slaves), Aristotelian ethics seems superior to Kant's, which despite his epistemological recognition of humankind as both sensuous and rational, rests on a very purified and eviscerally abstract concept of the human being as a rational agent who therefore requires some freedom of choice of action.

The particular problems with the Aristotelian and Kantian enterprises, many of which Williams neatly outlines, need not concern us here. The more basic problem that pervades these and similar attempts to ground ethics in an account of intrinsic or essential human nature is our strong postmodernist suspicion that there really is no such thing. We have an even stronger suspicion that there is no ahistorical essence that is both universally found and timelessly (metaphysically or biologically) fixed in humankind and yet is also determinate and substantial enough to generate or justify, by mere logical derivation or elaboration, a definite ethical theory. We have come to see that even our best candidates for essential status, like rationality and happiness, seem promising only as long as we do not probe too deeply into the culturally and historically divergent accounts of what in fact really constitutes these things.

The lack of an ahistorical ontologically given human essence does not, however, foreclose all possibility of foundationally deriving from human nature an ethical theory for historical humankind. For that project could perhaps get by with some nonontological but still transhistorical, cross-cultural human essence; some sort of amalgam of linguistic, cultural, and biological universals found to be universally present in and necessary to human life whenever and wherever it has flourished, and one from which could be projected a definite and coherent picture of what constitutes the good life. But skepticism here is no less potent in the face of obvious historical and cultural divergence. Even in what we conceive as the same cultural tradition—say, that which Eliot once personified as "the mind of Europe"—we find very different answers to what is essential to or desirable for a properly human life. Moreover, given what Lyotard diagnosed as our postmodernist suspicion of grand legitimating narratives,[12] we cannot try to explain away such divergence by appeal to the variant but progressive manifestation of the human spirit in search of liberation or perfection (*Bildung*).

Yet though we may reject both ahistorical human essence and the idea of some human essence shared by all ages and cultures of human history there still remains the more modest but still very significant project of generating an ethical theory for our own specific age and culture. This "limited" aim is surely what we most want, for what we want to know is how to live our own lives rather than those of our ancestors or descendants, which are obviously not ours to live. But even drastically narrowing the focus to our contemporary American society, we find there is just too much significant variety to talk confidently of any formative essence that could tell us what and how to seek in seeking the good life. We are perhaps unified in a commitment to freedom and the opportunity for the pursuit of happiness. But such notions, as communitarian critics of liberalism frequently complain, are helplessly vague and abstract; and the unity they apparently provide quickly disintegrates into variant rival visions of what freedom, happiness, and opportunity really mean.

There are at least two good reasons why not even such localized human essences can be found. First, not only in a mammoth country like America but in any advanced civilization, there is a very high order of division of labor, a division of occupational roles. The notion of a general functional human essence that Aristotle and other ethical theorists assumed and built upon seems no longer viable when men *and women* have so many different functional occupations that are so difficult to reconcile. How do we reconcile the functional essence of the farmer and the stockbroker, the creative artist and the factory hand, the priest and the cosmetician, the scientist and the casino operator? Much more disturbing is the fact that we not only collectively experience a conflict of divergent (occupational) functional essences, but we feel it just as powerfully on the individual personal level. The conflict between a woman's functional essence as defined by her profession, and that defined by her role as mother is perhaps the most familiar and acute of such contemporary problems of identity. But there are countless other examples of how our professional roles or self-definitions sharply conflict or simply do not coherently mesh with our self-definition as friends, family, or political agents, thus making it seem impossible to find humankind a functional essence in some coherent amalgam of its social roles.

To say that a postmodernist cannot generate a general or even personal ethic from his or her specific functional role because we all inhabit collectively and individually a plurality of inadequately integrated roles is to say with Wittgenstein and Lyotard that we inhabit such a motley variety of language games and are shaped by so many forms of discourse that we no longer can say definitively who we are. We cannot tell what is the good life for us, because the nature of us is so questionable and unsteady with our changing roles and self-representations. It is questionable, Rorty would argue, because it is not definitively there to be discovered but instead open to be made and shaped, and should therefore be shaped aesthetically. Moreover, according to Rorty not only is there no point in trying to penetrate our social roles to find a common human essence, which is not there, but even the idea of an underlying coherent individual essence of particular personhood (one's own true self) is a myth, which Freud effectively exploded. One's own self or personality seems to be revealed as an uneasy combination of a number of conflicting (conscious and unconscious) "quasi persons" composed of "incompatible systems of belief and desire," which discredits the whole idea of a person's one "true self" (*R*, 5, 11, 19). Rather than something unified and consistent emerging from an autonomous, stable, and rational core, the self is seen as "centerless," a collection of "quasi selves," the product of "random assemblages of contingent and idiosyncratic needs," shaped and modified by "a host of idiosyncratic, accidental episodes" transformed by distorted memories (*R*, 4, 12, 14). For Rorty, this Freudian decentering, multiplication, and randomization of the self "opened up new possibilities for the aesthetic life" as an ethic, for with no true self to discover and conform to the most promising models of "moral reflection and sophistication" become "self-creation" and "self-enlargement" rather than "self-knowledge" and "purification" (*R*, 11–12).

Antiessentialism as to human nature thus leads to an ethics of taste. It would be wrong, however, to see this as a logical derivation. If human nature's absence of essence means it implies no determinate ethic, it therefore cannot imply an aesthetic one. Yet, it still may be said to lead to an ethics of taste, for in the absence of any intrinsic foundation to justify an ethic, we may reasonably be encouraged to choose one that most appeals to us; and it is plausible to think that such appeal is ultimately an aesthetic question, a question of what strikes us as most attractive or most perfect.

2. It is time to turn from antiessentialism to the second general attitude that has worked to undermine traditional ethical theories and thereby help recommend an aestheticized ethics of taste. I have called this attitude the underdetermination of ethics by morality. It has two aspects that respectively concern the extension and dominance of moral considerations in ethical thought. The first aspect finds its most general expression in contemporary moral philosophy's increasing recognition that morality as traditionally conceived does not really cover the full gamut of ethical concern. For the ethical involves a wide range of considerations of value and goodness in respect to how one should live, many of them clearly personal and egoistic or at least not universalized (e.g., special concern for one's own interests or one's family's) and many of them nonobligational (e.g., munificence and uncalled for acts of kindness or heroism). But traditional moral thinking, as Williams and Wollheim have most recently maintained, constitutes a much narrower special "subsystem" of the ethical, governed by obligation and universalizability. For Williams, the narrower "special system" of morality "peculiarly emphasized certain ethical notions rather than others, developing in particular a special notion of obligation" (*Wi*, 6–7, 14). Wollheim concurs in taking "morality in the narrow sense . . . to be that which has obligation as its core," and he contrasts it very sharply with the realm of value and goodness

in terms of their differing psychological genealogy and consequent potential for human satisfaction. "One (morality) derives from introjection [of a menacing figure], the other (value) derives from projection ["of archaic bliss, of love satisfied"]. One is in its origins largely defensive and largely coercive, the other is neither. One tries to guard against fear, the other to perpetuate love."[13] And if Wollheim's account of morality emphasizes its menacing beginnings and baneful aspects, Williams is still more explicit (and perhaps more extreme) in asserting with insouciant bluntness "that we would be better off without it" (*Wi*, 175).

Williams's rejection of "morality, the peculiar institution" or "special system," is not so much theoretically motivated by its distressing psychological sources and effects as by its logical peculiarities and insufficiency in accounting for our ethical thinking. What makes this mere insufficiency so vitiating is that, while morality clearly underdetermines ethics, it constitutes and sees itself as a system globally exhaustive in its determinations. It presents itself as a consistent system of obligations (and consequent rights), which can tell us what we should do in any instance. That we should or ought to do something implies that we *can* do it, and therefore these obligations will be hierarchically ordered so as to prevent their conflicting in any final or irresolvable sense, for they cannot be allowed to issue in contradictory actions, which as incompatible cannot be performed. "Moral obligation is inescapable" and whether you want to subscribe to the system or not, it includes you in its categorical universalizing logic and imputes you moral blame if you do not act according to its comprehensive system of obligations (*Wi*, 177–78).

Williams is chiefly occupied with successfully challenging two of morality's globally categorical presumptions: its claim to exhaustive extension of application, and its supreme or all-overriding potency wherever applied. He shows how morality cannot defend the first claim against obvious cases of kindness and generosity that are non-obligatory or even in conflict with some prior definite obligation; and he exposes the failures of philosophical efforts to salvage the claim through the unconvincing positing of an elaborate hypothetical system of differently ordered obligations (particular obligations, general obligations, negative obligations, prima facie obligations, obligations to self, to others, etc.), so that any action we might look upon with favor or distaste will be seen as deriving or deviating from some relevant (or ordered complex of) obligation.

Closely connected with morality's assumption that it exhausts all ethical action and choice, that any worthy act can ultimately be justified only in terms of some obligation, is the presumption that in any ethical question moral considerations should always override all others and determine how one should act or live. Thus, if the performance of a noble unobliged act of kindness prevents me from meeting a trivial obligation—say, arriving to work on time—a vague general obligation relating to kindness must be posited to justify my act's obvious worth. The idea that certain things can be good regardless of obligation and can even outweigh obligation in ethical deliberation is utterly foreign and intolerable to the system of morality. Williams calls this morality's maxim "that only an obligation can beat an obligation" (*Wi*, 187) and its transparent falsity constitutes the second part of postmodernism's case for the underdetermination of ethics by morality. Ethics, as distinguished from morality, recognizes that there is more to the good life than the fulfillment of obligations, and indeed "can see that things other than itself are important . . . [to life] as part of what make it worth living" (*Wi*, 184). This does not mean that ethics need reject moral considerations entirely, but simply their claim to entirety and overridingness. What is denied (and this time in Wollheim's words) is "the view that morality is ultimate or overruling" (*Wo*, 225).

The result of this demotion of the moral to merely one significant factor in ethical deliberation on how to live the good life is to make such deliberation much more like aesthetic judgment and justification than syllogistic or legalistic discourse. Finding what is right becomes an affair of finding the most fitting and appealing gestalt, of perceiving the most attractive and harmonious constellation of various and variously weighted, changing and changingly weighted, features in a given situation or life. It is no longer the deduction of one obligation from another more general obligation or group of obligations, nor the outcome of a logical calculation based on a clear hierarchical order of obligations. Similarly, ethical justification must come to resemble the aesthetic in appealing to perceptually persuasive argument in its attempt to convince, an attempt that relies on and aims to sustain and extend some basic consensus, and yet also recognizes and serves to promote a tolerance of difference of perception or taste emerging from it. In the manner of aesthetic interpretation and evaluation, it is crucial to us that our fellows understand our ethical perspectives and choices, and see them as reasonable, but no longer so crucial that they accept them as universally right and valid for all. Ethical judgments can no more be demonstratively proven categorically true through unexceptionable principles than can aesthetic ones. Ethics and aesthetics become one in this meaningful and sensible sense; and the project of an ethical life becomes an exercise in living aesthetically. Perhaps this is what Wollheim has in mind when for one brief moment he very vaguely and tentatively suggests that ethics be viewed "like art" (*Wo*, 198).[14]

III

This, however, is not (or at least not all of) what Rorty recommends as the aesthetic life, which he depicts in more radical and substantive tones. Basing his rejection of morality on the perhaps more clearly Sartrian than Freudian themes that humankind has no essence and that a person is the product of random and idiosyncratic contingencies, Rorty does not react with Sartrian nausea but rather upbeat radiance in embracing the (again Sartrian) conclusion that we must create ourselves. Such creation could, of course, be achieved by the acceptance of even the most traditional or ascetic of moralities, so the necessity of self-creation in no way entails or recommends what Rorty advocates as "the aesthetic life." Moreover, the life painted by Rorty seems to represent only one of at least three basic genres of aesthetic life, which have found ardent and influential philosophical evangelists over the ages, and indeed even in this century.

What, then, is Rorty's vision of the aesthetic life and how does it compare to others? We would be fairer to quote how Rorty characterizes it before supplying any critical caricature or comparison of our own. His aesthetic life rejects "an ethics of purity" and self-knowledge for "one of self-enrichment" and "self-enlargement." "The desire to enlarge oneself," says Rorty, "is the desire to embrace more and more possibilities, to be constantly learning, to give oneself over entirely to curiosity" (*R*, 11). This quest for self-enlargement involves a dual "aesthetic search for novel experiences and [for] novel language" to redescribe and thereby enrich those experiences and their experiencer (*R*, 15). Similarly, "the development of richer, fuller ways of formulating one's desires and hopes" makes "those desires and hopes themselves—and thereby oneself—richer and fuller" (*R*, 11). The aesthetic aim is not to "see things steadily and see them whole" but to see them and ourselves through ever new "alternative narratives and alternative vocabularies" designed "to produce radical change" (*R*, 10–11). Those "exceptional individuals" who can take the breathless pace and confusion of compulsively proliferating and inhabiting a babel of vocabularies bent on protean radical change will be able "to make their lives works of art" (*R*, 11).

If our postmodernist culture has been aptly characterized as narcissistic, we should not be surprised that Rorty sees the ethical "search for perfection in oneself" as having already found it in himself. Rorty himself turns out to be the hero of his postmodernist narrative of "this aesthetic life, the life of unending curiosity," a narrative that works to identify "the aesthetic life" with "the life of the curious intellectual" (*R*, 11–12). This intellectual hero is "increasingly ironic, playful, free, and inventive: (*R*, 12), and displays both Lyotardian skepticism of all grand narratives (except his own bildungsroman of self-enlargement) and Lyotardian restless greed to take the most tricks in as many new language games as he can learn to play. This curious and ironic intellectual, to fill in the character of the Rortian postmodernist hero perhaps more fully than he would like, is as bold and iconoclastic in thought as he is timid and docile in life and the transformation of social and political realities. Rorty makes clear that his ethics of taste is a "private morality"; his aesthetic life is not a social project but a powerfully individualistic one for private gratification rather than group welfare.[15]

We have seen enough of Rorty's portrayal of the aesthetic life to recognize the genre as essentially Romantic picaresque, a tireless insatiable Faustian quest for enriching titillation through curiosity and novelty, a quest that is as wide-ranging as it is unstructured through the lack of center it so celebrates. However, this absence of structuring center prevents it from being the sort of *Bildungsroman* it seems to want to be. For the maximized spawning of alternative and often inconsistent vocabularies and narratives of the self, an aim that explicitly seeks to undermine the idea of the true self and replace it with an open, changing, growing, multiplicity of selves or self-descriptions, makes the whole idea of an integral enduring self seem completely empty and suspect. But without such a self that is capable of identity through change or changing description, there can be no self capable of self-enrichment or enlargement, and this would nullify the Rortian aesthetic life of self-enrichment by rendering it meaningless. Further analysis and critique of this version of the aesthetic life should, however, require at least brief notice that there are others.

One different and perhaps more familiar version of the aesthetic life is a life devoted to the enjoyment of beauty: beautiful objects of nature and art, as well as those hybrid products of nature and art we are loath to regard as objects of either—beautiful persons. This aesthetic life was very influential in the early part of our century through the fashionable Bloomsbury coterie who confess to having imbibed it from G. E. Moore's account of the ideal in human life. For Moore (who, like Rorty, repudiates any ethics based on the idea of "the true self") this ideal consisted of "certain states of consciousness, which may be roughly described as the pleasures of human intercourse and the enjoyment of beautiful objects"; because "personal affections and aesthetic enjoyments include *all* the greatest, and *by far* the greatest, goods we can imagine" in life.[16] Both these components of the aesthetic life are constituted by very complex and rewarding organic unities. However, the pleasures of personal affection require "that the object must be not only truly beautiful, but also truly good in a high degree," where a proper appreciation of human beauty must include appreciation of its "purely material" form and the "corporeal expression" of its mental qualities (*M*, 203–4).

If this Moorean-Bloomsbury aesthetic life strikes us as distinctively modern and even chicly contemporary in engaging with our hedonistic penchant for beautiful things and beautiful persons, we should remember that it too represents a romantic genre, more particularly a late romantic ideal of aestheticism. Unwilling to accept the universal dominance of the mechanized world picture, unable to accept the traditional religious and moral claims to spirituality, and unready to be sullied by philistine politics, the aesthetes sought individual and collective salvation through the satisfying gemlike flame of art and sensation instead of through God or state. Their ideal of the aesthetic life differs from Rorty's not only in being somewhat less preoccupied with "the curious intellect" but in being more appreciative of beauty, pleasurable sensation, and the leisurely luxury of satisfaction. It is essentially the ethic of Pater and Wilde, an exquisite flower of aestheticist decadence, which remains undeniably and captivatingly sweet, and may be the only flower still capable of growing in our postmodern wasteland. However, as versions of the aesthetic life tend somewhat to overlap and be compounded, we find in Wilde's maxim that "life itself is an art" a clear suggestion of a third notion of the aesthetic life, which I shall call, for contrast and commendation, the classical.[17] The idea here is not so much a life of aesthetic consumption, but a life that is itself a product worthy of aesthetic appreciation for its structure and design as an organic unity. This notion of the aesthetic life seems also to be advocated by the postmodernist Foucault who explicitly links it to ancient greek culture whose "ethics . . . was an aesthetics of existence," the expression of "the will to live a beautiful life, and to leave to others memories of a beautiful existence."[18]

The Greeks, as Williams and Wollheim both note in discussing ethical reflection, were strongly inclined to conceive and assess the good life holistically, as a unified whole. The idea that an individual's life needs to be seen, organized, and evaluated in terms of such an organic rather than simply mechanical or aggregative unity gave Solon's famous injunction to "call no man happy until he is dead" its special force. For a disastrously inappropriate end could distort beyond repair the satisfying unity of the life led thus far.

One of the basic projects of Greek ethics is to try to find such a unitary life that is maximally free of the threat of disunifying misfortune; and one general strategy to achieve such unity is to establish a center and contours for life by a kind of overarching aim or interlocking set of aims, a limiting concentration on a narrower range of goods (naturally those less susceptible to misfortune).

This kind of slimmed-down, centered, limit-respecting life of unity is labelled by Rorty "the ascetic life" (*R*, 11) in unfavorable contrast to "the aesthetic life" he advocates. But such characterization is misleading and unfair. It is simply wrong to assume that a life emphasizing strong unity and thus adopting the limits this requires cannot be an aesthetic life, that it cannot be enjoyed and praised as aesthetically satisfying or even recommended for its aesthetic appeal. One could well choose the life of an earth-rooted family-bound farmer over an air-hopping, spouse-swopping academic simply in terms of its aesthetic joys of order, coherence, and harmony, which stem from a centrally structured and limited project of development, whose unity is both enhanced and largely constituted by cyclical and developmental variations on its central theme or narrative. To live life aesthetically or even to adopt as an ethic "the aesthetic life" is not necessarily to adopt the Faustian aesthetic life of Rorty with its aim of maximizing alternative narratives and "tinkering" changes of the self, its relentless search for "novel experiences and novel language," and its repudiation of a center (which can be made rather than discovered). Among the multiplicity of genres of the aesthetic life that Rorty fails to recognize there are surely some that prefer order, grace, and harmony to opulence, radical change, and novelty.

This non-Rortian perspective on the aesthetic life can be linked directly to the classical definition of beauty as unity in variety, a definition reaffirmed by Coleridge and other romantics, and still the best definition we have. Moreover, such an ideal of beauty neither is nor can be opposed in principle to the aim of richness and variety, for this is precisely one side of the ideal. What its maintains, however, is that variety not be maximized beyond the limit it can be coherently held together in some convincing unity. Applied to a human life, then, this classical ideal does not necessarily require severe or narrow limitations of experience, if our material and social circumstances allow the forging of more complex unities. Such unity would neither be foundationally given nor static. It could be the sort of genealogical, self-constituted, and self-projected unity in variety that Nietzsche (surely a classically steeped romantic) seems to be offering us as the ideal life or character.[19] Such unity can even admit of a self of multiple narratives, as long as these can be made somehow to hang together as a higher unity from the right narrative perspective, one that makes that self more compellingly rich and powerful as an aesthetic character. What this aesthetic standard of the good life cannot admit is the loss of unity of self, which Rorty so glibly resigns as lost or (perhaps more accurately) cheerfully abandons.

But if Rorty's one-sided insistence on enlargement and variety shows him unappreciative of the aesthetic claims of unity and the dangers of its loss, this is not something he can breezily brush aside as merely a matter of genre preference within a range of viable forms of the aesthetic life. For, as I earlier suggested, the loss of such unity would seem to render his entire project of self-enrichment logically incoherent and unworkable by denying any reasonably stable and coherent self to enrich.

Once we abandon a foundationalist essentialism about the self, we can only constitute the self, as Rorty himself admits, in terms of narrative about it. It follows that the unity and coherence of the self will depend on the unity and coherence of its narratives. It is largely for this reason that Alisdair MacIntyre, who similarly rejects any foundationalist account of personal identity, insists on "a concept of self whose unity resides in the unity of a narrative".[20] Not only is this unity essential to the classical ideal (affirmed by MacIntyre) of seeing "each life as a whole, as a unity," but without such unity and coherence of narrative there is no intelligible self to speak of for Rorty's aesthetic life to enrich, enlarge, or perfect. If we abandon the aim of a unified or consistent self-narrative for Rorty's discordant chorus of inconsistent "quasi selves" constituted by alternative, constantly changing, and often incommensurable narratives and vocabularies, with no complex narrative "able to make them all hang together" (*R*, 8), then the project of self-enrichment becomes mythical and incoherent with the myth and incoherence of a single self collecting these riches together. The self-unity needed to speak meaningfully of self-enrichment or perfection (perhaps even to speak of the self at all[21]) is, however, something pragmatically and often painfully forged or constructed rather than foundationally given, and it surely involves developmental change and multiplicity, as all narrative unity must. A unified self is not a uniform self, but nor can it be an unstructured collection of egalitarian quasi selves inhabiting the same corporeal machine or social security number. Rorty's confederacy (rather than centralist union) of quasi selves thus seems less the formula for a Freudian ideal of self-perfection than the recipe for a Freudian pathology of schizophrenia.

Rorty almost seems to recognize the necessity for self-unity when he asserts that the only post-Freudian version of human dignity

is "a coherent self-image" and when he tries to appropriate MacIntyre's unifying virtue of "integrity or constancy" as part of his aesthetic life's "search for perfection" (*R*, 17, 19). But he implicitly denies
coherence in advocating a self composed of "a plurality of persons . . . [with] incompatible systems of belief and desire" (*R*, 19);
and the only constancy that he in fact prescribes is the constancy of
change, of novel alternative self-descriptions and narrations, the constancy of inconstancy, which essentially nullifies the unity and integrity of the self.[22]

In learning so much from Freud, Rorty might have probed why
Freud seemed much less eager to dispense with a unified, integrated
self. Why, for example, did he first opt for the positing of the unconscious rather than simply multiple consciousnesses or personalities
residing in the same body, and why did he never portray our psychological constituents as ideally "egalitarian" and all "sweetly reasonable" as Rorty does, as rational quasi persons engaging in free conversation (*R*, 7–9, 22), unordered by repression and censorship,
which of course, imply some organizational hierarchy governing discourse? One reason may be that Freud implicitly realized what a
pricelessly important and yet perhaps fragile achievement the unity
of self was, how difficult and painful such a unified self or self-
narration was to construct, and yet how necessary it was to lead any
plausible version of a good or satisfying life in human society. It is
certainly presupposed in Rorty's ideal of the Faustian aesthetic life,
no matter how much he wants to reject it. In fact, what makes his
portrayal of this life not only coherent but possibly attractive to us is
that it centers around one kind of self-narrative and vocabulary, that
of the intellectual and the intellectual quest.

The apparent incoherence of Rorty's project of self-enrichment
through multiplying congeries of inconsistent alternative self-nar-
ratives should be enough to dissuade us from adopting his version of
the aesthetic life as the postmodernist ethical ideal. But his advocacy
of this "private morality" of self-perfection seems still more problematic when he appeals to social and historical solidarity as somehow enhancing "the aesthetic life," giving an individual's life more
meaning and "a romantic sense of grandeur" by seeing that personal
narrative as bound up with the life narratives of other individuals and
embedded into the larger narrative of some community or tradition
(*R*, 19–20). Here we must ask with puzzlement, Where is the coherent integrated individual narrative (among the myriad inconsistent narratives of quasi persons) that we wish to bind with others in a
project of solidarity? Where is there a self that is unified and firm
enough not only to allow a momentary self-satisfied glimpse of con-

vergence with others but to guide the narrative enactment of continued and deepening bonds of solidarity? The Rortian self needs to get its own act together, attain its own narrative solidarity and coherence, before it can hope to cohere with others in more than a fleeting cohabitation of the same geography or language-game.

Moreover, given the familiar dialectic of self/other, the coherently unified selves that we are and that are necessary for larger projects of solidarity are themselves largely the product of such communal solidarity. The private self that Rorty wants to enlarge and perfect is thus "always already" social and must be so as soon as it has a language for its private thoughts; and Rorty is therefore unwise to maintain that his "private morality" of the aesthetic life is basically independent of the "public morality" of society and "culture" (R, 10–11). Indeed not only his particular private morality but his privatization of morality are obviously reflective of the society that shapes his thinking—advanced capitalist, liberal democracy.

To contend, as I have, that Rorty's particular ethic of the aesthetic life is neither very new nor conclusively argued is not to deny that all versions of the aesthetic life are similarly problematic nor to assert that novelty is required of a good ethic the way it is often (and perhaps excessively) required of a good work of art. I myself, by way of concluding confession, do not altogether mourn the postmodernist aestheticization of the ethical as a falling off from past ethics dictated by God or pure reason. Indeed, I too subscribe to a vision of the good life that could be characterized as aesthetic: one that attempts to integrate a reasonable variety of interests and enterprises into a pleasingly shaped, dynamically developing, and organically united narrative that I would like to call my life.

Notes

1. See L. Wittgenstein, *Tractatus Logico-Philosophicus* (London: Routledge & Kegan Paul, 1963), pp. 146, 147, proposition 6.421. The English translation in this dual language edition, "Ethics and aesthetics are one and the same," makes the assertion of identity much stronger than the German original, which says only "Ethik und Asthetik sind Eins." Future references to the *Tractatus* will be designated by *T* and the appropriate propositional number.

2. L. Wittgenstein, *Notebooks 1914–1916*, 2nd ed. (Chicago: University of Chicago Press, 1979). Page references to this text will be given with the abbreviation *Notebooks*.

3. See *T*, 6.45, and Wittgenstein's "Lecture on Ethics," written 1929–30 and posthumously published in *Philosophical Review*, 74 (1965): 3–12. In this lecture and in *N*, 83, Wittgenstein refers to the mystical through the notion of the wonderful or miraculous (*das Wunder*).

4. See Jean-François Lyotard, *The Postmodern Condition* (Minneapolis: University of Minnesota Press, 1984), pp. 10, 40–41.

5. The classic presentation of the logical differences or nonparallelisms between ethics and aesthetics is found in Stuart Hampshire's "Logic and Appreciation," reprinted in ed. W. Elton, *Aesthetics and Language* (Oxford: Blackwell, 1954), pp. 161–69.

6. I have discussed this and other aspects of Wittgenstein's later aesthetic theory in "Wittgenstein and Critical Reasoning," *Philosophy and Phenemonological Research*, 47 (1986): 91–110.

7. See Eliot's famous Preface to the second (1928) edition of *The Sacred Wood* (repr. London: Methuen, 1968), p. viii.

8. This distinction between "private morality" and "public morality" is a fairly common one, and has recently been employed by Rorty in arguing for his own aestheticized ethic, which will be critically scrutinized in what follows. Though I employ the distinction here for its pragmatic value, I doubt, for reasons that will later emerge, that the project of private morality is as clearly separable and independent from public morality as Rorty would have us believe. See Rorty, "Freud and Moral Reflection," in eds. J. H. Smith and W. Kerrigan, *Pragmatism's Freud: The Moral Disposition of Psychoanalysis* (Baltimore: Johns Hopkins University Press, 1986), pp. 1–27. The private/public morality distinction is made on pages 11–12. Future page references to this work will be designated in my text with the abbreviation *R*.

9. Postmodernism is surely not unprecedented in pointing to the intermingling importance of the aesthetic for the ethical. For Plato and generally for the Greeks, the ideas of the good and the beautiful were not so clearly differentiated, as can be seen from the fact that they were frequently referred to collectively in the composite term *kalon kai agathon* ("beautiful and good"), and that *kalos*, the specific term for the beautiful, was used perhaps as much as *agathos* to denote moral goodness. Once the Greek ethical world governed by the goal of eudaemonia gave way to ethics dominated by the ideas of divine commandment and duty or obligation, it was much easier to separate the ethical from the aesthetic and even to regard them as conflicting principles. The famous postclassical connections made between aesthetics and ethics express a salient awareness of their perceived divide. Kant saw beauty as a symbol of morality; Schiller saw an aesthetic education as a means to morality; and Kierkegaard saw an aesthetic attitude to life as an inferior alternative to the ethical life. Postmodernism's ethics of taste thus seems distinctive in its attempt at really merging the two principles in defiant awareness of a long

tradition of philosophical bifurcation (which would distinguish it from the Greek overlap), so that the aesthetic is neither a symbol of, means to, or surrogate for an ethic, but rather the constitutive substance of one. Yet though distinctive, it hardly appears unique. Indeed, it seems to be (at least as we shall see in Rorty's version) largely a rehash of fin de siècle aestheticism, which shares the same feverishly anxious lust for pleasurable novelty, and the same weary and faithless skepticism we postmoderns claim as our own.

10. R. Rorty, "Freud, Morality, and Hermeneutics," *New Literary History*, 12 (1980): 180.

11. B. Williams, *Ethics and the Limits of Philosophy* (London: Fontana, 1985), p. 29. Future page references to it will be designated by *Wi*.

12. See Lyotard, *Postmodern Condition*, pp. 27–41.

13. R. Wollheim, *The Thread of Life* (Cambridge: Harvard University Press, 1984), pp. 215–16.

14. Wollheim does not in fact use the term "ethics" but makes the same essential distinction as Williams by speaking of "morality broadly conceived" to include also value apart from obligation as opposed to "morality narrowly conceived," which is dominated by obligation and founded on introjection. See, for example, *Wo*, 221. It is worth noting that Williams portrays the desirable form of ethical reflection in the very manner in which aesthetic reflection is usually presented. Ethical thinking, for Williams, should eschew both the extremes of abstract systematic theorizing from unexceptionable general principles and of smug unreflective adherence to ethical intuitions or prejudices, in seeking "for as much shared understanding as it can find" (*Wi*, 112–17). This is the classical model of aesthetic reasoning, which cannot demonstrate its verdicts by general principles but does not therefore concede they are whims of taste or prejudice that cannot be adequately justified.

15. See not only *R*, 10–11, but Rorty's paper "The Priority of Democracy to Philosophy," eds. M. Patterson and Robert Vaughan, *The Virginia Statue of Religious Freedom* (Cambridge: Harvard University Press, 1987), and, still more recently, his *Contingency, Irony, and Solidarity* (Cambridge: Cambridge University Press, 1989). In the paper on democracy he emphatically advocates the "privatization of questions about the meaning of life" or ethical preference, where the role of society is only to give individuals "the space necessary to work out their own salvation" and "try out their private visions of perfection in peace" (pp. 36–38 of manuscript). Rorty, however, recognizes that private projects of self-fulfillment can find a most satisfactory form through involvement in larger social projects, but he still sees the domains of public and private morality as essentially separate and independent. The difficulty in so viewing them, even for Rorty's own project, will be discussed below, and is further discussed in relation to his recent book in R.

Shusterman, "Postmodernism and the Aesthetic Turn," forthcoming in *Poetics Today*.

16. G. E. Moore, *Principia Ethica* (Cambridge: Cambridge University Press, 1959), pp. 188–89; henceforth abbreviated *M*.

17. Oscar Wilde, *The Works of Oscar Wilde* (London: Collins, 1948), p. 934. Wilde's advocacy of the aesthetic life seems to combine aspects of all the three genres I have distinguished. He variously urges (1) a life of the pleasures of aesthetic consumption and the inspired momentary states of stasis and inactivity they afford, (2) the need for a life to form an aesthetically pleasing whole, and sometimes (3) something approaching the Rortian-Faustian aesthetic life when he recommends that such unity be found in constant change. Indeed, Wilde already expounded Rorty's postmodernist ethic in the 1890s when he stated that the ideal aesthete "will realize himself in many forms, and by a thousand different ways, and will be curious of new sensations and fresh points of view. Through constant change, and through constant change alone, he will find his true unity" (p. 987). The coherence of such a recipe for unity is, however, dubious, and (as Wilde later sadly discovered) its results could prove disastrous for life. It should be noted that Pater also anticipated Rorty's Freudian-Faustian aesthetic life in advocating a "quickened, multiplied consciousness," the thirst for the intense excitement of novelty, and the pragmatic experiential value of knowledge, not as providing any permanent truth (which is unattainable) but simply as "ideas," "points of view," or "instruments of criticism" (in Rorty's terms "vocabularies") for enriching our experience and quickening its appreciation. See W. Pater, *The Renaissance* (London: Macmillan, 1910), pp. vii–xv, 233–39.

18. See M. Foucault, "On the Genealogy of Ethics: An Interview of Work in Progress," in ed. P. Rabinow, *The Foucault Reader* (New York: Pantheon, 1984), pp. 341–43.

19. This interpretation of Nietzsche is most attractively presented in Alexander Nehamas, *Nietzsche: Life as Literature* (Cambridge: Harvard University Press, 1985), pp. 136–37, 177–99. He writes: "The unity of the self, which therefore also constitutes its identity, is not something given but something achieved, not a beginning but a goal" (p. 182). This goal "of the unified self is still compatible with continual change" and the quest for new and diverse experience. It allows a self, in Nietzsche's own words, "*all* the strong, seemingly contradictory desires—but in such a way that they go together under a yoke" (p. 221), held fast, as are the conflicting actions they may engender, in some coherent unity that may be very complex. There are, however, problems in how Nehamas views Nietzsche as grounding this ideal of self-unity on more fundamental logical, genealogical, and perhaps even ontological principles. I discuss these problems in "Nietzsche and Nehamas on Organic Unity," *Southern Journal of Philosophy*, 26 (1988): 379–92.

20. A. MacIntyre, *After Virtue* (London: Duckworth, 1982), p. 191. The following quotation is from p. 190.

21. I do not wish to maintain that all selves, by definition, are or must be adequately unified. For certainly we can and do speak sensibly of divided selves that are ridden with conflict or even split into multiple personalities. For logical individuation of selves in the most basic sense all we need is some primitive notion of a unitary rather than unified self, having some sort of unicity and admitting of varying degrees of unity, where such unity is largely a product of social- and self-construction.

22. He also seems to recognize the need for stability of character when he praises Freud for enabling us to maintain greater stability in unstable times by acknowledging the unconscious sources of many of our instabilities and thereby promoting a stabilizing "tolerance of ambiguities" (R, 9). Rorty's central mistake is to construe the need for "tolerance" of ambiguities and alternative narratives as the need for "celebration and maximization" of such things. He makes the same sort of mistake with respect to the need for new vocabularies, as I have argued elsewhere. See R. Shusterman, "Deconstruction and Analysis: Confrontation and Convergence," *British Journal of Aesthetics*, 26 (1986): 311–27; and *T. S. Eliot and the Philosophy of Criticism* (New York: Columbia University Press, 1988); pp. 208–15.

8

Aftermaths of the Modern:
The Exclusions of Philosophy in Richard Rorty, Jacques Derrida, and Stanley Cavell

Timothy Gould

The relations of philosophy to the postmodern are a good deal uneasier than those of other theories and practices. It is philosophy—and not, for instance, poetry or architecture or even theology—whose very existence has been most impressively doubted or found suspicious by postmodern practitioners. It might well turn out that a certain suspicion of philosophy was characteristic of sensibilities that thought of themselves as postmodern, or even that a postmodern epoch could be characterized as one from which philosophy was, finally and definitively, *missing*—or maybe only off-limits. This would, of course, be far from a merely negative result, either about philosophy or about postmodernism. We could go so far as to depict such a thought as a revision or an application of Marx's claim that, "just as the nations of the ancient world lived their prehistory in the imagination, in mythology, so we Germans have lived our posthistory in thought, in *philosophy*."[1] We might then try to conclude that the postmoderns of Europe and the United States imagine their lives as occurring in the aftermath of philosophy, thereby treating philosophy as a principal feature or symptom of the "modern" era.

It is perhaps too soon to work with such large and schematically historical conclusions, but it is not too soon to think about the pervasive and generalized suspicions that postmodernism directs toward philosophy. It seems clear enough, for instance, that this suspiciousness is exactly part of what some philosophers find fascinating in the phenomena of postmodernism. After all, it is almost the normal condition of philosophy, at least since Descartes, that philosophers themselves should periodically find its questions empty, its methods illegitimate, and its enterprises dubious in their very conception. Only the most fastidious among the professionals will have made themselves immune to such moments of doubt or lapses of conviction in the activities of philosophy. (And even among those who have most completely professionalized their lives, it is sometimes possible to discern a residual capacity for doubt, expressed, for instance, as doubts about their colleagues or their students.)

For many of us, however, the suspicions characteristic of postmodernism will come at times as a confirmation of our own suspicions and at times, perhaps, as a kind of relief from the less communicable anxieties of philosophy. And we may also begin to feel that there is something to learn from these apparently "external" postmodern objections to philosophy's continued existence. At the very least, a philosopher who deserved the title "postmodern" ought to keep open, or at least not constrict, philosophy's access to the cultural phenomena of postmodernism.

It is not merely that these cultural events and devices first gave postmodernism its name, at least in the United States.[2] From my angle, what gives postmodernism its main thrust are the postmodernist practices (however theoretical their bent) rather than what are characterized as postmodern philosophies (however pragmatic their explicit aspirations). And if these specific events and things remain local disturbances in the so-called art world and have no further effect on our political and cultural life, then the term "postmodernism" is likely to remain a sort of parody of earlier "modernist" efforts to name our own period and to place ourselves within a coherent and ultimately reassuring historical diagram.[3] Postmodern philosophers cannot, all by themselves, be expected to fill in the contours of the epoch whose main historical tendencies they have been at pains to discern and to sketch.

I do not, of course, wish to deny that in recent years it has become increasingly difficult and perhaps increasingly pointless to make such distinctions between postmodern "philosophies" and the various postmodern practitioners (including, of course, the practitioners of what is now sometimes called "theory"). But one might nevertheless still wish to retain the ability to distinguish, at least for certain purposes, a performance by Vito Acconci from a lecture by Richard Rorty. (Presumably, it has not yet become that difficult to distinguish a *lecture* by Acconci from a lecture by Rorty.)

However we sort out this tangle of issues, it does still seem to me that this generalized "postmodern" suspicion of philosophy provides us with one way of understanding Richard Rorty's current reputation and his entanglement with our immediate concerns. Along with Jean-François Lyotard, he is the principal figure associated with the possibility, and even the fact, of a postmodern philosophy.[4] The stories that Rorty tells about the modern and the postmodern have become almost ubiquitous—stories about modern philosophy's futile and self-defeating search for "foundations"; or about the postmodern replacement of theory by conversation or narrative; or about the advantages of solidarity over objectivity. His work now often sets the terms for discussion, even for those who wish to criticize him.

There a number of ironies stemming from Rorty's position on the agenda of those who wish to ask questions about the existence of postmodern philosophy. From Rorty's perspective such questions must appear to be at best of bibiliographical interest, containing little more of intellectual substance than the time it takes us to ask them. On the other hand, we might take note of something like a professional-oedipal motive for some of the attacks on Rorty. This is a situation that Rorty might well relish as confirming his sense of how items and figures get onto a "philosophical" agenda in the first place. I will return obliquely to these issues in the second half of my essay.

From someone in my political and philosophical condition, Rorty's posture betokens not so much doubt about the projects of philosophy as disdain for anyone who could take those projects as other than childish. One burden of this paper is to say something about why I find Rorty's stories so unhelpful and something about the specific political and intellectual liabilities that we would incur by working with them. My own interest in asking whether there is a postmodern philosophy derives from my interest in asking whether, and how, there can still be such a thing or practice as philosophy. Clearly, I find myself on a different and mostly opposite path from Rorty's, and it may seem to some readers that I have prejudiced the question in favor of the existence of philosophy, whether postmodern or otherwise. I should therefore make it explicit that I am trying to follow out some strands of my response to postmodernist practices and the questions they might pose for a philosopher, without accepting in advance the dismissals of philosophy that are so often retailed in postmodern arenas. Such dismissals are not without their interest but they are likely to prove powerless to effect their claims. The sense of oneself as rejecting the impositions of philosophy is no more effective by itself than the sense of oneself as rejecting any other regime, whether of thought, feeling, form, value, force, or power. And the wish to reject philosophy, however laudable at some moments or for certain purposes, is not to be taken at face value, as if philosophy were so intellectually moribund and politically corrupt that we need not examine our motives in opposing it.

There are, roughly, two strands or features of postmodernism that I wish to explore. First, postmodernists have presented themselves as trying to undo what might be called the operations of exclusion in the cultural and political fields of representation. Second, many American practitioners of postmodernism have often taken themselves to be opposing or undoing the "entrenchment" of various modernisms in painting or sculpture or music. A helpful place to learn about both these features is Frederic Jameson's "Postmodernism and Consumer Society".[5] Jameson speaks of postmodernism's "effacement . . . of some key boundaries or separations, most notably the erosion of the older distinction between high culture and so-called mass or popular culture."[6] I will emphasize a different sort of separation, and I will emphasize the fact that the boundaries in question are rarely perceived as neutral. They often work by ruling something in and, consequently, by ruling something out. To Jameson's description of the "established" or "dominant" forms of modernism, I add the term "entrenched." This use of the term is intended, in part, to commemorate one of Clement Greenberg's much maligned formulations of the issue of modernism.[7]

I find the following circumstance especially thought-provoking: although a great deal of postmodernist writing is aimed specifically at the accomplishments of modernism (and at modernist accounts of art and culture, like those of Clement Greenberg and Michael Fried), the proponents of the postmodern in philosophy have tended to content themselves with undifferentiated and, for the most part, crude portraits of "modern" philosophy. There has been little effort to characterize the possibilities—and hence the limitations—of a specifically "modernist" project in philosophy, much less to characterize the specific difficulties of philosophizing in the aftermath of such a project.

A notable exception here is Stephen Melville's book *Philosophy Beside Itself: On Deconstruction and Modernism.*[8] Melville works to situate Derrida's enterprises in terms derived as much from Stanley Cavell's description of a modernist moment in philosophy as from Greenberg and Fried's accounts of modernist painting and sculpture. For the moment, I will merely point to a couple of features of the situation that Melville is characterizing—namely, the power of some postmodernist writing to isolate uncanny moments of blindness and persistent repetition *within* the successions of modernism. It is one of Melville's further insights that if a project follows closely enough on the heels of a particular "modernist" project to constitute a "postmodernist" challenge, it is unlikely to be interestingly free of the tendency that it challenges. This is by no means inevitably a criticism of a specific postmodernist practice. But the persistence of "modernist" issues in a postmodernist practice may tend at least to undermine the self-conception or self-presentation of that particular practice.

The postmodern effort to undo exclusions and the postmodern challenge to particular modernist achievements and theories are often found together, and under certain circumstances they may coalesce. (We may see this happening in some remarks by Craig Owens—quoted below—where he characterizes the postmodernist challenge to the tyrannical exclusions of the "signifier" by contrasting it with what he takes to be the celebration of the signifier on the part of some modernists.) It would be satisfying—perhaps suspiciously satisfying—if my attempts to apply these two features of postmodernism to the situation of philosophy were also ultimately to coalesce. Within the scope of this paper, however, it will be necessary to treat the two strands of analysis for the most part as if they were independent.

I will not try to demonstrate in any detail how important the idea and the facts of exclusion are to the theoreticians of the postmodern. I quote at length from the essay just mentioned by Craig Owens:

> The postmodernist work attempts to upset the reassuring stability of [the] mastering position [of the representational systems of the West]. The same project has of course been attributed . . . to the *modernist* avant-guard, which through the introduction of heterogeneity, discontinuity, glossolalia, etc. supposedly put the subject of representation in crisis. But the avant-guard sought to transcend representation in favor of presence and immediacy; it proclaimed the autonomy of the signifier, its liberation from the "tyranny of the signified"; postmodernists instead expose the tyranny of the *signifier*, the violence of its law. . . . It is precisely at the legislative frontier between what can be represented and what cannot that the postmodernist operation is being staged—not in order to transcend representation, but in order to expose that system of power that authorizes certain operations while blocking, prohibiting or invalidating others. Among those prohibited from Western representation, whose representations are denied all legitimacy, are women. Excluded from representation by its very structure, they return within it as a figure for—a representation of—the unrepresentable (Nature, Truth, the Sublime, etc.).[9]

It seems to me an open question whether any individual postmodernist operation could "expose," even temporarily, the operations of the system that Owens is depicting. He characterizes it as essentially a unified system of representation, signification, exclusion, and power. Furthermore, he appears to think that this unity is—at least from certain angles—*self-evident*, despite the system's equally evident powers of mystification. I do not so much wish to disagree with his claim as to wonder about the methodological routes he must have traveled to arrive at it. We might also wonder about the political and personal consequences of maintaining such a view. However he got there, his picture is clear enough. It is a picture of an operation of exclusion, performed by the structure of Western representation upon the passive (and indeed victimized) subjects of exclusion. With equal clarity, the writer implies that he has now secured access to the excluded and prohibited material, despite the difficulties inherent in a culture where "visibility is always on the side of the male, invisibility on the side of the female."[10]

I will cite one more approach to the idea of undoing or transgressing a field of exclusions. Stephen Melville has related postmodernist practices directly to the accounts of modernism, cited above, by Greenberg, Fried, and Cavell. Melville's openness to the claims of philosophy and to the accomplishments of modernist artists makes his discussions more detailed than is common. Here is one of his formulations of an issue about postmodernism and modernist painting:

> We cast postmodernism at a deeper level if we say that the allegorical impulse is one which would acknowledge explicitly the futility of trying to sort out the "mere" from the "pure"—an impulse to embrace the heteronomy of painting. . . . [The] acknowledgement demands that we accept—as best we can—that the field we call "painting" includes, and cannot now be defined without reference to, its violations and excesses—performance work in particular.[11]

Melville traces the implications for his work—and also for postmodernism—of Derrida's insights into such projects of breaching. Melville's attention to the difficulties of thinking through the "inclusions" required by a specific challenge to modernism might encourage us to examine some specific efforts to undo the exclusions of philosophy. The allegorical impulse that he describes contains a demand that we examine in detail the mechanisms and also the accomplishments of exclusion. For an impulse to allegory without any detail would be uncomfortably close to an impulse to irony—at least to the sense of irony that Melville has developed out of the work of Paul de Man.

Beyond these difficulties and discomforts, Melville's work insists on something analogous to an old insight about intentionality: you cannot merely exclude (or merely include) in general, any more than you can merely intend something in general. What is excluded, like what is intended, is always—somewhere—something particular. In what follows, I will be implicitly trying to apply this insight of Melville's to Rorty's picture of how the exclusions of philosophy are to be overcome.

It should not, I suppose, require the success of any particular postmodernist practice or theory to see that philosophy often seems to gets its work done by excluding something. To paraphrase J. L. Austin, one might say that this work of exclusion was the preoccupation of modern philosophers, except for the sneaking suspicion that it was their occupation. Thinking for the moment of philosophy in English, a partial list of its exclusions would contain, not quite at random, the psychological, the rhetorical, the literary, the political, the merely contingent, the historical, and the question and questions of women. This list is not meant to deny priority to some elements or relationships among the elements. At different moments, different elements have seemed to me to provide the key to the list of exclusions. But the idea of a hierarchy of exclusions may be misleading here—as is, I suppose, the idea of a list.

During a period in which philosophy has declared so much to be "outside" philosophy (or not appropriate for philosophy, not really philosophy at all), one might well understand, and sometimes share, the wish that philosophy should simply stop or be stopped.[12] Let those who want to call themselves philosophers stick to their little residue of technical problems. Let the rest of us go about our business, and let all those excluded become included. Let the "insiders" be henceforth the outsiders, or, best of all, let there be no more opposing of the inside to the outside, no more centers, and no more excluded premises. Let circumference thrive.

Rorty is very good at capturing this mood, and part of his appeal surely lies in his capacity for depicting a kind of utopian future for academic cultural studies:

> It may be [Rorty suggests] a culture which is transcendentalist through and through, whose center is everywhere and circumference nowhere. In such a culture, Jonathan Edwards and Thomas Jefferson, Henry James and William James, John Dewey and Wallace Stevens, Charles Pierce and Thorstein Veblen will all be present. No one will be asking which ones are the Americans, nor even, perhaps, which ones are the philosophers.[13]

Rorty's optative mood is familiar to me, and I would not disown it. From within such a mood, one can appreciate the attractiveness of Rorty's remark that when a philosopher gives his own "scholastic little definitions of philosophy," he is merely employing "a polemical device . . . intended to exclude from the field of honor those whose pedigree is unfamiliar."[14] When the mood wears thin, I find myself regarding Rorty's impatience as less therapeutic than it might initially seem. Here again, his advice amounts to the suggestion that we forget about the problems of philosophy. We would be better off regarding them henceforth as romantic or childish and therefore, presumably, as silly. In any event, such problems are not worth the attention of a grown-up's mind.

This is, I suppose, sound advice, at least for some spirits. But the trouble with such advice, as a general rule, is that the person who needs it, is in no position to follow it. It is no more directly usable than any other advice—to forget about your problems and to get on with your life. Moreover, I find it increasingly hard to ignore the hints that Rorty's recommendations are themselves a form of resistance, a form of denial that a particular symptom is really all that important. We might consider, for instance, a remark like this one:

> Concepts like causality, originality, intelligibility, literalness and the like are no more dangerous, and no more suicidal, than sunsets or blackbirds. It is not their fault that in another country long ago, they were believed to have magical powers.[15]

Considering that a principal point of these remarks is to get readers of Derrida to regard the history of philosophy with less urgency, we might ask where the ideas of "suicide" and "magic" come from. Inasmuch as these are not the terms in which Derrida thinks about the mystifications and the dangers of the philosophical enterprise, we might want to speculate about the appropriate object of this reassurance. It seems to me that the remarks are more suitably aimed at a disaffected practitioner of the Anglo-American tradition. They would have more significance if they were directed at someone who shared the frustrated hopes for analytic philosophy displayed in Rorty's earlier work. When directed at someone who wants to pursue Derrida's relentless unheavings of metaphysics, Rorty's gestures seem rather designed to ward something off.

Rorty's point about philosophers excluding the "unfamiliar" is also quite selective in its targets. Consider so obvious and crucial a case as that of Plato's banishing the poets from the *Republic:* Are Sophocles and Homer to be exiled for anything like their unfamiliarity? Or would it be more plausible to suggest that Socrates has in mind their all but unquestionable capacity to command the attention and the passions of a Greek audience? Indeed, we would, I believe, do better to think of this power as a function of their insidious familiarity, as persuasive as the prevailing winds.[16] Even if we turn closer to home, we might ask whether it makes much sense to think, for instance, of Carnap as excluding Heidegger or of Searle as excluding Derrida on the grounds of their unfamiliar intellectual lineage.

Rorty's preoccupation with the chivalric romance of philosophy—as evidenced in his reference to the "field of honor"—is part of what positions his work so oddly in relation to that of Derrida or Cavell. For whatever the considerable distances separating these two writers, they both take seriously the possibility that Rorty denies—namely, the existence of specifically philosophical mechanisms of exclusion and defense. To demonstrate in detail the relationship between Cavell's and Derrida's accounts of such mechanisms would, I believe, go a long way toward providing a usable measurement of the distances between them. This would take me far beyond the scope of this paper, but the following remarks, however sketchy, will at last point to the kind of issues that must eventually be dealt with.

In Derrida, it is, of course, "writing" that has been the victim of a "logocentric repression" in favor of the *phoné* and, in particular, of speech. Derrida insists that the traces of this repression are only one sort of "symptom" among many, although from the standpoint of his work they are perhaps the most salient and the most revealing. Derrida also indicates his distrust of the word "symptom," and while he insists on the concept of repression—as opposed to "forgetting" or "exclusion"—he also insists that "logocentric repression is not comprehensible on the basis of the Freudian concept of repression."[17] This is one source of what Derrida characterizes as his "theoretical reticence" to employ psychoanalytic concepts "otherwise than in quotations marks."[18] Others are better situated than I to investigate this side of Derrida's work. To me it seems impossible to get very far with his work, apart from appreciating the extent to which he is constantly assessing what he calls the "relative autonomy" of philosophy.[19]

Something like this assessment seems to be a constant feature of his efforts "to determine from a certain exterior [*dehors*] that is unqualifiable or unnameable by philosophy what this history has been able to dissimulate or forbid, making itself into a history by means of this somewhere motivated repression."[20] It is worth consulting Derrida's French at this point: he wrote "se faisant histoire par cette répression quelque part intéressée,"[21] which might better be translated "making itself into *history*, etc." [my italics]. I take Alan Bass's translation to muffle the Heideggerian point about history, which echoes Derrida's earlier essay on Levinas. There he had written about "the violent way [in which philosophy] opens history by opposing itself to nonphilosophy, which is its past and its concern, its death and well-spring."[22] Some of philosophy's most persistent creations are the Western concepts of history (and what other concepts do we have to work with?), against which philosophy stakes its essential thoughts and from which it thinks to escape.

Throughout his work, Derrida is faithful at once to the mechanisms through which philosophy constitutes itself apart from—and yet by means of—the resources of "non-philosophy". (These mechanisms are often reduced by some of his readers to a list of "binary oppositions" or "philosophèmes".) To my mind, he is also and at the same time faithful to what he calls the "adventure" by which any individual thought is launched on the paths of philosophy. Consider such words as these:

> Thus, those who look into the possibility [*qui questionnent sur la possibilité*] of philosophy, philosophy's life and death, are already engaged in, already overtaken by the dialogue of the question about itself and with itself; they always act in memory of philosophy, as part of the correspondence of the question with itself. . . . This is where the objectification, secondary interpretation, and determination of the question's own history in the world all begin; and this is where the combat embedded in the difference between the question in general and "philosophy" as a determined—finite and mortal—moment or mode of the question itself also begins. The difference between philosophy as a power and adventure *of* the question and philosophy as a determined event or turning point *within* this adventure.[23]

These remarks are relevant not only to the discussions of a "postmodern" philosophy but to every effort to reduce the history of philosophy to its various periods. Whatever romance and whatever other evasions might be served by the thought of such adventures of repression and autonomy—of inside and outside—it is not the romance in Rorty's fable of the unfamiliar "pedigree."

In the work of Stanley Cavell, what philosophy represses can also be variously described.[24] One consequence of its repressions is that philosophers find themselves unable to question what we might characterize as the "sound" and the "look" of reason, hence unable to perceive what lies beyond the scope of argument or the boundaries of a current set of problems.[25] In Cavell's work, the emergence of arguments and problems in analytic philosophy is a sign that a memory of a more precarious position is being resisted. Philosophers argue. (This truth remains, for many, the essential element of any definition of philosophy.) But philosophers do not argue with the material that the reign of argument and logical analysis must begin by excluding. One name that Cavell gives to the condemned activity that seeks this excluded matter of the text is precisely "reading." But this activity and its related passivities are at the same time versions of the excluded matter. So far as I know, neither philosophers nor literary theorists have tried to trace the connection between the repression of reading in Cavell and the repression of writing in Derrida.[26] One reason why the connections have not been examined is that Cavell speaks centrally of the recovery of voice from its shunning in modern philosophy. And Derrida is taken by many to have shown that such a project of recovering the voice must itself be in the service of "metaphysics."

This last divergence between Derrida and Cavell will remain only superficially understood, until we have a more usable account of the ways in which any resistance to metaphysical thinking is liable to contain the elements of metaphysics. (This seems to me inevitable in the way that any therapy must at some stage be conducted in the language of the patient. But perhaps this thought will seem too "humanistic."[27]) The difference about "voice" and metaphysics, however, points to some other differences between Derrida and Cavell that may prove less tractable. Eventually, for instance, someone will have to trace the relation between Husserl's treatment of voice and Derrida's diagnosis of the system of "hearing-oneself-speak" and, on another front, the persistent Fregean wish for a *Begriffschrift*, a concept-writing that could essentially replace—or repress—the vagueness and other inadequacies of common speech. For there is no doubt that Cavell continues to respond to this wish as a prime version, at least within contemporary philosophy, of the repressions of metaphysics. (It remains, for one thing, the most powerful vehicle for the wish to turn philosophy into something more like a "science.") And examining such differences about Frege and Husserl will also involve us in some questions about audience. It seems to me significant that while Derrida got into one kind of political trouble for insisting that Heidegger's thought of presence was "uncircumventable," Cavell's insistence on Wittgenstein's relation to Heidegger helped to render Cavell's work almost instantly inaudible, if not quite invisible, to Anglo-American philosophers.

Taken together or taken separately, the writings of Derrida and Cavell suggest an area of investigation that can be perceived only by those who appreciate what Derrida calls the "relative autonomy" of philosophy. They would not (or perhaps even could not) investigate a slip of the tongue, who had trained themselves to regard all acts of speech as equally bungled. Wherever we might end up if we pursued the relation between their enterprises, it seems to me that a sympathetic reader of either one of them might want to get past Rorty's version of how philosophy excludes what is "unfamiliar." For the time being, I will take matters just a little further and suggest that we consider the possibility that what philosophy expels is exactly the familiar. Philosophy is bound up with the knowledge of the things that you cannot simply fail to know. If you go on, like Cavell, to describe this as the knowledge of what has been repressed, you have not yet said anything specifically related to psychoanlytic insight. Up to this point, the claim may still be merely that it takes work not to know what we cannot simply fail to know. And so, in consequence, it also takes work to *know* such things, or to let yourself know them. We might think of this as the other work of philosophy, which might well turn out to be connected to what Derrida calls its adventure.

But at some point, whether in Cavell's terms or in Derrida's and whether about reading or about writing, I think that some among us will want to spell it out: philosophy's concern with the familiar is a concern with what was previously familiar—the always-already, as Heidegger was the first to put it. And this is the region that Freud explores under the heading of the "uncanny," which involves the perception of "a hidden, familiar thing" as it emerges from the repression that rendered it hidden.

Just how far one will be prepared to go down this route, and on what terms, is far from clear in advance. Psychoanalysis remains as suspicious to Anglo-American philosophers as, say, romantic poetry and much more suspicious than certain versions of Marx or Nietzsche. Rorty himself has given us a version of Freud without a working concept of repression, a significant achievement even for someone with Rorty's capacity for assimilating and domesticating the projects of others. Rorty's Freud is useful primarily in the construction of "richer and more plausible narratives of this *ad hoc* type."[28] These narratives are supposed to emerge from the "enlarged vocabularies" of the intellectuals who are, in a sense, defined by their interest in deploying such vocabularies. What other accounts might have described as "repressed material" is on Rorty's account more grist for the mills of narration. It provides another "conversational partner," whose plausible voice merely happens to have been inaudible until now. In short, Rorty's "pragmatic" account of psychoanalysis renders it as tame as any Anglo-American philosopher could wish.

If we managed to take these issues of philosophy and psychoanalysis beyond the precincts in which they have been confined, we might find a way of posing a useful version of the question of "postmodern" philosophy. For now we can see that Cavell and Derrida indeed share a particular perception of an aftermath of "modern" philosophy: How—and from what position—can we understand philosophy and psychoanalysis as struggling for each other's knowledge and for the limits of this knowledge? Without trying to argue for the centrality of this question, let me try to say a little more about where it comes from and about what it might lead to.

Suppose we accept for the moment the suggestion (which I believe I share with Stephen Melville) that Derrida's relation to Heidegger and Cavell's relation to Wittgenstein can be characterized in part as responses to the dominant modernisms in their philosophical environment. Then it seems to me striking that both Cavell and Derrida can be understood as wishing to undo some of the "same" operations of exclusion, in particular, the various exclusions of psychoanalysis. To be sure, these exclusions were performed for apparently very different reasons. Heidegger linked it as much to the moral as to the technological impulses of psychotherapy. (He also linked it to what he called Anglo-American *Logik,* or what can still be called "logical analysis." This last connection is so breath-takingly oblivious of the ideologies of either group of "analysts" that it ought to repay some closer study." Wittgenstein's contempt was directed not so much at Freud's work as at the hermeneutical attractiveness of Freud's results. In a sense, he despised the very consequences that Rorty adulates, the construction of ever more plausible narratives as a means of avoiding a life that has become inaccessible to speech. These disparate motives for rejecting psychoanalysis should not be ignored, nor should we ignore the relative superficiality of the terms of the rejections. These terms are suspiciously far from the most interesting critical moments in either Heidegger or Wittgenstein.

Nevertheless, it seems to me worth investigating the ways in which Derrida and Cavell, in lifting a certain prohibition to analytic insight, keep discovering versions of philosophy's exclusion of the passive. More precisely, they both chart a series of relationships between the human repudiation of passivity, and the philosophical wish to renounce or reinterpret a "prior" situation in which "active" and "passive" are not distinct or even exactly conceivable. (Mostly—but not, I think, entirely—such repudiations are characteristic of maleness, and, indeed of men.[29]) Derrida goes so far as to characterize this repression as the founding repression of philosophy. We are to think of something like a "middle voice, a certain nontransitivity, [which] may be what philosophy at its outset distributed into an active and a passive voice, thereby constituting itself by means of this repression."[30] And he connects this to Nietzsche's critique of philosophy as an "active indifference to difference, as the system of an adiaphoristic repression or reduction."[31] There is a great deal of work to be done with such suggestions. I would argue, for instance, that one of the most visible traces of this repression (at least in Anglo-American philosophy) is the vision of full-fledged human "action," as distinct from the bodily movement. This is one of the privileged places where the idea of an activity that wholly excludes every trace of passivity finds its philosophical accommodation. This problematic is sometimes called the "theory of action." To show its connection to the suppression of reading—conceived of as what Cavell calls a "foreign" and apparently passive rigor—would be a labor of no small dimensions. It would be useful to be able to connect this perception of the double repression of passivity and of reading to Derrida's own doublings of philosophy. Through such connections (and, of course, not through these alone), one might even begin to see how we could describe a "modernist moment" in philosophy. If we were able to characterize such a moment as sufficiently persistent and as distinct from both the ancient and the modern texts of metaphysics, then we might turn systematically to the question of the self-conscious aftermaths of modernist philosophy. And that, for me, would be one useful way of posing the question of a postmodernist philosophy.

I do not claim to know where these issues will emerge, if they are followed out in the detail they require. I claim that they are worth trying to follow out, at least for anyone who is still interested in philosophy and its various sequelae. And I claim that to take up Rorty's story too soon—or too seriously—would prevent us from pursuing these issues. For that matter, Rorty's stories might easily keep us from providing ourselves with the terms in which Derrida's project could begin to raise some issues for American philosophy. As evidence for this latter claim, I will conclude with a further glance at Rorty's own fate as a reader of Derrida.

Consider what Rorty makes of Derrida's involvement with Rousseau. He appropriates Derrida by attributing to him the view that "writing . . . is to this kind of simple 'getting it right' [the sense of] . . . just the right piece fitting into just the right slot . . . as masturbation is to standard, solid, reassuring sex."[32]

He adds that this is why writers are thought to be "effete" compared to "men of science." This is an interesting contrast, but it does not have much to do with what Derrida is up to in *Of Grammatology*.[33] It would take a while to say what these enterprises are, but I think a sympathetic reader might want to explore exactly the notions of passivity and activity that are falsely at work in our understanding of masturbation, in the masculine (mis)understanding of women, and of what Derrida calls the "narrow gulf that separates doing from suffering."[34]

Rorty, on the other hand, uses the idea as a rather flat allegory for the possibility that male philosophers will get more self-conscious about what they are doing, which is scarcely the nonconsumation that Derrida has wished for. Derrida, Rorty says, avoids the danger of becoming just another philosopher of language by becoming a "philosopher of philosophy, where philosophy is just the self-conscious play of a certain kind of writing." In this light, Rorty's Kantian/non-Kantian contrast—one version of his modern/postmodern contrast—"now appears as the contrast between the man who wants to take (and see) things as they are, and thus make sure that the right pieces go in the right holes, and the man who wants to change our vocabulary for isolating pieces and holes."[35] It will not escape the reader's notice that this remark, however allegorical, makes its immediate sense only from the point of view of one's activities. And if Rorty were to reply that his intent was merely to isolate and satirize this set of male preoccupations, then I ask in return: Why does he stop where he stops? Surely the question of what goes where and when—and the related question of who is satisfied by whom and by what—are not solely matters of macho posturing. Or, at the very least, one ought to recognize that it is equally a matter of male self-satisfaction to declare that anything goes, where and when I say it goes. Rorty's perspective ignores the possibility of any other anxiety than the one about technical performance. Whatever his overt political opinions about feminism, Rorty's work tends to deny the possibility of discovering that there are other routes to epistemological satisfaction than the ones that postmodern, male philosophers are now familiar with.

This remark about pieces and holes is far from an isolated or ephemeral moment in Rorty's work. It is merely one of the most egregious. Consider his account of the world, with and without "gaps," and of Wittgenstein's remedy for this sort of oscillation in our masculine theories of knowledge:

[Wittgenstein] does not say: the tradition has pictured the world with gaps, but here is how the world looks with the gaps closed. Instead, he just makes fun of the whole idea that there is something here to be explained.[36]

Now we see something on the level of philosophy about what Rorty means by changing our vocabulary for talking about "holes": we are to stop talking about them altogether. Moreover, Rorty's remarks suggest that there is little point to any further examination of the familiar use of the woman's body as a figure for the truth of the world. There may be various possibilities at play in such a recommendation. But whatever the derivation of Rorty's position, the laughter that Rorty attributes to Wittgenstein makes plain the wish that there be nothing of importance there to account for—or to be seen.

This spot in Rorty's work brings me back to an earlier theme, and I will let it stand in place of a conclusion. We need to plot, at once more seriously and with better humor, the graph that connects male-centered epistemologies (and hence male-centered skepticisms and critics of skepticism) to male horror at the female genitalia and the consequent development of curiosity by way of compromise and compensation. And such matters would also take us back to the issues of uncanniness, which I have briefly touched on. Both Derrida and Cavell have tried to ask these questions of the uncanny in the face of philosophy's exclusions and repressions. And both of them take measures to allow for and to diagnose the resistances that Rorty would have us circumvent. Their writings prepare us for the fact that our questions about the uncanny are always liable to become uncanny questions. And as Heidegger pointed out long ago, the uncanny is frequently the near neighbor of the anxious.

Will these be questions about philosophy, or sex, or politics, or therapy or perhaps, after all, about aesthetics—about what we still have a taste for? Can a philosopher ask such questions and still be understood as a philosopher? These are the issues I have wished to raise for a postmodern philosopher—for any philosophers who find themselves stranded between philosophy's creation of the idea of history and its repression of the particular historical circumstances of philosophy's own culture. I hope that in asking these questions I am not—or anyway not necessarily—excluding myself, from philosophy or from the arenas of the postmodern, or from politics, or for that matter from any help that I can get. Nor, of course, do I wish to exclude anyone else who cares to ask.[37]

Notes

1. *Contribution to the Critique of Hegel's Philosophy of Right: An Introduction*, in *The Marx-Engels Reader*, ed. Robert Tucker, 2nd ed. (New York: Norton, 1978), p. 58.

2. See Jerome Mazzaro, *Postmodern American Poetry* (Urbana: University of Illinois Press, 1980), pp. vii and 15–28.

3. See Paul de Man's reservations about the term "postmodernism" in *The Resistance to Theory* (Minneapolis: University of Minnesota Press, 1986), pp. 119–20.

4. Despite some common concerns and despite Rorty's use of the term "mentanarrative," it seems to me that Lyotard's work is animated by a very different sense of philosophy's relation to either culture or politics. He writes, for instance, that "the postmodern is that in the modern which puts forward the unpresentable in presentation itself; which denies itself the solace of good forms" (*The Postmodern Condition* [Minneapolis: University of Minnesota Press, 1984], p. 81). It is beyond the scope of this paper to explore the implication in Lyotard's account that our understanding of the postmodern is bound up with the issues of the sublime, which he construes in Kantian terms. For an account of how we might think of the sublime as involving "presentable" aspects of the "unpresentable," see Neil Hertz, "The Notion of Blockage in the Literature of the Sublime," in *The End of the Line* (New York: Columbia University Press, 1985).

5. In *The Anti-Aesthetic*, ed. Hal Foster (Port Townsend, Wash.: Bay Press, 1983).

6. *The Anti-Aesthetic*, p. 112.

7. See Clement Greenberg, "Modernist Painting": "The essence of modernism lies, as I see it, in the use of the characteristic methods of a discipline to criticize the discipline itself—not in order to subvert it, but to entrench it more firmly in its area of competence" (reprinted in *The New Art*, ed. Gregory Battcock [New York: Dutton, 1966], p. 101). Something analogous to Greenberg's "positivism"—evinced here in the idea of "competence"—persists in many versions of postmodernism (for example, in a certain idea of "performance" or of effectiveness). What I just called Greenberg's "positivism" was, so far as I know, first diagnosed by Michael Fried in "Shape as Form", *Artforum*, 5/3 (November 1966).

8. Stephen Melville, *Philosophy Beside Itself; On Deconstruction and Modernism* (Minneapolis: University of Minnesota Press, 1986).

9. Craig Owens, "Feminists and Postmodernism," in *The Anti-Aesthetic*.

10. Ibid., p. 72.

11. "Notes on the Reemergence of Allegory, the Forgetting of Modernism, the Necessity of Rhetoric, and the Conditions of Publicity in Art and Criticism, *October*, 19 (Winter 1981).

12. This is a good place to recall the reasonably evident fact that the field of philosophy excludes actual people, as well as specific concerns and methods. It excludes or has excluded not just the subject of woman but particular women; and not just history or historical materialism, but particular historical materialists, or members of the Communist Party, or teachers who refused to take a loyalty oath in the 1950s.

13. Rorty, *Consequences of Pragmatism* (Minneapolis: University of Minnesota Press, 1982), p. 70. It seems to me more than merely polemical to point out, for instance, that neither Margaret Fuller, Gertrude Stein, or Marianne Moore make it into this circumferenceless circle, however widely it was intended to be drawn. The image of a culture who center is everywhere is not very helpful in thinking specifically about those who are excluded from our actual culture. That Rorty's intention is to parody Augustine is worth noting. But just as atheism is not a particularly good cure for the various theologies that we have internalized, so what I might dub Rorty's aculturalism is not a particularly good cure (or even much of a diagnosis) for the various exclusions of American culture.

14. Rorty, *Consequences of Pragmatism*, p. 92.

15. Richard Rorty, "Deconstruction and Circumvention," *Critical Inquiry*, 11 (September 1984): 20–21.

16. See *Republic*, iii, 40lb-d, where, however, it is only the good influences that are compared to the breezes. The bad influences are images [*eikosi*] and living among them is compared to grazing in an "evil meadow," which is also an image of a dangerous familiarity. (Paul Shorey's translation provides the meadow with "poisonous herbs.")

17. *Positions* (Chicago: University of Chicago Press 1978), pp. 196–97.

18. *Writing and Difference*, p. 197.

19. *Positions*, p. 102.

20. Ibid., p. 6.

21. *Positions* (Paris: Minuit, 1972), pp. 14–15. A further problem arises from the translation of *interessee* as "motivated," which loses the connection to the *écriture à soi intéressée*.

22. *Writing and Difference*, p. 79.

23. Ibid., pp. 80–81.

24. See my "Stanley Cavell and the Plight of the Ordinary," in *Images in*

Our Souls, eds. Joseph Smith and William Kerrigan (Baltimore: Johns Hopkins University Press, 1987).

25. See Wittgenstein, *Philosophical Investigations*, #134: ". . . one feature of our concept of a proposition is, *sounding like a proposition [der Satzklang].*" See also Cavell, *The Claim of Reason* (New York: Oxford University Press, 1979), pp. 121–25.

26. See below, pp. 18–19, and also Gould, "Where the Action is: Stanley Cavell and the Skeptic's Activity," *Bucknell Review* (Spring 1988).

27. Cf. *Positions*, p. 10.

28. *Pragmatism's Freud: The Moral Disposition of Psychoanalysis*, eds. Joseph Smith and William Kerrigan (Baltimore: Johns Hopkins University Press, 1986), pp. 9, 11–12, and passim.

29. See "Where the Action Is."

30. *Margins of Philosophy* (Chicago: University of Chicago Press, 1982), p. 16.

31. Ibid., p. 17.

32. *Consequences of Pragmatism*, p. 106.

33. See Eve Kosofsky Sedgwick, *Between Men* (New York: Columbia University Press, 1985).

34. *Of Grammatology* (Baltimore: Johns Hopkins University Press, 1976), p. 165.

35. *Consequences of Pragmatism*, p. 107.

36. Ibid., p. 34.

37. My thanks to Kathleen Whalen, Garrett Stewart, Hugh Wilder, Stephen Melville and Joshua Wilner for timely comments and encouragement.

Part IV

Paintings and Performances

9

Painting in the End:
Fates of Appropriation

Stephen Melville

As long as we have known of modernism, we have known also of the the existence of the word "postmodernism" and have tried under various circumstances and within various regions to pronounce it. As far as I known—and I have not taken a particularly scholarly interest in this matter—the first attempts to make the word count come out of literature, through John Barth and, somewhat differently, in the interests of the explicit project of metafiction. Neither of these efforts succeeded more than regionally. In the late 1960s the term gains a certain currency in discussions of dance, and within those discussions seems to get some real purchase: it clearly picks out a group of dancer—say, Twyla Tharp, Lucinda Childs, Laura Dean, Trisha Brown, and some others—who are bound together by something like an explicit awareness that there has been Merce Cunningham (although it does not necessarily follow that Cunningham's dance is thereby understood to have been merely modern).

The embeddedness of the activities of these dancers in openended exchanges between dance, visual art, performance, and music no doubt contributed to the emergence of some broader sense of the postmodern, but the usage here is still relatively confined. It is perhaps architecture that first succeeds in putting the term into some wider cultural currency, but this usage is essentially reactive, its unity lying more in its rejections than in its actual practices, which run the gamut from Venturi's sloganizing "Main Street is almost all right" to the grandiosities of Jencks or Graves. The term "postmodernism" seems to me gain real cultural centrality and to open a more than merely reactive line of thought and action only when it is taken up within the visual arts and their criticism in the late 1970s and 80s—as if only here were we able to see it as not just naming a desire but deploying a grammar.

I think there are reasons for this, so my main concern in this paper will be with exploring that grammar a bit. I give this hip-pocket history in part to get my topic on the table, but also to drop a few points along the way about the status of exemplification within our talk about postmodernism. It is, for example, interesting to me that some discourses about the postmodern support themselves through a primary reference to architecture, and I wonder about the interests that motivate that choice and the limitations it would impose upon our grasp of the postmodern. It interests me also that the application of the term to theory itself is a belated effect of this history, and I wonder, suspiciously, about the odd ease with which this lets theory situate itself in relation to its objects. At the same time I cultivate my own complicity between theory and object, and indeed take such complicity as itself a feature of the postmodern: so the question here is not about whether or not there is such complicity but about how it is to be acknowledged and what kinds of grasp one can and cannot imagine that acknowledgment to secure.

Finally, I am very struck by both the slowness with which the term "postmodernism" gains political force, the dominance of this political grasp when it is eventually secured, and the interest this grasp takes in being able to guarantee the critical directness of both its postmodern objects and its postmodern self. In talking primarily about the fates of appropriation within the world of the visual arts, I want to explore again the grammar grace of which postmodernism discovers itself as a broad cultural fact; I want also and more incidentally to make a little trouble for what I take to be the current theoretical settlement—or desire for such settlement—of the question of the postmodern.

It seems to me that it is a very definite set of practices and theorizations of them that open the real prospect of the postmodern. Something comes to a head when Sherrie Levine begins re-photographing Walker Evans and exhibiting the results under titles like *After Walker Evans* and over her own signature. There are of course obvious ways in which nothing new is happening here; we seem to be faced with but one more in a chain of increasingly familiar events—Duchamp exhibiting a urinal, Warhol showing Brillo boxes, whatever other examples we might want to point to that show something we might describe as the commodification of art, or its submission to institutional determinants, or as the demystification of the production of art, or. . . . And indeed these various descriptions have been taken up as ways either of rescuing these earlier acts for postmodernism or of relegating Levine's gesture to the modern (and sometimes this latter move understands itself as a disqualification of her work, while at other times it is taken to place her as a renewer of a radical tradition that has very largely betrayed itself).

Illustration 1, Sherrie Levine, "untitled" *(After Walker Evans)*, 10" x 8", photograph, 1981, courtesy Mary Boone Gallery

There are, however, two features of her gesture that seem to me to either disturb these descriptions or add to them something that finally outraces them. These would be, first, its intimacy with photography and, second, its readability as an act of appropriation. In the polemic situation of the late 1970s and early 1980s (and even now to some extent), the first of these was taken to be the dominant feature and the second merely a consequence. The intimacy with photography meant the end of painting and so the end of a whole system of aesthetic values—originality, expression, irreproducibility, rarity, etc.—that assigned painting a place of privilege within the articulation of both modernism and art.

This view, while not exactly silly, is, I think, hard to take seriously. The history of photography—or of photographies, as some would have it—is studded with the claims to the defeat of painting or art in general (claims that dovetail nicely with the general shape of Hegel's claim to the end of art). While it may be true that the shape of modernist painting is in some measure determined by an attempt to find ground apart from the mimetic success the camera seems to ensure, it does not necessarily follow that the end of modernism is accomplished in and as the exhaustion of this effort. Indeed, it seems more plausibly the case that photography can intervene in the practice of art at the deep level this view asks us to imagine only by coming to some explicit awareness of its own internal linkage to those practices: the very conditions necessary to claim that photography has at last supplanted painting cut against that claim.

This is why appropriation is not simply a strategy to be thought of as subjacent to the fact of the camera. It is an understanding or discovery of the camera, that binds it ineluctably into a history. It is the acknowledgment of this ineluctable historical binding that can be said to write a certain end to modernism—but this is also to begin writing a new text that will be structured not by the mutual exclusion of painting and photography, art and reproduction, but by their permanent entanglement within one another's term. This entanglement cannot be grasped without grasping as well the complication it imposes upon the project of theory.

Appropriation taken abstractly as a determinant factor is equally empty, unable to distinguish itself from any of the Dadaist gestures by which it has been preceded. Its promise is of a certain radical irony that would ensure its status as pure parody or critique, an unhampered claim to the end of art. But this claim is the recurrent note of late modernism and its very purity is the best guarantee of a lack of critical purchase. The contrast I am airing here tends to fall out as a contrast between a "realistic" and political view of postmodernism and another that stresses the logic of the simulacral, the two meeting in the peculiar phrase "cultural politics" and a certain insistence on the centrality of a "critique of representation." It is then odd that one of the seminal impulses toward such a critique unfolds out of an anxiety about how within modernity the end of a reduced and subjectivizing aesthetics will be realized in a "politics of culture."[1]

I want to argue that postmodernism begins where the myth of

the end of art itself comes to an end, not by stopping but by being recognized as a permanent condition of the practice of art, a relay through which art can no longer dream of not passing and in which it must imagine its habitation. This is to define the postmodern by insisting upon its orientation to finitude—say, its refusal to wish for any condition not marked as "post.-"

One must learn then to read the full complexity of the "after" that figures in so many of Levine's titles, to see that if it marks a certain sort of end, it marks also a certain continuation, reimagining the relevance of terms like "imitation" to the practice and appreciation of artworks. In this sense, the work I recognize as postmodern can also be called antiromantic in its refusal of a familiar enough emphasis on genius, originality, and the notion of mastery that flows from them. This refusal is acted out critically in both art historical and feminist terms through Levine's choice of objects to appropriate. Levine's fundamental orientation is, however, primarily to modernist work, and is in relation to another artist that a certain relation to romanticism can be perhaps most clearly articulated. In moving from Sherrie Levine to Ross Bleckner here, I am ignoring a wide range of differences that in other contexts would count more seriously for me.

From the beginning, Ross Bleckner's paintings are cast within a certain melancholy we may be tempted to call romantic. The images we are given are, if not exactly of the marriage of mind and nature, at least of the urgency of their mismatch. These same images extend the painter's grid toward an exploration of the entrapment of nature within architectural form, placing themselves in implicit relation to the practice of photography and the structure of the camera. As Bleckner works to unfold this relation through a painterly counter-allegory of light, he inevitably articulates as well a story about romanticism and the power it continues to exercise over our imagination of art. As Levine's critique of modernism continues it within its own post-, so Bleckner's continuing romanticism turns it toward a certain dispersion and critique.

The paintings explore, to my eye, the dark room painting now inhabits, into which light penetrates intermittently through a shuttered opening and registers obscurely upon an opposed surface. Somewhere along this path, in the empty middle of the room, there is a place where this light held itself (always in the past, guaranteed only—if at all—by the registration it falls short of) briefly, invisibly, in constellation, passing through the possibility of an image already lost. The three disparate series in which Bleckner more or less simultaneously works explore each moment of this story, tracking the possibilities of presence and absence, loss and possession, in each place.

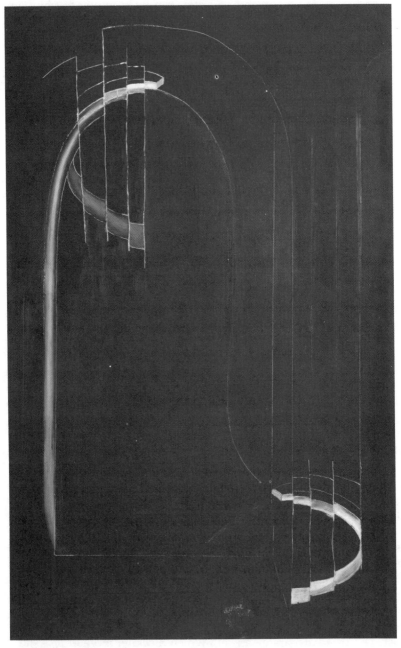

Illustration 2, Ross Bleckner, *Aegean*, 84″ x 52″, oil/canvas, 1979, courtesy Mary Boone Gallery

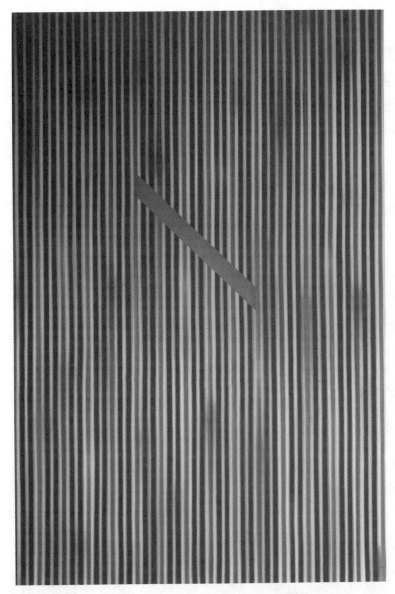

Illustration 3, Ross Bleckner, *Wreath*, 108″ x 72″, oil/canvas, 1986, courtesy Mary Boone Gallery

Illustration 4, Ross Bleckner, *Mister Mister*, 87" x 60", oil/canvas, 1983,
courtesy Mary Boone Gallery

Illustration 5, Ross Bleckner, *Crocodile Tears*, 48" x 40", oil/linen, 1985, courtesy Mary Boone Gallery

The most obvious comparison here is to Turner—although there are perhaps ways in which Friedrich is still more apt.[2] My discussion here follows closely Ronald Paulson's work in *Literary Landscape*.[3] The contrast between Bleckner and Turner seems quite straightforward: Turner gives us with ever more directness the natural sun, the central informing light in which we live and which is literally and figuratively the informing ground of his painting; Bleckner fights his fractured way toward a light that is artificial, significantly unilluminating its dark ground, isolated from its natural source or analogue (I will be tempted to read both ways here), and which can find no way to the powerful vortical unity of Turner's art.

What Paulson has I think interestingly and powerfully explicated in Turner's art is the sublime blinding and self-blinding dimensions of his blazing sun—the ways in which, as Burke has it, "extreme light, by overcoming the organs of the sense, obliterates all objects, so as in its effects exactly to resemble darkness" (cited by Paulson, p. 85). The phrase "exactly to resemble" interests me here; it is, one imagines, a way of trying to say that light, however extreme and overwhelming, remains something other than darkness even while attributing to it everything that belongs to darkness.[4] One might then say—this seems to me in fact what Paulson is saying— that Turner's effort to aim ever more directly toward the sublimity of the sun ends by showing the opacity of the sun's mode of visibility— either by making that sun and light itself continuous with and finally indistinguishable from the haze through which it shines (Paulson follows Hazlitt in calling this haze Turner's medium and glosses it as "the veil of allegory covering and concealing truth" [p. 83]), or else, in more directly painterly terms by inevitably courting "the insoluble paradox of light versus the representation of light" (p. 95) that leads light to its entrapment within the thick opacity of the means of its representation (one might think by contrast of Claude's refusals or diminishments of the sun in favor of the painting of its effects and the resulting difference in texture and finish). Paulson thus writes:

> "Turner seems to interpret the incomplete, even fragmentary, quality of the painting (what is not present, not shown, not carefully or completely defined) as an indication either that the actual vision or its experiential quality has been lost, and that what remains—or has been transmitted—is at best a shadow of that vision; or that something made him stop before he had completed the representation and now makes him disguise it. [p. 102]

It is within the frame of this enactment or realization of the impossibility of painting that Paulson then locates Turner's appeal to supplemental words and glosses.

Bleckner's painting similarly displays a certain radical dispersion—enacted both within his series and in the differences among them—and thus begins to appear as a repetition of Turner's. We do not easily know what to say about its critical force, as it might have

Illustration 6, Ross Bleckner, "untitled," 48" x 40", oil/linen, 1986, courtesy Mary Boone Gallery

seemed directed toward that past (we can as easily say that Bleckner rediscovers or continues Turner's art as that he critiques or parodies it)—as indeed we similarly cannot know what to say about the critical force of Levine's appropriations as they face their modernist past. One might then stop here; the general line of approach and apology here has been loosely deconstructive, and such a line might be thought to have reached its limit in the generation of some suitable aporia. But the line we are on is not epistemological or theoretical; it is the line of that which underlies our imaginations of theory and epistemology, so what we are seeing in these paintings and in this history is a story about the fate of light and that which it supports.

The camera is a machine that willy-nilly produces images that can be discovered to compel recognition of such stories; as Rosalind Krauss and others have argued, what it delivers in promising the sheer fact of vision is a world of signs—the surrealist practice of solarization turns out emblematically to give us not something to see but something to read—Bataille, like Bleckner and Turner, works within the self-division of the sun.[5] (Our lucidity shadows itself forth on the photographic plate.) Bleckner's achievement may, then, be that he has found in the camera the resources to take up more powerfully into painting the necessity of its failure (Bleckner enacts within painting the parables of memory and repression that Paulson reads in Turner's textual supplements[6]). But this would matter to us precisely as an achievement of painting within a certain posthumousness that we would then be increasingly tempted to read as nothing other than its history.

It is this messing about the sharpness of the difference between life and death that imposes the word "fate" upon us (as, indeed, I would suggest it is as someone bearing news about our fate—the fact above all that we have one—and not as a skeptic that de Man compels our interest). If in the beginning photographic appropriation looked like the opening into a new era and a freeing of us from our past and those practices in it that would now be dead to us, it has, in Bleckner as in Levine, found another end. One may view this as a betrayal of a critical stance, a surrender of historical position or of the gains of theory. But one may also, and I think more powerfully, see it in a linkage of the fates of vision and of theory, and so also a lesson about the hard terms of criticism: carried along, inscribed, on this story of the fate of light is another story about the fate of theory as that through which we are still tempted to guarantee the purity of our critiques, and which, like light, matters only in a world that confounds such guarantees and such purity. Appropriation would in this sense be not just a movement that like any other has a fate to be lamented or proclaimed, but a thought about fate and a whole constellation of issues surrounding it–organizing what or how critique and parody can mean for us now. It would also place a new or newly explicit emphasis on that fate of any work, which is its submission to criticism, and on that fate of criticism and theory, which is its submission to writing.

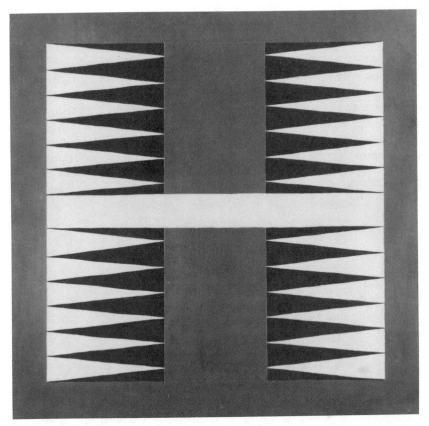

Illustration 7, Sherrie Levine, "untitled," 20″ x 20″, casein/lead, 1987, courtesy Mary Boone Gallery

May 1987

Postscript: The Chances of the Game

Sherrie Levine's most recent work consists in two series of identically sized paintings on lead (stuff of the grave, no doubt, but stuff also of Turner's problematic white light). The first series continues in the new format the apparent abstraction of Levine's earlier generic stripes and checkerboards, but the second series–geometric and abstract to be sure, but backgammon boards nonetheless—literalizes the first: 8 × 8, these are indeed checkerboards. Moving through the gallery we move through representations of the game we know cannot keep from thinking art to be.[7] What we are given here are the surfaces on which the game is played, but no certainty as to whether it has ended or has yet to begin. And the game is divided: here it answers to a perfectible calculus, but there it answers to a throw of the dice and a willingness to wager.

The show is Levine's first since moving to Mary Boone's prestigious space. This too will appear to be a move in a game, and no doubt there will be those—there must be those—who will see in it that calculation through which appropriation cedes its critical resources and admits its own complicity, its own appropriation. But there is always the chance that this is painting, light breaking, a clearing within which one can stand, a surface that exceeds itself and on which history does not stop playing.

Notes

1. See Martin Heidegger, *The Question Concerning Technology and Other Essays* (New York: Harper & Row, 1977), p. 116.

2. I owe this thought to William Galperin.

3. R. Paulson, *Literary Landscape* (New Haven: Yale University Press, 1982.).

4. Heidegger's question about technology articulates itself at times as a late attempt at renewing our ability to recognize, within what we take to be our lucidity, its exact resemblance to darkness. Such an experience of the sublime might then shatter the comfort of our aestheticism, the certainty of our calculations. See, e.g., *The Question Concerning Technology*, pp. 135–36, 154.

5. See R. Krauss and J. Livingstone, *L'amor fou: Photography and Surrealism* (Washington, D.C.: Corcoran Gallery of Art; and New York: Abbeville Press, 1985).

6. See Ross Bleckner, "Transcendent Anti-fetishism," in *Blasted Allegories: An Anthology of Writings by Contemporary Artists,* ed. B. Wallis (New York: New Museum of Contemporary Art; and Cambridge: MIT Press, 1987).

7. One wants to note here the appearance in the previous year of the Boston show entitled Endgame, including work by both Levine and Bleckner as well as other representatives of the diverse tendency called NeoGeo. See *Endgame: Reference and Simulation in Recent Painting and Sculpture* (Boston: Institute of Contemporary Art; and Cambridge: MIT Press, 1986).

10

Anselm Kiefer: Postmodern Art and the Question of Technology

John C. Gilmour

Recent debates about postmodern culture have featured different assessments of the set of ideals originating from the Enlightenment. On the one side, Jürgen Habermas has defended an updated version of the Enlightenment ideal of reason: he perceives it to be the only basis for promoting social improvement. In describing what he calls "the project of modernity," Habermas speaks of the efforts of Enlightenment thinkers:

> [they endeavored] to develop objective science, universal morality and law, and autonomous art according to their inner logic. At the same time, this project intended to release the cognitive potentials of each of these domains from their esoteric forms. The Enlightenment philosophers wanted to utilize this accumulation of specialized culture for the enrichment of daily life—that is to say, for the rational organization of everyday social life.[1]

Habermas hopes to revitalize these ideals to help create a society fulfilling the ideal of "communicative rationality."[2] When Habermas asks whether we should "try to hold on to the *intentions* of the Enlightenment, feeble as they may be, or should we declare the entire project of modernity a lost cause?,"[3] he defines the watershed that separates him from advocates of the postmodern. His desire to revitalize, rather than give up, these ideals leads him to denounce developments in both postmodern thought and art.

In contrast, a thinker like Jean-François Lyotard criticizes the role of the Enlightenment ideal of reason within the contemporary world, arguing that we need to reconsider the secondary status it accords to mythical and narrative thinking and to reevaluate the place it gives to technological systems. Although he agrees, for the most part, with Habermas's perception of the interlocking ideas forming "the project of modernity," Lyotard argues that in the postmodern world the legitimating principles that governed modern thought have lost their credibility. He speaks of a "grand narrative" of the unity of all knowledge based on the story of the mind and of a parallel "grand narrative" justifying modern social practices: "the name of the hero is the people, the sign of legitimacy is the people's consensus, and their mode of creating norms is deliberation. The notion of progress is a necessary outcome of this."[4] Perhaps no feature of modern history better expresses the convergent operation of the ideals of rational knowledge and historical progress than modern technology.

According to Lyotard's analysis, the concurrent development of scientific reason, modern capitalism, and technological and electronic systems has produced such unfavorable results that we must question the ideology that fostered it. Postmodern artists, too, have challenged our complacent acceptance of this ideology. In what follows, I will consider the work of Anselm Kiefer as a challenge to the worldview of modernity, with particular emphasis on the way his imagery utilizes discarded ancient perspectives to challenge the place of technology in our lives. In addition to considering his art in relation to Lyotard's ideas, I will also make use of Heidegger's analysis of technology and of Jean Baudrillard's criticisms of modernity.

Technology and Nature

Anselm Kiefer's *Pittsburgh* confronts us with the skyline of an industrial wasteland, whose power lines, upright supports, and factories define the upper space, rising over a rift below. The abstract form of the lower section could symbolize a strip mine, which has yielded up its fuel for industrial production or, alternatively, a mound of industrial debris dumped along the river valleys of that beleagued city. Staged in Kiefer's theater of cruelty (as Artaud described his confrontational theater), these images generate disturbing questions we repress at our own risk. The murky wash covering the surface, like the film that appears on the windows of all our Pittsburghs, raises doubts about what is seen and what is hidden. The downward flow of the yellow pool of liquid at the top, contradicting the upward thrust of the power posts, reminds us of the sun's rays that would bathe this space, cutting through the grey atmosphere, if it were one of nature's foggy mornings. Yet what we confront here is not nature herself, but human artifacts thrown up to challenge nature.

Like so many of Kiefer's works, this one seems bent on fulfilling

Artaud's dream of turning the theater into a *"site of passage* for those immense analogical disturbances in which ideas are arrested in flight . . . in their transmutation into abstractions."[5] The disturbances finding their site in Kiefer's recent collages include within their scope tensions between ancient and modern ways of thought, between figurative and abstract art, and between the cultural goals of a space age and the natural settings from which they arise. *Pittsburgh,* beginning in photographic realism, presents a twilight scene, partially obscured from view by collage pieces pasted over the bottom half and by the painted liquid emanating from the sky above. Kiefer undermines our sense of realism by his deliberate violation of its photographic terms, thereby setting up reverberations between his own activity and the depicted space of industrial reality. While we may think of nature as the common base for both industrial and artistic creations, Kiefer establishes a conflict between our desire to be at home within nature and our desire for more Pittsburghs.

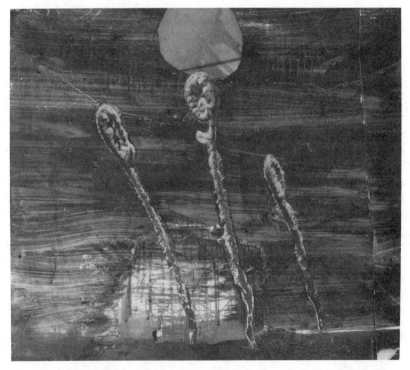

Illustration 8, Anselm Kiefer, *Johannisnacht,* 66.5 x 75.5 cm., acrylic, emulsion, shellac on photo collage on burlap, 1978-85, courtesy Anselm Kiefer Studio

This feature is nowhere more evident than in his *Johannisnacht* (Illustration 8). He creates in it a metaphoric matrix from collage elements that display three erect fern fronds, reaching like dancers into the sky, whose movement celebrates the Dionysian festival of Midsummer's Night, against the background of a collage cutout of an industrial pylon, opening like a second scene within the overpainted substructure. The effect Kiefer achieves through these juxtapositions is to deconstruct the source of our desires, exposing the conflict between nature-desires and the "Pittsburgh-of-desire" for us to contemplate.

He helps to show that nature has been submerged in favor of a culture dominated by what Lyotard calls "the principle of optimal performance." This means that technology is "a game pertaining not to the true, the just, or the beautiful, etc., but to efficiency."[6] The hidden order of values implicit in this performance principle, although masked under the ideal of rational progress, concerns the operation of capital. Lyotard adds:

> What happened at the end of the eighteenth century, with the first industrial revolution, is that the reciprocal of this equation was discovered: no technology without wealth, but no wealth without technology. A technical apparatus requires an investment; but since it optimizes the efficiency of the task to which it is applied, it also optimizes the surplus-value derived from this improved performance.[7]

Even scientific research is implicated in this interface between technology and wealth, for research requires technological instruments. The intertwining of the value of knowledge with capitalism's performance principle is one reason Lyotard expresses suspicion about the rationalist values of Enlightenment culture.

Kiefer's collages confront us with questions about our relationship to nature within the technological project. Heidegger has argued that "we shall never experience our relationship to the essence of technology so long as we merely conceive and push forward the technological, put up with it, or evade it."[8] Neither the enthusiastic promotion, the toleration, nor the evasion of technology meets the challenge of understanding its transformative power, which extends even to changing humanity itself. Heidegger sees fundamental alteration in everything:

> The earth and its atmosphere become raw material. Man becomes human material, which is disposed of with a view to

proposed goals. The unconditional establishment of the unconditioned self-assertion by which the world is purposefully made
over according to . . . man's command is a process that emerges
from the hidden nature of technology.[9]

Part of what is hidden within the technological project is the mentality of modernity, which even in its artistic manifestation celebrates
the self-assertive act of creation, refusing to acknowledge nature as a
limit of any kind. By evoking a more elemental relation to nature in
Johannisnacht, Kiefer raises doubts about the modern attitude.

Our penchant for treating technology as neutral is exposed by
Heidegger as a pattern of self-deception, even as it is by Kiefer's
Pittsburgh. Heidegger sees it as an *enframing* project, by which reality
gets arrayed for human consideration in a specific way: reality is that
which reveals itself within the framework of research activity.[10]
Kiefer appears within two of his collages to have reversed this enframing act, exposing the genealogical background of technological
enframing by hanging it on the wall for us to see. In *Mast* the photographed image of a power pole, overpainted in black, suggests a
metaphoric exchange between this conveyer of electrical power and
the superstructure of a ship. Or in another version of *Pittsburgh,* the
upward reach of a tree, an industrial pylon, and several supports for
power lines are set in counterpoint to the downward flow of molten
lead, which seems to ooze from the sky above. Both the solidified
crust of the lead and the scorched surface reflecting the effect of its
heat break the visual dominance of the pylon, partially obscuring it
from our view. This latter image is particularly typical within Kiefer's
whole oeuvre, for it sets up an association between these industrial
remnants and the transformations produced by earlier alchemists,
who were also bent on turning natural elements into more valuable
substances. By establishing this parallel between the "Pittsburgh-of-
desire" and the desires of the alchemists, Kiefer creates a complex
paradox for our consideration: alchemy in Pittsburgh.

It *is* a paradox, rather than a simple parallel, because the assumptions of alchemy and other prescientific forms of thought differ
markedly from the assumptions of our technological age. Kiefer no
more permits us to champion, tolerate, or evade the technological
than Heidegger does, for he stages a number of paintings that confront the conflict of worldview between earlier forms of thought and
our own. For example, his 1985 painting, *Yggdrasil* (Illustration 9),
invokes the ancient Nordic myth about the world ash tree, named in
the title, which serves as the source and nurturing support for many
life processes. Yggdrasil, however, is no omnipotent force, for it is

under threat from a dragon below, which gnaws at its roots and from animals from feeding on its leaves. Nor is the place of the tree of life within nature guaranteed by forms of natural law, which give secure support to Yggdrasil's overflowing benevolence. Kiefer displays the tree under threat, from an abstract, scorched blob of lead, reaching down from the sky, the upper space blackened from the heat of a fire, whose glow appears to envelop the tree and to ignite its upper branches. His overdetermined image, like Kiefer's 1985 collage depicting Yggdrasil in front of a Pittsburghlike landscape, confronts us with the ecological hazards engendered by our technological designs. The fiery tone of the sky behind this version of Yggdrasil joins the image of the heat from the alchemist's fire to the eerie glow of the night sky in old Pittsburgh, where the steel mill's blast furnaces often appeared to ignite the surrounding sky. This imagery juxtaposes two views of the human relationship to nature. Although both involve transformations of natural materials, the ancient view involved reverance for nature, whereas the modern view treats nature as raw material to be exploited for human ends.

Nature and Symbolic Exchange

Kiefer's frequent use of imagery from ancient times effectively requires that we examine the guiding assumptions of modern thought, including those of modern art. His own recent artistic practice results in a number of huge landscapes, which remind us of the scope and reach of the painters of the abstract sublime, but within a framework including figurative reference and historical allusion. In one of these paintings, *Outpouring* (1982/86), Kiefer captures our ambivalent feelings within the space age by presenting a painted black cloud hovering between heaven and earth, its shape alternately suggesting the black smoke of some subterranean fire, or scorched elements emanating from the sky. This latter suggestion reminds us of the lead overlays in the collages, especially those used in the 1985 exodus series to symbolize the pillars of cloud and fire that guided the ancient Israelites from Egypt. Except for the emanating lead, nothing of the hidden god is evident, making us doubt whether the Israelites were following Jahweh's signs or some imagined dream of their own, like the alchemist's dream of gold. For us these doubts are heightened in an age in which, as Heidegger claimed, our technological self-affirmation undermines trust in the ancient gods. Kiefer has dealt with this problem in his painting, *To the Supreme Being* (1983), which depicts an empty temple haunted by the absent god. For us, the black cloud in *Outpouring* may reflect instead some burned-up space vehicle, a nuclear explosion, or else a fire burning beneath the surface of the earth. This latter reading, supported by spots of red punctuating the fissures along the diagonal of the land mass, fits the theme of the transformation of earth's elements by fire within the alchemical tradition. The up-and-down movement between heaven and earth is reinforced by strands of dried plants, arranged along the whole face of the painting within the vertical axis. Alongside the cloud, Kiefer has fastened a sculptured funnel, readily associated with the refining and heating of elements within the alchemist's workshop.

The dissonant energy conveyed by *Outpouring* evokes a hidden conflict between the values of modern humankind and more archaic views of nature. Perhaps this conflict is never far from the surface, even though we have become expert at ignoring it. In exploring this theme, I would like to borrow from Jean Baudrillard's analysis of the outlook of modern science toward nature. He argues that modern science "presents itself as a project progressing toward an objective determined in advance by Nature. Science and technology present themselves as revealing what is inscribed in Nature: not only its secrets but it deep purpose."[11] Yet what is inscribed there reflects the human purposes involved in technology and capitalist production. The result, says Baudrillard, is; "Everything that invokes Nature invokes the domination of Nature."[12] This attitude creates a separation between humankind and nature uncharacteristic of archaic cultures. The alternative Baudrillard sketches is a view of nature within primitive cultures where humans are intimately involved with natural forces and where the mode of life was shaped by symbolic exchange. He adds that "in his symbolic exchanges primitive man *does not gauge himself in relation to Nature*. He is not aware of a Necessity, a Law that takes effect only with the objectification of Nature."[13] Baudrillard holds that even Greek rationalists never produced the separation between humankind and nature found in modern science.[14]

Baudrillard's depiction of cultures built around symbolic exchange helps us to see what is at stake in Kiefer's appeals to alchemy and to ancient myths. They help to expose our transformation of nature "according to the code of production," and Baudrillard points out that our idea of history has been coded in the same way.[15] While nature provides the spatial locus for production, history provides the temporal framework. Baudrillard argues that those cultures based on symbolic exchange have experienced the world in a radically different way. He observes:

> Nothing is ever taken from nature without being returned to it. Primitive man does not chop one tree or trace one furrow with-

out "appeasing the spirits" with a counter-gift or sacrifice. This taking and returning, giving and receiving, is essential. It is always an actualization of symbolic exchange through gods. The final product is never aimed for. There is neither behavior aiming to produce useful values for the group through technical means, nor behavior aiming at the same end through magical means.[16]

The reciprocity involved in this outlook between humankind and nature and between community members contrasts with modernity's understanding of reality and rational consensus. Kiefer's deconstruction of the technological project helps us to see this contrast.

As was true in Kiefer's earlier scorched-earth paintings, we encounter in his recent work images of destructive actions and forces, reflecting one outcome of our historical efforts to build a world to our own liking. Kiefer seems to be insisting that in creating we destroy, requiring that we assess the one against the other in our judgment of what we have accomplished. The destructive potential of our technological designs arises from the confident self-assertiveness Heidegger warned about. Our project entails that "the world is purposefully made over according to . . . man's command," but without the limits to human power that were acknowledged in earlier forms of culture.

Eliade has argued, for example, that the ancient blacksmith created purification rituals to protect himself against the dangers inherent in his art: "Fire turned out to be the means by which man could 'execute' faster, but it could also be something other than what already existed in Nature. It was therefore the manifestation of a magico-religious power."[17] Kiefer's theater of cruelty stagings raise doubts about where we are today, and what risks our project engenders. His use of Nordic myths helps to pose questions about the status of the earth, and about unknown forces that may manifest themselves amid our remaking of the world.

In *Midgard* (1983/85), for example, Kiefer alludes to the Edda myths, in which the gods raised up Midgard ("Middle Ground") between the underworld and heaven. Kiefer depicts this by portraying a stone, cast up on the shore of the sea, with no sign of purpose and no apparent support. This earth-stone appears merely to be there, the genealogical descendant of something that emerged from the deep. The division of the world between upper and lower domains, derived by Kiefer from the cosmic division described in the Jewish Kaballah,[18] as well as from the Edda, is symbolized by the clear division of the painting into a horizontally separated diptych. The narrow band of sky above the horizon of the receding sea displays nothing, whereas the dream-space of the upper region, composed of a thick impasto looking like the surface of fired pottery, holds its place as a dense mass hovering over the sea. The neck of a serpent appears, thrusting into the sky like a missile breaking into the void. Emerging from behind the lower sky, as if appearing from behind a curtain, the head of another serpent undulates its way through space. What are we to make of this complex imagery, which is scarcely coherent within modern terms? As is so often the case, Kiefer offers us the clue by inscribing the word "Ragnarök" in the upper right corner, a term that refers to the cycle of existence described in the Edda when the gods will be attacked by their enemies. The resulting war, led by the descendants of an evil goddess, will include a confrontation between Thor and Mithgarthsorm, a giant serpent who surrounds the earth. This world snake, like the dragon that threatens Yggdrasil, appears and reappears in different guises within Kiefer's oeuvre.

While there is an obvious association between the earth-threatening snake of the Edda and the evil, satanic forces that the Judeo-Christian tradition attributes to the Garden of Eden serpent, Kiefer's handling of this imagery opens up surprising dimensions extending beyond such an obvious reading. For example, in three recently completed collages, the snake becomes a lyrical figure, floating through photographed lights within astral space. In this space above the sky, where modern humankind aspires to fly, the unknown forces may set off, as they once did for the ancient masters of the fire, doubts and fears out of keeping with our self-affirmative confidence. One of these works, entitled *Ourouboros*, depicts a snake that bites its own tail, a gnostic symbol for the condition of primal darkness, where humankind in its ignorance encounters an undifferentiated world of confusion and uncertainty.[19] The appearance of Ourouboros in space, harking back symbolically to the confused mixture of prime matter achieved through the alchemist's breakdown of the elements, reflects Kiefer's preoccupation with the destructive tendencies that attend the exploration of outer space. Ourouboros might turn out to be, within the space age, Mithgarthsorm in another guise. It may also remind us of the possibilities of symbolic exchange, so long left behind.

Yet when we try to assess where we stand in light of Kiefer's installation of alchemy within Pittsburgh, our judgment is easily confused, for Kiefer's appeal to gnostic signs, the practices of alchemy, Nordic myths, and the Jewish Kaballah can hardly serve as the basis for a literal restructuring of our worldview around such mythological elements. On the contrary, the stones within the painting called

Cherubim and Seraphim (1983), labeled with the titles of those exalted members of the celestial hierarchy, seem to suggest that our highest values will have to be created from the materials of the earth, for we can no longer believe in the heaven in which they allegedly resided. While such a stance raises conceptual difficulties we have no way to resolve, that is the function of any theater of cruelty, which is more concerned to confront our evasions than to give us resolutions to the problems it reveals. Kiefer's painting exemplifies Heidegger's warning, issued when he argued that both what the earth *is*, and consequently what it is to be human, has undergone a fundamental alteration because of modern technology. One danger, cited by Heidegger, is that the subjection of everything to the calculability of scientific methods has the result that: "the revealing that holds sway throughout modern technology does not unfold into a bringing-forth in the sense of *poesis*. The revealing that rules in modern technology is a challenging, which puts to nature the unreasonable demand that it supply energy that can be extracted and stored." This produces a fundamental change in our relationship to nature, Heidegger adds, because "a tract of land is challenged into the putting out of coal and ore. The earth now reveals itself as a coal mining district, the soil as a mineral deposit."[20] But we know, when we encounter the stones of *Cherubim and Seraphim*, that nature remains more than a "standing reserve"[21] for our projects.

We experience the mysterious, unfathomable openness of nature when we stand before the expanse of the sea, which both shelters and threatens Kiefer's Midgard, cast onto the shore by its forces. Just as the celestial stones, appearing on the blackened landscape of *Cherubim and Seraphim*, promise the renewal of the fallow, burned furrows, so the poetic reach of the Midgard paintings, exceeding our definition of everyday realities, promises renewal of a world at risk. While the skylines of our Pittsburghs tend to obscure the poetic dimension of human thought, the act of reinstalling alchemy within Pittsburgh may evoke new possibilities that fall outside our technological dreams. In its noblest aspect, that is what modernist sensibilities within art have been about, through the poetic inspiration of painters whose vision, sometimes guided by religious inspiration, has reached toward that openness of thought exemplified in Kiefer's postmodern canvasses.

Although we may never again subscribe to the beliefs contained in ancient mythologies, those same mythologies may confront us with forces that have shaped, and are still shaping, our responses to the world. If we are to comprehend Midgard, thrust up as a lonely stone within the cosmos, we must risk raising doubts about the closure we thought we had gained when we believed we could, at last, master nature. That is why Kiefer is one of the most important artists of our time, because he is willing to confront what so many of us want to avoid. This fulfills Heidegger's claim for art, which he puts in these terms:

> Because the essence of technology is nothing technological, essential reflection upon technology and decisive confrontation with it must happen in a realm that is, on the one hand, akin to the essence of technology and, on the other, fundamentally different from it. Such a realm is art. But certainly only if reflection on art, for its part, does not shut its eyes to the constellation of truth after which we are *questioning*.[22]

Kiefer's revival of this poetic sense to challenge the enframing limits of the technological age breaks the vessels that would turn the earth into the wasteland of our Pittsburghs, promising instead the renewal of the emanating powers on which we depend.

Conclusion

The challenge mounted by postmodern art against the world view of modernity has one of its manifestations in Kiefer's deconstruction of the technological project. That project depends upon an idea of the preexisting rational structure of nature, which humans can come to know through methodical investigation, in contrast to an open, ambiguous relationship that manifests itself in ancient ideas of symbolic exchange. The attempt by Kiefer to revitalize this ancient outlook conflicts with the revitalization of Enlightenment ideals advocated by Habermas. Kiefer's approach agrees with Lyotard's because both try to create a role for narrative knowledge and for myth, which Enlightenment ideals of reason would never permit. Rather than giving the exclusive power to scientific knowledge, they are intent on exposing the way knowledge so defined lends support to existing power structures. Where does that leave us? Lyotard describes the situation in this fashion:

> A postmodern artist or writer is in the position of a philosopher: the text he writes, the work he produces are not in principle governed by preestablished rules, and they cannot be judged according to a determining judgment, by applying familiar categories to the text or to the work. Those rules and categories are what the work of art itself is looking for. The artist and the writer, then, are working without rules in order to formulate the rules of what *will have been done*.[23]

Illustration 9, Anslem Kiefer, *Yggdrasil*, 1985.
Acrylic, emulsion, shellac, lead on photo. 103 x
83.5 cm. Courtesy of Anselm Kiefer Studio.

Lyotard has shown how the rules that are supposed to govern humankind within modernity include both natural and historical structures. Yet contemporary Europeans detect an absence of the bourgeois structures in the postwar period.

This is the theme of a roundtable discussion between several contemporary artists (Joseph Beuys, Jannis Kounellis, Enzo Cucchi, and Kiefer). In considering the loss of moral and conceptual legitimating structures in the postwar period, Kiefer is led to conclude that the artist suffers the following plight: "The structures are broken. The class that establishes structures is missing. And what makes our profession so difficult today is that we must set up the laws and, at the same time, oppose them."[24] Rather than reverting to the intentions of the Enlightenment, as Habermas would have it, Kiefer and his fellow postmodern artists find it necessary to create the rules for "what will have been done." The question of technology is only one of the issues that requires this response of the artist in the postmodern moment.

Notes

1. Jürgen Habermas, "Modernity—an Incomplete Project," *The Anti-Aesthetic: Essays on Postmodern Culture*, ed. Hal Foster (Port Townsend, Wash.: Bay Press, 1983), p. 9.

2. Ibid., p. 8.

3. Ibid., pp. 9–10.

4. Jean-François Lyotard, *The Postmodern Condition* (Manchester: Manchester University Press, 1984), p. 30.

5. Antonin Artaud, *The Theater and Its Double* (New York: Grove Press, 1958), p. 109.

6. Lyotard, *Postmodern Condition*, p. 44.

7. Ibid., p. 45.

8. Martin Heidegger, *The Question Concerning Technology* (New York: Harper and Row, 1977), p. 4.

9. Martin Heidegger, "What Are Poets For?," in *Poetry, Language, Thought*, tr. and ed. Albert Hofstadter (New York: Harper and Row, 1971), p. 111.

10. Heidegger, *Question Concerning Technology*, pp. 19ff.

11. Jean Baudrillard, *The Mirror of Production* (St. Louis: Telos Press, 1975), p. 55.

12. Ibid., p. 56.

13. Ibid., pp. 58–59.

14. Ibid., p. 64.

15. Ibid., p. 69.

16. Ibid., pp. 82–83.

17. Mircea Eliade, *The Forge and the Crucible*, 2nd ed. (Chicago: University of Chicago Press, 1978), p. 79.

18. For excellent discussion of this derivation, see Gudron Imboden, "Exodus from Historical Time," *Anselm Kiefer*, eds. Paul Maenz and Gerd de Vries (Cologne: Walther König Buchhandlung, 1986), pp. 14ff.

19. Bettine Knapp, *Theater and Alchemy* (Detroit: Wayne State University Press, 1980), p. 9.

20. Heidegger, *Question Concerning Technology*, p. 14.

21. Ibid., p. 17.

22. Ibid., p. 35.

23. Lyotard, *The Postmodern Condition*, p. 81.

24. *Ein Gespräch: Joseph Beuys, Jannis Kounellis, Anselm Kiefer, and Enzo Cucchi*, ed. Jacqueline Burckhardt (Zurich: Parkett-Verlag, 1986), p. 12. The original reads: "Die Strukturen sind kaputt. Die strukturstiftende Klasse fehlt. Und was unseren Beruf jetzt so schwierig macht, ist, dass wir beides sein müssen: Wir müssen Gesetze aufstellen und gleichzeitig auch dagegen sein."

11

Vito Acconci and the Politics of the Body in Postmodern Performance

Philip Auslander

The question of whether there can be viable political art practices under postmodernism is a vexing one. To a great extent, the image of culture offered by the theory of postmodernism echoes that developed in poststructuralist theory. The term "postmodernism" designates "a culture that is utterly coded" in which artists may manipulate "old signs in a new logic"[1] without hoping "to create new discourses out of our mere desire,"[2] a culture that encodes both artistic discourses and their audiences, and is seemingly capable of absorbing any disruptive action into its economy of signs. The postmodern political artist has no choice but to operate within the culture whose representations he or she must both recycle and critique. The awkward relationship between the desire for political activism and the acknowledgment that we cannot transcend the terms of our cultural context manifest in discussions of postmodern political art can also be seen in poststructuralist discourse on politics in general, a discourse that apparently can support political action only at highly localized, micropolitical levels.[3] Much of the most incisive of recent political art and the most articulate of recent theory has emerged from such specific areas of investigation, especially from various feminist inquiries. All postmodern political art, however, whether micropolitical or global in aspiration, confronts the same issue: the problematic of representation. As Hal Foster points out, a postmodern political art cannot rely simply on the (re)presentation of a program, a critique, a desired utopia or perceived dystopia—it must interrogate the means of representation themselves as structures of authority "to question the assumption of truth in the protest poster, of realism in the documentary photograph, of collectivity in the street mural"[4] and, by so doing, to expose the ideological discourses that both define, and mediate between, images and their receptors. The political artist can no longer demand "Paradise Now" without simul-

185

taneously examining the intersecting discourses that produced any particular image of paradise and through which it is reproduced.

In performance, physical presence, the body itself, is the locus at which the workings of ideological codes are perhaps the most insidious and also the most difficult to analyze, for the performing body is always both a vehicle for representation and, simply, itself. Even in the most conventionally mimetic forms of modern western theater, the actor's body never fully becomes the character's body. As Herbert Blau puts it:

> In a very strict sense, it is the actor's mortality which is the actual subject [of any performance], for he is right there dying in front of your eyes. . . . Whatever he represents in the play, in the order of time he is representing nobody but himself. How could he? that's his body, doing time.[5]

We can reiterate Blau's emphasis on the body's materiality without necessarily accepting his position that its mortality is the inevitable subject or content of all performance. The performing body is always doubly encoded—it is defined by the codes of a particular performance, but has always already been inscribed, in its material aspect, by social discourses (e.g., science, medicine, hygiene, law, etc.). Typically, modern performance theory has evaded this double encoding by focusing either on one set of codes or the other, either on the body as representation, as "the somatic support for a discursive logos," or on the body as an irreducibly originary presence, the instinctually charged "prime referent in an autonomous theatricality" thought to transcend the discursive.[6]

Each of these theorizations has a long history in the annals of modern performance theory: Constantin Stanislavski may have been the first to systematize the body's long-standing submission to *logos,* to "the unbroken line"[7] of action derived from a dramatic text. Adolphe Appia, writing around the turn of the twentieth century, may be the progenitor of the other position. Whereas Stanislavski prompts the actor to explore his or her own emotions introspectively, Appia exhorts the performer to achieve a neutral state, to "depersonalize," in order to allow the body to speak in its own language.[8] Stanislavski's assumptions concerning the relationship between actor and text underlie most conventional Western theater; theoretically, this current may culminate in the semiotics that sees the actor's body primarily as an iconic sign for the character's body.[9] The current initiated by Appia is that of the avant-garde, of Antonin Artaud, who holds that the body is the source of "true hieroglyphs,"[10] which can have a direct psychic impact on the spectator, and of the early Jerzy Grotowski, whose version of the same concept is the "ideogram," which translates the performer's psychic energy directly into physical imagery.[11] As Wladimir Krysinski points out, the "autonomous theatricality" of Artaud and Grotowski is not "the simple rejection of psychological theater. On the contrary, autonomous theater should be examined as an evolution of psychological theater"(143). Indeed, one can already see a trace of the notion that the body is a site of autonomous expression in Stanislavski's assertion that the rational faculty must convince "our physical natures of the truth of what you are doing on the stage" (127)—the body is the arbiter of truth.

These theorizations are also allied in a more important way— both want to derealize the performer's body, to make it disappear. The goal of psychological theater is to make the actor's body disappear into the character's; the goal of autonomous theater is, in Grotowski's words, to make the body vanish and burn in a flash of pure psychic apprehension (16). If, as Michel Foucault and others have argued, a part of the object of social discourse is to discipline the body, to make it manageable, modern performance theory as a social discourse has managed the body by robbing it of its materiality, by subjecting it to the discipline of text, whether the dramatic text or the text of archetypal psychic impulse. Although avant-gardist performance theory frequently claims to liberate the body and thus to challenge the social or political hegemony, it fails adequately to conceptualize this liberation by failing to see the body as ideologically produced. As Blau has written, "There is nothing more coded than the body. . . . The ideological matter amounts to this: we are as much spoken as speaking, inhabited by our language as we speak, even when—as in the theatre of the 60s—we sometimes refused to speak, letting the bodies do it."[12]

The problem is not that modernist performance theorists, especially Grotowski, fail to acknowledge that the body is encoded by social discourses, but rather that they suggest that these codes are only an overlay on the body, that there is an essential body that can short-circuit social discourses. This essential body is a metaphysical, even a mystical, concept: it is asocial, undifferentiated, raceless, genderless and, therefore, neutralized and quietist. The effect of these theorizations is to return the body to the disciplines of the social discourses they claim to circumvent.

In order to recover the possibility of seeing the performing body as an instrument of counter-hegemonic artistic production, the history of the body in performance must be conceived as a part of the history of the body itself, a history understood, as Catherine Gallagher and Thomas Laqueur suggest in their introduction to *The Making of the Modern Body*, as a study of how the body "has been perceived, interpreted, and represented differently in different epochs, [of how] it has been lived differently, brought into being within widely dissimilar cultures, subjected to various technologies and means of control, and incorporated into different rhythms of production and consumption, pleasure and pain."[13]

A history, in short, of the body's materiality and of difference. The development of modern ideas of acting and performance was simultaneous with the transformation of the "representations and routines of the body . . . during the late eighteenth and early nineteenth centuries . . . transformations [which] were linked to the emergence of modern social organizations" (vii). And just as "twentieth century thinkers have not really taken up a position outside the nineteenth century's discourses of the body and sexuality" (xv), so contemporary performance theory has not escaped the terms of the modern discourse initiated by, say, Diderot's *Paradoxe sur le comédien* of c. 1773.[14]

If the modern body can be shown to have been produced by the ideological discourses of the late eighteenth and early nineteenth centuries, discourses only recently made visible by contemporary scholarship, the "postmodern body" is the body actively and currently *conceived of as* produced by ideological encodings, which it cannot simply transcend. In the remainder of this essay, I would like to suggest that the body in some postmodern performance can be understood, using Foster's model of postmodern political art, as a body that exposes the ideological discourses producing it, through performance that insists on the body's status as a historical and cultural construct and that asserts the body's materiality. The political function of such art is, as Fredric Jameson has noted, pedagogical, to provide us with "cognitive maps" that will help us "to grasp our positioning as individual and collective subjects and regain a capacity to act and struggle" within the dislocating postmodern sensorium.[15] I will use selections from Vito Acconci's "body art" of the early 1970s as my examples. In choosing Acconci, whose work was contemporaneous with work such as Grotowski's, which I have already described as modernist, I am once again suggesting that the distinction between a modernist and a postmodernist artist is an epistemological, not a historical, difference. Whereas the modernist artist believes that ideological and cultural codes may be transcended, or even annulled, through transgression, the postmodernist artist recognizes that he or she must work *within* the codes that define the cultural landscape.

Some of Acconci's simpler pieces, which might be called "activities" rather than "performances," demonstrate the body's materiality very directly and straightforwardly.[16] In *Rubbing Piece* (1970), Acconci rubbed a spot on his arm until he produced a sore there. In *Waterways* (1971), a video tape, he allows his mouth to fill with saliva until he can no longer contain it, then spills it out into cupped hands.[17] Both pieces are, in Blau's terms, examples of the body "doing time": both direct attention to the body's existence in time—the time it takes to raise a sore or to produce a mouthful of saliva. As Acconci himself notes, the body becomes a measuring device. *Rubbing Piece* took place in a restaurant; Acconci's "private activity measures the public activity at the restaurant—'sore time' rather than 'clock time'" (9). In *Hand and Mouth* (1970), a short film, Acconci pushes his hand into his mouth until he chokes (18). In *Runoff* (1970), Acconci ran in place for two hours, then pressed his sweaty body against a painted wall—the sweat stained the wall; some of the paint adhered to his body (36–37).

All these events involve uses and aspects of the body that are, in and of themselves, seemingly independent of social discourses, ideology, and the like. The body's bruisability, its reflexes, its production of saliva and perspiration, go on regardless of these other issues. But, as Germano Celant points out, it is precisely *because* its does these things that the body is absorbed into a cultural economy of representation that emphasizes cleanliness and order—the body's productions must be masked, suppressed, and eliminated by a culture that fears to associate "itself with the excretive functions of city life, functions which produce millions of tons of garbage."[18] The body as source of uncleanliness is made to disappear in such a culture; Acconci's insistence on presenting "the body as a system, sweating and spermatic, fecal and salivating" (Celant, 78) exposes the existence of social structures designed to make us forget all those things, as well as their own failure really to maintain cleanliness for, as Celant indicates, filth is getting the better of our urban environments (78).

The major way of suppressing the body's materiality is through representation. As Brian DePalma recently showed us, bodies can be reconstructed through representation to be exactly what we want them to be: clean, smooth, perfect, erotic. Acconci problematizes representation by leaving no doubt as to which body is carrying out the activity and will bear the mark of it afterward: there is no question of the body as iconic sign here. In his work, the body produces its own crude representations: sweat stains on the wall; the bite marks pressed into ink and printed in *Trademarks* (1970; 10–11). Acconci printed one bite mark onto a woman's body, the real bite on one real body giving rise to a represented bite on another real body, the whole representation perhaps standing for the male's repressed violence toward the female. For *Trappings* (1970), Acconci withdrew into a closet, where he played with himself, dressing up his penis, talking to it, making it into a "character" (57). Acconci acted out the popular mythology of the penis, the idea, as Cynthia Heimel would have it in *Sex Tips for Girls*, that the penis has a psychology and morality all its own, the sense that men have of being in thrall to a part of the body.[19]

In *Conversions*, a film of 1971, Acconci engages the question of gender representation more complexly. He tries in three ways to convert his body into a female body: by burning the hair away from his breasts and attempting to enlarge them; by trying out various physical activities and postures in front of the camera with his penis tucked between his thighs; and by having a woman kneel behind him and take his penis into her mouth, thus producing a penisless image for the camera (26–29). The experiment is of course a failure: Acconci ends up looking nothing like a woman, and this failure is part of the point. Acconci fails because he accepts the facts of his body as they are and tries to work around them. He wants his becoming a "woman" to have some inner reality—he wants to *feel* what it is like to have a woman's body. What limited success he does have in converting his body is the result of mediation: by facing an unmoving camera, he can create a very roughly female-looking image of his body. "I'm forced to play to the camera—my performance depends on an attempt to handle, control personal information" (28). The same control is necessary in the third part of the performance, though it is effected by other means: "a girl [sic] kneels behind me: I acquire a female form by inserting, losing, my penis in her mouth." (28). Because we can see the woman crouched behind him in the film, the representation— once again—is a failure; the means used to create it are too visible.

Although I cannot defend Acconci's use (and that is what it is) of the woman in this film, I do not think this piece can simply be reviled as misogynistic or as a particularly noxious reification of a culturally reinforced image of woman as submissive to even the most degrading of male desires. The premise Acconci is playing with here may be the most antifeminist one possible: he, a man, proposes to co-opt the female body itself through representation, to demonstrate nothing so modest as the claim advanced by some literary critics that men can "do" feminist criticism better than women, but that men can actually *be* women, can occupy and thus nullify that position of difference. Acconci's ludicrous failure to become a woman, or even a representation of a woman, stands as testimony to the "ineluctability of difference," to use Paul Bové's phrase (see note 3). While Acconci's piece is obviously strongly masculine in point of view and certainly cannot be said to place the woman in anything resembling a "subject position," it nevertheless postulates a limit to male dominance over women and the shaping of representations of women. As Stephen Melville remarks of Acconci in a related context, "What he wants is to touch the other as what he cannot control and to make his inability to control that other a proof of the other's existence."[20]

Acconci's attempt to lose his maleness, to "become" a woman, becomes, in its failure, a document of difference. Even if Acconci *did* lose his penis, would that make him a woman, or even a representation of one? What is the relationship between "female form" and female gender? To what extent does Acconci's ability to experience his own body as a woman's body depend on his creation of a successful representation for the camera? And what of this representation? Do we, as spectators, accept an image of a penisless man as an image of a woman? The spectator's complicity in Acconci's work is always one of its major issues (Melville, 80). The questions do not stop at the level of Acconci's obsessive performance, but ripple out to include broader issues of gender representations, the ideological currents that underlie them, and, as spectators, our reception of such representations.

Acconci's deconstruction of representation is not unproblematic by any means. Anthony Kubiak states in a recent article, in reference to the acts of violence perpetrated against the body in Acconci's and other "body art," that "marking the body in performance alienates it from itself and forces it to become a sign (or rather, a sign of a sign) of its physical presence."[21] Kubiak is concerned with the relationship between the scarred body as representation and terrorism as representation. This is an important concern; Kubiak is describing the inevitable risk involved in work that does not profess to transgress the limits of cultural representation. One must also wonder about the relationship of Acconci's work to pornography. I would argue that Acconci's work is not pornographic if one's definition of pornography includes the idea that pornography's appeal to (male) desire enables it to reify its representations of women. While Acconci's films and performance documentations often share the grainy, shadowy look and voyeuristic aura of low-rent porno, they have no erotic appeal whatever, at least not for me, but operate purely as obsessive meditations on the body and representation. By contrast, DePalma's film *Body Double*, which I alluded to earlier, deconstructs the ways in which women's bodies are objectified for the male gaze through pornographic representation, but also participates in the very economy of pornographic representation it supposedly exposes.

At its most incisive (though critical standards for "body art" are hard to articulate), Acconci's work avoids becoming what it deconstructs because Acconci is so much aware of the impact of mediation on the shaping of the image he presents and draws attention to that impact through his "sloppiness"—his "failure" to keep the woman out of the frame so that his "transformed" body can appear to be real and autonomous. DePalma's slickness, on the other hand, undermines his own deconstruction by turning it (perhaps intentionally) into spectacle, thus playing back into the hands of hegemonic representations.[22]

In his comments on his own performance work, Acconci refers many times to the distance that inevitably intervened between himself and the spectator. In the notes on *Rubbing Piece*, he says, "the viewer might want to draw back, leave me alone" (9). In commenting on *Trappings*, he notes that the spectator "shouldn't want to have anything to do with me—I'm something to throw off, withdraw from" (57). Discussing *Seedbed* (1971), a performance in which Acconci masturbated under a ramp in a gallery, he observes that "at the end of the day when I left the ramp . . . the people who were still there would look at me very strangely, draw back, obviously . . . what can you possibly say to a masturbator?" (73). We are drawn voyeuristically to Acconci's obsessiveness, but back away from the person who performs such acts publicly, as art. We are inclined to treat Acconci as a prostitute, as someone who performs with his body for our shameful pleasure. But the image of the prostitute illuminates Acconci's work in a more important sense as well.

Christine Buci-Glucksman observes in an essay entitled "The Feminine as Allegory of the Modern":

> Prostituted, dispersed, and fragmented bodies themselves express the destructive impulse of allegory—with its loss of aura, veils, immortality. But this destructive utopia is also critical; though regressive, it admits of a positive aspect—[what Walter Benjamin calls] "the dissipation . . . of appearances," the demystification of all reality that presents itself as an "order," a "whole," a "system."[23]

Craig Owens has claimed that allegory is the basic mode of postmodern art.[24] That is too large a question to address here, except to say that Acconci's prostituted, dispersed, and fragmented body does take its place in the kind of allegory described by Buci-Glucksman: a regressive image that, because of its insistence on the materiality of the body, cannot help but critically engage those ideological discourses that would suppress or coopt that materiality, an image that therefore takes a step toward demystifying the economy of representations that enforces such suppression.

Notes

1. Hal Foster, "Re: Post," in *Art After Modernism: Rethinking Representation,* ed. Brian Wallis (Boston: David R. Godine, 1984), p. 194.

2. Charles Russell, "The Context of the Concept," *Bucknell Review,* 25/2 (1980): 191.

3. See, e.g., Jean-François Lyotard and Jean-Loup Thébaud, *Just Gaming* (Minneapolis: University of Minnesota Press, 1985); Paul A. Bové, "The Ineluctability of Difference: Scientific Pluralism and the Critical Intelligence"; and Bruce Robbins, "Feeling Global: John Berger and Experience," in *Postmodernism and Politics,* ed. Jonathan Arac (Minneapolis: University of Minnesota Press, 1986), pp. 3–25 and 145–61, respectively. See also Arac's introduction.

4. Hal Foster, "For a Concept of the Political in Contemporary Art," *Recodings* (Port Townsend, Wash.: Bay Press, 1985), p. 143.

5. Herbert Blau, "Theatre and Cinema: The Scopic Drive, the Detestable Screen, and More of the Same," in *Blooded Thought: Occasions of Theatre* (New York: PAJ Publications, 1982) 134.

6. Wladimir Krysinski, "Semiotic Modalities of the Body in Modern Theater," *Poetics Today,* 2/3 (1981): 141, 143.

7. Constantin Stanislavski, *An Actor Prepares* (New York: Theatre Arts Books, 1936), pp. 238–39.

8. Adolphe Appia, *Music and the Art of the Theatre* (Coral Gables: University of Miami Press, 1962), p. 41, and *The Work of Living Art* (Coral Gables: University of Miami Press, 1960), pp. 54, 130.

9. See Keir Elam, *The Semiotics of Theatre and Drama* (London, N.Y.: Methuen, 1980), pp. 21–23. Elam grants that iconism is "wholly conventional" (23) and that convention is, in part, ideological (52). He insists, however, that anything that occurs on stage is a sign: "whatever cannot be related to the representation as such is converted into a sign of the actor's very reality—it is not, in any case, excluded from semiosis" (9). Wilfried Passow argues that semiosis is not simply a given of the performance context, that in

some cases, we do respond to the actor's body as a real body, not an iconic sign for a real body (see "Analysis of Theatrical Performance," *Poetics Today*, 2/3 (1981): 244–47). Krysinski (n. 6, above) argues that the body's instinctual charge undermines its subjugation to the *logos* of the dramatic text; he wants to develop a semiotics that can account for this process.

10. Antonin Artaud, "Le Théâtre et son double," *Oeuvres Complètes* (Paris: Gallimard, 1964), 4: 48.

11. Jerzy Grotowski, *Towards a Poor Theatre* (New York: Simon and Schuster, 1968), p. 39.

12. Herbert Blau, "Ideology and Performance," *Theatre Journal*, 35 (1983): 458.

13. Catherine Gallagher and Thomas Laqueur, Introduction, *The Making of the Modern Body: Sexuality and Society in the Nineteenth Century* (Berkeley: University of California Press, 1987), p. vii.

14. Joseph Roach has done an admirable job of tracing the relationships between scientific and medical discourses and ideas on acting in the 17th and 18th centuries in his *The Player's Passion: Studies in the Science of Acting* (Newark: University of Delaware Press, 1985). Roach, however, does not investigate the relationship between those discourses and ideology.

15. Fredric Jameson, "Postmodernism or the Cultural Logic of Late Capitalism," *New Left Review*, 146 (1984): 91. For a more developed account of Foster's and Jameson's views of political art under postmodernism, see my "Toward A Concept of the Political in Postmodern Theatre," *Theatre Journal*, 39 (1987): 21–24.

16. See Michael Kirby, "The Activity: A New Art Form," *The Art of Time: Essays on the Avant-Garde* (New York: Dutton, 1969), pp. 153–69. Acconci describes some of his own work as activities, though he uses the term differently than Kirby.

17. *Avalanche*, 6 (1972): 9, 12. All my accounts of Acconci's performances derive from the documentation in this special issue, which includes notes by Acconci and an interview.

18. Germano Celant, "Dirty Acconci," *Artforum*, 19 (1980): 76.

19. Cynthia Heimel, *Sex Tips For Girls* (New York: Simon and Schuster, 1983). "One must, first and foremost, understand the psychology of the penis" (121). "The penis knows its Ten Commandments." (186).

20. Stephen Melville, "How Should Acconci Count For Us?," *October*, 18 (Fall 1981): 83–84.

21. Anthony Kubiak, "Disappearance as History: The Stages of Terror," *Theatre Journal*, 39 (1987): 87.

22. See Dana B. Polan, "'Above All Else to Make You See': Cinema and the Ideology of Spectacle," in *Postmodernism and Politics* (n. 3, above), pp. 55–69.

23. Christine Buci-Glucksman, "Catastrophic Utopia: The Feminine as Allegory of the Modern," in *The Making of the Modern Body* (n. 13, above), p. 226.

24. Craig Owens, "The Allegorical Impulse: Toward a Theory of Postmodernism," in *Art After Modernism* (n. 1, above), pp. 203–35.

Part V

Architecture: Construction/ Deconstruction

12

Place, Form, and Identity in Postmodern Architecture and Philosophy: Derrida *avec* Moore, Mies *avec* Kant

Edward Casey

> There are, moreover and always,
> two functions which overlap.
>
> **Jacques Derrida**

> [A building] must embody the
> difficult unity of exclusion rather
> than the easy unity of exclusion.
>
> **Robert Venturi and
> Denise Scott Brown**

I

"Place," "Form," "Identity" are strange names to engage in a book on postmodernism. For they are archetypally metaphysical names—in many ways, the most telling names in the history of metaphysical thinking. Not only do they help to inaugurate Greek metaphysics at its inception (place as *topos* and form as *eidos* collude in giving rise to the identity of "substance" construed metaphysically), but their imprint is still felt in Kant's *Critique of Pure Reason* at the end of the eighteenth century.

At the end of Kant's text, which sets forth a massive critique of dialectical metaphysics, there is a slender but significant chapter entitled "The Architectonic of Pure Reason." By "architectonic" Kant means "the art of constructing systems [of knowledge]," and this strictly "in accordance with the essential ends of reason."[1] Within an architectonic of reason thus conceived, we find all three metaphysical names in play. "Place," first of all, is operative in the systematicity of

199

architectonic, its orderly organization as a conceptual topography. When Kant says that "by a system I understand the unity of the manifold modes of knowledge under one idea,"[2] he is pointing to such a topography. Architectonic as a system of knowledge is a system of the *places* of knowing, as Kant makes explicit in adding that the idea that determines "the unity of the manifold modes of knowledge" is to be grasped as determining not only the scope of knowledge as a whole, but also "the *positions* which the parts occupy relatively to one another."[3] These "positions" are the precise *topoi* that pin knowledge down to determinate spots in a hierarchy of concepts—much as physical *topoi* pin down the tumultuous and irregular movements of *chora* or primordial space in Plato's *Timaeus,* and represent the end points of motion of Aristotle's *Physics.* In all three cases, place serves to delimit and regulate an otherwise unruly scene, whether this be conceptual or physical or metaphysical.

In the perspective of Western metaphysics, place can achieve this powerfully stabilizing effect only by dealing with the *forms* of things. Just as the elementary geometric forms collude in the constitution of particular places in the Platonic cosmology—and places grasped in terms of their innermost boundaries are analogous to forms qua shapes in the Aristotelian physics—so the Kantian architectonic of pure reason posits the connivance of form and position in the conceptual scaffolding of systematic knowledge. For what determines the positionality of the parts of knowledge is the idea not of a whole as such but of "the *form* of a whole" in Kant's revealing phrase —a whole that *as a form* is "thus an organized unity (*articulatio*) and not an aggregate."[4] Instead of a mere heap of items, architectonic delivers to us a fully articulated whole of internally related terms.

It is precisely by means of such a formal wholeness of articulated positions that *identity* is attained in turn. The architectonic whole, writes Kant, "may grow from within, but not by external addition. It is thus like an animal body, the growth of which is not by the addition of a new member, but by the rendering of each member, without change or proportion, stronger and more effective for its purposes."[5] The action of architectonic is therefore to engender internally coherent, self-identical wholes, which function as embryonic, quasi-organic units. Identity or full growth is achieved by the internal articulation of parts that maintain homologous locations: a rule that applies as decisively to organic entities as to self-identical substances in the Platonic or Aristotelian worldview—and to the even more rigorously self-identical concepts with which the *Critique of Pure Reason* is preoccupied.

By pointing thus to the archetypal complicity of place, form, and identity in classical and modern metaphysics, I am suggesting that there is something archly metaphysical in this very complicity, something that Heidegger would sum up in the name of "determinate presence" (*Anwesenheit*). I have further intimated that Kant, situated at a pivotal point of the modern metaphysical tradition (he is at once its most trenchant critic and its most cogent practitioner), embeds all three signifiers in his notion of architectonic as the systematic unity of pure reason. This unity is identical with metaphysics itself: "metaphysics," says Kant almost redundantly, "is the philosophy which has as its task the statement of [pure a priori] knowledge in its systematic unity."[6] By "systematic unity" Kant means architectonic unity.

Here we cannot help but ask: Is the term "architectonic" innocently chosen, a matter of pure reason alone? We suspect otherwise after Vico, Nietzsche, and Derrida, who have taught us that there are no innocent or philosophically pure metaphors. The word "architectonic" is founded on the very same Greek etymons as is "architecture"—that is, *archos*, 'chief', plus *tekton*, 'builder'. It follows that the architect is literally the "master builder." Kant, who brought the word "architectonic" into central philosophical usage, does not hesitate to draw on the architectural resonances of the word; he speaks, for instance, of a "foundation for building [a system]" and of the "complete edifice of knowledge."[7]

Which is primary, then, "architectonic" (as Kant presumes in placing "the architectonic interest of reason" above all other interests, including those he disdainfully calls merely "technical"[8]) or "architectural" (on whose semantic resources Kant is dependent in his very description of architectonic)? The question is poorly posed, insofar as asking for primacy is itself an instance of a tenacious metaphysical tendency. The fact is that each term infects the other by displacement. For "architectonic" is ineluctably architectural in its conception of a systematic unity of closely interwoven parts, just as "architecture" itself is intrinsically architectonic in its nisus to control and organize spaces by the manipulation of systematically related building materials. The master builder of one enterprise is at the same time the master builder of the other enterprise. The metaphysician, who builds with diaphanous concepts, is a close cousin of the architect, who builds with obdurate materials. Both require what Kant calls a "schema" in order to relate constructively to the real: that is, to put place, form, and identity into a coherent unity in the concrete praxis of thinking and building.[9]

II

But in the epoch of postmodernism certain things have changed. Not only would we no longer look assiduously to find in either building or thinking the rigorous system of place, form, and identity; we would question the very idea of "system" itself as well as the system-building terms "place," "form," and "identity." Postmodern philosophers attempt to undermine metaphysics—often in the name of another noninnocent metaphor, "deconstruction"— so as to call all of these terms, and thus the notion of architectonic that holds them together, into question. The displacement thereby effected is a displacement out of the metaphysical assurance of systematicity itself and into the margin of metaphysics. Similarly, postmodern architects lay siege to the received doctrines of classicist and especially modernist architecture as representing obsessions with *closed* forms of systematic unity—and as bringing with them their own closed canons of practice, including rigorously formulated rules dictating the proper form, identity, and place of buildings and parts of buildings. There is displacement here as well—as exhibited in Charles Moore's brilliantly deconstructive "Piazza d'Italia," plunked down in the midst of New Orleans—and a concomitant fascination with the architectural *parergon,* the work alongside the main work, a by-work or "facade" (as Freud called phantasy vis-à-vis its memorial origins): the entire Piazza is an elaborate by-work as well as an ironic joke-work.

No longer does a single architectural idea or ideal reign—any more than it does in philosophy, where it would be futile to command obeisance to the principle of what Kant called "derivation from a single supreme and inner end"[10] or to what Heidegger designates derogatorily as "onto-theology," according to which there is a single supreme being from whom all other beings are derived by creation or deduction or analogy. In both cases, the architectonic and the architectural alike, the ideal itself, precisely *as ideal,* has been, if not discredited, set aside—and thereby dis-located, dis-placed.

To dislodge the architectonic from its hegemony was for Kant tantamount to degeneration into what he called *Rhapsodie,* a word that means in its origin "that which is stitched together." "Our diverse modes of knowledge," forewarns Kant in the *Critique,* "must not be permitted to be a mere rhapsody, but must form a system."[11] It is striking that charges of ill-organized *pastiche*—itself a way of merely stiching things together—are characteristically made of postmodern works and texts, whether in architecture, philosophy, or literature. "Random assortment!" "Merely thrown together!" is the kind of reproach one has come to expect from critics of postmodernism such as Kenneth Frampton, who accuses Charles Moore of indulging in "flaccid ecclecticism."[12] Frampton cites, with barely disguised contempt, Moore's own statement of the pastichelike design process of the Piazza d'Italia:

> I remembered that the architectural orders were Italian, with a little help from the Greeks, and so we thought we could put Tuscan, Doric, Ionic, and Corinthian columns over the fountain, but they overshadowed it, obliterating the [fountain's] shape of Italy. So instead we added a "Delicatessen Order" that we thought could resemble sausages hanging in a shop window, thus illustrating its transalpine location. But now I think there is going to be an Italian restaurant and no sausages. . . . There was a little bit of money left over so we thought we would bang up a temple out front to show that our piazza was behind it. There was enough money too to make a campanile beside the temple to show off our existence and to make more patterns with the verticals of the skyscraper behind. Someday there will be shops around it, like Ghiradelli Square, but for the moment it is just sitting by itself and a little lonesome.[13]

One could imagine Jacques Derrida making a similar statement about the production of *Glas:*

> I remembered that the philosophical ideas were German, with a little help from the Greek, and so I thought I could put Platonic, Aristotelian, and Plotinian canopies over the body of Hegel, but they overshadowed it. . . . So instead I added a "Genet Order" that I thought could well resemble sausages hanging in a shop window. . . . There was a little bit of space left over on the page so I thought I would bang up the text of Hegel's *Philosophy of Right* right out front to show that my philosophical pi(a)zza was behind it. There was enough space too to make inserts beside Hegel's text by means of *parergoni* that showed off my learning and to make more patterns with the verticals of the colossal columns behind. Someday there will be still more paratextual margins around it, like Heidegger Square, but for the moment it is just sitting by itself a little lonesome, looking for a reader.

But even if there is considerable intuitive truth in the perception of postmodern architecture and textuality as stemming from an unbridled *rhapsodein*, abetted by an adroit *bricolage*, still the buildings

and books of Moore and Derrida are constructed as convincing facades from the very ashes of their deconstructive fervor and wit. Even
if they are only stitched together, they do hang together (and hold
together) as by-works. One way they do so is by a process of "double
coding" in Jencks's term: "post-modern architecture, in an attempt to
communicate, is double-coded, an eclectic mix of traditional or local
codes with modern ones."[14] Ecclecticism need not be flaccid if it can
only exemplify the rigor of respecting at least two codes at once—one
code "a popular, traditional one which, like spoken language, is
slow-changing, full of clichés, and rooted in family life, [the other] a
modern one full of neologisms and responding to quick changes in
technology, art, and fashion."[15] Thus what Jencks describes as "pastiche and travesty . . . whimsy and nostalgia"[16] is redeemed in the
case of the Piazza d'Italia by its dual coding of Greek and Italian
columnar orders on the one hand and of neon-lit supergraphics on
the other, the one code at once sustaining and subverting the other.
In the Piazza—as also in Moore and Turnbull's Kresge College at
Santa Cruz—we can sense the presence of what Derrida calls "reversal" (i.e., between the two terms of a binary opposition) and of a dis-
ordering "dissemination" of dazzling aftereffects.

  It is remarkable that *Glas*, published in 1974 (the year when
Kresge College was completed), is itself constructed on a double code
deriving from texts of Hegel and Genet, each undermining the other
(for example, with regard to the issue of "family life" mentioned by
Jencks as part of a traditionalist coding: an issue explicitly at stake in
the passages from Hegel's *Philosophy of Right* on which Derrida
draws). At the same time, each supports the other by being juxtaposed page after page in a continual *Nebeneinanderstellung* whose
impact is as dismaying for the reader of *Glas* as standing in the central
"street" of Kresge College is for the uninitiated Santa Cruz college
student. In both cases, we witness the radical undoing of Kant's
notion of architectonic as system—or more exactly, as metasystem.
"By a system," writes Kant, "I understand the unity of the manifold
modes of knowledge under *one* idea."[17] The "one" is a supervisory
concept or system, an architectonic whole under which all particular
concepts or subsystems are to be arranged and contained.

  If "postmodern" means anything, it means (in Lyotard's felici-
tous formulation) "incredulity toward metanarratives."[18] So it is
hardly unexpected that Derrida, the master unbuilder of the metanarrative of metaphysics, should advert to what he calls pointedly "*two*
functions" on the very first page of a text that is itself (de)constructed
out of two columns of print:

Two unequal columns . . . of which each . . . incalculably reverses, returns, replaces, remarks, recuts the other. . . . There
are, moreover and always, two functions which overlap. . . .
One assures, guards, assimilates, interiorizes, idealizes, takes
up (*relève*) the fall into the monument. The fall maintains itself,
embalms and mummifies, "monumemorializes," is named—
tomb (*tombe*). . . . The other—lets fall (*tomber*) the rest. It risks
returning to the same. Tomb (*Tombe*)—the columns, the water-
sprouts (*les trombes*) twice over—remains (*reste*).[19]

The mention of "monument," of "columns," and even of "water-
sprouts" (all of these are prominent features of the Piazza d'Italia)—
as of the "colossal" and of "pylons" elsewhere in Derrida's writings—reminds us that Derrida, the archdeconstructor, is constantly
drawn to architectural motifs in his dis-mastering of metaphysical
presence.

Nor is it surprising to learn that Derrida has collaborated with
Peter Eisenman, one of the leading American postmodern architects.
What brings the otherwise disparate work of postmodern architect
and postmodern philosopher together is the subversive-dis-
seminative use of double coding in building and writing: they meet in
(or on) the tomb (*tombe*) of double inscription, which is at once the
motor and the legacy of deconstruction in every field to which it has
been extended. The "grand narratives" of which Lyotard speaks—
and of which classicist and modernist architecture are exemplary
cases in point—*fall* to the undoing doubling of deconstruction. Or
more exactly, postmodern architect and philosopher meet in *twice*
falling—in a space that is at once beyond rhapsody and short of
metasystem, in an interspace of free fall epitomized by the infamous
"absent column" that slices through Eisenman's House VI in Washington, Connecticut. The columnar splitting of House VI carries forward, at once *in absentia* and *in concreto*, the column-splitting of *Glas*.

III

But let us return to our point of departure. "Place," "form,"
"identity" stand, in their metaphysical and architectonic splendor,
like three columns of concepts—not unlike the august triads of Kant's
metaphysical Table of Categories (itself a raid on Aristotle's merely
"rhapsodic" list): unity, plurality, totality; reality, negation, limitation; possibility, existence, necessity; etc.[20] And not unlike those
pages of *Glas* that feature three columns of print. The triad of place,

form, and identity doubtless has its particular "position" in the architectonic of pure reason—as well as in its architectural analogues in
classicism and modernism.

Yet these three terms are of interest to us, at this particular
point, for their postmetaphysical and antiarchitectonic valency: for
what they become in the deconstructive turn.

Identity. In the postmodern perspective, the very identity of concepts, their status as what Kant calls "synthetic unities" of cognition,
comes into question. The identical as the sheerly selfsame overflows
the borders of its own definition—as Heidegger has argued in opposing the Same to the Identical and as Derrida proposes in insisting that
conceptual identity depends on repetition. So too in postmodern architecture the self-identical, self-identified building is taken apart—
either literally (as in the self-deconstructing, "notched" Best department store building in Sacramento, Calif.) or metaphorically (i.e.,
through a renewed respect for ornamentation in architecture).[21]

Form. It follows forthwith that form is also in question: from
having been (in Plato and Aristotle) the decisive determinant that
brings messy matter into eidetic shape, it becomes itself an undecidable. Like the delightfully ambi-guous French word *tombe,* we cannot
decide in advance on the form of things, whether these be words or
built structures. Hence the use of indeterminate boundaries in much
postmodern architecture (e.g., the way in which Kresge College
backs gracefully into the redwood.

Place. The precise conceptual topography of Kantian architectonic gives way to what can only be called *dis*-placement, the radical
unlocatability of the signifier in its frenzied metonymic enchainment
(as Lacan might put it). We witness displacement at work in recent
architecture both spatially and temporally: the latter in the weird
juxtaposition of styles that allows Mario Botta to bring together Pal-
ladio with modernism (and *still* to achieve a distinctively postmodern
dis-narration); the former in the shattering of a settled sense of place
that is so manifest in Michael Graves's accalimed Portland Building,
about which Frampton remarks that it shows "a surprisingly insen-
sitive attitude towards the site."[22] But is this so surprising after all if
place itself is made subject to deconstruction—if the "scenographic"
takes over from the "tectonic"?[23]

IV

The postmodern deconstruction of identity, form, and place is a
dismembering not just of three classical metaphysical concepts and of
their architectural analogues in classicist architecture (i.e., of Greek

columnar "orders" or of Vitruvian principles of order, arrangement, and economy).[24] It is, at the same time, an undoing of specifically modernist thought and building. The Cartesian criteria of clarity and distinctness—and the idea of "objective reality" as finding its support in the accurate mirroring of material entities in mental representations—ensure that in the well-ordered early modern world-picture of Descartes, identity and form, the two columns on which objectivity is supported, survive intact as absolute metaphysical premises.

The same conceptual columns shore up the theory of modernist architecture. As Mies van der Rohe has said, "the authentic approach to architecture should always be the objective."[25] An indispensable part of the Miesian ethos of architectural objectivity—whose criteria are organization, clarity, and economy[26]—is a demand for order. Where order for Descartes would be methodological or metaphysical (and would be expressed in a hierarchically arranged system of the sciences), for Mies it is tectonic. Or rather, it is architectonic, as becomes evident in this statement of 1938:

> We shall emphasize the organic principle of order as a means of achieving the successful relationship of the parts to each other and to the whole. . . . *We must have order*, allocating to each thing its proper place and giving to each thing its due according to its nature.[27]

Mies, invoking the equivalent of Cartesian objectivism, also approaches Kant's idea of systematic totality—a quasi-organic totality in which each constituent item (e.g., each particular building part) is "articulated according to the organization of the work."[28] It ensues that the work is at once, and inseparably, architectonic and architectural. It is what guarantees the *identity* of each part by according to it its "proper place" in the work as a whole: identity *is* place. Identity is having a proper place in the archi-tectonic/tectural whole. By the same token, *form* is achieved by the interaction of all parts working in concern: "form is not the aim of our work [this would be classicism] but only the result."[29] Form, like identity, is a function of the work-as-a-whole, a whole foreshadowed in Descartes's model of the unity of the sciences and brought to speculative completion in Kant's idea of the ideal systematic whole of pure reason.

We detect in Miesian modernism, however, a dissident chord that threatens to disharmonize the modernist symphony so mellifluously played out in advance by Descartes and Kant. Despite Mies's stress on form—for example, as lucidity of formal structure—he also says blatantly that "form, by itself, does not exist."[30] This last sentence could not have been written by Descartes or by Kant. Mies would doubtless apply to these latter two architects of modernist thought the denunciatory term "formalism."[31] Like Bergson or Husserl—both of whom also opposed formalism by recourse to criteria of liveliness borrowed ultimately from biology—Mies has recourse to *life* as a foundational metaphor: "only what has intensity of life can have intensity of form."[32] Pursued further, this idea (whose origin is to be found in Frank Lloyd Wright, a critical influence on Mies from 1910 onward), replaces the image of architecture as only *quasi*-organic with the idea of it as unabashedly organic.[33]

Mies also, and even more vehemently, engages in the deconstruction of place. As we have just seen, the only sense of place to which he accords formal recognition is that which locates an item in a systematic architectural order: place is literally *al-located* in this order. It does not exist outside it—except as mere construction site. In the case of place, however, the work of deconstruction had begun long before the architectural modernism of Mies. In fact, it started with Descartes himself—with his conception of space as homogeneous and isotropic, and thus as leaving *no place for place*.

The very notion of place, which had been so important in classical Greek philosophy and architecture,[34] is no longer pertinent or viable in philosophy after the seventeenth century. It has been superseded by the idea of infinite "space," which swallows up all particular places. Descartes still distinguishes between "internal" and "external" place, but neither of these terms designates anything like a secure locus, much less a locus on which a building might be set.[35] By the time we reach Kant, place has dropped out of philosophers' vocabulary altogether, thus clearing the way conceptually for the characteristic modernistic neglect of placement in architecture—of doing "next to nothing" (*beinahe nichts*) about it in Mies's celebrated phrase. Mies himself collapses place into identity: apart form the site of construction, place is nothing but the proper location of the elements of the architectural work in that work. It has no status of its own as that "within which the work itself is situated. Modernist architects have lost their classicist counterparts' concern with the adequate placement of buildings in relation to their surroundings.

It ensues that the thorough deconstruction of place, form, and identity undertaken in postmodern architecture and thought did not arise de novo. It had its beginnings in philosophical modernism's systematic dismantling of both "place" and "form." Mies and his philosophical predecessors had already initiated the close scrutiny of these archmetaphysical notions by a resolute refusal to accept ancient Greek conceptions of *topos* and *eidos*.

But all the modernists, architects and philosophers alike, left "identity" intact; and it is with *its* effective suspension that we can say that postmodernism makes its own distinctive move. In undermining identity—a step expressly undertaken by Derrida as by Moore—postmodernism topples the last remaining pillar of the classical triad of columns that undergird the jointly maintained edifice of architecture and philosophy.

Perhaps we should speak, in sum, of postmodern architecture not as "antiaesthetic" (an unfortunately chosen term, given that much of postmodern building is quite pleasingly aesthetic) but as "antitectonic"—in express opposition to the architectonic impulse in architectural modernism. "Mies *avec* Kant" is an appropriate subtitle for the story of the modern in philosophy and architecture—in "philotecture" as we might call their combined pursuit—just as "Moore *avec* Derrida" begins to describe the disjunctive, doubly inscribed trajectory of the postmodern in the two fields.

Along this trajectory, the double columns of architecture and philosophy are being reconfigured in a new order of things coming and to come. In the vision of such an order, each column, true to its postmodern form and (non)identity, supports and supplants the other in a common deconstruction of the assurance of place, of *stabilitas loci*. Just as the identical has dissolved in the swerve of the same, and as form has become increasingly ironic and eclectic, there is no longer any assurance of place.

Notes

1. Immanuel Kant, *Critique of Pure Reason* (New York: St. Martin's, 1965), pp. 653 and 663. "The Architectonic of Pure Reason" is itself contained in the section of the *Critique* entitled "Transcendental Doctrine of Method" and which, along with the "Transcendental Doctrine of Elements," spans the entirety of the Critical project. Architectonic is thus part of method—part of *how* we should practice philosophy in contrast with *what* philosophy consists in (i.e., its elements, intuitions, and concepts). It is essential to Kant's modernist vision that the "how" of philosophy is just as important as its "what."

2. Ibid., p. 653.

3. Ibid.

4. Ibid. My italics.

5. Ibid., pp. 653–54.

6. Ibid., p. 661.

7. Ibid., pp. 429 and 430, respectively.

8. Ibid., pp. 430 and 654, respectively.

9. On architectonic versus technical schemata, see ibid., p. 654.

10. Ibid.

11. Ibid., p. 653.

12. Kenneth Frampton, *Modern Architecture: A Critical History* (London: Thames & Hudson, 1985), p. 293.

13. Ibid.

14. Charles Jencks, *The Language of Post-Modern Architecture* (New York: Rizzoli, 1977), p. 133.

15. Ibid., p. 130.

16. Ibid.

17. *Critique of Pure Reason*, p. 654; my italics.

18. Jean-François Lyotard, *The Postmodern Condition: A Report on Knowledge* (Minneapolis: University of Minnesota Press, 1984), p. xxiv.

19. Jacques Derrida, *Glas* (Paris: Galilée, 1974), pp. 7–8.

20. Kant claims that his own table of categories "is developed systematically from a common principle, namely, the faculty of judgment. . . . It has not arisen rhapsodically, as the result of a haphazard search after pure concepts, the complete enumeration of which, as based on induction only, could never be guaranteed" (*Critique of Pure Reason*, p. 114). Once again, mere rhapsody is contrasted with architectonic unity—here the unity of judgment, which as "pure" can never be founded on mere induction in the impure empirical realm.

21. On this respect, see Robert Venturi, Denise Scott Brown, and Steven Izenour, *Learning from Las Vegas* (Cambridge: MIT Press, 1977), pp. 114–15. I have been made acutely aware of this development and its overall import from discussions with Kent Bloomer of the Yale School of Architecture.

22. Frampton, *Modern Architecture*, p. 308.

23. On the distinction between tectonic and scenographic, see ibid., p. 307.

24. Cf. Vitruvius, *The Ten Books on Architecture* (New York: Dover, 1960), p. 13. The Vitruvian principles also include eurythmy, symmetry, and propriety.

25. Mies van der Rohe, "Frank Lloyd Wright" (1940), cited in Philip Johnson, *Mies van der Rohe* (New York: Museum of Modern Art, 1947), p. 195.

26. "The office building is a house of work, of organization, of clarity, of economy" (statement from "The Office Building" [1928] cited in ibid., p. 183).

27. From "Inaugural Address as Director of Architecture at the Armour Institute of Technology," cited in ibid., pp. 194–95; my italics.

28. "The Office Building" in ibid., p. 183.

29. "Aphorisms on Architecture and Form" (1923), cited in ibid., p. 184.

30. Ibid.

31. "We reject all aesthetic speculation, all doctrine, all formalism . . . form as an aim is formalism; and that we reject" (ibid., pp. 183–84).

32. "A Letter on Form in Architecture" (1927), cited in ibid., p. 187. For Mies, the basic question is "whether the form is derived from life or invented for its own sake" (ibid.).

33. By "quasi-organic" I mean the mere *likening* of a constructed entity to a biological organism. Thus Kant says that the architectonic of human knowledge "is *like* an animal body" (*Critique of Pure Reason*, p. 653; my italics).

34. Vitruvius gives specific instructions regarding the most desirable location of cities, temples, theaters, and houses in books 1, 4, 5, and 6 (respectively) of his *Ten Books on Architecture*. On the role of *topos* in Plato and Aristotle, see my forthcoming book, *Getting into Place*.

35. On Descartes's distinction between external and internal place, see his *Principles of Philosophy*, 2:10.

13

Building it Postmodern, in LA?
Frank Gehry and Company

Roger Bell

Placing the postmodernist idiom within the milieu of southern California, one can only wonder if the question, architecturally at least, can survive the driving assault of a city so indebted to the techniques of producing the illusory.[1] Here I am thinking not only of Hollywood, which gives us our divertissements and castles in the hills of Malibu, but the articulate code itself by which Disneyland co-opts the very distinction between reality/illusion with its strength of images. The many facades LA shows to its visitor all appear to share this logic, from the fast food joints that dot the boulevard to Philip Johnson's Crystal Cathedral sounding the skies of Garden Grove.

LA's sprawling grid of a city must work its magic upon a population seemingly in constant automotion. This is the place where a MacDonald's, the oldest surviving (thirty-one years), is included on the National Register of Historic Places, and an architectural style derives its name "Googie" from the postwar prototype of the coffee shop on Sunset Boulevard.[2] In LA, time seems to be snagged on the tectonic plates at the edge of the continent, rendering "history" a trace of residual nostalgia for the passing of the latest trend, a mere afterthought to an energized present, its aftershock, the instant "classic." This is a city seen, and best understood, through the window of the passing car, its symbolism and its environment spread out in orientation to the automobile. This is the culture of the "strip" and Venturi's lessons "from Las Vegas" brought to the scale of the metropolis. Taking Venturi's detour:

> Passing through Las Vegas is route 91, the archetype of the commercial strip, the phenomenon at its purest and most intense. We believe a careful documentation and analysis of its physical form is as important to architects and urbanists today

as were the studies of medieval Europe and ancient Rome and Greece to earlier generations. Such a study will help to define a new type of urban form emerging in America and Europe, radically different from that we have known; one that we have been ill-equipped to deal with and that, from ignorance, we define today as urban sprawl.[3]

Just such a place, this new "form" that Venturi implores us to recognize and for which purpose he takes us on a tour of Vas Vegas, exists in an advanced stage of emergence in LA, complete with a growing sense of traditions articulating its mythical self-understanding. This is an architectural place in which the automobile, parking lots, and signs dominate the buildings. LA takes the symbolism of its architectonic facade and distributes it over the entire suburban landscape, orienting its significance toward the life of the streets, which have an intensity and diversity not found elsewhere. LA's challenge to the possibility of a postmodernist reading involves deciphering its polysemic voices, recognizing the manner by which the complex symbolism of its facade conflates the illusory and the real, and extracting the fuller significance of its broader archi-textural "form." But this would be an iconography of the present as emergent, rather than a historicist past, one that, rather than inventing itself, seeks to *find* its voice in the present. Such an iconography would constitute a break or rupture by which a tradition is seen as having already been established from within a present seemingly without memory, any past being always the immediate, without the revolutionary didactics of an avant-garde.

Now to the question, Has such a moment arrived? Is there any evidence within the architectural record of LA that its modern condition, the condition of modernism, is opening for reappraisal the significance of this "form" noted by Venturi some fifteen years ago? Is there a postmodern architecture to be found practiced in LA that rejects invention for the ongoing process of demythologizing the present consciousness, a building that informs the public through a symbolism of coded questions put to the contemporary culture? Of course such an architecture would be postmodern with regard to its emphasis upon questioning over the pretense of solutions and interpretive closure. The emphasis of the *post*modern is upon the sense and urgency of retrieval, but for LA such retrieval is of the immediate, not a neoclassicism.

At its inception postmodern architecture was presented as a rejection of the ideological limits of modernism, which strove to solve social problems by a relation of function to form. Building is understood as an organization of structural power whereby its formal relations serve the appointed function of its designer. This was a world in which there was thought to be no room for the decorative, the frivolous, the playful. "Design" was raised to a level comparable to that point in the Renaissance when art and science shared the same telos, but for modernism the social sciences were pertinent. Clearly, I think, the postmodernist critics are correct in judging the widespread failure of such a modernism, which still produces homogenization of the world environment. But what do we look for in postmodern tectonics? Is it a form displaced from function? Or is it the simple admittance of the decorative, of the conspicuous, its lauding of praise on capitalist excess and power? Or is it a new humanism, a building that communicates a sense of place through building the site, both environmentally and historically on a human scale?

Now the versions of postmodern architecture are quite familiar, names like Charles Moore, Robert Stern, Charles Jencks, Michael Graves, et al. In fact discussions of the postmodern moment in culture generally refer to architecture as a point of stability for marking this historic transition across the diverse cultural arenas. But is this benchmark artificial? Is the architectural example any more decided than that of literature, science, art? I think not and intend here to exploit LA to make my case.

But first, why this choice of exemplary regionalism? Why LA? The answer involves four recent events that all indicate, although somewhat differently, that something is up architecturally in LA, something worthy of careful attention and thought. First and most obvious is the recent publication of a glossy, beautifully illustrated book subtitled "The New Architecture and Interior Design from Los Angeles." This text, with all the pretense of a coffee-table book, brings together into its folds with a seeming unity of purpose the most eclectic of architectural design. It argues its case complete with contrasting documentation of a "heritage" from which this body of "new wave" work derives. But being LA and the "heritage" regional, the traditions are primarily modern and this "new wave" of work issuing from the late 1970s to the present is termed *Freestyle*, indeed the title of the book. Here the author of the argument (Pilar Viladas, a senior editor for *Progressive Architecture*), begins her introduction by stating that this work involves experiments quite different than the ones of the more academically oriented postmodernists.[4] Upon initial scrutiny this would appear to be the case, but the question of this difference, after careful study of the text and its images, returns but one theme: the question of postmodernism itself.

The second and third motivating events involve the success of

Frank Gehry, the key figure in this "new wave" of LA architects. Gehry is the figure on the cover of *Progressive Architecture* (October 1986), an entire issue dedicated to his recent work and philosophy: "What You Know, You Question."[5] So the question remains: Why is the east coast paying such attention to Frank Gehry and his "Freestyle" experiments? But this is too weak. Why is the east coast paying such tribute to the work of Frank Gehry? Well almost the east coast: "The Architecture of Frank Gehry" closed at the Walker Art Center in Minneapolis, November 16, 1986. And as Pilar Viladas writes, this time in the Introduction to his work in *Progressive Architecture*: "he is the first American architect of his generation to be the subject of a one-man exhibition at a major American museum."[6] Actually this show will travel from Minneapolis to Houston, Toronto, Atlanta, and close in LA's new Museum of Contemporary Art, the first U.S. building by Arata Isozaki of Tokyo, which opens in December, just missing being mounted in Gehry's very own Temporary Contemporary quarters, which were themselves such a critical success that this renovated warehouse has become a permanent annex.

But the fourth connection is the most intriguing and questionable: LA's Pershing Square competition selecting SITE Projects, Inc., of New York, best known for their store fronts for Best Products, with the remark in "Pencil Points" that "all Los Angeles seems united in praise of SITE's scheme."[7] Is this announcement in Gehry's issue of *Progressive Architecture* unconnected, simply spurious to my question of regionalism? For the moment judgment must be deferred, leaving the question to function as a clue.

Returning to the question of postmodernism, interestingly Habermas opens his article, "Modernity—An Incomplete Project," with a reference to the 1980 Biennial in Venice:

> In 1980 architects were admitted to the Biennial in Venice, following painters and filmmakers. The note sounded at this first Architecture Biennial was one of disappointment. I would describe it by saying that those exhibited in Venice formed an avant-garde of reversed fronts. I mean that they sacrificed the tradition of modernity in order to make room for a new historicism. Upon this occasion, a critic of a German newspaper, *Frankfurter Allgemeine Zeitung,* advanced a thesis whose significance reaches beyond this particular event; it is a diagnosis of our times: "Postmodernity definitely presents itself as Antimodernity." This statement describes an emotional current of our times, which has penetrated all spheres of intellectual life. It has placed on the agenda theories of postenlightenment, postmodernity, even of posthistory.[8]

The significance of this event for Habermas hangs on the charge of "sacrifice" and the consequence of historicism. In architecture, at least, the view that modernism sacrificed itself has equally compelling evidence that certainly predates the opening of "Strada Novissima" in the Venice Biennial's "Presence of the Past." In fact the date generally accepted is quite specific: July 15, 1972, at 3:32 P.M., as is the place: the demolition of the Pruitt-Igoe Housing of St. Louis, the award-winning housing project built between 1952 and 1955.[9] However, one can well imagine Habermas's shock walking down this unusual street bound on both sides by these twenty-two facades. Having seen the show when it traveled to San Francisco in the summer of 1982, I remember being struck by the curiosity and design interest of just this appropriation of classicism. But as false fronts, the question of historicism did not arise for me. These structures just were not real enough; after all we were in California, if only northern California, and, alas, the show received rave reviews in our local press. The neoclassicism that dominated this show was still just an idea, a street of billboards advertising the work that was ever so slowly developing from polemic to reality: Graves's The Portland Building nearing completion as the first large-scale postmodern building. Is this regionalism once again; some shows travel well while others do not? This one evidently did. One can imagine the Venice public coming in off their medieval canals and piazzas to disgruntled exclamations of "So what else is new?," borrowing the New York vernacular. In contrast San Franciscans are always reaching for the prestigious association of such classicism, especially in their buildings; how else to distinguish themselves from the south?

However, not the entirety of this "Presencing of the Past" was neoclassical. One of the facades I remember distinctly could hardly support Habermas's charge of historicism in the normal understanding of the word. At the time this particular "front" simply produced a chuckle in me and a sense of recognition, a moment of irony and light-hearted humor. Later, much later, it came to me that this facade communicated a greater significance than the wealth of historical allusion gathered together in the majority of the other exhibits. This was Gehry's exhibit, a facade of straightforward framing, the unillustrious material of standard building: the "2x4." How could Habermas have missed Gehry? Here was an exhibit aimed at such a Marxist revisionism, at a communication undistorted by the contrivances of the rhetorical, stripped down to the rudimentary works: Gehry with his sleeves rolled up.

At the time, besides the irony, and of course the California identification, what caught my eye were the 2x4s, the fact that their real dimensions were slightly off the "local" standard, obviously spe-

Figure 2

cially milled in Italy for the purpose and shipped to the U.S.A. to mark their difference: regionalism calling attention to itself again. One wonders what the Italians made of it? In researching the question I found that a central element of Gehry's piece was lost in translation to San Francisco. In Venice there was a prominent window of the true classical exhibit hall upon which Gehry's facade was centered as a framing of a frame, the stage set upon the centerpiece, complete with diagonal bracing, which traced an illusionist perspective toward the window. Gehry shows his penchant for the "installation" and his conversance with LA artists, especially Robert Irwin who himself in 1976 contributed an installation to the Venice Biennal.

The "installation" is the final distillation of minimalism where the traditional art object itself is abandoned. In Irwin's work the object becomes perception itself, a phenomenological exploration of our reading of space by the application to the gallery space of such marginal elements as plaster, paint, lighting, wire, scrim, etc. As Irwin himself describes it, the installation "conspires to skew one's expecta-

tions, to raise some and lower others, so that your perceptual mechanism becomes tilted, and you perceive the room as you otherwise
might not have."[10] The difference of the "installation" is this removal
of the traditional "frame"; art can no longer be understood as "representation," which is seen as a second-order phenomenon. Its work
becomes "attention to the incidental, the peripheral, everything that
was beside the point," so as to "reestablish the inquiry on the perceptual level."[11] That is, only perceptual presence itself is left within the
artist's framework, and the artist's challenge is to resuscitate this
presence out of a past of habituations and in so doing to bring the
process of spatial reading to notice. This is an artistic strategy well
suited to architecture and Gehry's facade, which "installs" itself in
front of the sixteenth-century window, equally redirects our perceptual gaze by means of its illusory devices to question its "perspective"
on the past.

Interestingly, the Italians did notice Gehry's question; Germano
Celant's review of the exhibit concludes:

> In the end the most radical intervention is decidedly that of
> Frank Gehry, the California architect who has refuted monu-
> mentalizations and imitations by proposing a woodframe skel-
> eton through which to view the sixteenth-century architecture
> of the arsenal "in perspective" thus turning this postmodernist
> rebirth into what might be called a "renaissance of the
> Renaissance."[12]

What was ironic is rethought and Gehry's "perspective" *is*
serious, refuting representation's "imitation" to rebuild a spatial perspective on the tradition of Renaissance architecture, thus deriving,
from what Celant aptly terms the difference of a "renaissance," a
revival of the problematic of perception, but from a phenomenological perspective rather than the objectivism of representation and its accompanying codes of architectural decor appropriated
by the neoclassicists. Also, notice that the organizing elements of
Gehry's installation are the simple 2x4s of conventional building, arranged according to the code, whereby the perceptual illusion is rendered by building's coded requirement of "diagonal bracing." Gehry,
then, refers the perceptual problematic to the building process, its
development as language. The irony of his slight of hand is that the
building code achieves this "illusion" of a spatial perspective of depth
while in fact the depth is "real," the discrepancy being the difference
of the two distinct build-ings. This reference of perspective to architecture also is in keeping with the Renaissance/renaissance theme

whereby Brunelleschi's discovery from just within the doors of Florence's Duomo, granting a "true" representation of the bapistry, the shock from its illusion, derived a corresponding architectural formalism. So what has come of this sense of postmodernism, the one that escaped Habermas's notice? Does it also escape the judgment of antimodernism, which Habermas so quickly cites? The answers here are straightforward but confusing.

In a recent interview in *his* issue of *Progressive Architecture* Gehry restates his defiance as an antipostmodernist, as Pilar Vilidas puts it in her introduction, "a modernist with a small 'm.' "[13] But all these "isms" can be misleading. Is it postmodernism that he means to disassociate himself from or really the neoclassicist version of architects such as Graves and Moore? The answer can be read in his interview:

> "I'm committed to the twentieth century," he says with typical defiance. "It's an anti-Post-Modernist thing."
>
> At the same time, he's troubled by the implications of his stance, or at the very least puzzled by them. "They say a painting done two hundred years ago is as important as a painting done today, so there's no progress, there's just art," he says, remembering a recent discussion he had with Graves and Moore. "So I counter that and say, 'Well, I agree with that, but there is change, and change leads to differences, and you build on things, and the world is a progression of some kind, good or bad, and we're related to the world, therefore we're in that same kind of progression. I'm interested in progress even if those other guys aren't. I mean progress in the scientific sense. You invent, you formulate ideas, they're slightly different, they come out of somewhere. It's not necessary that new is better. It's just that we're tied to a rollercoaster and can't get loose. I'm into this reality and I don't understand it."[14]

But he is clearly trying to understand it. And, judging by the work, Gehry is making progress. Our question is whether this progress can be viewed through, not a break with the past, the agenda of an avant-garde, but rather the telos of a science, of an inquiry tradition-bound. This would not be a science of the social upon which modernism focused its attention, but of "nature" such as initially provoked the question of perception in the Renaissance. But unlike Brunelleschi's experiments in perspective illusion, Gehry builds his illusions in "real" space, making them presentational rather than representational, compounding the difficulty of decoding spatiality.

Furthermore, is the "rollercoaster" LA, the challenge of Venturi's trip to Las Vegas, to understand the strip as a tradition? This understanding is clearly not utopian, the small *m* of his modernism, which includes its failures, not its rejection, an architectural "heterotopia"[15] immediately at odds with modernity. Is Gehry playing that double game of the "deconstructivist," employing the modern against itself to accomplish his purposes? Is this really the ruse that lies behind his puzzlement?

But here we are jumping ahead of the things themselves, the architecture. In the work can we locate the trace of those indices of a postmodernism, yet not stylized according to historicism: the importance of language, contextualism, and bricolage. Such a postmodernism would be, in the words of the movement's key spokesperson, Robert Stern, the "attempt to reconcile the modernist experience with the academic traditions of the earlier past of the century . . . notable for its marriage between ordinary, currently accepted building types and a sense of composition that elevates housing to the realm of art by virtue of its connections to the vernacular?"[16] With these questions in mind we now return to the work itself.

In 1980 LA saw the completion of Johnson/Burgee's Crystal Cathedral, a most elegant use of mirrored glazing over a white, interior lace of space-framing, a high-tech, modernist achievement of Gothic proportions, which with its price tag of $16 million attests to the monumental faith and resolve of its congregation. Its review in the December 1980 issue of *Progressive Architecture* declares it "the most talked of building of the year,"[17] and for a church whose roots go back to the roof of the snack-bar of the Orange Drive-in Theater, this building contains an *interior* space of definite spiritual significance. This is a place of spectacle and so the media have employed it. For this writer, who discovered it beckoning in the distance while searching for Disneyland, it was the parking facilities, complete with drive-up speakers, oriented behind the giant French doors that magically open Sunday morning behind the altar for those of the congregation who prefer the old traditions of drive-in religion, that brought my feet back to ground, to the asphalt of LA's ways. But from the vantage of hindsight it wasn't to be the Crystal Cathedral that proved to supply the needed mirror to LA's architectural psyche. Rather, it was a much more modestly scaled project, definitely nonmonumental, a mere residential remodel that also appeared on the cover of *Progressive Architecture* in the same year: Frank Gehry's Santa Monica home.[18]

So to settle this question of postmodernism in the terms of Venturi's question of LA, we must go home with Frank Gehry. That his house is provocative is evidenced by the bibliography of articles,

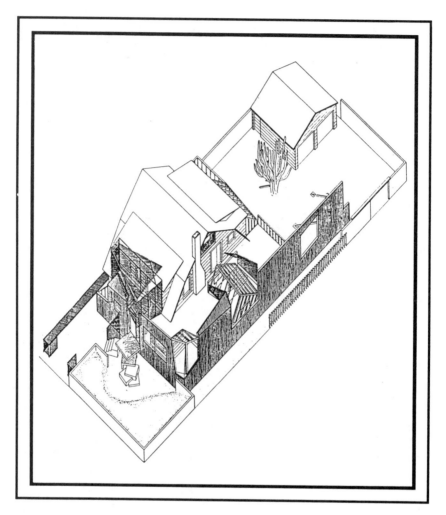

Figure 3

reviews, and letters to the editor in the local press that followed the
first year of its completion, 1978. Reactions to the image of the house
interestingly almost always prove to be quite visceral and initially
negative. I can remember quite distinctly the first time I actually saw
the house. Of course I was driving, headed for San Vicente, a main
artery of Santa Monica noted especially for its health-conscious jog-
ging set in their designer, warm-up suits running the grassed, medi-
an strip, fitting in well with the manicured look of the residential
neighborhoods. Coming around a corner to see the house's front
facade of irregular angles, corrugated steel siding, and chainlink fenc-

ing rising to and over the roof line is a disorienting experience. There is a spatial discontinuity; one is momentarily removed from the Santa Monica of comfortable, 1920–30, tree-lined neighborhoods. The house on its corner signals a spatial rupturing of place; it unsettles the ease of the gentrification of this once middle-class area. Initially you tend to hover between abject fascination, as with an accident, and wanting to quickly drive on. But we must stop and get out of the car. Ironically the garage around back is the only conventional structure; of course I parked on the street.

When examining one's initial reaction to the house it is hard to get away from the force of the corrugated siding. This is a building material not noted for its residential applications, at least not yet.[19] It is the wrapping material of the industrial park, the flotsam of the temporary structure, the siding of the shed not yet decorated.[20] Its use here in Santa Monica, on the corner of Ocean and 26th, confounds the viewer; how does one relate it to the residential dwelling? And then there is the "Cyclone" chainlink fencing, another building material common to industrial applications. But here Gehry uses it not as fencing material but primarily as an apparently nonfunctional, absurd screening of the second floor with a large section catapulting over the roof, not unlike the wrapping of home plate in baseball diamonds. When it comes to wood the front facade welcomes with a panel of raw, unfinished plywood set next to the front door where one would expect a door lite. The materials are "high-tech" but their use here constantly brings one back to the euphemism of this label. There is a casual, yet formal, order to the facade, but not one that allows transcendence of the materials and their roots in the environment. Unlike some "high-tech" architecture that strips the materials of these associations through a slickness of treatment or originality of metaphor, Gehry's application is straight architectural. They remain the building materials that they are; Gehry simply expands their application and bestows on them a definite aesthetic.[21] What at first appears inappropriate, ugly, and clapped together like any temporary structure, gives rise to a striking sense of formal rigor. The trapezoidal shapes of the facade, its window/skylights, the panels of chainlink, the arrangement of the stacked staircase all form a quite tight and complex sculptural composition in the constructivist tradition. But despite the rigor of the composition you do not forget the industrial park of LA, rather your eye is challenged to search out such order from within its facades the next time you are driving through. So the face of Gehry's build-ing mirrors the contemporary environs of the city rather than the homes of his neighbors: a "post&suburban" construction.

Peering through the mysterious fencing wrapping the second

story one finds the original house. Does this new facade simply serve to protect the old? Or is Gehry communicating a new orientation for residential design, a new question of function that such designing must face? As a remodel, the quintessential design problem for a builder, Gehry's house, originally 2100 square feet, gains an 800 square-feet addition, plus a 680 square-feet deck. But these statistics do not do justice to the transformation of the house. The new front facade accounts for very little of this gain in footage. Its purpose, as is the case with the wrapping of all three sides of the original house, is to be "read." The single family dwelling is to be understood through this association with its workplace counterpart, the spaces of the industrial park. When approaching the house for other than the first time, it is easy to imagine an interior filled with the stuff of the "shop": the parts, materials, and tools, all arranged around their processes and activities, the ongoing life of work. In this case the association would be the artist's studio, the "atelier", LA style.

Is Gehry telling us that the home is a place for creative growth and expansion, a home oriented to the flexibility required for changing activities, growth, and life itself? Does his facade announce a home built with the "industrial strength" needed to preserve the traditions of the nuclear family, to raise kids into the twenty-first century? That he has two sons and the house integrates so many elements of the playground, complete with catwalks and tunnels to and from the second-floor decks, would seem to indicate this importance of play. The chainlink fencing itself, the most playful, nonfunctional element of the facade, jutting up and over the original house's second story, is visually surprisingly tactile, an invitation to climb to the building's highest reaches, reviving those youthful adventures whereby the playground and the building site are seen as interchangeable. I can still vividly recall the sensations of a game of tag played out upon the skeleton of a freshly framed house, the rich smell of freshly cut Douglas fir and the ever-present fear of falling. That Gehry acknowledges inspiration derived from the unfinished state of developer-built houses indicates not simply the aesthetic failure with which these projects are generally clad, but also a retrieval of the structure's youthful possibility, a playful layering of a spatiality that resists closure.

Gehry states in an interview that the chainlink was the solution to the problem of finding a translucent material that was stronger than glass.[22] The aesthetic importance of this "glazing," however, must also be emphasized. One need only see a photograph of the house before the fencing was erected to see its integral place in the overall organization of the facade's layered spatiality. But it is the facade's playfulness that brings the adult back to sources, to the childhood state of curiosity and surprise, bridging the gap of generations. However, this reference to traditions is of the lived variety and pertains to the house's remarkable interior and its perceptual surprises.

Once inside Gehry's house one sees the full significance of the relation between the old and new. The original house of the 1920s remains; its siding and windows become the interior wall of the new kitchen, the old front door is just inside the new front door. One can either pass through the entrance way into the original living area or turn right and descend into the new kitchen along the side of the old house, which is whimsically floored in asphalt, tracing the old driveway, which never was. Gehry's sleight of hand is to bring the two historys, the 1920s and the late 1970s, into communication within a single structure. This communication operates on perceptual, spatial, and symbolic levels. The resultant structure, its dwelling, derives from this complex communication: a decidedly postmodern phenomenon.

Like Gehry's piece for the Venice Biennial this "remodel" works to place a perspective upon the past, to bring it into communion with the present. The two structures, the old and the new, initially transform each other through a synthesis of continual perceptual surprises. The illusion that Gehry plays with involves that of both perceptual perspective and expectation. The interior spaces open to each other and to the exterior, for instance the roof decks, in such a way to accomplish a quite pleasing sensation of surprise and warmth of layered enclosure with its quite delicate filtering of light through the alignment of windows and screening of wire glass and chainlink. Much of the interior's surprise is accomplished by the skewed angles of the new glazing and skylights, which converse throughout the resultant building. Its difference from the Venice Biennial installation is the relative complexity of its illusions and the recency of LA's past in comparison to Venice's, but this is the regionalist component to Gehry's version of postmodernism. Also, compounding the ambiguity of this question of traditions for Gehry is the attention to the symbolic level, which questions our expectations concerning dwellings upon the syntactic level of the building process itself, again the symbolism of the Venetian 2x4.

In the commentary and analysis upon this house, of which there is a great deal, the label of "deconstructivist" seems universally applied. The most recent, extensive analysis by Gavin Macrae-Gibson in his book *The Secret Life of Buildings* compares Gehry's accepted deconstructivism to the art of the American sculptor Gordon Matta-Clark, works like "Office Baroque," and "Bingo X Ninths," actual houses sliced up and exposed in various fashions.[23] But, as inviting as this comparison on the surface would appear, it is misleading. Gehry's approach to architecture is decidedly sculptural, but of the "additive" persuasion.

Constructivism lends itself to this work because of the medium: architecture, and in particular the examples employing standard framing construction. One simply needs to look at his models to see this. Gehry is a *builder,* and it is especially apparent in his house, which looks as if he himself did build it. While he did not, many decisions were clearly made on the site. That elements of the original house have been removed and elements of the new additions seem unfinished serves to reference the building process, its language, by which to further enhance the communication between the traditions of the old and the new. While some critics argue that his work appears to be in a figurative process of falling apart, I would point out that the symbolism of materials, which speaks of the temporary quality found in the environment of the "strip," refers not to deterioration but of rearrangement, being put together in alternative forms. Where Gehry does remove part of the skin of the old interior, some plaster and lathe of the original walls, it is a careful "deconstruction," a taking apart in reverse order to expose the syntax and mechanics of building itself. Nothing is ever lost or destroyed, the trace of the structure of the original is always preserved while transformed.

Any sense of "deconstruction," then, is not literal, as most would have it, and here Gehry differs from the work of SITE with their crumbling facades and exploded views.[24] However, what these two firms do share is the philosophical sense of "deconstruction" à la Derrida.[25] The "deconstruction" operates upon the conceptual level of significance. The question is metaphysical, a challenge to our assumptions about dwelling(s) as articulated space, and ultimately living in the contemporary world. The past enters Gehry's work as a tradition to both borrow and question. And the presence of this past is inescapable, the conventions of building at the syntactical level; closure is no longer a meaningful possibility. As dwellings are to serve the living process, they never were really susceptible to closure—that is, the evidence of remodels. In fact Gehry's love of leaving exposed the Douglas fir of standard framing lumber actually falls within the California tradition of exposed post and beam construction of such turn-of-the-century architect/builders as Maybeck, and Green and Green. What Gehry does is reverse the tendency of the Green and Green super bungalows, as in the Gamble House of Pasadena, to glorify the wood as fine furniture with their choice of mahogany and hand finishing. Gehry simply employs the standard materials of framing, fir, complete with the stenciled grading marks, and leaves them unfinished.

It must be noted that this use is not always economic, for the complexity of the structures so constructed are labor intensive, a carpenter's nightmare, as can be seen in the obliquely angled skylights of his Santa Monica House. But this use of materials updates this use of wood, which was always meant to convey a sense of casual informality and flexibility associated with California living. Gehry attempts to build according to this Derridean *différance*, actually designing in the deference of a completion. Here the only point of contact with such a strategy and Johnson's Crystal Cathedral is the remnant of the drive-in parking lot; without that the building would be fully closed upon itself, with the Gothic cathedral's arabesques of colored light from the stained glass' communion with heavenly light replaced by the transmissions of media television from within this sanctuary of mirrored glass.

For the architect working in LA, traditions come right to the edge of the present. Consequently, if one attempts to follow Venturi's question and deconstruct our assumptions about the context of building and living: that internexus of home, neighborhood, and city traced by the constant movement of the auto-motive, the postmodern emergence becomes decidedly ambiguous. Just this ambiguity of history in LA is exposed most forcefully again in the Venice Biennial exhibition with that difference of the 2x4s to which my eye could not adjust. This facade without its skin becomes its own historical reference, to the building process, to peripatetic perception, to the language of materials, and to the importance of the immediate past for the LA resident who must excavate its layers of significance, as do the Italian, but in LA without the depth of ages. So in Gehry's house how long does the eye take to accommodate to the difference of the nominal 2x4 in the new and the real 2x4 in the old, traditions, then, being such continuity in *différance?*

So back in my car heading toward San Vicente and downtown LA I think again of Pershing Square and the appropriateness of SITE's latest commission. Despite the competition of these art centers, LA the young upstart, they do understand each other. SITE's winning design based on an earlier design for Best products in LA called the "Parking Lot Showroom" where a parking lot is rolled out like a rug and the waves in the carpet before it lies flat become the entrances and glazing for the building. For Pershing Square the relation is reversed, the cars being put underneath and the park on top. These artists from Manhattan, one of the last places where persons can live without a car, do understand the mythology of LA and the essence of

Venturi's question. Looking over the surroundings passing by me I wonder how other regions of LA architecture will accept and develop the postmodernism of Gehry's antipostmodernism, indeed how such a deconstructive "double game" will translate to other regions of the country to supplant neoclassicism.

Notes

1. I want to thank my colleagues at Sonoma State University, Harold Alderman and Diane Romain, for their careful and helpful reading of an earlier draft of this paper.

2. *Googie: Fifties Coffee Shop Architecture* (San Francisco: Chronicle Books, 1986).

3. Robert Venturi, *Learning from Las Vegas* (Cambridge: MIT Press, 1986), p. xi.

4. Tim Street-Porter, *Freestyle: The New Architecture and Interior Design from Los Angeles* (New York: Stewart, Tabori, and Chang, 1986), p. 60.

5. *Progressive Architecture*, Oct. 1986, pp. 69–101.

6. Ibid., p. 70. See the catalogue for the show, *The Architecture of Frank Gehry* (New York: Rizzoli, 1986). Also, it must be mentioned that Gehry's work was the subject of an exhibition in New York in 1978 at P.S. 1, Long Island City, and the subject of an article in *New York* magazine, Oct. 23, 1978, called "California Corrugated," in which the author writes: "The choice of Gehry, rather than a New York architect, for the opener of an architecture series at P.S. 1, the showcase sponsored by the Institute for Art and Urban Resources, is significant, for Frank Gehry's work deals with questions like the juxtaposition of clashing objects and the nature of process—issues that artists confront often but architects rarely admit to. It is also significant in that it affords New Yorkers a rare view of work from the West Coast" (p. 96). This was one of the earliest critical articles on his work and in *New York*.

7. "California Corrugated," p. 36.

8. Hal Foster, *The Anti-Aesthetic* (Port Townsend, Wash.: Bay Press, 1983), p. 3.

9. See Charles Jencks, *The Language of Post-Modern Architecture* (New York: Rizzoli, 1977), p. 9.

10. Lawrence Weschler, *Seeing is Forgetting the Name of the Thing One Sees* (Berkeley: University of California Press, 1982), p. 152.

11. Ibid., pp. 147 and 61. That this is not easily accomplished can be seen in the account of his Venice Biennal work:

> Irwin merely outlined, with a piece of string stretched into a taut rectangle, the dapple of treefiltered light on a patch of ground. At that point he still felt he needed the string, not so much because he needed to leave a trace of himself as because he needed to mark that particular corner of ground as in some sense a heightened field. But many people mistook the string itself for the work of art ("When I point my finger at the moon, don't mistake my finger for the moon" is a Zen aphorism that Irwin is fond of citing). By mid-1976 Irwin himself was prepared to jettison—along with figure, line, focus, permanence, and signature—the very requirement of any overt activity of making as a necessary prerequisite for artistic viability. [p. 175]

12. *Frank Gehry: Building and Projects* (New York: Rizzoli, 1985), p. 182.

13. *Progressive Architecture*, p. 70.

14. Ibid., p. 98.

15. Michel Foucault, *This is Not a Pipe* (Berkeley: University of California Press, 1982), p. 4.

16. *American Architecture: After Modernism, A+U*, March 1981, p. 13, an extra edition guest-edited by Robert Stern. This collection includes Gehry's work, and in Stern's introduction within his taxonomy of postmodernism: irony, abstraction, and citation, Gehry is identified, along with Venturi, in the ironic category, the "de-constructions of Frank Gehry" (p. 28). Also of Interest is Stern's reference to a "progress" different from the standard modernist version but nonetheless pertinent to the postmodern sensibility. Both Gehry and Stern served as judges for the 1980 PA annual awards and their discussions of especially the Graves award-winning design is most revealing. See *Progressive Architecture*, January 1980.

17. *Progressive Architecture*, December 1980, p. 76.

18. *Progressive Architecture*, March 1980, pp. 81–85.

19. Interestingly Charles Moore used it on an interior wall of his own house above a staircase.

20. See Robert Venturi, Part II, "Ugly and Ordinary Architecture, or the Decorated Shed." Here Gehry employs the material of the shed as the facade itself, inverting the normal equation, whereby the original "Dutch colonial" house with its pink, shingled siding and gambrel roof becomes the hidden shed.

21. See, e.g., Richard Roger's work, Pompidou Center and PA Technological Laboratory and Corporate Facility, Hightstown, near Princeton,

N.J., also the interior for the Knohl International Showroom in Soho (New York) by Paul Haigh.

22. From Esther McCoy's essay on Gehry in his *Progressive Architecture,* October 1986, p. 75:

> Chain-link fencing fits both availability and absurdity. It was an answer, however, to a search that had plagued Gehry: where to find a translucent material tougher than glass. An office that could discover cardboard crating as a material for furniture is up to stretching from glass to chain link. In phase one it was used for screens, but in phase two the constructivist play began. Gehry said of the ten layers of chain link used at the Cabrillo Marine Museum, "The figures on the other side are ghostly. You can see into the souls of the people on the other side." Nothing is more ghostly than the cars inside the parking structure at Santa Monica Place; they shimmer into sight, then fade into ghostly presences behind the sea-colored steel links.

23. Gavin Macrae-Gibson, *The Secret Life of Buildings: An American Mythology for Modern Architecture* (Cambridge: MIT Press, 1985), pp. 1–29.

24. See *SITE: Architecture as Art* (New York: St. Martin's Press, 1980), pp. 7–17. Also SITE's more recent work, a McDonald's outside Chicago with the standard kit but with pieces left hovering, not quite together.

25. See Jacques Derrida, *Speech and Phenomena* (Evanston, Ill.: Northwestern University Press, 1973); *Writing and Difference* (Chicago: University of Chicago Press, 1978); *Of Grammatology* (Baltimore: Johns Hopkins University Press, 1976).

14

The Deceit of Postmodern Architecture

Diane Ghirardo
for Ghazi and Ferruccio

In the worlds of literary criticism, art criticism, and even linguistics, the argument for the last several years has been that something radically new has happened in the world of culture in general, and more specifically in literature, and this new, or postmodern condition, differs significantly in context and in the way it manifests itself from preexisting, or modernist, practices. Commentators usually identify architecture as one discipline most vividly dominated by postmodernism, and they tend to discuss architecture in tandem with the other arts, an approach that is fundamentally flawed. It is impossible to assess architecture with the same optic one might turn on literature, painting, or sculpture. For one thing, there is no way to decontaminate architectural and economic realities.[1] Every building erected has first been directly manipulated by bank officers, often leasing agents, developers, planning commissions, and local, state, or national political officials, and buildings continue to play a significant role in the environment long after they are completed.

My paper argues that the rupture from the modern movement in architecture happened long before the 1960s: prewar modern movement architecture, because of its associations with social-democratic housing projects, and its critical posture toward the dominant bourgeois culture and toward the social implications of construction, differed enormously from the commodified version that developed after the war. What the popular and architectural press persists in calling postmodern architecture marks a reversion to the use of conventional signs drawn from the history of Western architecture as a means for supplying the building with "meaning." More importantly, however, this position reinforces the prevailing belief that architecture is an art, and that it is illegitimate to ask questions about the source, purposes, social and cultural roles of a building, let alone its political function. Instead, contemporary architectural discourse focuses on the problem of "meaning."[2] Furthermore, the attempt to discuss architecture by reference to postmodernism in other disciplines aids and abets this process by continuing to treat architectural objects as if postmodernism enjoyed autonomous aesthetic significance in the landscape.

First, let us look briefly at some of the characterizations of postmodernist developments in architecture. For critics such as Hilton Kramer of the New Criterion, postmodernism represents a loss of quality, a dangerous slide from the dizzying heights of artistic autonomy into the quagmire of low or mass culture, which for Kramer is simply a monolithic agglomeration of kitsch—ultimately destructive not only of art but also of the minds and intelligence of the populace as a whole. The only possible response to this pernicious threat is eternal vigilance against any and all hints of degradation in high modernism's elevated standards.[3]

Kramer's position can be characterized as a new elitism, struggling to maintain the high cultural standards set by writers such as Joyce and Mann, artists such as Kandinsky and Klee, and architects such as Le Corbusier, Wright, and Marcel Breuer.

Others take a more positive view of these same architectural events: for them, postmodernism represents a salutary departure from precisely those constraints of high modernism that encouraged reverence for the art objects in its emblematic position as carrier of high, or elite, culture.[4] Postmodernism in this view is celebrated as an art that is populist, communicative, or nondogmatic.

Charles Jencks is the most prominent exponent of this view. Jencks and other enthusiasts of postmodernism perceive a relationship to mass culture and an emancipatory potential because of postmodernism's disjunction from the domain of high or elite culture—more precisely, because of its presumed immediacy and accessibility.[5] I make this comment with some misgivings, because writers such as Jencks attempt to confuse matters by defining postmodernism as both elitist and "popular"; despite these subterfuges, the avowed intention is to "communicate."[6]

For others still, the rupture represents a break from the critical tradition of modernism, particularly in its earliest phases, as a vanguard of oppositional cultural criticism. Critics such as Kurt Forster have voiced this concern over a period of several years in a number of essays; it is a view not unrelated to that of Jürgen Habermas, who argues that the formerly outrageous works of modernists have been recuperated and injected into the mainstream (especially through the universities); thus domesticated, they have lost their critical thrust.[7] Certainly the allegiance of conservatives to modernism such as

Kramer would tend to support this reading. It is worth noting that Kramer's support for modernism, and indeed the support of Jencks, Robert Stern, and others for postmodernism, seems predicated more on the canonic definitiveness of certain formal features than upon any oppositional political position (as found in modernism, for example). The closeness on a number of issues of this particular group of postmodernists, whom I have elsewhere described as being exclusively concerned with formal matters, to the political and aesthetic conservatism of critics such as Kramer, as well as to another "radical" wing in architecture (discussed later in this paper) is an important and troubling point to which I shall return.

While Kramer's position and those of Jencks and other formalists are based essentially on aesthetic issues, the last one, which speaks of cultural criticism and opposition, addresses art in its capacity to play an active and critical role in the life and culture of a society. In this view, persons respond to the products of the culture industry—mass or otherwise—largely passively and affirmatively. A critical art of whatever type would instead foster a critical awareness of the manipulative and administered character of the culture industry, and perhaps of broader phenomena of control in a late capitalist society.[8]

Turning now more directly to architecture, let me first respond to the widely held view that the rupture from modernism began in the 1960s with the stylistic programs of Robert Venturi and those who followed him. This group rejected modernism on many of the grounds cited above—that it was uncommunicative, dogmatic, exclusivist—but also because it was boring and dull.[9] The modern movement of which they spoke, the commodified post–World War II versions as developed in America, had little in common with the prewar movement, which, within some limits, maintained a critical posture toward the architectural culture, the social implications of construction, and housing. One thinks, for example, of the work of Ernst May in Frankfurt (including the Bruchfeldstrasse, Romerstadt, and Hohenblick housing projects), and that of Walter Gropius in Dessau, Bruno Taut, Martin Wagner and Gropius in Berlin, and the Dutch architects of the same period.[10] All these designers, and many others, made polemical associations between the new architecture and a radically transformed society in the wake of World War I. Germany was certainly the crucible for much of the modern movement, but Holland also sponsored modern architecture as part of a broader social and political agenda.

As a corporate architectural emblem and an instrumentalized aesthetic, which played a key role in the so-called urban renewal schemes (often a euphemism for "black removal," or the removal of the poor from potentially lucrative building sites in center cities) from the late 1940s on, the postwar version of modernism had virtually nothing in common with the contentious, polemical, and oppositional movement of the 1920s and 30s. In postwar America, the modern movement was institutionalized and shifted from a position of opposition to one of affirmation, indeed, to the emblematic representation of corporate, multinational capitalism we know so well. This transformation of architecture from opposition to corporate emblem in America parallels a similar transformation that occurred with Keynesian economics after World War II. During the 1930s the American business community opposed Keynesian programs that called for large-scale compensatory spending on the grounds that it was fiscally unsound and potentially threatening to the political and social order; but in the postwar period, business fashioned a compromise with deficit spending and developed a conservative, investment-oriented model of Keynesianism, which served its own ends. Corporate capital in America, in other words, recuperated both economic and architectural programs in a fashion that robbed them of their most important and critical thrusts.

It is easy to forget today that the modern movement of the 1930s constituted an attack on bourgeois architectural institutions, practices, and priorities, and that its adherents believed that they could effect major social transformations through their innovative aesthetic. As Alan Colquhoun argued nearly twenty years ago, when the modern movement rejected historical manifestations, their "theory was based on the belief that shapes have physiognomic or expressive content which communicates itself to us directly."[11] Indeed, the fact that during the Weimar Republic agencies and socialist city administrations sponsored so much of the new architecture lent some validity to this belief, and that the Nazis in turn suppressed the style seemed to testify to the transparency of the political message in the particular formal arrangements. They believed, then, that they would transmit not only a revolutionary formal message, but a revolutionary social message as well, grounded in praxis. This is the true locus of the rupture. In the conformist cultural politics of postwar America, architecture came to be seen as radically depoliticized: certainly during the cold war no architecture manifestly associated with leftist or communist political systems could have been adopted wholesale by corporate capitalism without first expunging those political associations.

The mechanism of the transformation of modernism from a politically charged, oppositional movement involved more than aesthetic issues. Hitchock and Johnson presented the so-called International Style as a purely aesthetic phenomenon in the 1932 exhibit at MOMA, but its adoption by corporate capital depended also upon the capital accumulation and concentration in America after World War II, and the penetration and exploitation of world resources.[12] The earliest patrons of the new style were commercial and manufacturing giants such as liquor, airline, tire, oil, metals, and food companies, department stores, and apartment buildings both for the poor and the wealthy.[13] Changes in the skylines of America's major cities diagram in telling and unambiguous form the changes in capital accumulation over the last forty years: the skyscrapers are now not only taller, but they also sport the signatures of banks, financial networks, and anonymous corporate giants no longer associated with a particular object or enterprise but with highly concentrated yet somehow anonymous accumulations of wealth and power. However profoundly conservative in political, fiscal, and social dimensions such institutions may have been (like the government of Mussolini's Fascist Italy), they have been eager to present a "modern" public face in buildings as well as in advertising campaigns and stock reports that suggest the cachet of the "new" and "up-to-date."[14] Modern architecture came therefore to be seen as generically "modern" and as lacking any particular political associations.

At the same time that the transformation of American skylines was underway, these architectural emblems of modernity traveled with other American cultural debris to the Third World, to Singapore, Hong Kong, India, and elsewhere, where they both displaced indigenous traditions and testified to the hegemony of international, American-based capital institutions. It is no irony that these very same corporations could turn around and embrace a postmodern aesthetic, not, in my view, because it "communicated" better than modernism, but because it was newer. Gerald Hines recently acknowledged that trendy designs by trendy architects simply lease faster and at higher prices.[15]

During the very same decades in which architecture was progressively drained of any critical content, when attention focused on increasingly empty formal games, major social and economic changes have taken place, not only in the United States, but also in other countries, and architecture, if it has responded at all, has responded with aesthetic affirmation, or in some cases, belated attention—for example, to some aspects of the energy crisis. On the whole, the profession has adopted the position that architecture consists of the manipulation of formal, symbolic elements: a position not dissimilar to that of structuralists who argued that the content of a text is not the actual story recounted but the form, and the relations between the words themselves. The appeal of structuralism for many postmodern theorists, such as Jencks and Paolo Portogehesi, rests precisely on this compatibility.

I am less concerned with what is discussed in the architectural world than what is not: the decision-making process; the impact of building upon the community in the widest possible terms; the role of others who participate in building, including city officials, leasing officers, bank officials, developers. Buildings are regularly treated as three-dimensional paintings, as objects of silent contemplation and as the product of those brave little form-makers, the architects. As I have observed elsewhere, builders and developers could not in their wildest dreams have designed a strategy of such academic and intellectual status that it would successfully direct analysis toward trivial matters of surface and away from much more vexing matters of substance.[16]

All too often, confronted with these observations, the architect responds that he or she is trained to produce forms, to design poetic spaces, and to release his or her creative potential. In this view, the artist/architect in modern society is engaged in an enterprise of independent self-expression: this is a distinctly modern characterization of the role of the architect, who traditionally and openly has been engaged in the task of legitimizing a whole range of authority structures in the Western tradition.[17] To deny that architects serve such authority structures today is naive at best. The profession attempts to carve out a distinct and highly limited area of responsibility, one in which architecture appears as an autonomous art that must remain uncontaminated by a world of construction where, as architects hasten to point out, they have no power anyway.

The view that architecture is an autonomous art espoused by practitioners who refuse to engage in or to acknowledge the political realities of the building process has an academic corollary in another postmodern theory currently being propounded by Daniel Libeskind, Alberto Perez-Gomez, Bahram Shirdel, Mary Alice Dixon-Hinson, and others.[18] At first blush it will seem strange to link a narrow professional practice in which the architect decorates surfaces with the complicated, often intelligent, and highly abstract theories of this group, whose strategy is more subtle but equally troubling. Yet the linkage can be explained.

The narrow professional who refuses to engage political issues often argues that society's building program comes to the architect so preformed, with so little room for maneuvering, and with virtually no power in the hands of the architect, that it is impossible for the architect to do anything but to retreat to the confines of his or her limited practice.[19] For the second group of academic postmodernists, the world in which the architect attempts to build is also profoundly corrupt: the commodification of the environment has touched building along with everything else. Architecture today is a "realm where 'angels once feared to tread,'" which has been transformed into "a supermarket of commodities, or worse, a whorehouse of opinions about them." Architecture's problem, in the words of Daniel Libeskind, is its "existence in a corrupt society, and how to resist this corruption."[20] By contrast with a commodified construction process, architecture, in the words of Perez-Gomez, "is the re-creation of a symbolic order, deployed in the most immediate and concrete universe of essences. . . . [It] is not the embodiment of information; it is the embodiment of meaning."[21]

In essence, this view responds directly to the world of practice I described above, a world in which architecture—which Libeskind describes as "that divine luxury of faith, highest crystallization of the material liberty of humanity, its imagination and spirit"—has been fatally contaminated by the sordid realities of late capitalism.[22] It may appear to be something of a paradox, however, that in essence, the response of the two groups is radically parallel. Both assert the autonomy of architecture, both take refuge in a position of absolute purity: the practitioner in the autonomy of the manipulation of formal elements of various derivations and admixtures, the academic postmodernists in the refusal to build at all, and in their turn to drawings, to models.

In the work of Dixon-Hinson, this refusal to build, this confinement of the task of the architect to the world of drawings and models, is characterized as a political act: the drawings of Daniel Libeskind, for example, can have no built parallel in the constructed three-dimensional world; they therefore rob architectural representation of its associations with power structures and with proposals for a future or recordings of a past.[23] I have no particular quarrel with this position: it is intelligent and takes seriously today's cultural condition. But this view constitutes more than a private poetics or even the lone political act of a designer such as Libeskind. It is more than a poetics: it is a politics, it is a pedagogy, it is a practice. And in the form in which it is presented to students and practiced by the followers of Libeskind, it accomplishes much the same ends as the narrow practice of which it is so critical: it permits the patronage, exploitation, development, and commodification to continue undisturbed. Why is this so? Because the object of attack for Libeskind et al. (the self-described "Circle"), is not architecture in the world, but architecture as some transhistorical mystical ideal.

Sharing the same conservative views of Kramer and the cynical architect who builds with indifference, the academic postmodernists paint themselves into a corner in which to practice at all in the corrupt world is impossible. But one problem with purity is that to be maintained, the germfree environment must remain intact: one infection will kill a patient too fragile to survive in the real world. And this academic postmodernism has already contracted its first viruses; the drawings and models produced by the Circle can have only one end, and that is in the marketplace their authors so disdain.[24] Libeskind's work appears in museums, galleries, private collections, and is sold as reproductions and in various kinds of publications; significantly, it is also "consumed" by his students in their own drawings, which bear a remarkable resemblance to the work of the master. Increasingly cut loose from traditional academic institutions, the architects who refuse to practice can survive only by forming their own schools—funded by high tuitions and hence available only to the very wealthiest of students.[25] There is some irony in a critique that exalts the perceptions of the uneducated savage, then savages the educated, only to propose as an answer another educational system.[26] If the purity of their system is to be maintained and the argument followed to its rigorous and inevitable conclusion, the academic postmodernists should leave architecture altogether, supporting themselves by means that have nothing to do with architecture and never selling their work, at best only acknowledging its detachment from the former "cultic" functions of art, in Benjamin's categories, by permitting it to be exhibited as fully secularized postauratic art.

At the same time, both the narrow practitioner and the academic postmodernist refuse to acknowledge the impossibility of complete purity: the degree to which each refuses to engage in the world, however corrupt and contaminated, is the degree to which both are finally inconsequential. More specifically, inasmuch as the theories of both specifically militate against any intervention in reality, both are complicit with that reality. Unfortunately, both are inconsequential in extremely noisy fashion, and in a way that directly masks the locus of "corruption": the one in the professional journals, the other in academic publications and journals.

Both offer concrete rewards to their followers: the practitioner willing to suspend any discourse about who builds what, where, for whom, and at whose expense, can be guaranteed an architectural practice anywhere from modest to prosperous, the recognition of his or her peers if he or she emerges as a particularly able form-maker and, in the best of circumstances, recognition outside the profession itself. Michael Graves and Philip Johnson are two of the best contemporary examples. The academic postmodernists, on the other hand, offer the possibility of constructing an alternate universe in which clear decisions have been made about what is real and valuable, what is architecture and what is not (drawings and models as described above are architecture, nothing else is), and the apparently wonderful liberty of producing this architecture in the complete absence of any political or social context with no constraints, no messy realities to intrude on the practice. Both claim to confront the contamination of political reality, but while Johnson acknowledges that he becomes a "whore" and embraces the corruption, Libeskind claims to be a virgin who turns his back on it and, in effect, pretends that it does not exist.[27] One might well argue the merits of the two responses, but there is little doubt that both total capitulation and total denial leave the object—the structure of building in the world of late capitalism— intact. Worse, neither is able to offer any grounds upon which to make distinctions between these or other positions.

One need not return to the redemptive hopes of modern movement architecture in order to combat the troubled situation today. Nonetheless, the focus of contemporary discourse in architecture seems significantly less important and certainly offers less potential for change than did modern movement strategies. The classic turn today is to seek "meaning" in design instead of the better world promised during the 1920s and 30s. The sense that architecture has suffered an irredeemable loss, which could be summarized in the problem of "meaning," buttresses current developments in practice and nonpractice, and also in architectural theory.

In the early nineteenth century, in Notre Dame de Paris, Victor Hugo traced the decline of architecture to its having lost its meaning: Hugo branded all postmedieval architecture as hopelessly vacuous.[28] Henry Adams, too, took medieval architecture as a model: in Mont St. Michel and Chartres, he voiced a more troubling fear. A fragmented modern society, he lamented, had lost its capacity to express cultural values and hopes of the sort conveyed by medieval Europeans in the great Gothic cathedrals.[29] More recently, Manfredo Tafuri has identified a loss of purpose in architecture both with the decline of symbolic meaning that was still characteristic of the precapitalist world and with the failure of modernist belief in the power of aesthetic innovation to inaugurate social change.[30] Finally, Alberto Perez-Gomez investigated the usurpation of symbolism in architecture by the functionalization of architectural theory, in particular since 1800. With the loss of poetic content, architecture's meaning was left to arid formal games and nothing more.[31] Both for Tafuri and for Perez-Gomez, the redemptive promises of the modern movement also proved illusory, and both appeal to the Middle Ages as a time when architecture was "whole."

All these views, it need hardly be added, hinge upon a highly idealized portrayal of the Middle Ages, and a profound antipathy to the consequences of the division of labor: in short, a rejection of the fundamental changes of modern life.[32] Part of their appeal to the community of students and practicing architects must rest upon the disarming simplicity of the view: if one could only return to practicing the craft as it was done hundreds of years ago, both the practice and the product would be more "meaningful." And, inasmuch as the change would take place in the soul of the individual architect without the necessity of any social transformations or collective action, it would also be a painless shift that would not call any social or political arrangements into question.

There are three general categories of responses among practitioners to the "crisis of meaning." The first locates meaning in the intervention of conventional signs drawn from the long history of primarily Western architecture. This might occur in the elevation (the eyelid dormers of Robert A. M. Stern's Bozzi house, which repeat the eyelid dormers of nineteenth-century Shingle Style houses, or his Tuscan order on a molded plinth for The Dining Hall at the University of Virginia), in the plan (Stern's plan for the Bozzi house is based on H. H. Richardson's plan of the Crane Library), or in the accretion of various decorative elements within and without the building. Among the many examples that illustrate this are the gothicizing elevation of Philip Johnson's Republic Bank in Houston; the vinyl flooring that simulates terrazzo pavement in Stern's Dining Hall again; or the Diane von Furstenburg boutique by Michael Graves.[33]

I have little sympathy for this particular way of evoking "meaning": to find "meaning" in the appliqué of historical elements seems curious to me at best; whatever a Doric column may have meant in ancient Greece, in ancient Rome, in Renaissance Italy, or eighteenth-century England, it hardly "means" the same thing today. In fact, I would suggest that it simply has a generic association with "antique" or, at best, "classical" to the average viewer today. This architectural language that purportedly communicates meaning better than modernism did is in fact more like Esperanto than any "natural" language, and what communication it manages occurs in fragments to a small, elite population. But what are the theoretical underpinnings of this definition of meaning? Rather spindly, as underpinnings go, but the argument seems to run as follows: the modernist box was empty of meaning and inexpressive; therefore, to restore meaning and expression to building, one must turn to the past, when forms still held meaning, and graft those forms onto contemporary buildings—a view that completely ignores the fact that "meanings" of the past do not automatically accrue to the building along with forms. The assumption seems to be that meaning resides in form, a notion parallel to that which Edward Said describes in the thought of the medieval Islamic school, the Batinists, who held that meaning was concealed in words.[34] This group of practitioners simply shuffle and reshuffle a deck of symbolic attributes to sell a product.

A second response to the problem of meaning has its origins in the early part of the twentieth century. For modern movement architects such as Le Corbusier, Gropius, Mies van der Rohe, and to the extent that it figured in their discourse, meaning derived from the design process itself, as well as from technology and materials. Inasmuch as materials, fabrication techniques, and production conditions had altered, the old styles lacked relevance; ornaments were simply useless excrescences. Gropius summarized the task of architecture in 1926:

> It is only through the constant contact with newly evolving techniques, with the discovery of new materials and with new ways of putting things together, that the creative individual can learn to bring the design of objects into a living relationship with tradition and from that point to develop a new attitude toward design . . . [which included] the organic design of things based on their own present-day laws, without romantic gloss and wasteful frivolity.[35]

Even more pointedly, Le Corbusier affirmed that "building construction is the purposeful and consistent combination of building elements. . . . Thus the architect has at his disposal a box of building units. His architectural talent can operate freely. It alone, through the building program, determines his architecture." These remarks followed his outline of the five points for a new architecture—five technical considerations available for the architect to use in design.[36] Even Frank Lloyd Wright, with his emphasis on the totally designed environment, relied upon an "organic" design strategy that included an "organic" ornamentation to give meaning to his work. Of course, for Wright, habitation was a central concern, one that has been lost in more recent evocations of a similar preoccupation with the design process itself as a source of meaning. The same concern preoccupied the modern movement architects I mentioned above: challenged by a series of real problems that confronted their society, including the adoption of new materials, housing shortages, how to adapt city planning to the automobile, among others, they did not believe "meaning" as such to be central. To the extent that they did discuss it, they often found "meaning" to be a result of the design process itself.

In its contemporary manifestation, one might best find a similar attitude expressed in the theories of Peter Eisenman and Daniel Libeskind, with the important difference that "meaning" has now become central. For Eisenman, particularly in his first four houses of the late 1960s, design consisted of the formal transformation of a cube from a simple state to a more complex one. In subsequent houses, Eisenman moved beyond the use of a simple cube to planes split and turned inside out as in House VI. Just as earlier modernists specifically identified meaning with the machine imagery, so Eisenman denotes the problem of meaning in the conceptual and actual loss of center in his houses after House VI. With "loss of center," he refers to what he perceives as the rupture in the relationship between humankind and object; through a process of decomposition (the reverse of "transformation"), Eisenman identifies within the architectural objects itself the cultural condition in which neither "intellectual systems [nor] physical artifacts are [capable] of being comprehended from some central place, either conceptual or tangible." The house, such as House El Even Odd, stands suspended between the two possibilities of either fullness or void, a condition of permanent indeterminacy.[37]

Eisenman's designs are less houses to live in, less sites of inhabitation, such as Wright's were, than conceptual models of his perception of the human condition at this moment, currently conditioned by his reading of Derrida. Here Eisenman argues that postfifteenth-century architecture, including modernism, operated under the influence of three fictions: representation (a billboard for a message), reason (a rational source for design), and history (a mirror for the Zeitgeist). Ensnared in a wider crisis of value, architecture ended up bereft of legitimacy. In response to this condition, Eisenman proposes a "not-classical" architecture, which only attempts to be a representation of itself, its own values and internal experience. Note that it is still a representation, however. In effect, he proposes an architecture that steps outside history with arbitrary, valueless starting points.[38]

Just as deconstructionist critics in literature engate in self-referential discourse about texts, explicitly rejecting any connection between a text and its social context, so Eisenman's proposal for architecture steps out of the lived world into a world of autonomous artifacts. Eisenman declares, along with Foucault and Derrida, that we have moved away from anthropocentric, and, as Derrida argues, moved away from the burdens of a centered subjectivity.[39]

A somewhat different attitude within this second category of responses to the "crisis of meaning" comes from Daniel Libeskind, who sets out from the position that architecture has been reduced and functionalized over the last two centuries—a process that he and others believe was launched by L. N. L. Durand and his codification of architectural types. Perez-Gomez concludes that only after Durand's work was it important for architecture to be "nice" or "pleasurable" rather than "meaningful."[40] For both Liebeskind and Perez-Gomez, the answer is to step out of the totalitarian system of contemporary design and, in Liebeskind's words, to undertake a "metaphysical quest" and to shake off the "rules, regulations, taboos, and accepted codes of orderly design."[41] Dalibor Vesely calls Liebeskind's drawings "deconstructive constructions," for of course Libeskind cannot shrug off the rules of structure and build houses; most of the work is confined to drawings or, in some cases, model "machines" of various kinds.[42] Vesely says that the object (or drawing) that results from this process "reverts to an infinite series of latent possibilities which are not peculiar to it and therefore entails its transformation. The object's conventional meaning then becomes entirely subordinate to its transformational meaning." Libeskind's drawings—geometrical projections in transformation—"create new meanings, they create new contexts in which meaning may occur."[43]

I emphasize the reference to "meaning" in the above passage because it quickly becomes clear that, like Venturi, Stern, and others, Eisenman, Libeskind, Perez-Gomez, and the Cranbrook school are engaged in a quest for "meaning" in architecture, meaning that has been lost and must be "restored." All are fully aware, and even sometimes acknowledge, that there is ambiguity to meaning; that, as Libeskind says, "things are dense,"[44] or, as Vesely says, the resultant drawings reveal a "bizarre interplay of forms, which can be identified, and meaning, which can only be anticipated."[45] But there are some troubling contradictions about Libeskind's position: for one thing, despite the acknowledgment of the ambiguity of meaning, Libeskind frames his indictment of contemporary architectural practice as follows:

> The process whereby the making of architecture comes to resemble a laboratory experiment reflects the general secularization of culture, whose symptoms include the relativization of meaning, the devaluation of tradition, and the virulent attack on all forms of symbolic, emblematic, and mythical experience.[46]

Though on the one hand acknowledging ambiguity in meaning, on the other he indicts relativized meaning; it would seem that it is the predominance of a particular meaning that Libeskind seeks to overthrow, but on behalf of another absolute meaning. The clues to his intentions are found in his writing, but more importantly, in his practice, where students become less fellow seekers after knowledge than disciples (and they are even called such in discussions), where his "analytical, interpretive, symbolic, and nonrepresentational" treatment of architecture becomes, itself, the new truth. Whatever permutations this new truth will undergo will be carefully guided and, as has become obvious, it is conceived as a closed discourse not open to question or criticism from without.[47]

The third category of responses is more difficult to characterize. In the simplest terms, architects in this category do not "pursue" the problem of "meaning"; they neither attempt to apply it to nor discover it in the buildings they design. Although diverse in other respects, these architects are united by the fact that "meaning" is not the overt object of their design; these architects seem to acknowledge that "meaning" is something set in motion but not conclusively shaped by the architect, and therefore its future cannot be anticipated or determined. What, then, do the designers seek? It differs from designer to designer, and indeed, from problem to problem, building to building. One might use the work of Frank Gehry, Mark Mack, Aldo Rossi, or a younger architect from Houston, Carlos Jimenez, as examples.

Take Gehry's Indiana Avenue houses: clad in prefabricated industrial materials, they exhibit three finishes—stucco, plywood, and asphalt shingles, all very mundane materials used forcefully and imaginatively. And, as in his own house, Gehry exposes joints, trusses, unfinished walls, and uses what almost seem to be "found" materials, including chain link fencing and corrugated metal."[48] Gehry implicitly acknowledges the carelessness, literally the artlessness, of construction today: on the other hand, he is not trying to find "meaning" in this, nor is he "representing" another condition—he is simply permitting this fact to be made manifest in some of his designs.[49]

Mark Mack (formerly Batey/Mack) was trained in Austria in a program of study that combined design and construction—a hands-on approach unusual in the United States. Given the limitations of the "craft" of construction today, Mack has nonetheless achieved extraordinary results using materials of the utmost simplicity and equally unpretentious design techniques, such as variations on the idea of eroding the cube and on combinations of the cube and the pergola. His materials—corrugated metal, cement block, concrete, adobe—are used with elegance and originality, and he confronts such questions as how to provide greater privacy in the living room (which is quite public in most California houses), or how to position the house on the site with the least disruption to the environment. Note that Eisenman too eroded the cube —but to a very different end: Eisenman is making a statement about his view of the human condition; Mack is simply designing a house.

Carlos Jimenez, a young Central American architect practicing in Houston, follows along the same lines: he adopts simple forms based upon suburban and rural types found in Houston and in Central America, as in his own house and studio, or he takes the language of an industrial shed and transforms it into a spatially rich setting for the Fine Arts Press. It is still an industrial building, but one that carries the language to its highest possibilities.[50]

In the work of Mack and Jimenez, one finds not only intelligence, unpretentiousness, and a thoughtful use of simple materials, one also finds buildings that have been beautifully crafted. And this crafting comes not from the skill of the builders, but from the care and attention of the architects to the design, so that when the drawings reach the builder, they need only accomplish their tasks with reasonable care.

One final example of an architect who also thinks a great deal about architecture but without, again, seeking to place "meaning" in his work is Aldo Rossi. One of his earliest major public buildings was the addition to the existing cemetery of the city of Modena, in northern Italy. A cemetery for Rossi is a house for the dead, indeed, a city of the dead. The elemental architectonic forms, as in the elegant stereometric volume of the ossuary, reflect his investigations into building typology. For him, it is a constant that remains beyond the particular and the concrete. The primary elements of architecture are repeated again and again in his work; Rossi is engaged in a determined search for the most essential and elemental forms, based on "repetition and fixation," as he recovers what he calls "the immovable elements of architecture." For Rossi, architecture provides a fixed scene for human events, and because the architect cannot foresee them, the architecture must stop short of anticipating the events. The grand stepped podium leading to the gymnasium in the school at Fagnano Olona is both an elegant introduction to the building and the place where class photographs are taken, a ritual as traditional and natural in the United States as in Italy. In the school at Fagnano Olona and in the one at Broni, one finds the same elemental forms; at Fagnano Olona, the rotunda, the cubic block, and the conical smokestack are grouped along the major axis and several subsidiary ones, almost as if it were a miniature city.[51] But like the full city, this school-city does not attempt to project meanings onto the inhabitants: rather it summarizes and transforms elements of the past for contemporary uses.

I have entitled this essay "The Deceits of Postmodern Architecture" because it is my belief that the discourse on meaning, the focus on surface, and the emphasis on explanatory systems drawn from other disciplines, draw a veil over the true facts and most troubling issues of the building process. What is not being discussed? There are at least two important issues: one is the problem of building as construction, and the second is the building as a politics, not just a poetic, of choices. Let me briefly discuss the first.

I recently visited several projects by the Miami firm Arquitectonica. Their buildings are a classic example of the triumph of image over substance. In just one simple case, a group of townhouses (the Haddon Street Townhouses in Houston), the third-floor bedrooms partially extrude from the building mass and are distinguished as a blue cube with windows. Because these cubes extrude, they have to confront the problem of water, rain, and the elements, much as a roof would. Either Arquitectonica did not care, or did not know how to deal with the problem: how to maintain the blue cube's crisp aesthetic effect and still make it watertight. The cubes leak, and leak extensively. They leak into the rooms and into the walls, so that the facade will literally rot from within. The roofs of all of the townhouses also had to be completely replaced within three years. Such design problems characterize other Arquitectonica work: a speculative office building in Houston, the Mesa Building (1984), reveals rusting stairs, stained stucco (again, the same problem; flashing is a recurring problem in their work)—in short, problems that are not trivial. But their buildings appear on the television show "Miami Vice," and the firm enjoys great success: as long as the buildings look good for the photographers, there seems little interest in anything more substantial. On the most basic level, the system of publishing and commissioning speculative projects in the United States facilitates a cavalier attitude about construction, as indeed does the educational system, which teaches the student to draw, but not to understand materials or construction.

But the second issue, building as politics, is far more troubling to me. To the degree that the current discourse focuses on "meaning" it avoids the very real issues of who builds what, where, for whom, and at whose expense. Edward Said talks about the worldliness of the work of art, about the fact that works of literature are produced in a particular historical moment, and they live on through other historical moments.[52] To study them or to think about then as autonomous artifacts is to miss their most meaningful dimensions. Is the persistent emphasis on "meaning" a way of avoiding the most difficult issues in the building process? In fact, I find that the architecture of today has not lost meaning, but perhaps the values and messages are not very satisfying: our choices about land use, the work place, property ownership, public spaces, speculation, financing, and even quality of construction do indeed express our culture's values of exploitive hedonism and profiteering. Putting it another way, architects offer highly circumscribed and fundamentally trivial definitions of "meaning."

But there are different problems of meaning to confront. What does it "mean" when the Los Angeles City Council seriously proposes transferring thousands of homeless in Los Angeles to a World War II–era barracks ship moored in the Los Angeles harbor while, at the very same time, the planning commissioner was embroiled in a dispute, not over the homeless, but with developers over the proliferation of minimalls (over two thousand of them in Los Angeles, each costing between one and two million dollars)?[53] What does it "mean" that an estimated two hundred thousand illegal refugees occupy unconverted garages (at an average of five persons per garage), while Toronto-based Manufacturer's Life plans a $160 million office tower in downtown Los Angeles?[54] What does it "mean" that downtown business interests and the Community Redevelopment Agency spent hundreds of thousands of dollars on a competition for the renovation of a downtown park, Pershing Square, while thousands of homeless slept on the sidewalks? In fact, part of the plan was to remove the homeless from Pershing Square, not by providing housing but by making the square inaccessible to them.

The central problems of urban morphology today concern the nature and direction of change in cities such as Los Angeles and Houston, and other cities that will be following their example and confronting similar problems. In neither of these two cities, let alone in others, do architects or their professional organizations seem to be participating in the decision-making processes that will determine the shape of the future. Discussions about meaning help to mask the central issues, and the relative powerlessness of the architect in the client-architect relationship encourages practitioners to remain passive. They often claim that it is impossible to act within the current constraints, but in effect all they do is justify their own unwillingness to act. Their efforts remain concentrated upon producing the fetishized objects of the average trendy practice, such as the endless loft conversions in New York City ministered to by a growing army of Ivy League architects.

The discourse on meaning seems to provide a convenient escape from the tough questions of urban and suburban development, urban form, and how to guide practitioners to become responsible participants in the shaping of the American landscape. Postmodernism has brought the issue of meaning to the forefront of discussion in the United States in the architectural community, has privileged this over other concerns as the central focus for the architect, and ultimately has contributed to the impoverishment and marginalization of the profession.

Notes

I have been working on the issues explored in this paper for some time. I presented parts or versions of this paper at Tulane University in 1986, at the Tampa Architectural Club, the University of Houston, and the University of Minnesota in 1987. The perceptive criticism and comments of these audiences helped clarify many of my points. Vincent P. Pecora read and commented on an earlier draft of this paper; I owe him a debt of thanks for the errors that he identified. Any remaining errors of fact are mine also.

1. The other arts are arguably no less contaminated. See Terry Eagleton, *Literary Theory* (Minneapolis: University of Minnesota Press, 1983) for an elaboration of this viewpoint.

2. Meaning surfaces in most contemporary discourse about architecture, but for an acute example see Gavin Macrae-Gibson, *The Secret Life of Buildings* (Cambridge: MIT Press, 1985), and my review, "Visions and Revisions," *Design Book Review,* 10 (Fall 1986): 57–59. See also Alberto Perez-Gomez, *Architecture and the Crisis of Modern Science* (Cambridge: MIT Press, 1983), esp. pp. 3–7.

3. Hilton Kramer, "The Whitney's New Graves," *The New Criterion* (September 1985): 2.

4. See Stanley Aronowitz, *The Crisis in Historical Materialism* (South Hadley, Mass.: Bergin and Garvey, 1981), and Leslie Fiedler, *A Fiedler Reader* (New York: Praeger, 1981).

5. Charles Jencks and William Chaitkin, *Architecture Today* (New York: Braziller, 1982), p. 12.

6. Jencks, *Architecture Today,* p. 16.

7. See Kurt W. Forster, "Traces and Treasons of a Tradition," in P. Arnell and T. Bickford, *A Center for the Visual Arts, The Ohio State University Competition* (New York: Rizzoli, 1984), pp. 135–39; Jürgen Habermas, "Mod-

ernity—An Incomplete Project," in Hal Foster, ed., *The Anti-Aesthetic: Essays on Postmodern Culture* (Port Townsend, Wash.: Bay Press, 1983), pp. 3–15.

8. For a thorough and provocative exploration of this point, see Richard Wolin, "Modernism vs. Postmodernism," *Telos*, 62 (Winter 1984–85): 2–29.

9. Robert Venturi, *Complexity and Contradiction in Architecture* (Cambridge: MIT Press, 1977); Robert Venturi, Denise Scott-Brown, and Stephen Izenour, *Learning from Las Vegas* (Cambridge: MIT Press, 1972).

10. See Barbara Miller Lane, *Architecture and Politics in Germany 1918–1945* (Cambridge: MIT Press, 1985), esp. pp. 87–124; Ronald Wiedenhoeft, "Workers' Housing as Social Politics," in *VIA IV: Culture and the Social Vision* (Cambridge: MIT Press, 1980), pp. 112–25.

11. Alan Colquhoun, "Typology and Design Method," in Alan Colquhoun, *Essays in Architectural Criticism* (Cambridge: MIT Press, 1981), pp. 43–50; the citation is on p. 48.

12. Henry-Russell Hitchcock and Philip Johnson, *The International Style: Architecture Since 1922* (New York: Norton, 1932).

13. One thinks of Ludwig Mies van der Rohe's Seagram Building in New York (1954–57); Philip Johnson's Pennzoil Building in Houston (1976); Skidmore Owing and Merrill's One Whilshire Building in Los Angeles (1964) and their Alcoa Building in San Francisco (1964). One could chart the financial topography in the United States over the last hundred years by examining the patronage of the skyscraper in major cities.

14. Diane Yvonne Ghirardo, "Italian Architects and Fascist Politics: The Rationalists' Role in Regime Building," *Journal of the Society of Architectural Historians*, 39 (May 1980): 109–27.

15. Victoria Geibel, "In Hines' Sight," *Metropolis* (March 1987): 38–41, 55–57.

16. Diane Yvonne Ghirardo, "A Taste of Money: Architecture and Criticism in Houston," in *Harvard Architecture Review*, 6, pp. 88–97.

17. For a sophisticated modern view, see Albert Perez-Gomez, "Abstraction in Modern Architecture," in *The Carleton Book* (Ottowa: Carleton University, 1986), pp. 182–93; and *Architecture and the Crisis of Modern Science*, esp. pp. 3–14, 323–26.

18. In addition to the publication already cited, see Perez-Gomez, "Architecture as Drawing," *Journal of Architectural Education*, 36/2 (1982): 2–7. For the work of Mary Alice Dixon-Hinson, see her article "Vico's Discovery," *Volumezero*, pp. 2–15, and "Erasing the Ghost of Perrault," *Harvard Architecture Review, 5: Precedent and Invention* (New York: Rizzoli, 1986), pp. 80–95. For Daniel Libeskind, see his publications: *Between Zero and Infinity* (New York: Rizzoli, 1981); *Chamber Works, Architectural Meditations on Themes from*

Heraclitus (London: Architectural Association, 1983); *Theatrum Mundi* (London: Architecture Association, 1985); "Notes for a Lecture: Nouvelles Impressions d'Architecture," *AA Files*, 6 (1983): 3–13; "Colloquium: Architecture and Abstraction," *Pratt Journal of Architecture: Architecture and Abstraction*, 1 (1985): 58–63.

19. Many contemporary architects argue about this view; Thom Mayne adopted such a position at a session on housing/houses at the annual meeting of the Association for Collegiate Schools of Architecture in March 1987.

20. Daniel Libeskind, "An Open Letter to Architectural Educators and Students of Architecture," *Journal of Architectural Education*, 40/2 (Spring 1987): 46.

21. Alberto Perez-Gomez, "Architecture as Embodied Knowledge," *Journal of Architectural Education*, 40/2 (Spring 1987): 57.

22. Libeskind, "Open Letter," p. 46.

23. Dixon-Hinson, "Perrault," pp. 90–91; also, lecture at Southern California Institute of Architecture, March 1987.

24. *Chamber Works* is a series of prints by Libeskind sold as a set with essays by Libeskind and prominent theorists and practitioners; other originals are sold regularly. The contradiction is clearly troubling, but even in a public forum, Libeskind refuses to answer questions—or perhaps is unable to—about any aspect of his program; "Points of Reference: UCLA Architecture Forum," April 2, 1987.

25. Architecture Intermundium was launched in Milan in the fall of 1986 by Libeskind. Although extensively advertised as a school, at the UCLA forum Libeskind denied that it is a school—even though the students pay a fee of several thousand dollars to attend for one year.

26. Libeskind talks of being a "monk," or a "medieval mason," and his JAE article (n. 20, above) is an indictment of current architecture schools based upon a rather foggy view of history lost in the mist of an idealized past.

27. See *The Charlottesville Tapes*, commentary by Jacquelin Robertson (New York: Rizzoli, 1985), p. 19; Libeskind's response is, in effect, equally cynical.

28. Victor Hugo, *Notre Dame de Paris*.

29. Henry Adams, *Mont St. Michel and Chartres* (Princeton: Princeton University Press, 1981). See also his *The Education of Henry Adams* (New York: American Heritage Library, 1988).

30. Manfredo Tafuri, *Architecture and Utopia: Design and Capitalist Development* (Cambridge: MIT Press, 1976).

31. Perez-Gomez, *Crisis*, p. 11.

32. This is of course less true of Adams, who was prepared to accept the changes if only he could begin to identify the axis of change.

33. For the work of Michael Graves, see K. Wheeler, P. Arnell, T. Bickford, and Michael Graves, *Buildings and Projects 1966–1981* (New York: Rizzoli, 1982); for Robert A. M. Stern, See P. Arnell and T. Bickford, *Robert A. M. Stern, 1965–1980* (New York: Rizzoli, 1981).

34. Edward Said, *The World, the Text, and the Critic* (Cambridge: Harvard University Press, 1983), esp. pp. 1–53.

35. Walter Gropius, "Principles of the Bauhaus," in U. Conrads, ed., *Programs and Manifestoes on 20th-century Architecture* (Cambridge: MIT Press, 1970), p. 95.

36. Le Corbusier and Pierre Jeanneret, "Five Points Towards a New Architecture," in Conrads, *Programs,* p. 101.

37. Peter Eisenman, *House X* (New York: Rizzoli, 1983); *Five Architects* (New York: Rizzoli, 1975).

38. Peter Eisenman, "The End of the Classical: The End of the Beginning, the End of the End," *Perspecta 21* (Cambridge: MIT Press, 1984), p. 167.

39. Michel Foucault, *The Order of Things* (New York: Random House, 1973); Jacques Derrida, "The Ends of Man" in *Margins of Philosophy* (Chicago: University of Chicago Press, 1982); but esp. the critique by Richard Wolin, "Modernism."

40. Perez-Gomez, *Crisis,* p. 299. See also my assessment of postmodernism, "Past or Post Modern in Architectural Fashion," *Telos,* 62 (Winter 1984–85): 187–96.

41. Libeskind, *Zero,* p. 27.

42. Dalibor Vesely, "The Drama of the Endgame," in *Between Zero and Infinity,* p. 105.

43. Vesely, "Endgame," p. 105.

44. Libeskind, *Zero,* p. 27.

45. Veseley, "Endgame," p. 105.

46. Libeskind, *Zero,* p. 27.

47. This became painfully apparent at the UCLA symposium, published in 1987 in the *UCLA Architecture Journal.*

48. *Frank Gehry* (New York: Rizzoli, 1986); Kurt Forster, "California Architecture," *UCLA Architecture Journal,* 1986) esp. pp. 13–19.

49. See esp. "Four Houses," *Architectural Record* (November 1985), pp. 132–43; and Forster, "California Architecture," esp. pp. 11–13.

50. See the article "Architect's Studio and House," *Architectural Record* (March 1986), pp. 124–27.

51. Aldo Rossi, *A Scientific Autobiography* (Cambridge: MIT Press, 1981); P. Arnell and T. Bickford, eds., *Aldo Rossi: Buildings and Projects* (New York: Rizzoli, 1985). See also the unpublished lecture by Kurt Forster at the USC symposium on criticism (April 1986).

52. Said, *The World*, esp. pp. 35–36.

53. "Plan to Keep Homeless Afloat," *Los Angeles Herald*, June 24, 1987; "City Mini-mall legislation creates major controversy," *Los Angeles Times*, June 27, 1987.

54. "Garages: Immigrants In, Cars Out," *Los Angeles Times*, June 24, 1987.

Part VI

The Politics of
Postmodernism

15

Power, Discourse, and Technology: The Presence of the Future

Stephen David Ross

To write on "postmodernism"[1] confronts the twin obstacles that we are still unsure how to think of modernism and by no means clear about how to think of its future. "Modernism" and "postmodernism" bear different meanings in relation to advertising, architecture, film, literature, painting, and philosophy. To think of the future is a function of how we think of the past, and "modernism" in relation to this century's art is very different from a "modernism" that goes back to the Enlightenment.

Among the dominant figures that characterize "postmodernism" are the recuperation of excluded voices and the image of a future to be achieved in the demise of modernism. Yet discussions within "postmodernism" have already begun to establish their own exclusions—I list just a few: modernism, humanism, mastery, teleology, representation, reason, instrumentality, and technology. The nature of this exclusion, especially in relation to instrumentality and technology, faces "postmodernism" with a divided relationship to its future—one that can be relevant only in the mode of representation and without which representation would be without meaning.

There can be found in the American pragmatists, whose views bear so many affinities with "postmodernism," a different sense of the future and of the instrumentality necessary to its achievement. Instrumentality, teleology, and technology are divided moments, risky and experimental, capable of including their others within themselves, hostile to the perfectibility that too frequently characterizes both modern rationality and the Greek sense of *technē*, local forms of rational practice. Here emphasis may be laid, not on the image of control within technology, but on that of disruption, a figure central within "postmodernism." What I wish to consider here, in the shadow of the question of the future, is whether "postmodernism" goes far enough in disrupting its own tendency toward canonicity, whether it lacks political force because it has too thin a relationship to its future. The question I wish to raise is that of technology and the future in the context of the perilousness of every relation involving power and desire.

I

Among the themes that define "postmodernism," two closing ideas found in Foucault's major works play a fundamental role. One is concerned with power, the other with the subject:

> What political status can you give to discourse if you see in it merely a thin transparency that shines for an instant at the limit of things and thoughts? Has not the practice of revolutionary discourse and scientific discourse in Europe over the past two hundred years freed you from the idea that words are wind, an external whisper, a beating of wings that one has difficulty in hearing in the serious matter of history?[2]
>
> Since man was constituted at a time when language was doomed to dispersion, will he not be dispersed when language regains its unity? . . . Ought we not to admit that, since language is here once more, man will return to that serene nonexistence in which he was formerly maintained by the imperious unity of Discourse? Man had been a figure occurring between two modes of language; or, rather, he was constituted only when language, having been situated within representation and, as it were, dissolved in it, freed itself from that situation at the cost of its own fragmentation: man composed his own figure in the interstices of that fragmented language.[3]

"Postmodernism" includes three major themes defined here by Foucault: the intimate relationship between power and truth, the fragmentation of discourse, and the disappearance of the subject.

Two of these ideas are not new, but go back to the eighteenth century, to the point at which "man" was constituted a sovereign subject of rational discourse. The inseparability of power and truth and the disappearance of the subject are themes that characterize Hegel's *Phenomenology*. Theoretical knowledge is but a moment in the development of practical freedom. With its culmination, Spirit will overcome the alienation that characterizes the history of the subject. What replaces it are the great forms of recollection described in the closing images that define Absolute Spirit:

Since its accomplishment consists in Spirit knowing what it is, in fully comprehending its substance, this knowledge means its concentrating itself on itself, a state in which Spirit leaves its external existence behind and gives its embodiment over to Recollection. . . . The goal, which is Absolute Knowledge or Spirit knowing itself as Spirit, finds its pathway in the recollection of spiritual forms as they are in themselves and as they accomplish the organization of their spiritual kingdom.[4]

Absolute Knowledge is the close of the epoch in which the Subject defined itself through another, and begins an epoch in which it defines itself through itself, by recollecting its own history:[5]

In thus concentrating itself on itself, Spirit is engulfed in the night of its own self-consciousness; its vanished existence is, however, conserved therein; and this superseded existence— the previous state, but born anew from the womb of knowledge—is the new stage of existence, a new world, and a new embodiment or mode of Spirit. Here it has to begin all over again at its immediacy.[6]

The dominant images that describe the close of the march of Spirit are recollection and repetition and the disappearance of the oppositions that have characterized the incipient moments of the dialectic. There is a famous aporia present in this conjunction, expressed by Arendt as the abolition of the forces that have defined the movement of history.[7] More striking, however, and so fundamental to Hegel's theory as to characterize many otherwise divergent interpretations, is the sense of an absolutely new beginning conjoined with an extraordinary emphasis on recollection. In this sense, thought is always after the fact, and moves into the future with its face resolutely directed toward the past. The most famous words on this subject are in *The Philosophy of Right:*

When philosophy paints its grey in grey, then has a shape of life grown old. By philosophy's grey in grey it cannot be rejuvenated but only understood. The owl of Minerva spreads its wings only with the falling of the dusk.[8]

The issue, unresolved by Hegel, is of the situation of the present, between past and future, from within an emergent view of both practice and theory. The relationship of Spirit to its future, even from within its culmination, remains enigmatic, since the only form of understanding that allows for the synthesis of its divided moments is recollection. Even the infinite task of recollecting the past from within an emergent future is always too late. The circles of recollection transform the past but have no overt practical relation to the future. Foucault confronts the same aporia, which many of his critics have mistakenly regarded as nihilistic. His method is entirely historical, yet the form of understanding it provides—concerned with power—is practical, directed toward the future.[9] Here, despite their deep affinities, there is a fundamental difference between the continental and pragmatist post-Hegelian strains. The former is characterized by a deep ambivalence toward the future, a consequence of a profound nostalgia for the past. As in Hegel, so in Foucault and most of the other "postmoderns"—Derrida, especially—the future confronts us with an absolute abyss, overcome only by a certain nostalgia, strikingly manifested in Heidegger's image of a future:

> One essential way in which truth establishes itself in the beings it has opened up is truth setting itself into work. Another way in which truth occurs is the act that founds a political state. Still another way in which truth comes to shine forth is the nearness of that which is not simply a being, but the being that is most of all. Still another way in which truth becomes is the thinker's questioning, which, as the thinking of Being, names Being in its question-worthiness. By contrast, science is not an original happening of truth, but always the cultivation of a domain of truth already opened, specifically by apprehending and confirming that which shows itself to be possibly and necessarily correct within that field. When and insofar as a science passes beyond correctness and goes on to a truth, which means that it arrives at the essential disclosure of what is as such, it is philosophy.[10]

Throughout all these originary forms, there is an ambivalence toward the practical future that is striking given Heidegger's emphasis on the primordiality of time.[11] None of these forms is practical, concerned with influencing, even controlling the future. None of these forms is instrumental. All may be read as nostalgic rather than as future-directed, disclosive rather than disruptive.

A more striking expression of Heidegger's denial of the *practical* and *instrumental* future can be found in *Being and Time:*

> *Authentic Being-towards-death—that is to say, the finitude of temporality—is the hidden basis of Dasein's historicality.* Dasein does

not first become historical in repetition; but because it is historical as temporal, it can take itself over in its history by
repeating.[12]

Even where repetition is never the same, futurity is emergence
but not instrumentality. There is neglect of the movement of the
present *toward* the future—a relation that is traditionally regarded as
instrumental. Here instrumental practice is as disruptive as it is repetitive. Practical being toward the future is toward the finite
vicissitudes of life as much as death, caught up in the terror of disruption but faced with the practical imperative to undertake action. There
is an inescapable tension between a historical awareness, even constantly emergent, and an instrumental awareness that intervenes in
the future, however aware it must be of its history. What is missing in
the nostalgic view is a rich enough sense of the disruptions and
fragmentations that belong to the instrumentality of both science and
technology. What is missing in most views of modern technology is a
deep enough sense of the history of power.

II

To emphasize the future is to emphasize both power and practice. It is notable that technology is not included in the above list of
originary ways in which truth happens, for it is included in Heidegger's most famous essay on technology: "Technology is a mode of
revealing. Technology comes to presence in the realm where revealing and unconcealment take place, where *aletheia*, truth, happens."[13]
Technology is a form of truth. Modern technology is also a form
of truth, characterized not by "a bringing-forth in the sense of *poiēsis*,
[but] is a challenging, which puts to nature the unreasonable demand
that it supply energy which can be extracted and stored as such."[14]
This conception of modern technology shares the ambivalence toward the future that characterizes much of post-Hegelian continental
thought. Both notions, in *poiēsis* and modern technology, contain
unmistakable references to the future, the one a "bringing-forth," the
other a "storing energy" supplied by nature. The image in relation to
poiēsis is one of originariness and production; the image in relation to
modern technology is one of storage and repetition. Yet why is it
unreasonable that nature should supply not only energy, but forms
and materials, that can be stored for the future? And why is instrumentality a less originary form than art, especially since it points
directly at the unknown future? Heidegger's answer is that modern

technology drives on "to the maximum yield at the minimum expense."[15] "Regulating and securing even become the chief characteristics of the revealing that challenges"—that is, modern technology.[16] The images are mechanical: "unlocking, transforming, storing, distributing, and switching about. . . ."[17] Modern technology creates a machine, all of whose parts lock together.

Heidegger rejects the view of technology as mere instrumentality on the grounds that it fails to grasp the unconcealment inherent within technology, but he rejects as well the instrumentality in modern technology. Instrumentality is associated primarily with antecedent norms, with technical perfectibility. A natural response to such a view is that it is the *business* of the future to be dangerous.[18] In *The Discourse on Language*, Foucault speaks of the "particular, fearsome, and even devilish features" of discourse.[19] Yet when he asks, "What is so perilous, then, in the fact that people speak, and that their speech proliferates? Where is the danger in that?,"[20] he answers not by reference to the future, where danger threatens, but to the regulations of the past:

> I am supposing that in every society the production of discourse is at once controlled, selected, organized, and redistributed according to a certain number of procedures, whose role is to avert its powers and its dangers, to cope with chance events, to evade its ponderous, awesome materiality.[21]

If there is a reference here to the future, it lies within the phrase "chance events." Otherwise, Foucault's sense of the danger of discourse lies within the rules that have constrained its powers. Nevertheless, the indeterminateness of the future faces us in all our practical undertakings, but especially in politics and technology: a future filled with chance dangers and unforeseeable contingencies. The future is at once the presence and disruption of rules.

Could it be that Heidegger's rejection of the instrumentality in modern technology and of the originariness of science is due to the efforts of science and technology to control the future? And if this is so, how can we answer except as James and Dewey did, that anything other than such an attempt is absurd? Is there a fear of the future that corresponds, within the "postmodern" emphasis on finiteness, to what it regards as the ontotheology of the tradition? If there is an instrumentality that faces the future without historical awareness, is there analogously a historical thinking that denies its own violence toward the future? Nostalgia for the past replaces nostalgia for the unconditioned, producing a nostalgia for the future.[22]

III

The question common to postmodernism and technology is of the presence of the future. In this sense, both are practical, and there is no escape in human life and experience from such practicality. In this same sense, to recognize, along with Foucault, that power is everywhere[23] is to recognize the insistent relativity of the future, not only the future of the present but of the futures of the past that occupy every history. This futurity of the past is fundamental as well as recurrent throughout Hegel's *Phenomenology*. Yet the future of the present is found there only in its absolute unintelligibility, while practical judgment, including technology, requires the intelligibility of a future in which any rule may be broken. The paradox of modern technology is that it claims in the guise of science to bring the future under the rule of instrumentality, while it is both largely devoid of historical awareness and the primary source of the disruptions that will falsify any expectations of the future. It follows that instrumentality is no more perfectible then are art and truth. Practice—including all forms of instrumentality and technology—lies imperfectibly between past and future.

It is suggested that there is, within an emergent view of the future, emphasizing incommensurateness and disruption, a nihilism without rules. The suggestion, which has skeptical undertones, is laudable if the absence of rules means the absence of oppression. The future is open to the disruption and cancelation of every rule including the forceful presence of oppressive rules. The promise of the future is that every regulation is finite. The corresponding danger within the limits of regulation is that practice will emerge before us in its naked unintelligibility. Universal rules mask the indeterminatenesses of practice—that is, of politics—behind the oppressiveness of repetition. To abandon repetition is to face the future with the responsibility for its construction without the regulation provided by the past. If between past and future the present is a ruleless disruption, then practice loses its intelligibility. In fact, every present is filled with rules and dominations, with manifold oppressions, facing the disruptions of an emergent future. Historical recollection presents us with ever-changing stories of the disruptions of the past. The gulf between these and our present relationship to our own future is the focal center of instrumentality.

Modern technology is permeated by the paradox that it would achieve control over the resistant and perilous future by means of rules, while it is the origin of the most violent disruptions in contemporary life. It promises repetition but presents convulsion. Yet convulsion and disruption are themselves repetitious. This circularity makes the future intelligible, and demands of us knowledge of a history that is never repeated—a knowledge that modern technology itself does not require.

Modern technology is paradoxical and self-refuting to the extent that it denies both its past and its future disruptiveness, sometimes in the name of efficiency, sometimes in the name of science. Technology in general is not analogously paradoxical, because it does not promise an equivalent form of instrumentality. There is, in the Greek sense of *technē*, the idea of an end independent of both the past and future, at least determinate in advance. This sense of *technē* introduces the notions of perfectibility and measure into technology, notions dominant within much of modern technology's sense of itself. In this sense, *technē* both denies its disruptive relationship to the future and the effects of past powers upon its own techniques. It presents us with a defective sense of instrumentality. Collingwood calls this sense of an end separate from the means that produce it "craft."[24] He does not consider its relationship to technology. Many writers have suggested that modern technology is dominated by a vision of an instrumentality that is devoid of both history and emergence. The reality is quite different.

The Greek sense of *technē*, in which the end is both separate and independent of the means, is found in both Aristotle and Plato. This image of practice as technique has been repeated throughout the Western tradition, frequently in the name of science, more recently in the name of technology. Yet just as it is inadequate in relation to art, it is inadequate to practice in general and to technology in particular. I take technology to be the material side of practice, concerned with means that define the future. On this reading, the openness of the future both contaminates every technique with disruptions and cancelations and is a consequence of the disruptions within material practice. Even the ideal of a small technology that would maintain a harmony between the human and natural worlds is caught up in the paradox of rules: the greatest of human achievements works by disruption and revolution. This paradox expresses the deepest truth of practical judgment, the reason why politics is the most disruptive of the forms of human life. Power is irresistibly disruptive, even while it exercises authority. Perfectibility is as irrelevant to technology as it is to reason.

IV

The History of Sexuality, Volume I is, like its successor volumes, ostensibly about sexuality and desire. It is, however, explicitly about power as none of the others are. What Foucault says about power deserves application to technology:

> It seems to me that power must be understood in the first instance as the multiplicity of force relations immanent in the sphere in which they operate and which constitute their own organization; as the process which, through ceaseless struggles and confrontations, transforms, strengthens, or reverses them; as the support which these force relations find in one another, thus forming a chain or a system, or on the contrary, the disjunctions and contradictions which isolate them from one another; and lastly, as the strategies in which they take effect.[25]
> Power is everywhere; not because it embraces everything, but because it comes from everywhere.[26]
> —Power is not something that is acquired, seized, or shared, something that one holds onto or allows to slip away; power is exercised from innumerable points, in the interplay of non-egalitarian and mobile relations.
> —Relations of power are not in a position of exteriority with respect to other types of relationships (economic processes, knowledge relationships, sexual relations), but are immanent in the latter. . . .
> —Power comes from below; that is, there is no binary and all-encompassing opposition between rules and ruled at the root of power relations. . . .
> —Power relations are both intentional and nonsubjective. . . .
> —Where there is power, there is resistance, and yet, or rather consequently, this resistance is never in a position of exteriority in relation to power. . . . These points of resistance are present everywhere in the power network. Hence there is no single locus of great Refusal, no soul of revolt, source of all rebellions, or pure law of the revolutionary. Instead there is a plurality of resistances, each of them a special case: resistances that are possible, necessary, improbable; others that are spontaneous, savage, solitary, concerted, rampant, or violent; still others that are quick to compromise, interested, or sacrificial; by definition, they can only exist in the strategic field of power relations.[27]

This is a metaphysics of power both because power is everywhere and because it contains its other. Power is everywhere not least because being is relational, and relations are powers. Even more important, wherever there is power, there is resistance: power dividing against itself. That is why it is everywhere and why there is no great point of Revolution. Such a point would not be resistance, but would be another mobilization of power.

There are strategies and constellations of power. The pervasiveness of power does not mitigate its oppressiveness. The fields of force within a social realm establish oppressors and victims, dominant and marginal voices. Foucault's images of power and resistance speak not against oppression but against a defective understanding of practice. To locate power precisely suggests an equally precise location of resistance, the point at which practical judgment is required. Yet strategies of power and control permeate their social context, permeate not only political but theoretical and moral relations. The point at which rebellion will be effective belongs as much to the system of power as does the force that puts down the rebellion.

Two fundamental principles in Foucault's view of power constitute its importance. One is explicit: the dispersion and pervasiveness of power, "everywhere"; its immanence within practical life. The second is implicit in the first: the reciprocity of power. It is this reciprocity that defines resistance. Power is both always divided against itself and always reciprocal. Where the slave is under the authority of the master, the master's authority is defined by his slave. Foucault is by no means the first to recognize either the pervasiveness or the reciprocity of power. He is the first, perhaps, to codify their relationship in terms of resistance. What follows is that the materiality and density of discursive relations as well as desire are to be understood as power relations, mobilizations of influence divided within and without by resistances. This is a metaphysics of power because it has to do with the nature of limits and relevance. It is these limits within material relationships of power that define both the strategies that comprise oppression and the resistances that divide every strategy.

The images of pervasiveness and strategy also describe technology. Technology is everywhere, not because it includes everything but because it comes from everywhere. It is equivalent with material practice, and there can be no effective practice that is not material, or a human being who is not practical. Technology cannot be identified with certain material products as against others, with refrigerators and automobiles, computers and VCRs, but not with clothing, housing, schooling. That power is everywhere entails that it is inseparable from truth and desire. That technology is everywhere entails that it is inseparable from power, desire, and truth. Technology is material power itself, the form power takes in practice. And while there is power everywhere, even where there is no directed practice, where human life is directed toward the future, there we inevitably find technology.

Wherever there is power, there is resistance. That is because resistance is also a form of power. Similarly, wherever there is technology, there is more technology, but technology dividing against itself. There is no form of discourse, no truth, desire, power, or practice, that is not divided within and against itself. The image of an oppressive form of unreason opposed by the forces of light is replaced by immanent divisions of reason and unreason belonging to each other and by desire dividing against itself. Similarly, despite its hegemony, modern technology is not indivisible, but, through its relations to power, but also desire and truth, continually disrupts itself in relation to both its indeterminate and terrifying future and its apparently settled past.

V

It is time to return to "postmodernism." We can do no better than to consider Lyotard's two definitions. One works directly from his view of the modern:

> I shall call modern the art which devotes its "little technical expertise" . . . to present the fact that the unpresentable exists. To make visible that there is something which can be conceived and which can neither be seen nor made visible: this is what is at stake in modern painting.[28]
> What, then, is the postmodern? . . . It is undoubtedly a part of the modern. . . . Postmodernism thus understood is not modernism at its end but in the nascent state, and this state is constant.[29]
> The postmodern would be that which, in the modern, puts forward the unpresentable in presentation itself; that which denies itself the solace of good forms, the consensus of a taste which would make it possible to share collectively the nostalgia for the unattainable; that which searches for new presentations, not in order to enjoy them but in order to impart a stronger sense of the unpresentable.[30]

The other, still reflecting his understanding of modernism, follows from the view that scientific discourse requires legitimation but cannot legitimate itself, so depends on "metanarratives": "Simplifying to the extreme, I define *postmodern* as incredulity toward metanarratives."[31] He goes on to say, most revealingly, in the following paragraph, that "Thus the society of the future falls less within the province of a Newtonian anthropology (such as structuralism or systems theory) than a pragmatics of language particles."[32] Here, I believe, we come to the center of those views of "postmodernism" that cannot include technology within themselves. It is ironic that such a view should be present even within Lyotard, for whom the relationship between postmodernism and technology is decisive.

A prevailing theme in both of Lyotard's definitions of postmodernism—and it is by no means obvious that they are equivalent—is that of language and representation. A feature of "postmodernism" is its dependence on the linguistic turn, expressed at the extreme in Foucault's image that as language regains its unity, "man" will return to "his" serene nonexistence. In Lyotard the primary figure in much of his writing is that of a "language game," at times supplemented by that of "speech-act." What cannot be ignored is that the etymology of both these compounds disappears in the "postmodern" emphasis: we are to forget that language games are a species of games and speech acts are a kind of act. Lyotard even goes so far as to define injustice as forcing another to speak ("play") one's own language game, preventing that other from establishing his or her own mode of expression.

This transformation contains a deep insight: the inseparability of power, desire, and truth. It nevertheless presents us with an equally profound loss: neglect of the games and acts in which desire and truth are effective but in which language plays a marginal role. The linguistic turn emphasizes the historicality and contingency of truth, but it both overinflates language (as compared with other forms of expression) and neglects the future in a fundamental way. The reason for the latter is not hard to find: the diachronic perspective from within which language is to be understood in contrast to a synchronic perspective is historical in a recollective, not a practical, sense.

Wittgenstein is acknowledged to be a major force behind both the linguistic turn and "postmodernism," though relatively little has been done to fulfill the promise that his analyses offer to either the unpresentable or to the dispersion of power. Wittgenstein has written little on power and desire, primarily on representation. The term "language game" is his, though he by no means gives it the kind of force found in Lyotard: so to speak, equivalent with "form of life." There is, in Wittgenstein, little sense of how a language game belongs to its future. The richer images pertain to forms of life and to language itself, as for example:

> Remark: The picture we have of the language of the grown-up is that of a nebulous mass of language, his mother tongue, surrounded by discrete and more or less clear-cut language games, the technical languages.[33]

Similarly, a speech act is not the only kind of act. What "postmodernism" appears to have forgotten, in its enthusiasms for the interactions of practice and representation, is that there are other forms of representation than language. Also neglected is the reciprocity in the principle that power, desire, and truth are inseparable: not only are desire and truth forms of power, but power is a form of truth. Technology is a form of episteme, with or without language. The reciprocal of the recognition that discourse is dense and material, effective and powerful. Among the major contemporary forms of such originariness is modern technology.

VI

There are two themes within Lyotard's view of "postmodernism": the dispersion of language and the presentation of the invisible. The former has two sides, one of ancient origin, the identification of human being with the *logos*, the other the denial that either humanity or language has a determinate essence. "Postmodernism," as the proliferation of language games, explicitly emphasizes the second but implicitly includes the first. The images that surround us, definitive of both "modernism" and "postmodernism," are Kafka's machine of torture that writes the Word upon the flesh of its victims correlated with the proliferation of torture throughout repressive political regimes in the last few decades. In relation to the latter, a crucial phenomenon must be noted: the movement from a torture in which truth plays a fundamental role, either explicitly or by reflection, to a torture that mimics the first but serves only to arouse fear and terror. In Guatemala and El Salvador, death squads torture and murder their victims as if they might have something to say, but speech is of no consequence whatever. Brutality is institutionalized for its own sake. Power contains its own desire and truth.

There is another principle of fundamental importance that I think "postmodernism" has neglected. Not only are power, desire, and truth entwined in practice, language, and history, but each is autonomous in some respects relative to the others. What is involved is the nature of limits, and although every limit exists to be broached—the inevitable and important challenge to disciplinary and political distinctions—every limit does indeed limit. The two sides of limitation are constraint and disruption, determinateness and indeterminateness.

This indeterminateness in determinateness, and conversely, is the invisibility of which Lyotard speaks. Modernism and postmodernism are both concerned with the presentation of the invisible,

the indeterminateness in determinateness. Proliferation and fragmentation are the fundamental images in terms of which
"postmodernism" seeks to dissolve its relation to modernism, as if it
might lie within a discourse to defy consensus. Here "low" music
imposes itself as a form in which defiance of conventional norms itself
establishes consensus, not least the result of modern technology and
sophisticated marketing. These conjoin to demand the widest possible consensus—worldwide and international. Within this oppressive
tendency, I would argue, there are countervailing and divisive tendencies. But that is less the point here than that there is no possibility
of fragmentation and proliferation of language games without material embodiments that are effective only through the means of
technology.

What is invisible in technology perhaps more than any other
form of practice, silent within its material presentations, is the future.
We return to the silence of the future that, I believe, is too serenely
present in "postmodernism," drowned out by its verbosity. One way
to deny the future is to deny the past. Here the rise of science represents modernism's primary version of atemporality, though with
Dewey and Heidegger I would extend the denial of the disruptiveness of the future back to the beginnings of history. And I would
add that art and literature have throughout the tradition warred with
the images of reason that followed from such attempts to avoid the
terrors of the future.

Another way to deny the future, however, is to talk about it too
much without a deep enough sense of its material disruptiveness.
This verbosity can be found within the entire Western philosophic
tradition, close to what Foucault calls the empty beating of wings in
the serious matter of history. For there is a serious matter of history
indeed, and it includes words. Discourse belongs to the efficacy of
history and the disruptiveness of the future. For this insight,
"postmodernism" may be of inestimable value. Reciprocally, however, that there are strategies of power, fragmented and dispersed,
must include realization of the importance of efficacy wherever
power is involved. Power is practical only in relation to the future,
and within practice efficacy is of fundamental importance—not efficiency and not effectiveness, but a concern with what does and what
does not affect the future. Here Hegel again casts a giant shadow that
falls across modernism into postmodernism, suggesting that there is
a clear and unambiguous sense of what is efficacious within historical
practices and what is not. To the contrary, we reply to Hegel and also
to Marx, efficacity is always divided and ambiguous, part of what
constitutes the indeterminateness of the unknown future. Yet divid-

ed and ambiguous as it may be, it is a fundamental dimension of power and all-important to material practice.

Here, I believe, is where modern technology confronts us with the indeterminateness of the future. And I believe that the revulsion against modern technology among those who would profess postmodernism is a perpetuation of the very modernism that they would hope to succeed, and in two fundamental ways. One is an inversion of the principle that words are mere transparencies: the belief that they matter to the future. Indeed they do, in material and efficacious ways. But if words are practical, then it is of fundamental importance to practice to know what is more effective and what is less.

The other is the same repudiation of the indeterminateness of the future that haunts modernism throughout, realized in its multiple images of utopias and dystopias, along with the recurrent theme of transcendence. We must think the future without shrinking. Yet we cannot do so without thinking the past—without *re*thinking the past, repeatedly—and without facing its indeterminateness. However we think the past and future, the forms of thought that establish today's meanings may undergo radical transformations, in unpredictable ways. And more than any other form of practice, whether through its reflexive forms of representation or simply as a discursive consequence of material procedures, modern technology is a site where the future is to be realized, where finiteness presents itself in its terrifying irresistibility.

VII

In conclusion, if "postmodernism" is the proliferation of those forms of human being in which the invisible is manifested, in all its disruptiveness, then modern technology is the inescapable form in which past and present determinations have only marginal relevance. The future is invisible in the visibility of the present—an invisibility with the power to invade both past and present. Practice is always situated in the abyss between an unknown yet determined future and a partly known but still unrealized past, awaiting the disruptive futures that will define its meaning. Just as practice must find its form, and will do so under criticism from within and without, technology will both define the shape of the future and disrupt it, under criticism from within and without. In this sense, modern and postmodern criticisms of modern technology that sound simplistic frequently have a profound purpose: to find the alternative forms within it that can bring the future under practical control, and to reexamine the past sacrifices that have made the present possible, so that we may hope to anticipate the sacrifices that the future requires.

The plurality of past, present, and future—many pasts, presents, and futures—requires a plurality of voices, of forms of reason, each with its limitations, each a critical standpoint for the others. Here technology remains an irresistible site at which the dreams and hopes for the future and the lessons we have learned from the past face their greatest danger: of ceasing to be relevant. The past is present in the mode of nostalgia in our attempts to recapture past marginal voices that appeared to be irrelevant. The threat of the future, which cries out for such nostalgia, is the threat of being altogether forgotten. Here both modern and postmodern technology must continue to terrify us, not least because we cannot relate practically to any future without them and because they embody our greatest powers. Within the coerciveness of all such powers lies the threat of transformations that will make any of us entirely irrelevant to the future.

Notes

1. I will employ a distinction in this chapter between "postmodernism" and postmodernism, the former representing the object of contemporary discussions, frequently of a millennial nature, the latter simply what will follow "modernism." Something certainly will follow modernism, whether of a radically different nature (the disappearance of the subject, the end of the metaphysical tradition), a cyclical repetition of past forms, or merely more of the same. The purpose of this paper is to characterize the difference between "postmodernism" and postmodernism in relation to power and practice, especially in relation to technology.

2. Michel Foucault, *The Archaeology of Knowledge* (New York: Pantheon, 1972), p. 209.

3. Michel Foucault, *The Order of Things* (New York: Random House, 1970), pp. 385–86.

4. G. W. F. Hegel, *The Phenomenology of Mind* (London: George Allen & Unwin), 1931, pp. 807–8.

5. Hegel calls this new beginning, founded on Spirit's rethinking its own history, "Development" (G. W. F. Hegel, *The Logic of Hegel* [London: Oxford University Press, 1892], pp. 288–91).

6. Hegel, *Phenomenology of Mind*, p. 807.

7. Hannah Arendt, *Between Past and Future* (Cleveland and New York: World Publishing, 1963).

8. *Hegel's Philosophy of Right*, T. M. Knox tr. and ed. (London: Oxford University Press, 1952), p. 13.

9. It is only in relation to *Anti-Oedipus* that Foucault suggests a practical relation to the future, characterizing that book as "a book of ethics, the first book of ethics to be written in France in quite a long time . . . (. . . being anti-oedipal has become a life style, a way of thinking and living . . .)," cf. Gilles Deleuze and Félix Guattari, *Anti-Oedipus* (Minneapolis: University of Minnesota Press, 1983, p. xiii). Nevertheless, the relationship of this anti-oedipal context to the past, genealogically and archeologically, remains enigmatic.

10. Martin Heidegger, "The Origin of the Work of Art," in *Poetry, Language, Thought* (New York: Harper & Row, 1971), pp. 61–62.

11. Sartre criticizes Heidegger for placing too great an emphasis on the future ekstasis, rather than upon the present. See Jean-Paul Sartre, *Being and Nothingness* (New York: Philosophical Library, 1956), p. 142. Yet for this reason, *Being and Nothingness* lacks political sensibility. ". . . it is only by human reality that the Future arrives in the world," (p. 124). This is a view of the future that denies both its reality and its danger.

12. Martin Heidegger, *Being and Time* (New York: Harper & Row, 1962), p. 438.

13. Martin Heidegger, "The Question Concerning Technology," in *Basic Writings*, D. Krell ed. (New York: Harper & Row, 1977), p. 295.

14. Ibid., p. 296. I will, for purposes that will become clear, distinguish between technology and *modern technology*, a notion that includes within itself the ambivalences toward the future that can be found in "postmodernism." There is, then, an affinity as well as a polar opposition between "modern technology" and "postmodernism."

15. Ibid., p. 297.

16. Ibid., p. 298.

17. Ibid.

18. Marshall McLuhan, *Understanding Media: The Extensions of Man* (New York: McGraw-Hill, 1964). Despite repeated searching, I have been unable to find the passage McLuhan ascribes to Whitehead.

19. Michel Foucault, *The Discourse on Language*, appendix to *The Archaeology of Knowledge*, p. 215.

20. Ibid., p. 216.

21. Ibid.

22. Since using this phrase, I have found it in Berel Lang, "Postmodernism in Philosophy: Nostalgia for the Future, Waiting for the Past," *New Literary History*, 18 (1986–87): 209–23.

23. Michel Foucault, *The History of Sexuality* (New York: Random House, 1978), 1:93.

24. R. G. Collingwood, *The Principles of Art* (London: Oxford University Press, 1958), chapter 2.

25. Foucault, *History of Sexuality*, pp. 92–93.

26. Ibid., p. 93.

27. Ibid., pp. 94–96.

28. Jean-François Lyotard, "Answering the Question: What is Postmodernism?," appendix to *The Postmodern Condition: A Report on Knowledge* (Minneapolis: University of Minnesota Press, 1984), p. 78.

29. Ibid., p. 79.

30. Ibid., p. 81.

31. Lyotard, *Postmodern Condition*, Introduction, p. xxiv.

32. Ibid.

33. Ludwig Wittgenstein, *The Blue and Brown Books* (Oxford: Blackwell, 1960), p. 81.

16

Does it Pay to Go Postmodern If Your Neighbors Do Not?

Steve Fuller

An important test for the pragmatic value of an ideology is whether its adherents are likely to benefit, even if the ideology is clearly a minority voice in the society. For example, ideologies that postulate a "vanguard" class, such as Marxism and various modernist aesthetics, often benefit from their minority status, insofar as the ideology can easily explain—in terms of progress against the resistance of tradition—the current difference in beliefs between the small number of adherents and the large number of nonadherents. This, in turn, serves to drive the adherents to persevere that much more, which ideally issues in their ultimately becoming the dominant ideological voice.

However, it is not clear that adherents to a postmodernist ideology equally stand to benefit from being in an intellectual environment currently dominated by other ideological voices. Indeed, I shall argue that the crucial pragmatic difference between modernism and postmodernism lies in the fact that postmodernists flourish only in intellectual environments where postmodernism is the dominant, if not only, ideological voice. Given the content of postmodernism, which stresses both the desirability and necessity of pluralism, this no doubt appears to be a surprising and ironic conclusion. It underscores the extent to which postmodernism has yet to be conceptualized as a truly *social* theory. One route to such a conceptualization would be for postmodernists to persuade their neighbors in the academy, or their collective representative, that postmodernism is an ideology from which they could all benefit. As we shall see, this is easier said than done. At the end, another route will be proposed, more in the spirit of postmodernism, though less in the spirit of a neighborhood of academicians.

Modernisms typically hold that "enlightenment" requires a

break with traditional authority structures, which can be accomplished by discovering how those structures work and then systematically transforming them.[1] The only obstacles to such systematic transformation, on the modernist view, are ignorance and inertia, both of which can eventually be overcome by enough rationally informed wills. In contrast, adherents to the various forms of postmodernism—as the name itself suggests—conceive of themselves as living at a time when much of the modernist project has already been realized. In particular, the legitimacy of the traditional authorities has been subverted, and means are generally available (esp. information technologies) for legitimating any variety of new authorities.

However, postmodernism is distinctive in its reflection on the fact that the modernist project has been only *partially* realized; for rather than the critique of authority issuing in the replacement of a traditional authority structure by a more "rational" one, the critique has simply led to the fragmentation of authority. And whereas the modernist contrasted the historically contingent and accidental character of past authorities (products of ignorance and inertia) with the rationally informed character of future ones, the postmodernist sees all authorities as equally contingent and accidental—though the latest forms of ignorance and inertia have resulted from the very fact that there are more texts proposing ways to "enlightenment" than ever before.

An important consequence of these differences between modernism and postmodernism is that postmodernism eschews the interventionist tendencies of modernism. For example, Habermas and Lyotard represent the modernist and postmodernist approach to pluralism. After having mastered the nature of communicative competence, Habermas wants to set up procedures whereby any member of a speech community can exercise this competence. Lyotard notes that if this proposal were taken literally, it would require not only a massive redeployment of the current communication technologies, but an unprecedented surveillance of the operation of those technologies once the redeployment had been made, so as to prevent any "systematic distortion" from ever arising again.

In contrast, Lyotard (and this also seems to be the tenor of Rorty and Bernstein) asks us only to change our *attitude* toward the current distribution of voices in the ideological marketplace.[2] Inasmuch as we still naturally think that dominant voices have "earned" their legitimacy in virtue of some special access they have to reality, it is important to revise our view of dominance so that it becomes seen as the product of the most historically local considerations. Were some receding or silenced voices given the same historical opportunities as the dominant voices, they too would have appeared legitimate. However, the postmodernist's reliance on counterfactual demystification does not necessarily encourage one to vindicate any of the receding or silenced voices, but rather it only encourages one to dissociate their receding or silenced status from any judgments about their inherent value.

Problems for postmodernists arise once they conceive of themselves as being in an ideological marketplace populated mostly by modernists, along with some vestigial traditionalists and a few unrepentant postmodernists. Imagine that this marketplace is populated by the current array of academic disciplines, and imagine that there is one person (or office), a cognitive tsar,[3] who must decide how to allocate resources (both financial and legitimatory) among these contesting faculties. Think of the cognitive tsar as the person to whom the directors of both the National Science Foundation and the National Endowment for the Humanities must report. Now for a quick survey of the faculties:

1. The natural sciences, along with their social scientific emulators, are unabashed and probably unreflective modernists; thus, they promise new power by extending proven effective methods into new domains.

2. Postmodernists aside, the humanities are typically split along modernist and traditionalist lines.

An example of the division in humanistic allegiances appeared in *Newsweek*.[4] The story concerned two attempts at relieving the nation's cultural illiteracy. Out of the ranks of modernism comes E. D. Hirsch, who has written an intellectual "how-to" book subtitled *What Every American Needs to Know*. Hirsch does not so much promise depth as breadth, more facility than profundity with our store of ideas. From the traditionalist camp then comes Allan Bloom's *The Closing of the American Mind*, which blames our cultural illiteracy on modernists like Hirsch whose idea of understanding the Western tradition is a mere "passing knowledge," which enables today's savants-on-the-go to appropriate the dicta best suited for their own projects without having to idle over the subtle considerations that originally informed them.

The cognitive tsar cannot fail to notice the difference between the bill of goods that the modern and traditional humanist are trying to sell him. The modernist Hirsch is confident that putting his book in the hands of the teachers of tomorrow's leaders will hasten the spread of cultural literacy. As might be expected, the traditionalist Bloom is less sanguine about any major cultural revival, being quite content to entrust the fate of the Western tradition to a small but devoted band of humanists who each generation take the time to rehearse the reasoning—and not merely the conclusions—of a Socrates or a Nietzsche. What do postmodernists have to offer this debate that does not simply undercut the legitimacy of their opponents but actually does their own position some good?

At first glance, the cognitive tsar would be well disposed toward the postmodernists, if only on the basis of his impressive vital statistics, which show that his wing of the humanities is currently most fashionable among the next generation of college teachers. Moreover, the cognitive tsar can plainly see the truth in the postmodernist critique of traditionalism and modernism. He would simply need, on the one hand, to sample the variety of contradictory statements made over the last five hundred years on what exactly constitutes "the Western tradition" to show that the traditionalist's sense of historical continuity is self-deceptive. On the other hand, the cognitive tsar could conduct a longitudinal study on any of the modernist "fix-it" texts from Bentham to Dewey to discover that none have systematically transformed the culture as intended. For whatever reason, the postmodernist would thus seem to be right that the *humanist* has as little control over the future as the humanist does over the past of our culture. Indeed, the cognitive tsar might find one deconstructive project often associated with postmodernism—namely, revealing how claims to overarching control over the course of history arise in moments when one is losing control over the immediate circumstances—an effective antidote to the hubris typically affected by humanists in the marketplace.

But in end, the cognitive tsar realizes that the value of postmodernist critiques of the humanities pales in the face of the genuine control apparently afforded by the experimental methods of the natural sciences and their social scientific emulators. This is not to say, of course, that postmodernists have not also tried to overturn this bastion of cognitive authority. Yet it would be fair to say that postmodernism's campaigns against science have not only failed to impress the cognitive tsar but have backfired to the extent that they cast serious doubts on the overall well-foundedness of the postmodernist project. Take the debates over the last ten years on "The Strong Programme in the Sociology of Knowledge," originating from the Edinburgh Science Studies Unit.[5] In brief, the Edinburgh school has presented an array of case studies from the history of mathematics and the natural sciences showing that a theory attains scientific status not because independent researchers can demonstrate its truth, but because a wide variety of social interests can legitimate their pursuits by presuming the theory true. Taken together, these studies would seem to provide conclusive evidence that claims to knowledge may be merely "ideological" when only one or two interest groups support them, but they become "scientific" once they have support from many such groups: an ironic moral benefiting postmodernism's pluralist sensibility.

Yet, as I suggested above, the irony eventually rebounds on the postmodernist. For in pleading their case before the cognitive tsar, the natural scientists can easily observe that if a piece of knowledge can be so useful in the hands of so many, often opposing interest groups, then there must be something *interest-invariant*, if not actually interest-free, about the knowledge in question. This would seem to bring the "proven effectiveness" of scientific methods in through the back door. More generally, this clever rejoinder points to a flaw in the postmodernist's strategy: it appears that by adding enough local concerns together, a truth of rather general scope has been produced. But how did the ever-artful postmodernists allow themselves to be caught off guard in this manner?

In essence, the postmodernist mistakenly supposes what I have elsewhere call the *Viconian Fallacy:*[6] namely, just because something—here scientific knowledge—has been shown to be a human construction (and hence the product of local human interests), it is then fallaciously inferred that we have more cognitive control over it than we would, were that thing shown to have been of nonhuman origin. And by "cognitive control" I mean, in this case, the ability to predict or determine the course of scientific knowledge. Richard Rorty's writings, especially the three "contingency" lectures,[7] are a rich source of this type of fallacious reasoning to which postmodernists are generally susceptible. In particular, Rorty blends Hegel and Davidson (or Dewey and Wittgenstein) to produce the following intriguing argument:

1. The only things that can be true or false are sentences.
2. Sentences are human constructions.
3. Therefore (given 1 + 2), truth and falsity are human constructions.
4. The world essentially changes when the sorts of things that can be true or false changes.
5. Therefore (given 3 + 4), humans construct a new world with each new system of sentences.
6. "Anything can be made to look good or bad, important or unimportant, useful or useless, by being redescribed."[8]
7. Therefore (given 5 + 6), humans can construct whatever world they wish.

This argument is perfectly sound until its final step, which falsely presumes that because all possible worlds are human constructions, it follows that humans can determine which one turns out to be the actual world. The error here resembles the one involved in saying that because all officeholders in a democracy are elected by the people, it follows that the people always elect the candidate they want. The inference is faulty, of course, because it confuses the fact that each individual's vote contributes to the election's outcome with the fact that the outcome may not conform to any given individual's expectations—or preferences for that matter (especially if individuals try to vote "strategically" based on a false understanding of what their fellows think). An excellent example of this phenomenon is afforded by the history of intelligence testing, a perennial research favorite among sociologists of knowledge.

On the sort of local, interest-based account one expects from sociologists, Alfred Binet would be portrayed as having developed the IQ test as a method uniquely suited for French educational reform, for once it was possible to specify the extent to which a child's cognitive achievement falls below the norm for the child's age, the teacher could then design an appropriate course of study that will enable the child to catch up. No longer (so thought Binet) would slow learners be written off as intractably stupid. Of course, over the last hundred years, the IQ test has been used by many educational interest groups, most of which have been diametrically opposed to Binet's. Indeed, as the recent work of Stephen J. Gould most vividly shows, an unintended consequence of the IQ test having passed through so many hands is that it is no longer the passive tool of any particular interest, but rather it has become an object of study in its own right (a branch of psychometrics) with standards of interpretation that can be used to decide between the knowledge claims of competing educational interests. For example, arguments concerning the racial component in intelligence are typically adjudicated by seeing whether the difference in means for, say, blacks and whites in an IQ test is statistically significant. These developments in the "objectification" of intelligence testing take us far from Binet's original intentions, perhaps even to the point that would make him regret ever having introduced the concept of IQ.

In hearing this tale, the cognitive tsar would not let the poignancy of the last remark obscure its real lesson: namely, that "objectivity" in the scientist's sense triumphs in spite of (indeed, *because of*) the efforts of agents who have been characterized in terms acceptable to the postmodernist. The tale is the familiar one of a means designed for particular pursuits—in this case, the IQ test—unwittingly being turned into the standard by which the success of all pursuits are judged.[9] Moreover, this ironic conclusion recurs at a more explicitly ideological level, which may help explain the grave reservations that Christopher Norris and others have had about postmodernist politics.[10] These reservations have usually centered on attempts by Rorty and the rest to characterize their stance as "liberal," a notoriously slippery term even in the hands of the most careful theorist.

To start, take the two senses of "liberal" most frequently intended by Rorty:

equal-time liberalism—the doctrine that efforts should be taken to ensure that all parties to the conversation of humankind are *always* on an equal footing, no matter what transpires in the course of the conversation, even if it includes a radical change in the attitudes that the parties have to one another's views.

separate-but-equal liberalism—the doctrine that since a viewpoint is valid for the culture from which it arose but invalid (or at least inappropriate) for any other culture, it follows that efforts should be taken to protect the viewpoint of a culture from outside interference.

These two versions of liberalism are basically two ways of translating epistemic relativism into political terms. They share a commitment to egalitarianism that is sufficiently strong to justify the application of force to prevent equality from disintegrating under either (in the first case) the emergence of a dominant voice or (in the second case) cultural imperialism. The implication, of course, is that such disintegration would *naturally* occur without the liberal's intervention. Thus, insofar as postmodernists are liberals in either of the above two senses, their social policy is given to a certain amount of artifice. But note the irony here. For the postmodernist had earlier been able to show that the tradition of pronouncements on "the tradition" could be used against the traditionalist, that the modernist criterion of "proven track record" could be used against the modernst, thereby suggesting artifice on the part of both foes. Yet are not postmodernists themselves now susceptible to the charge of artifice? In other words, it would seem that for all their Wittgenstein-sounding noises, Rorty and Lyotard must make some deliberate interventions in order to "leave the world alone."[11]

We have so far only presented the "welfare state" side of postmodernist liberalism, the side that believes that a rich culture is one rich in viewpoints. But in order to simulate the ironic turn toward objectivism that we earlier saw in the case of the sociology of science, we must now turn to the "laissez-faire" side of postmodernist liberalism, whose noninterventionism is at the same time much more in line with the spirit of Rorty and Lyotard's wanting to leave the world alone. As can be seen, this position also bespeaks a certain sense of "egalitarianism":

equal-in-principle liberalism—inasmuch as all viewpoints are "created equal," in the sense that none has any a priori advantage over the rest, it follows that whatever success particular viewpoints turn out to have historically will be solely the result of their having adapted to contingencies in the marketplace of ideas.

Like the more strictly political versions of laissez-faire liberalism, this one extends a false hope, which is suggested in the ambiguity of the term "adapted" and which recalls the Viconian Fallacy. There is one sense of "adapt," the Lamarckian sense, that implies that individuals can intentionally adapt to their circumstances. This sense is implicit in postmodernist descriptions of agents as trying to capture the spirit of the time and thereby maximize their own advantage. Both postmodernist philosophers and sociologists agree here that if the agents are properly attuned to the sorts of arguments that will persuade their intended audiences, then they are likely to succeed. However, the second, more Darwinian, sense of "adapt" is not nearly so sanguine, insisting that what turns out *to have made* various individuals either adaptive or maladaptive to their intellectual environments is an unpredictable and emergent feature of their collective activities in those environments. Thus, while the IQ test began by enhancing Binet's instrumentalist views on education, it turned out to be an even more potent weapon in the hands of his foes, the racialists. And in the process, the statistical trappings of the IQ test have become the part of the standard by which any theory of intelligence is judged.

While postmodernists have downplayed this Darwinian sense of "adapt"—no doubt because its *Que será será* attitude to intellectual change hardly provides the cognitive tsar with any constructive policy recommendations—it nevertheless highlights the brute contingency that the postmodernist sees in the intellectual world. When Rorty says, parodying Spinoza and Hegel, that "freedom is the recognition of contingency," he is at most trying to persuade the cognitive tsar to take comfort in the fact that whatever he does not like about the current intellectual scene will eventually pass away. The problem, of course, is that Rorty can also say the same thing about whatever the tsar happens to *like* about the current scene.

In addition, when Rorty conflates the Darwinian and Lamarckian senses of "adapt," he can make it seem as though the mere expression of sentiment for or against a particular viewpoint determinately contributes to the fate of that viewpoint. And so, in another instance of the Viconian Fallacy, Rorty argues that the (allegedly) increasing dissatisfaction with natural scientific approaches to knowledge among both humanist intellectuals (such as himself) and more ordinary folks (such as creationists) means that the time is ripe to redefine our epistemic values, which Rorty believes should be based on "solidarity," which aims for a sense of community, rather than "objectivity," which has the effect of discriminating persons according to epistemic merit.[12] In reflecting on this bit of counsel, the cognitive tsar could not fail to note that Rorty neglects other, more plausible diagnoses of current attitudes to science, particularly diagnoses that point to science's implicit *strength*. For example, anti-science is the natural response of humanists who, after having once been well adapted to the intellectual environment, now fear disciplinary extinction. And as for pseudo sciences such as creationism, far from being anti-scientific, they are in fact failed attempts at *imitating* science, usually by adopting the strategy of "if you can't beat them, join them."[13] Rorty's, then, is a Lamarckian response to a Darwinian world.

Readers at this point may wonder whether I have unfairly characterized Rorty as running together several liberal and evolutionary theories, since, as we have just suggested, his repeated stress on "community" and "solidarity" would seem to go against the individualism and psychological atomism that undergird most forms of liberalism and evolutionism. However, I contend that the perceived tension is primarily in Rorty, and that a careful diagnosis also provides the postmodernist way out of one's problems with the cognitive tsar. To the charge leveled by Rorty's defender that I have given an "individualist" misreading of Rorty's "communalist" message, I say that Rorty has misunderstood the axis of our disagreement. Neither of us denies that anything worth talking about is done by groups of persons, but we seem to disagree as to what holds these groups together. More precisely, Rorty's rhetoric suggests one sort of "social glue," whereas his examples and explications suggest another. The two social adhesives I have in mind were coined by Ferdinand Toennies in the title of the book that launched academic sociology in Germany: *Gemeinschaft und Gesellschaft.*[14]

Gemeinschaften are held together by such "natural" relations as blood, habit, and tradition, while *Gesellschaften* operate by means of "artificial" relations like contracts, money, and rules. The title of Toennies's book has often been translated "Community and Society," which captures nicely the distinction between a form of life in which persons appreciate each other for what they are and one in which persons measure each other's worth as means toward their own ends. In the first form of life, persons naturally stick together regardless of the circumstances, while in the second, circumstances are exactly what can alter their relationships. In light of what we have been saying about Rorty, he is thus aptly classed as someone who "talks" *Gemeinschaft* in a world which, as evidenced by the three strands of liberalism we discerned, clearly runs in a *Gesellschaft* fashion.

The lesson for the postmodernist here is to realize that the cognitive tsar himself is a remnant of (supposedly) more *Gemeinschaft* days, when academics did indeed form a community of standards embodied in the tsar's trusted judgments, the history of which would be the canonical history of academic community. However, in a *Gesellschaft* world, the postmodernist must be prepared to take the evolutionary metaphor to its logical conclusion and admit that the intellectual environment varies just as much as (indeed, independently of) the contesting organisms. Consequently, the conceptual niches that the academics are trying to fill, the rivalries they involve, and the criteria that will ultimately make a difference to survivors all add up to a fragmented picture of the cognitive tsar. However, as we shall now see, another casualty is Rorty's notion of "solidarity"; for if the cognitive tsar goes, so too does the neighborhood. In conclusion, then, consider the five steps by which the centered self (i.e., Cartesian academics who know their own mind and know that they are right) is dissolved, first to level 2 (below), where the cognitive tsar has been presiding throughout this paper, and finally by relentless postmodernist logic, to the point of becoming a mere construction of a decentered audience for whom the tsar and his neighborhood are no more than phantoms:

1. I am in a privileged position to know what I mean and therefore in a privileged position to know whether it is true or false.

2. I am in a privileged position to know what I mean but in no such position to know whether it is true or false. That is for my audience to determine.

3. I am in no privileged position to know either what I mean or whether it is true or false. My audience is in a privileged position to determine those things. But I am in a privileged position to determine who my audience is.

4. I am in no privileged position to know what I mean, whether it is true, or *even* who is and is not part of my audience. In fact, the audience is in a privileged position to determine my own identity as a speaker.

5. Not only am I in no privileged position to know what I mean, whether it is true, or who is and is not part of my audience, but the audience itself is in no privileged position to determine who does and does not belong to it, which implies that my identity as speaker is at best fragmented.[15]

Notes

1. My main source for the distinction between "modernism" and "postmodernism," and especially my reliance on Habermas and Lyotard as their respective exemplars, is Christopher Norris, *The Contest of the Faculties* (London: Methuen, 1985), esp. pp. 19–46.

2. Jean-François Lyotard, *The Postmodern Condition* (Minneapolis: University of Minnesota Press, 1984), esp. pp. 60–67.

3. This term originated in Steve Fuller, "A Statement of Purpose," *Social Epistemology*, 1 (1987): 1–4.

4. David Gates, "A Dunce Cap for America," *Newsweek*, April 20, 1987, pp. 72–74. The article is a review-interview of E. D. Hirsch, *Cultural Literacy: What Every American Needs to Know* (Boston: Houghton Mifflin, 1987); Allan Bloom, *The Closing of the American Mind* (New York: Simon and Schuster, 1987).

5. On the Edinburgh School, see Barry Barnes, *About Science* (London: Oxford University Press, 1986).

6. For an account of this fallacy's link to Vico, see Steve Fuller, "Toward Objectivism and Relativism," *Social Epistemology*, 1 (1987): 351–61.

7. Rorty's three lectures, which concern the contingency of "language," "selfhood," and "community," appeared in the following issues of *London Review of Books:* April 17, April 30, and July 24, 1986.

8. This is a quote from Richard Rorty, "The Contingency of Language," *London Review of Books*, April 17, 1986, p. 3.

9. The story of a means becoming an end-in-itself is a familiar one in the sociological literature. Georg Simmel is especially noted for explorations of such mediating agencies as money and "third parties." See *The Sociology of Georg Simmel*, ed. Kurt Wolff (New York: Free Press, 1964).

10. See esp. Christopher Norris, *The Contest of Faculties* (London: Methuen, 1985), pp. 139–66.

11. For an analysis of such noises, see Jonathan Lear, "Leaving the World Alone," *Journal of Philosophy*, 79 (1982): 382–403.

12. Richard Rorty, "Solidarity or Objectivity," in *Post-Analytic Philosophy*, eds. John Rajchman and Cornel West (New York: Columbia University Press, 1985), pp. 3–19.

13. For more on the differences between anti- and pseudo-science, see Steve Fuller, "The Demarcation of Science: A Problem Whose Demise Has Been Greatly Exaggerated," *Pacific Philosophical Quarterly*, 66 (1985): 329–41, esp. part 3.

14. Ferdinand Toennies, *Community and Society* (New York: Harper and Row, 1963). The original was published in 1887.

15. Although decentering of the subject (and, less so, the audience) is a recurring theme in Foucault, Lacan, Derrida, and Lyotard, it has also begun to be raised by analytic philosophers, under the rubric of the role that context plays in constituting intentionality and reference. See *Subject, Thought, and Context*, eds. Philip Pettit and John McDowell (Oxford: Oxford University Press, 1986). Analytic analogues for our five stages include: (1) Kuhn and the positivists, or anyone who believes that meaning determines reference; (2) Putnam and Kripke, or anyone who believes that meaning is independent of reference; (3) Daniel Dennett and Tyler Burge, or anyone who accepts the later Wittgenstein's remarks on meaning; (4) Gareth Evans; (5) maybe Donald Davidson in his most recent work, where he denies the existence of language beyond intersecting idiolects. See "A Nice Derangement of Epitaphs," in *Truth and Interpretation*, ed. Ernest LePore (Oxford: Blackwell, 1986), pp. 433–46.

17

Religion and Postmodernism:
The Durkheimian Bond in Bell and Jameson

John O'Neill

In contemporary cultural criticism, whether neoconservative or neo-Marxist, it is generally agreed that our cultural malaise is at its height in postmodernism. But whereas Daniel Bell would argue that the collapse of the modern temper is to blame for the incivility of postindustrial society,[1] Frederick Jameson would consider late capitalism itself to be the source of the postmodern fragmentation of its cultural values.[2] However, despite this analytic difference and their opposing political values, Bell and Jameson are inclined to call for a renewal of religious symbolism to restore the social bond against postmodern values, which undermine equally the conservative and Marxist tradition.[3] Postmodernism appears, therefore, to create a neomodern opposition from both left and right. In turn it inspires a Durkheimian reflection on the ultimate value of the social bond, which is either backward-looking, as in Bell's neoconservatism, or else resolutely utopian, as in Benjamin, Bloch, Marcuse, and Jameson.

I think it is not unfair to Bell's argument to put it as follows. Capitalism has successfully changed itself and the world without destroying itself through the class and ideological conflicts predicted by Marxists. Indeed, capitalism has successfully moved into a postindustrial phase in which its information sciences continuously revise its technological future, thereby solving the problem of history and again disappointing its Marxist critics. The postindustrial phase of the capitalist economy appears, however, to be threatened more by the contradictions deriving from its postmodern culture and policy than early capitalism was endangered by the cultural tensions of modernism. In short, late capitalism may prove unable to integrate its postmodern culture with its technological base. This is because the efficiency values of the latter are difficult to reconcile with a culture of narcissism and a politics of egalitarianism.

While Bell insists that previous cultural critics were naive in supposing that modern society can collapse at any single point, his own articulation of the triplex of economy, policy, and culture, nevertheless envisages the possibility of the postindustrial techno-culture being sapped by postmodern hedonism and self-gratification. For, despite the contempt that modernist artists expressed toward bourgeois scientism and materialism, they nevertheless shared the same bounded individualism exemplified in the Protestant ethic and its affinity for industrialism. That is to say, there existed a tension in modernism between its religious and its secular values between its attitudes toward the self and society. But this tension has collapsed in postmodernism and its lack threatens to bring down postindustrialism. However, Bell is quite unclear whether it is modernism, or the collapse of modernism (and thus postmodernism), which undermines late (postindustrial) capitalism:

> Today modernism is exhausted. There is no tension. The creative impulses have gone slack. It has become an empty vessel. The impulse to rebellion has become institutionalized by the "culture mass" and its experimental forms have become the syntax and semiotics of advertising and haute couture. As a cultural style, it exists as radical chic, which allows the cultural mass the luxury of "freer" lifestyles while holding comfortable jobs within an economic system that has itself been transformed in its motivations.[4]

Here, then, modernity is damned it if does and damned if it does not underwrite capitalism. In the passage from Bell, however, we can hear more clearly his neoconservative lament for the moral values of a solitary bourgeois society in which the bond of religion is strong and resilient enough to bear the creative tensions of bounded Protestantism and spirited capitalism. At bottom, Bell attributes the crisis of capitalism to a crisis of religion, to a loss of ultimate meaning, which undercuts its civic will.[5] By this he means that the obligations of collective life are reduced to subjective rights, the will to endure calamity is softened into the demand for instant gratification, and religion is replaced by the utopiates of progress, rationality, and science:

> The real problem of modernity is the problem of belief. To use an unfashionable term, it is a spiritual crisis, since that new anchorages have proved illusory and the old ones have become submerged. . . . The effort to find excitement and meaning in

literature and art as a substitute for religion led to modernism as a cultural mode. Yet modernism is exhausted and the various kinds of postmodernism (in the psychedelic efforts to expand consciousness without boundaries) are simply the decomposition of the self in an effort to erase individual ego.[6]

Bell's conception of postmodernism seems to turn upon a rejection of everything in modernism except its puritanism as the matching ethic of bourgeois culture and industry. Everything else is thrown into a catch-all of hedonism, neurosis, and death, which exceeds the bounds of "traditional modernism" whose subversion, as he says, "still ranged itself on the side of order and, implicitly, of a rationality of form, if not of content." But the vessels of art are smashed in postmodernism and religious restraint vanishes from the civil scene. Humankind itself disappears as a transcendental value. Worse still—for Bell is not worried so much by philosophical extravaganzas—postmodernism ushers in a crisis of middle-class values! Here bathos is the result of Bell's attempt to combine historical, philosophical, and sociological generalities to create a vision of cultural crisis that is universal and yet decidedly American. What he gains in assigning a certain grandeur to the diagnosis of American problems, Bell loses when it comes to tackling them in any specific institutional setting.

For example, Bell claims that the road to postindustrialism involves three stages. In the first, we encounter a natural world; in the second, we deal with a fabricated world; in the third, our world is ourselves and our social interaction. Although one might have expected Bell to celebrate this last stage of sociability as a sociologist's (Simmel, Goffman) paradise, one finds instead that we have lost all sense of the social bond due to our progressive secularization:

> The primordial elements that provide men with common identification and effective reciprocity—family, synagogue, church, and community—have become attenuated, and people have lost the capacity to maintain sustained relations with each other in both time and place. To say, then, that "God is dead" is, in effect, to say that the social bonds have snapped and that society is dead.[7]

Because he is at pains to avoid a Marxist (even a critical theory) analysis of the sources of "instability" in the American social order, Bell is obliged to leave things at the level of a neoconservative lament over neoliberalism, hedonism, and postmodernism. Thus America's final crisis is blamed upon a moral crisis whose sources are found in any number of situations (ignorance, poverty, AIDS), which seek to exceed the social compact and the proper arbitration of public and private goods. Without naming the excesses of the corporate culture and its wilful barbarization of the masses, by keeping silence with regard to the industrial military adventures that enraged American youth, Bell falls into dismissing the critical culture of the 1960s in the same vein that Christopher Lasch trashes the culture of narcissism. Because they suppress relevant distinctions regarding the system of corporate power, whose production of the culture they despise determines its mass consumption,[8] Bell and Lasch cannot avoid the voice of a genteel modernism lamenting its own lost contexts of value with the fall into postmodernism.

Overall, Bell seems worried that the project of modernity will be overwhelmed by its own antinomianism. The latter may have served a positive good in its break with patriarchal and feudal authority, but without such authorities to kick against, antinomianism soon loses all sense of its own limitations. The result is that liberty turns to liberation against which we lack any overarching principle of legitimation. The death of God and now the death of humankind, rather than its expected resurrection, leaves society without value. This is the terrible price of the antibourgeois assault upon modernism. The curious thing, however, is that despite Bell's vision of the erosion of authority, we have not seen any expansion of social revolutions other than in the name of the very bourgeois and Christian values discounted by postmodernism. The reason may well be, as the Grand Inquisitor well knew, that the masses retain that coherence of meaning and value that Bell believes it is the task of his own exhausted elite to reimpose. Thus, whatever the changes in the institutions and rites of religion, its basic existential responses are perhaps less endangered because they are more necessary than ever.

Bell seriously underestimates the popular resistance (if not indifference) to the elite culture of unrestrained individualism, impulsive art, and moral nihilism, which he defines as modernity's gift to postmodernism. Apart from remarking upon the resurgence of idolatry in the Chinese and Soviet Party, he does not make enough of the power of religious values to sustain resistance among intellectuals as well as old women. Of course, one is not appealing to the current prevalence of cults and sects of one sort and another, which flourish while the official religions appear to wane. Yet Bell is bold enough to forecast the appearance of three new religions[9] or types of religious practice:

1. moralizing religion: fundamentalist, evangelical, rooted in the "silent majority";

2. redemptive religion: retreating from (post)modernity, rooted in the intellectual and professional classes; and the growth of intellectual and professional classes; and the growth of "mediating institutions: of care (family, church, neighborhood, voluntary associations) opposed to the state;

3. mystical religion: antiscientist, antiself, postoriented, rooted in the eternal cycle of existential predicaments.

If Bell's prediction were to be borne out, then we might hope for (post)modernism to erase the "beyond" of modernity, returning to the limits that the great civilizations have imposed upon themselves. To do so, however, (post)modernism would need to revive sacred institutions while not sacrificing our commitment to cultural pluralism. So far, no theorist has appeared with any positive vision of such a society.

In the meantime, we may turn to Jameson's reflections on postmodernism and his attempt to restore Marxism as what Bell would call a redemptive religion, for each of them is in fact aware of his respective appeal to Walter Benjamin's insistence upon the indestructibility of the aura of religion in human history. Ordinarily, social scientists and Marxists in particular are not kind to messianism. This has made the reception of Benjamin slower on this score than his studies of commodity fetishism. In short, Benjamin's analysis and his response to modernism have been separated, either to be expropriated in the analysis of postmodernism or else left to those whose sympathies lie with the unhappy consciousness deprived of any hope of redemptive institutions.

I turn now to Fredrick Jameson's reflections upon the place of postmodernism in the cultural logic of late capitalism because, as an unrepentant Marxist, Jameson draws some of the necessary distinctions I found lacking in Bell's account of the role of mass culture in late capitalism. Yet I want also to show that despite their opposing political values, Bell's neoconservatism and Jameson's neo-Marxism both resort to a Durkheimian lament over the dissolution of the social bond. Whereas Bell's ancient liberalism separates him from the Marxist vision of community, Jameson can invoke this communal vision as the ultimately emancipatory drive in the political unconscious of our culture. Postmodernism certainly reflects the sense of an ending. The question is, what is ended? Is it industrialism—in which case both capitalism and socialism are finished? Bell would probably take this view. Yet he can find nothing to celebrate in postindustrialism, because in the end he remains a high priest of modernism.

But then Bell, Habermas, and Jameson, despite their differences, are all open to the taunts of Lyotard who finds everything to celebrate in the postmodern dissolution of right and left consensus.[10] For Habermas, too, is unwilling to abandon the modernist project to which Marxism is committed. With quite different values than those of Bell, Habermas has also set about the destruction of the French branch of postmodernism, which currently infects North America and Western Europe.[11] Between such figures, Jameson's position is a little difficult, for certain aspects of postmodern cultural criticism must appeal to him inasmuch as it belongs to the received radicalism of literary studies with which he identifies himself. Overall, however, Jameson manages to extricate himself from the postmodern fascination and to oppose it with an eloquent, even if surprisingly religious appeal on behalf of Marxism as the transcendental ground of all human culture and community.

It might well be argued that such sociologies as those of Bell's postindustrialism, Lasch's culture of narcissism, and Toffler's third wave are themselves prime examples of the postmodern exorcism of ideology and class struggle essential to the culture industry of late capitalism. Thus Jameson insists upon drawing a number of distinctions in order to avoid both cultural homogeneity and cultural heterogeneity as twin aspects of postmodern mass culture. He therefore argues that:

  a) cultural analysis always involves buried or repressed theory of historical periodization;
  b) global and American, postmodern culture is the superstructural expression of American domination;
  c) under late capitalism aesthetic production has been integrated into commodity production;
  d) postmodernism cannot be treated as part of modernism without ignoring the shift from early to late capitalism and the latter's redefinition of the culture industry.

These distinctions enable Jameson, like Habermas, to argue that Marxism must survive as the neomodernist opposition to late capitalism, absolutely opposed to its superficiality, its imaginary culture, and its total collapse of public and private history.[12] Jameson and Habermas are therefore insistent that Marxist discourse cannot flirt with contemporary fragmentation and subjectlessness. Marxism is the transcendental story, a people's story, which remains lively with human hope; it is a utopian gesture without which humanity is unthinkable.

However, incapable of shocking the bourgeoisie, postmodernism certainly seems to *épater les marxistes!* Consider how Jameson contrasts Andy Warhol's *Diamond Dust Shoes* with Van Gogh's *Peasant Shoes* or rather Heidegger's reflections upon them.[13] Warhol's shoes are colorless and flat; they glitter like Hollywood stars, consumed by a light that bathes them in superficiality, denying them all interiority, making them appear crazy for any gesture that is rooted in a world beyond artifice. By contrast, Heidegger claims that the peasant's shoes tell a story that involves ordinary persons; they are continuous with institutions whose meaningful history is the broader framework in which they figure as human artifacts. According to Jameson, all this is lost in the world of video space-time, in the hyperspatiality of postmodern architecture, and in the self-consuming arts of postmodern literature and music. Like Bell, Jameson refuses the postmodern celebration of the fragment, the paralogical and paratactical arts that dissolve the modernist narrative, dancing upon the grave of identity, rationality, and authority. Yet Jameson insists that postmodernism should not be considered solely as a phenomenon of style:

> it [postmodernism] is also, at least in my use, a periodizing concept whose function is to correlate the emergence of new formal features in culture with the emergence of a new type of social life and a new economic order—what is euphemistically called modernization, postindustrial, or consumer society, the society of the media or the spectacle, or multinational capitalism.[14]

Here, as so often, Jameson's piling up of alternative epithets for the description of the socio-economic system leaves it unanalyzed in favor of its exploration in terms of two cultural phenomena—pastiche and schizophrenia to which we now turn. The fascination of these phenomena for postmodernist theorists is itself a sign of the inextricable sense and non-sense that characterize the ahistorical and anecological predicament of late capitalism.[15]

Pastiche involves the intertextuality, interpictoriality, the intermodishness of codes-without-context whose inappropriateness suggests they never had even a local value and hence always prefigured the contemporary value chaos. As I see it, such codes create the illusion that "Bogart" experienced himself and his social institutions with the same affectation exhibited by today's Rocky Horror Show for kids without a society and for whom character can mean anything else than caricature. The illusion of recycled popular culture is that bourgeois capitalism never created the institutional settings in which

"Bogey" was taken by himself and others for real. This is appealing because in the bureaucratic contexts of late capitalism, "Bogey" could only be a pastiche/parody of lost subjectivity and individualism. Postmodern sophisticates would, of course, claim that "Bogey" is all there was from the beginning—that is, the essential myth of individualism. Hence all that remains is to democratize the myth—every man his own "Bogey," every woman as "Bacall." All we can aspire to is autoaffection through style, fashion, fad, the moment, the scene, regrouped on the collective level through nostalgia, and everyday life as an open museum, a junk store, a replay.

While drawing upon the evaluative connotations of schizophrenia as a diagnostic concept, Jameson nevertheless disallows any intention to engage in cultural psychoanalysis beyond the confines of the literary community. Thus schizophrenia, as Jameson takes it from Lacan, is a linguistic pathology, the inability—through faulty oedipalization—to assign signifiers any temporal and spatial fixed points of identity and reference. Everything floats in an imploded present; action, project, and orientation collapse in the literal, nauseous, and real present in which teenagers are typically trapped. To keep them in this docile state is a task for our education system as a part of the larger system of mass culture to which it occasionally opposes itself, as I have argued elsewhere[16] regarding the functions of the disciplinary society and its therapeutic apparatus. What Jameson (like Bell and Habermas, but from a different interpretation of the same materials) finds at work in pastiche and literary schizophrenia is the collapse of the oppositional culture of modernism so that these two cultural elements of postmodernism now feed the cultural style of late capitalist consumerism:

> I believe that the emergence of postmodernism is closely related to the emergence of this new moment of late, consumer or multinational capitalism. I believe also its formal features in many ways express the deeper logic of the particular social system.[17]

By foreshortening the production process to the production of consumerism, the more difficult analysis of the social relations of production, power, class, and racism is reduced to the operation of an imaginary logic of the political economy of signifiers, and where everything floats on the surface of communication. Here Jameson's reliance upon Baudrillard[18] commits him to the company of Daniel Bell in a lament over the flood of narcissistic consumerism deprived of the mirrors that reflected the old order identities of societies that subordinated exchange value to the higher symbolisms of gift, sacrifice, and community. Rather, postmodern consumers find themselves as mere switching points at video screens, which miniaturize their lives in order to speed them up. The result is that their everyday lives are left devastated by the contrast between the archaic symbolic orders that consumers nevertheless inhabit and the imaginary flux in which they drift. Thus, inside those soft bodies, which wander through our shopping malls and whose minds are operated upon from the outside world, desire is deprived of all intelligence:

> This is the time of miniaturization, telecommand and the micro-procession of time, bodies, pleasures. There is no longer any ideal principle for these things at a higher level, on a human scale. What remains are only concentrated effects, miniaturized and immediately available. This change from human scale to a system of nuclear matrices is visible everywhere: this body, our body, often appears simply superfluous, basically useless in its extension, the multiplicity and complexity of its organs, its tissues, and functions, since today everything is concentrated in the brain and in genetic codes; which alone sum up the operational definition of being.[19]

Here, then, we have a curious effect. How can analysts as varied as Bell, Jameson, Lasch, Baudrillard, and Habermas join common chorus against late capitalism when their politics vary so widely from right to left? The answer seems to be that as cultural critics of late capitalist consumerism, they are all *neomodernists*. In turn, Marx's own modernism may well be the guiding influence. The centrality of Marxism to the project of modernity, as argued for by Habermas and Jameson, can also be claimed on consideration of Marx's writing, his imagery, style, and narrative conventions. Thus Berman and O'Neill have drawn attention to the modernist reading required in order to grasp Marx's polyvalent writings without reducing them either to narrow science or to mere mythology.[20] O'Neill has argued it is because Marx's text so obviously turns upon its modernist aesthetics the Althusserian reading of it as a text of science must be rejected,[21] but without, however, surrendering to Lyotard's reading of it as a lunatic text, a pure work of art.[22] The tension in the modernist sentiment is very well expressed by Berman in a recent effort to separate what is good from what is bad in modernity. Marx, Nietzsche, and Baudelaire still represent relevant dimensions of the modern world because, as he says:

> They can illuminate the contradictory forces and needs that inspire and torment us: our desire to be rooted in a stable and coherent personal and social past, and our instable desire for

growth—not merely for economic growth but for growth in experience, in pleasure, in knowledge, in sensibility—growth that
destroys both the physical and social landscapes of our past,
and our emotional links with those lost worlds; our desperate
allegiances to ethnic, national, class, and sexual groups, which
we hope will give us a firm "identity," and the internationaliza-
tion of everyday life—of our clothes and household goods, our
books and music, our ideas and fantasies—that spreads all our
identites all over the map; our desire for clear and solid values to
live by, and our desire to embrace the limitless possibilities of
modern life and experience that obliterate all values. . . . Experiences like these unite us with the nineteenth-century modern
world: a world where, as Marx said, "everything is pregnant
with its contrary" and "all that is solid melts into air"; a world
where, as Nietzsche said, "there is danger, the mother of morality— a great danger . . . displaced onto the individual, onto the
nearest and dearest, onto the street, onto one's own child, one's
own heart, one's own innermost secret recesses of wish and
will.[23]

What unites Bell and Jameson, despite the nuances in their response to the culture of postmodernism, is the will to order. In Bell
the order is backward-looking, in Jameson it is forward-looking. Both
are in search of a new social bond and both believe that it cannot be
discovered by severing our links with the past, as the most mindless
forms of postmodernism imagine. In this regard, even Lasch and
Habermas share the same modernist sentiment, despite different
ideas about its historical sources. Although orthodox Marxism and
neoconservatism are as opposed to postmodernism as they are to one
another, with respect to the value of the past each is shot through
with the contradictory impulses of modernism. Each may blame the
self-consuming artifacts of postmodernism for their cultural malaise.
But the fact is that industrialism, which institutionalizes discontent
and, so to speak, condemns us to modernity. Yet the neo-Marxists
seem just as unwilling as the neoconservatives to switch their gods.
As Marcuse saw, both continue to cling to the old god Prometheus.
Both fight to keep out the young gods Orpheus and Narcissus whose
premodern and postindustrial figures still fail to seduce Habermas
and Bell. This is so, even though the social forecast of postindustrialism calls for a more creative divinity.

In the light of the idea of nonrepressive sublimation, Freud's
definition of Eros as striving to "form living substance into ever greater unities, so that life may be prolonged and brought to higher devel-

opment" takes on added significance. The biological drive becomes a cultural drive. The pleasure principle reveals its own dialectic . . . the abolition of toil, the amelioration of the environment, the conquest of disease and decay, the creation of luxury. All these activities flow directly from the pleasure principle, and, at the same time, they constitute *work*, which associates individuals to "greater unities"; no longer confined within the mutilating dominion of the performance principle, they modify the impulse without deflecting it from its aim. There is sublimation and, consequently, culture; but this sublimation proceeds in a system of expanding and enduring libidinal relations, which are in themselves work relations.[24]

Given the neo-Marxist and neoconservative refusal of the new god, Eros, a void is created in which Jameson can work to refurbish the Marixt vision of a productive utopia. Thus he argues that the death of the subject, the end of humankind, the migration of reason into madness, the collapse of social and historical narratives into schizophrenic case histories, are acceptable visions of postmodern critique only if we work for a renewal of Marxist history and hermeneutics. Jameson, still apprenticed to Marcuse and Bloch, assumes the Promethean task of binding his own myth to the utopian future of industrialism. He thereby seeks to retain the historical identity of the original Promethean myth with its utopian science of action and community bound by hope and memory:

> Now the origin of Utopian thinking becomes clear, for it is memory which serves as the fundamental mediator between the inside and outside, between the psychological and the poetical. . . . The primary energy of revolutionary activity derives from this memory of prehistoric happiness which the individual can regain only through its externalization through its reestablishment for society as a whole. The loss or repression of the very sense of such concepts as freedom and desire takes, therefore, the form of a kind of amnesia . . . which the hermeneutic activity, the stimulation of memory as the negation of the here and now, as the projection of Utopia, has its function to dispel, restoring to us the original clarity and force of our own most vital drives and wishes.[25]

Whereas capitalism displaces its own myths with secular science, utopian Marxism keeps the bond between myth and science as a history-making institution. Utopianism, then, is not a romanticism or nostalgia that refuses to learn form history. Rather, what can be learned from history, which preserves rather than represses its own genealogy, is that romanticism and myth cannot be contained by secularism and that in the end they are to be joined to the sciences of action and collectivity that they prefigure:

> Thus, to insist upon this term of Breton which corresponds both to Freudian usage and to our own hermeneutic vocabulary, a genuine plot, a genuine narrative, is that which can stand as the very *figure* of Desire itself: and this not only because as the Freudian sense pure physiological desire is inaccessible as such to consciousness, but also because in the socio-economic context, genuine desire risks being dissolved and lost. . . . In that sense desire is the form taken by freedom in the new commercial environment.[26]

In short, Jameson argues that every genre of thought (myth, literature, science) has to be grasped as a psycho-historical master narrative (the political unconscious), which, when properly interpreted, is Marxism. Postmodernism cannot be a stage in this narrative because it abandons history as a human motive—that is, as the motive to make ourselves human individually *and* collectively.[27]

The latter conjunction is the social bond whose dissolution Bell and Lasch lament, whereas Habermas and Jameson continue to affirm its ultimate historical, normative, and analytic primacy. Jameson's particular strength, it must be said, lies in his will to carry the burden of the dialectical switching between the secularization and the reenchantment of the life-world and its modern vocation, while seeking to avoid Weberian pessimism as well as Nietzschean cynicism. He does so fully conscious that the age of religion has passed and that for this very reason we are tempted to produce an "aestheticized" religion, an imaginary or hallucinated community, in an age that is neither religious nor social. How, then, can Marxism exempt itself from such sentimentalism? Jameson's reply is that Marxism and religion can be embraced as elements of a "marital square" in which history and collectivity join individual and community action and understanding against inaction and ignorance that disposses the community and exploit it in favor of its masters. Jameson's fundamental claim is that all forms of social consciousness—both of oppressor and of oppressed—are utopian inasmuch as these groups are themselves figures for an unalienated collective life. Jameson is at pains to deny that such an affirmation merely represents a return to a Durkheimian symbolics of social solidarity, or to a neo-Marxist marriage of aesthetics and social hygiene. Marxism needs both a positive as well as a negative hermeneutics of social solidarity if it is not to

degenerate into postmodern fragmentation, or into an absurd nega-
tivity that would separate forever its scientific utopianism from its
primitive myth of communism:

> Only Marxism can give us an adequate account of the essential
> *mystery* of the cultural past, which, like Tiresias drinking the
> blood, is momentarily returned to life and warmth and allowed
> once more to speak, and to deliver its long forgotten message in
> surroundings utterly alien to it. This mystery can be re-enacted
> only if the human adventure is one; only thus—and not
> through . . . antiquarianism or the projections of the modern-
> ists—can we glimpse the vital claims upon us of such long-dead
> issues as the seasonal alternation of the economy of a primitive
> tribe, the passionate disputes about the nature of the Trin-
> ity. . . . Only if they are retold within the unity of a single great
> collective story . . . for Marxism, the collective struggle to arrest
> a realm of Freedom from a realm of Necessity. . . . It is in detect-
> ing traces of the uninterrupted narrative, in restoring to the
> surface of the text the repressed and buried reality of this funda-
> mental history, that the doctrine of a political unconscious finds
> its function and its necessity.[28]

Such passages are among the best in literary Marxism. Yet Jameson's
claims are clearly exorbitant. They are so because he cannot identify
any specific social forces to carry his utopianism—and so he throws
the holy water of Marxist utopianism over any group, whether oppressor or oppressed, insofar as they are "figures" of an ultimately
classless society! Such a vision verges almost upon the mystical or, as
he would say, the allegorical:

> All class consciousness of whatever type is Utopian insofar as it
> expresses the unity of a collectivity; yet it must be added that
> this proposition is an allegorical one. The achieved collectivity or
> organic group of whatever kind—oppressors fully as much as
> oppressed—is Utopian not in itself, but only insofar as all such
> collectivities are themselves *figures* for the ultimate collective life
> of an achieved Utopian or classless society.[29]

On the right and on the left, we are still waiting for history to
deliver itself. Whether politics or religion will be the midwife remains
undecided. After a bitter lesson, the sociologist puts his money on
religion. Jameson perseveres with the alchemy of a hermeneutics that
will deliver history, politics, and religion. And so the stage of history

takes another turn. The ghost of Marx returns; there is much talk in which Jameson is apparently more agile than Habermas who waits for a chance to articulate a final economy of truth, sincerity, and justice. Bell is silenced but offstage the laughter of Lyotard still reaches us. Marcuse, Bloch—and perhaps ourselves remain—saddened.

Notes

1. Daniel Bell, *The Cultural Contradictions of Capitalism* (New York: Basic Books, 1976), and restatements, "Liberalism in the Postindustrial Society," "Beyond Modernism Beyond Self", pp. 228–44 and 275–302 in his *The Winding Passage: Essays and Sociological Journeys 1960–1980* (Cambridge: ABT Books, 1980); also "Modernism Mummified," *American Quarterly* (January 1987).

2. Fredric Jameson, "Postmodernism, or the Cultural Logic of Late Capitalism," *New Jersey Review*, 146 (July-August 1984): 53–94.

3. Fredric Jameson, *The Political Unconscious: Narrative as a Socially Symbolic Act* (Ithaca: Cornell University Press, 1981).

4. Bell, *Cultural Contradictions*, p. 20.

5. Ibid., pp. 21–22.

6. Ibid., pp. 28–29.

7. Ibid., p. 155.

8. John O'Neill, "Televideo Ergo Sum: Some Hypotheses on the Specular Functions of the Media," *Communication*, 7/1 (1983): 221–40.

9. Daniel Bell, "The Return of the Sacred? The Argument on the Future of Religion," in *The Winding Passage*, pp. 334–35.

10. Jean-François Lyotard, *The Postmodern Condition: A Report on Knowledge* (Minneapolis: University of Minnesota Press, 1984).

11. Jürgen Habermas, "Modernity—An Incomplete Project," pp. 3–15 in *The Anti-Aesthetic: Essays on Postmodern Culture* (Port Townsend, Wash.: Bay Press, 1983).

12. John O'Neill, "Public and Private Space," in his *Sociology as a Skin Trade: Essays towards a Reflexive Sociology* (New York: Harper and Row, 1972), pp. 20–37.

13. Jameson, "Postmodernism, or the Cultural Logic of Late Capitalism," pp. 58–62.

14. Fredric Jameson "Postmodernism and Consumer Society," in *The Anti-Aesthetic*, p. 113.

15. Hal Foster, "(Post) Modern Polemics," pp. 121–38, in his *Recordings: Art, Spectable, Cultural Politics* (Port Townsend Wash.: Bay Press, 1985).

16. John O'Neill, "The Disciplinary Society: From Weber to Foucault," *British Journal of Sociology*, 37/1 (March 1986): 42–60.

17. Jameson, in *The Anti-Aesthetic*, p. 125.

18. Jean Beaudrillard, *For a Critique of the Political Economy of the Sign* (St. Louis: Telos Press, 1981).

19. Jean Beaudrillard, "The Ecstasy of Communication," in *The Anti-Aesthetic*, p. 128.

20. Marshall Berman, *All That is Solid Melts Into Air: The Experience of Modernity* (New York: Simon and Schuster, 1982); John O'Neill, "Marxism and Mythology," in his *For Marx Against Althusser, And Other Essays* (Washington, D.C.: University Press of America, 1982), pp. 43–58.

21. *For Marx Against Althusser*, pp. 1–17.

22. Jean François Lyotard, "Le desir nommé Marx," pp. 117–88 in his *Economie Libidinale* (Paris: Minuit, 1974).

23. Berman, *All That is Solid*, pp. 35–36.

24. Herbert Marcuse, *Eros and Civilization: A Philosophical Inquiry into Freud* (New York: Vintage, 1962),pp. 193–94.

25. Fredric Jameson, *Marxism and Form: Twentieth-Century Dialectical Theories of Literature* (Princeton: Princeton University Press, 1971), pp. 113–14.

26. Ibid., pp. 100–101.

27. John O'Neill, "Naturalism in Vico and Marx: A Discourse Theory of the Body Politic," in his *For Marx Against Althusser*; and his "Marx's Humanist Theory of Alienation" in *George Lukacs and his World: A Reassessment*, ed. Ernest Joos (New York: Peter Lang, 1987), pp. 59–76.

28. Jameson, *Political Unconscious*, pp. 19–20.

29. Ibid., p. 291.

Part VII

Questions of Language

18

Heidegger and the Problem of Philosophical Language

Gerald L. Bruns

> The relation to what is present that
> rules in the essence of presencing
> itself is a unique one, altogether
> incomparable to any other relation.
> It belongs to the uniqueness of
> Being itself. Therefore, in order to
> name the essential nature of Being,
> language would have to find a
> single word, the unique word. From
> this we can gather how daring
> every thoughtful word addressed to
> Being is. Nevertheless such daring
> is not impossible, since Being
> speaks always and everywhere
> throughout language. The difficulty
> lies not so much in finding in
> thought the word for Being as in
> retaining purely in genuine thinking
> the word found.

"The Anaximander Fragment"

According to a line of thinking that comes down to us from Leibniz, a philosophical language would be a logically perfect language—that is, a language with a syntax but no vocabulary, or in other words a purely analytical language, or a language whose deep structure would not be deep any more but would be completely open to view. A language, in short, with nothing to hide. Such a language would be completely under control; it would be control itself. Linguistic competence would be identical with performance, theory identical with practice. Rhetoric would be absorbed into grammar along with everything else. Discourse would no longer have to be monitored; it would be above suspicion. It would simply function, would be a pure functioning without substance, a pure transparency. Nothing that you could put into language would ever get lost in it; it would always be itself, a pure identity. In fact the idea of putting anything into language is oddly metaphorical. For in principle this would be a language already entirely written—that is, a construction without beginning or end in which everything would be already entirely contained. So a description of this language, a grammar of it, would also be a description of all that is; it would speak the plenum of Being. As we never tire of being told, there is nothing outside language. Imagine a language whose center is everywhere and whose circumference is the infinite abyss or sum of zero.

A prevailing picture of Heidegger has him searching for something like a primitive version of this language—that is, for "a single word, a unique word," the name of names that would, if only we could lay our hands on it, lay Being open to view. This "alliance of speech and Being in the unique word, in the finally proper name," is, Derrida says, Heidegger's metaphysical hope, his nostalgia for "a purely maternal or paternal language, a lost native country of thought." So he ransacks the antique fragments of Anaximander and Heraclitus in search of the "magic word" that will conjure up the essence of presencing itself.[1]

Actually, Heidegger's later writings on language—his reflections on *Sage* or Saying—are not easy to interpret. For example, the idea of laying anything open to view is deeply repugnant to Heidegger, and this is especially so when it comes to language. He thinks language should be thickened, not refined to transparency. This is what he takes poetry to be—namely, a thickening of language; the word for poetry is, appropriately, a pun: *dichten*, "to thicken." If you ask what poetry is for, the answer is that it is not for the expression or representation of anything—that is, it is not a primitive form of science or philosophy—not a species of signification, but a step back from signification, a renunciation of meaning. Poetry is "a breath for nothing" (Rilke), a speaking "without why." This does not appear to be just another formalism. In Heidegger's lingo, poetry in the sense of *Dichten* is not the production of poems (*poiēsis*); it is the letting-go or *Gelassenheit* of language that allows language to withdraw into itself or into its own, to close itself up and go its own way. Philosophically, this means going out of control. Already Plato had likened words to the statues of Daedalus that were so lifelike that they had to be restrained like slaves because they kept running off. This simile gives us our word for ambiguity or the wandering or waywardness of words, which philosophy from the beginning has tried to bring to a halt. Heidegger's idea, however, is that, instead of trying to control this waywardness (instead of trying to function like philosophy), thinking should allow itself to be appropriated by it—that is, it should let itself go, even if this means wandering in the wilderness or in the dark. ("It is more salutary for thinking to wander into the strange than to establish itself in the intelligible" [VA 218/76].)

This is what comes of the dialogue with poetry. Poetry exposes thinking to the otherness of language, its uncontainability, its self-refusal or withdrawal from the conceptual frameworks in which we are taught to make sense of things. Poetry as the thickening of language turns the thinker into a wanderer whose discourse is composed of puns rather than concepts. And this is what poetry has evidently done to the later Heidegger, whose discourse is a parody of philosophical language.

For example, a crucial notion in the later Heidegger is that of the rift or rift-design (*Riss* or *Auf-Riss*). However, the rift is not something that can be conceptually determined. The best we can do is to read it as a parody of the traditional concept of deep structure. In "The Origin of the Work of Art" Heidegger speaks of the "rift" of earth and world, where the earth is that which closes itself up before every effort we make to penetrate into it, whereas the world is that which is self-disclosing and opens to allow us to come into our own (where "coming into our own" means entering into mortality or withdrawal). The work of art inscribes this rift within itself; it is "structured" as a conflict of earth and world insofar as its work is to open up a world even as, at the same time, it withdraws itself, reserves itself to itself, solitary and strange, refusing every effort that we make, in our usual analytical style, to lay it open to view. The work in this respect is not an aesthetic object. It does not represent or express anything; it does not stand before us as an object of our critical gaze. Heidegger speaks of it as "self-standing," belonging only to itself. It possesses thingly and equipmental features, to be sure, and so we are apt to find it at hand and apparently subject to our will, we will imagine ourselves the finest connoisseurs, but the *truth* of the work occurs only in its *work*—that is, it occurs in the form of a double movement of unconcealment and refusal or dissembling.

Here the truth of the work is not simply disclosure in the sense of *alētheia*; rather, *alētheia* has to be taken now as a pun. The word is rifted by a hyphen (*a-lētheia*) that inscribes something older than truth—namely, the darkness or oblivion (*lēthē*) that belongs to the essence of truth, the shadow that lies at the heart of it (SD 78/81). The work *is*, but not as a being that "is"; rather, the more that it thrusts into the Open—say, into the "is" (if that is what the "is" is)—"the more cleanly does it seem to cut all ties to human beings" (Hw 54/66). The work of art is not anything human. In its truth it is absolutely other, absolutely strange. Of course, here is where most persons turn against Heidegger.

Now the work of art opens the way to the later Heidegger's reflections on the thing, the world, and language. Thing and world are not beings of any sort. We cannot say of them that they exist, or anyhow it is not enough, or not much, to say this. Rather, as the work *works*, so the thing *things* and the world *worlds*. Compare this to "it rains" where the substantive conceals itself, refuses itself, withdraws into the verb or, more accurately, into the event. Categories of existence, presence, objectivity, representation, and meaning are absorbed in all that happens in this event—called, famously, *Ereignis*. Paul Ricoeur, following Otto Pöggeler and others, thinks of *Ereignis* as "a philosopher's metaphor" like the analogy of being.[2] In fact, however, like so much else in the later Heidegger that Ricoeur finds offensive, *Ereignis* is a pun so dense no one has yet been able to unpack it, and no one ever will: it is sometimes translated as "event," sometimes as "appropriation," but it means something like getting into the dance or swing of things; it is a figure of letting-go. It is *not* another word for Being. On the contrary, to borrow a line from Emmanuel Levinas, it is "otherwise than Being" or "beyond Being" or "older than Being." Being does not figure very much in the later Heidegger. The idea of naming Being does not belong to the later Heidegger.

As for the world: it is not to be thought of as a place or container for things. The thing is worldless, self-standing like the work of art, separated from the world by a rift that nevertheless draws thing and world into a mutual belonging. Rift here means "dif-ference" (*Unter-Schied*), which is again a parody of a hoary old philosophical term, a "rifted" difference. As Heidegger indicates, "The word dif-ference is now removed from its usual and customary usage [*gewöhnlichen und gewohnten Gebrauch*]" (US 25/202), not so much to mean something new as to unfix its meaning so as to not-mean what we think: "The dif-ference is neither distinction nor relation" (US 25/203), Heidegger says. Thing and world are not related to one another, although they are intimate, only this intimacy is sliced lengthwise in a way that separates world and thing and settles them each into its own "apartness." So world and thing are singular rather than particular, recalcitrant and unsubsumable. The thing is not a Kantian object but an event, nor is the world anything constituted according to the forms of time and space and the categories of explanation. We are a step back from or outside representation and explanation.

In his essay "The Thing," which is a sort of parody of representational thinking, Heidegger designs, sketches, or rifts the world in a wild mixture of metaphors and puns in which earth and sky, gods and mortals, come together out of Hölderlin's fragments into a "mirror-play" and "round dance" that unites them, or rather "rings" them, as a fourfold (*Geviert*). We do not know what the fourfold is, either. Some call it Heidegger's "cosmology," but if so it is a worldview that is more pun than picture. What Heidegger calls the "world" is the mirror-play of the fourfold, the round dance of *Ereignis* (or, rather, *Ereignis*) in which everything comes together and belongs together, rings together and puns together, each in its own apartness: *Das Spiegel-Spiel von Welt ist der Reigen des Ereignens.* Heidegger thinks of this event as the setting free of the thing, where freedom means something like what Levinas means when he says that the Other is free of sameness or identity, and therefore something we have no power over, something that takes us out of the grasping mode of cognition. "Out of the ringing mirror-play," Heidegger says, "the thinging of the thing [as against its objectification before consciousness] takes place" (VA 173/180). Many persons want to capture this setting free of the thing by thinking of it as a sort of revelation— that is, as if it were still an event taking place before our eyes; but, if we listen to the pun, concealment belongs to this event as *lēthē* belongs to *a-lētheia*. The *Er-eignis* of thinging means the withdrawal of the thing even as we reach for it. The thing is now something otherwise.

Now it is to the strange idiom of thinging and worlding that the speaking of language (or Saying) belongs: *die Sprache spricht* in the same way that *das Ding dingt* and *die Welt weltet*. Heidegger's earliest lecture on language asks what it is for this speaking to occur. The hardest thing to understand is that we are not involved in this speaking as performing subjects. We belong to language by way of listening, not as speech-actors endowed with linguistic competence. Indeed, for Heidegger linguistic competence means, if anything, being open to all the puns that are ringing always and everywhere throughout language—for example, the pun on hearing (*Hören*) and belonging (*gehören*). It means hearing all the puns in *Er-eignis*, including the celebrated word for sign (*Zeichen*), which is itself a pun on showing (*zeigen*) and self-standing or owning (*eigen*). This punning inscribes and also breaks up the motif of the proper that Derrida hears in Heidegger's language.[3]

Poetry and thinking are modes of listening; they are not acts that we perform. Think of them as callings to which we must respond, or to which we are exposed and answerable the way we are to questions of time or being. The question itself is a kind of calling; it is never something we think up. Rather the question (whatever it is a question of) is always there. Like the question of death, one day it hits us and we are never the same again.

So it is with language, which speaks as a calling, where calling is like the raining that occurs without a rainer. Calling is uncanny discourse because the caller withholds itself, refuses itself in the manner of the work of art, whose work is also a sort of summons. The German word for this refusal is *Sichversagen*, which is a kind of Saying as Nay-Saying. And as the work of art is absorbed in its working, or as the rain is absorbed, if that is the word, in its raining, so is the caller in its calling, and language in its speaking. And so are we. I mean that we are absorbed or appropriated by this event, we disappear into it, are overwhelmed or transformed by it, transported out of the sphere or frame of our ordinary comportment, estranged from ourselves, out of control, a little mad perhaps, or perhaps, Hölderlinlike or Nietzschelike, not just a little but are apt to be found wandering apart in the wilderness as madfolk do, otherwise than human. Heidegger calls this "having an experience with language." It is also what is called thinking.

An experience with language does not occur in the speaking of it; it is not part of any plenum of discourse or copia of words and things. On the contrary, the experience occurs at the moment words get away from us, fail us, refuse themselves—the moment explored so dramatically by Mallarmé. It would be easy to show that the history of poetry is obsessed with this moment, and so is philosophy. It is the moment when language withdraws itself, frees itself from our control, grows impossibly strange and unspeakable (as in *Finnegans Wake*, with its powerful and pointless puns). Philosophy was invented to keep this moment from happening. Nevertheless, it is in this event that the nature of language (*das Wesen der Sprache*) unfolds itself. This unfolding is not easy for us to grasp because it is an unfolding as withholding (*Ereignis*). The phrase "nature of language" has to be taken not in its usual lucid philosophical sense but darkly in the manner of Heraclitus, as in the famous fragment no. 123, *phusis kruptesthai philei: "phusis* loves to hide." So it is with "the nature [*phusis*] of language." Heidegger says:

> There is some evidence that the essential nature of language flatly refuses to put itself in words—in the language, that is, in which we make statements about language. If language every-

where withholds its nature in this sense, then such withholding belongs to the very nature of language [*dann gehört diese Verweigerung zum Wesen der Sprache*]. Thus language not only holds back when we speak it in the accustomed ways, but this its holding back is determined by the fact that language holds back its own origin and so denies its being [*Wesen*] to our usual notions. But then we may no longer say that the being of language is the language of being [*das Wesen der Sprache sei die Sprache des Wesens*: the word "being" does not fit here], unless the word "language" in the second phrase says something different, in fact something in which the withholding of the being of language—speaks [*worin die Verweigerung des Sprachwesens—spricht*]. [US 186/81]

So it appears that we must not imagine language speaking as if it were some mythic personification of the father- or mother-tongue; it is, unimaginably, the *withholding* of language that speaks. In this event language is no longer itself; it is otherwise than language. Heidegger calls it Saying (*Sage*), which is a *Sichversagen*, a self-refusal of language that leaves us speechless.

Let me conclude by mentioning Heidegger's lecture "The Word," where he returns to the final couplet of Stefan George's poem, "Das Wort," this time to pick up on the word *verzichten*, to renounce: "*So lernt ich traurig den verzicht: / Kein ding sei wo das wort gebricht.*" Renunciation, Heidegger says, means giving up language as *logos*—that is, the power of framing representations. It means giving up language as the system of signs that "rule over things" (US 225/144). By means of renunciation, the poet opens onto "a different rule of the word," one that is not based on signs and has nothing to do with signification. Heidegger says:

> The poet must relinquish claim to the assurance that he will on demand be supplied with a name for that which he has posited as what truly is. This positing and that claim he must now deny himself. The poet must renounce having words under his control as representational names for what is posited. As self-denial [*Sichversagen*], renunciation is a Saying which says to itself: Where word breaks off no thing may be [*Kein ding sei wo das wort gebricht*]. [US 227–28/146–47]

Renunciation means getting out of the mode of worldmaking, giving up the idea of order at Key West. In Heidegger's case, this means rethinking the nature of poetry as he had figured it in his

Hölderlin essays from the 1930s, where the poet is characterized specifically in terms of the foundational power of naming: "Poetry," Heidegger says in "Hölderlin and the Essence of Poetry," "is the establishing of Being by means of the word [*Dichtung ist worthafte Stiftung des Seins*]" (EM 38/281). Here poetry is still being philosophized—that is, assimilated into foundationalism as a condition of possibility, the Kantian *Bedingung,* the act of positing or objectification of the world. Thus "when the gods are named originally and the essence of things receives a name, so that things for the first time shine out, human existence is brought into a firm relation and given a basis [*auf einen Grund gestellt*]. The speech of the poet is establishment [*Stiftung*] not only in the sense of the free act of giving, but at the same time in the sense of the firm basing of human existence on its foundation" (EM 39/28–29).

But now Heidegger says that this power is just what the poet surrenders: "The poet must renounce having words under his control as representation names [*darstellende Worte*] for what is posited." Poetry now means letting go of the ground; it means letting language go, which is the same as letting language speak and things thing: *das Wort be-dingt das Ding zum Ding* (US 232/151). Peter Hertz translates this line as "The word makes the thing into a thing," as if to turn Heidegger back into Kant, but the word is not productive or constitutive of things. Poetry is not *poiēsis,* not *Stiftung* and *Gründung.* "Renunciation," Heidegger says, "commits itself to the higher rule of the word which first lets a thing be as thing. The word 'be-things' the thing. We should like to call this rule of the word 'bethinging' [*Bedingnis*]" (US 232/151). It is not too hard to read this as a parody of foundationalism.

What is worth knowing about the word *Bedingnis* is that it is no longer a word; or rather it is a word but not a term (WD 88/130). Logically, it is a nonentity. "This old word," Heidegger says, "has disappeared from linguistic usage" (US 232/151). Goethe still knew it, he says, but only in the sense in which it would later become a philosophical term of art—namely, as condition. But as Heidegger uses it:

> Bethinging says something different from talking about a condition. . . . A condition is the existent ground for something that is. The condition gives reason, and it grounds. It satisfies the principle of sufficient reason. But the word does not give reasons for the thing. The word allows the thing to presence as thing. We shall call this allowing bethinging. The poet does not explain what this bethinging is. But the poet commits himself,

that is, his Saying, to this mystery of the word. In such a commitment, he who renounces denies himself to the claim which he formerly willed. [US 232–33/151]

In other words, we no longer know what *Bedingnis* means, what it signifies, and so for us it is a dead word; but precisely for this reason it comes alive for Heidegger. It is a word that has withdrawn itself, secluded itself in darkness—call it a word of self-refusal, as if this dark word could become the word of words, the word for "the higher rule of the word," or, as Heidegger says, the word for "the word's mystery" (US 233/151). Call it a word that language speaks, or a word for what happens when language speaks—but not a word for us. As a word, it leaves us in the dark. But we must not be afraid. All this means is that there is no lexicon, no discursive field, no semantic space, no conceptual scheme, no language game, no interpretive community, no *chōra* in which this word can be found or where its meaning can be recuperated and fixed, this time not to wander off and become lost. It is what a word looks like, or sounds like, when it has been set free: a *singulare tantum*. A pun on we know not what (thinging).

Now imagine, if you can, a philosophical language made up of such words. Of course, there is no imagining such a thing, but it appears that Heidegger would have liked to philosophize in such a language, were such a thing possible. This seems to have been the point of his effort to start up "a dialogue with early Greek thinking" (Hw 309/25)—that is, with the fragments of Anaximander and Heraclitus, whose words we can no longer reconceptualize, translate them as we will. These fragments are dark sayings—enigmas, sayings that do not speak or that have withdrawn from the world back into the earth whence they came. So there is no question of going back to these sayings as if to a starting point that would get the history of philosophy underway anew, this time not to go astray. The idea of starting history over again, of revolution, is a dream of mastering history; whereas in fact history is ambiguity, waywardness, withdrawal, errancy. So it makes a kind of sense that there is nothing programatic or even purposeful about Heidegger's conversation with the ancients; he is not recommending this conversation as a new way of doing philosophy (a new archaism). It is not clear what this conversation amounts to—other than a trackless reflection, a thinking without why, a wayward musing here and there upon a handful of overtranslated words: *phusis, logos, moira, eris, alētheia, hen*. What Heidegger does, in effect, is to "undertranslate" these words, as if to preserve them in their darkness. One could say that he lingers in their company, in their nearness, but instead of trying to remove their strangeness or remoteness, Heidegger allows himself to drift away into the dark, leaving us not knowing what to make of him.

Here is something like a context for the quotation that I began with. If language could find "a single word, the unique word" for "the essence of presencing itself," it would not be a word that we could take over and reiterate in order to experience at last the plenum that our historicality withholds from us; rather, the word would be like a window or threshold onto this withholding itself. The risk of thinking, its venture or daring, would be to cross this threshold. This would be like entering into an endless pun whose changes could never be terminated, whose multiple paths could never be exhausted or traced back to a beginning or worked out to a certainty. As if there could be no thinking that did not put its reason at risk.

Abbreviations

References to Heidegger's works as cited in the text. The first number refers to the German text, the second to the English translation.

ED   *Erläuterungen zu Hölderlins Dichtung.* Frankfurt: Klostermann, 1982. Contains "Hölderlin und das Wesen der Dichtung" and "Heimkunft / An die Verwandten." "Hölderlin and the Essence of Poetry" and "Remembrance of the Poet," *Existence and Being,* trans. Douglas Scott. Chicago: Henry Regnery, 1949, pp. 233–91.

EM   *Einführung in die Metaphysik.* Tübingen: Max Niemeyer, 1966. *Introduction to Metaphysics,* trans. Ralph Manheim. Garden City, N. Y.: Doubleday, 1961.

G   *Gelassenheit.* Pfullingen: Günther Neske, 1959. *Discourse on Thinking,* trans. John M. Anderson and E. Hans Freund. New York: Harper & Row, 1966.

ID   *Identität und Differenz.* Pfullingen: Günther Neske, 1957. *Identity and Difference,* trans. Joan Stambaugh. New York: Harper & Row, 1969.

Hw   *Holzwege.* Frankfurt: Klostermann, 1950. Contains the following:

"Der Ursprung des Kunstwerkes." "The Origin of the Work of Art," trans. Albert Hofstadter. *Poetry, Language, Thought.* New York: Harper & Row, 1971, pp. 15–87.

"Nietzsches Wort, 'Gott ist tot.'" "The Word of Nietzsche: 'God is Dead,'" trans. William Lovitt. *The Question Concerning Technology and Other Essays.* New York: Harper & Row, 1977, pp. 53–112.

"Wozu Dichter?" "What Are Poets For?," trans. Albert Hofstadter. *Poetry, Language, Thought*, pp. 91–142.

"Der Spruch des Anaximander." "The Anaximander Fragment," trans. David Farrell Krell and Frank A. Capuzzi. *Early Greek Thinking*. New York: Harper & Row, 1975, pp. 13–58.

NI   *Nietzsche I.* Pfullingen: Günther Neske, 1961. *Nietzsche*, trans. David Farrell Krell. New York: Harper & Row, 1979. vol. 1, *The Will to Power as Art.*

SD   *Zur Sache des Denkens.* Tübingen: Max Niemeyer, 1969. Contains "Das Ende der Philosophie und die Aufgabe des Denkens." "The End of Philosophy and the Task of Thinking," trans. Joan Stambaugh, *On Time and Being.* New York: Harper & Row, 1969, pp. 55–73.

SZ   *Sein und Zeit.* Tübingen: Max Niemeyer, 1984. *Being and Time*, trans. John Macquarrie and Edward Robinson. New York: Harper & Row, 1962.

US   *Unterwegs zur Sprache.* Pfullingen: Günther Neske, 1959. Contains the following:

"Die Sprache." "Language," trans. Albert Hofstadter. *Poetry, Language, Thought*, pp. 189–210.

"Die Sprache im Gedicht." "Language in the Poem: A Discussion on Georg Trakl's Poetic Work," trans. Peter D. Hertz. *On the Way to Language.* New York: Harper & Row, 1971, pp. 159–98.

"Aus einem Gespräch von der Sprache." "A Dialogue on Language," *On the Way to Language*, pp. 1–54.

"Das Wesen der Sprache." "The Nature of Language," *On the Way to Language*, pp. 57–108.

"Das Wort." "Words," *On the Way to Language*, pp. 139–56.

"Der Weg zur Sprache." "The Way to Language," *On the Way to Language*, pp. 111–36.

VA   *Vorträge und Aufsätze.* Pfullingen: Neske, 1954. Contains the following:

". . . dichterisch wohnet der Mensch . . ." ". . . Poetically Man Dwells," *Poetry, Language, Thought*, pp. 213–29.

"Die Frage nach der Technik." "The Question Concerning Technology," *The Question Concerning Technology and Other Essays*, pp. 3–35.

"Bauen Wohnen Denken." "Building Dwelling Thinking," *Poetry, Language, Thought*, pp. 145–61.

"Das Ding." "The Thing," *Poetry, Language, Thought*, pp. 165–86.

"Logos (Heraklit, Fragment 50)." "Logos (Heraclitus, Fragment 50)," *Early Greek Thinking*, pp. 59–78.

"Aletheia (Heraklit, Fragment 16)." "Aletheia (Heraclitus, Fragment 16), *Early Greek Thinking*, pp. 102–24.

WD   *Was heisst Denken?* Tübingen: Max Niemeyer, 1961. *What is Called Thinking?*, trans. J. Glenn Gray. New York: Harper & Row, 1968.

Wm   *Wegmarken.* Frankfurt: Klostermann, 1967. Contains the following:

"Was Ist Metaphysik?" "What is Metaphysics," *Martin Heidegger: Basic Writings*, trans. David Farrell Krell. New York: Harper & Row, 1977, pp. 95–112.

"Vom Wesen der Wahrheit." "The Essence of Truth," trans. John Sallis. *Basic Writings*, pp. 117–41.

"Brief über den 'Humanismus.'" "Letter on Humanism," trans. Frank Capuzzi and J. Glenn Gray. *Basic Writings*, pp. 189–242.

Notes

1. See "The Anaximander Fragment" (Hw 337/52). Derrida's comment on this line comes at the end of "Différance" in *Margins of Philosophy*, trans. Alan Basss (Chicago: University of Chicago Press, 1982), p. 27. On Heidegger's magic words, see Richard Rorty, "Deconstruction and Circumvention," in *Critical Inquiry*, 11/1 (1984): 10–13.

2. *The Rule of Metaphor*, trans. Robert Czerny et al. (Toronto: University of Toronto Press, 1977), pp. 311–14. Ricoeur tries to separate authentic speculative thinking in the later Heidegger from the poetized logic that "leads to a series of erasures and repeals that cast thought into the void, reducing it to hermeticism and affectedness, carrying etymological games back to the mystification of 'primitive sense.'" What Ricoeur deplores specifically is the way Heidegger tries to "sever discourse from its propositional character" (p. 313).

3. See "The Ends of Man," in *Margins of Philosophy*, p. 129. Heidegger's idea seems to be that when things come into their own (*eigen*) they are no longer properly themselves, no longer answerable to names or concepts, but are set apart, singular and strange.

19

The Naming of the Virgule in the Linguistic/Extralinguistic Binary

Virgil Lokke

So much in postmodern discourse hinges on the hinge. Our fascination with the role of the binaries, their taxonomic and generative power, their office as generator of hierarchy and closure has almost rendered it habitual that we separate our binaries with a diagonal, a separatrix, slant sign, slash or, as I prefer to call it, the virgule. A significant use of the virgule is as the dividing marker between the *either* and the *or*. This leaning wall, falling toward the future and yet never entering into it, both pushes apart and holds together the names that precede and follow its appearance. The virgule pushes apart to make all names contrastable, oppositional, different, and "clear and distinct." At the same time it holds together these names by an unspecified binding that is always more than pure adjacency, if only because pure anything, let alone pure adjacency, is difficult to find in these postmodern days. Significantly, all names seem to bear the imprint of having once shared a categorizing net, other than the one in immediate focus. If all names are shards of some half-remembered taxonomic moments bearing traces of class membership, class exclusion, and the generative force of negation, shimmering constantly for attention, then it would seem that the generative/degenerating flux of taxonomic processes would provide ample material for bridging the gap, the space marked by the virgule.

The deployment of the virgule is hardly a postmodern phenomenon, but there is something a bit different about our attitude toward it. If we can think of the dialogue between Hermogenes and Cratylus and begin to see Socrates as the functionary slant sign, separating and holding the two disputants together, we have entered the mode of the newly viewed virgule. In this "glueing" and "cutting" edge of the virgule appears the memory of the artifice of hierarchy, the archive of the inescapable containment of each term within the other, and a haunting trace of the deeply implicated either/or of the linguistic/extralinguistic binary. This master binary generates the proliferating versions of "the prison house of language" as well as the current projects for "proper" naming and for the "proper" description of the kind of relationship that obtains between that which lies "within" and that which lies "outside" language.

It is perhaps clear that the virgule itself must be contextualized within the "linguistic" in order to render "either/or-ness." It can be used, of course, to indicate the choices, one or more, that may "properly" fill the blank space that follows. But the virgule need not be strictly identified with a particular or exclusive binary. It can be argued that the virgule is the poststructuralist punctuation par excellence (although a strong case can be made for the hyphen), in that it can be deployed to suggest the endlessness of binariness, a serial proliferation of constrastives in horizontally endless adjacencies, as well as implicating the endless reversibility of insideness and outsideness, a reversibility that common practice denies through vertical hierarchization. Despite its leaning toward infinity, the common virgule tends to invoke a properly contrastive name to pair with the name that preceded it. Indeed, some might be tempted to argue that it would be a rare "virgule" indeed that would not seek both to specify the "proper" word or phrase that can follow and to posit an underlying synonymity for all alternative choices.

What I am concerned with here is the naming and the function of the virgule in poststructuralist discourse. I am interested in how major theorists seek to come to terms with the relationship of the linguistic to the extralinguistic conditions of human experience. It is the naming and function of this juncture that preoccupies many of the disputes, the charge and countercharge of contemporary discourse. It is this juncture that often becomes the focus of competing ideological,[1] philosophical, and anthropological articulations—reinscribing their foundational perspectives in the virgule's new names and function.

One reason that the linguistic/extralinguistic binary has been brought into focus here is the by now somewhat tedious charge that certain intellectual modes, particularly deconstruction, deny the extralinguistic, deny the significance of that which is extratextual, extradiscursive. Various poststructuralist modes, then, are judged according to the degree to which they presumably deny the importance and very existence of history, praxis, the body, the real, and, ultimately, the political.

The charge of exclusion of the political that so many critics level against deconstruction, the charge that the intense focusing upon the linguistic, or the symbolic, or the discursive, or the textual excludes the political is made possible only by an aggressively ideological description of the political. Critics who make the charge find Derrida and others threatening in at least two different respects: that deconstruction is too blatantly academic, or that the kind of redescription of the political implicit in deconstruction demands such an ever-increasing arena of redescription that university structures—departmental and institutional boundaries—are too dangerously and too radically breached.

One example, worthy of some exploration, is the curious possibility of a symbiotic relationship in which American Marxism may be viewed as a ward of the university, as a discursive practice within which the traditional disciplinary boundaries can continue to flourish as unthreatening hyphenated subcategories within a largely untroubled taxonomic matrix. As we all know, American Marxism has considerable trouble convincing others, let alone itself, that it is engaged and committed. What I am suggesting is that the very drawing of lines, the marking per se of metes and bounds *is* political, *is* ideological, and the calling of attention to the marking of bounds is *also* political. And it is the range of the political as exemplified in the naming and placing of the boundary markers, the description of the lines of differentiation, that marks my own discourse.

Theoretical speculations that either deploy the linguistic/extralinguistic binary at some critical juncture or seek ostentatiously to circumvent such a binary exist in rich abundance. A long list of major contemporary cultural critics in whose works the relations between the linguistic and the extralinguistic opposition occupy a key position almost instantaneously presents itself. One thinks of Adorno, Foucault, Lyotard, Gadamer, Habermas, and Heidegger—to name but a few. Again the significant role played in the works of important contemporary feminist critics by the linguistic/extralinguistic dyad can only be suggested by a short list including Kristeva, Irigaray, Cixous, and Clement, whose works examine the linguistic/extralinguistic binary in the context of gender. Beyond the borders of such an investigation lies the possibility of a comparative (male/female) exploration of the possible functions of gender in those theories that name, situate, and ascribe functions to the virgule in the linguistic/extralinguistic binary.

For the present, however, I shall limit my brief and tentative explorations to a few reprentative figures, including Derrida, Bakhtin, Bourdieu, Castoriadis, Jameson, Baudrillard, Lacan,

Luhmann, and Deleuze and Guattari. Each theorist can be related to the next by an impure space, which I have already contaminated with the political. Each can also stand in a translational relationship to the others, such relationship to be marked only by an invisible virgule.

Derrida, for example, gives us a rich lexicon of terms that seem to share a virgulean function. Terms such as "supplement," "trace," "parergon," and "margin" come quickly to mind. But *différance* seems most readily useful. *Différance* is like the virgule in that it is "neither a word nor a concept." It is, however, a juncture.[2] The virgule, then, is the punctuation that marks the double functioning of spacing and temporalization, the deferred and the different. It may also be suggested that it is this double functioning that marks the role of the virgule in the linguistic/extralinguistic binary. Each employer of the virgule gives it a different twist, a unique spin with differential stresses. My concern, then, is to point to the importance in postmodern discourse of the way in which the virgule, the space between the linguistic and the extralinguistic, is named and rendered functional.

In *Marxism and the Philosophy of Language,* Mikhail Bakhtin explains that "the only possible definition of consciousness is a sociological one. Consciousness cannot be derived directly from nature, as has been and still is being attempted by naive mechanistic materialism and contemporary objective psychology."[3] What is at stake here is not the nature of the world outside human interaction, outside and uninfected by social perception, or of a causal world that in any significant and meaningful sense can be revealed as determinative of perception, but rather an insistence upon the interactive social involvement of the production of ideology. Philosophy itself is an ideological construct whose traditional pretension is that of adjudicating truth claims about the nature of the really real. Ontological issues, epistemological issues, aesthetic issues, ethical issues are understandable as ideological issues. Bakhtin's analysis of the linguistic/extralinguistic binary suggests that however this binary is viewed, whatever appears on the right-hand side of the virgule, the extralinguistic side, this other, this unnameable, is the product of a convention of discursive practice, a product of the conceptualization of the negative, a concept invented by discursive humanity, an invitation in Kenneth Burke's terms to the "rottenness of perfection."

That which is not linguistic, that which is not symbolic, is marked not by the name that appears on the right-hand side of the virgule, but by the virgule itself, which as a mark of spacing and timing, of rupture, performs a function of leaning into the future of that which is to become discursive knowledge. It is boundary marker, signaling the intersection of the individual with the social, an intersection that constitutes the fluctuating, mobile, unstable arena of the production of the ideological, of the generatrix of meaning. Whatever falls outside this process is meaningless—only, of course, because it is in the arena of the not yet. So, for Bakhtin, the slant sign, the slash, the virgule, always falling forward, marks a space-time function. Bakhtin's emphasis upon the space-time ratio, his deployment of the chronotope as a classificatory strategy, indicates his insistence that space and time are understandable only in terms of each other, space and time hiding and revealing each other. The boundary as space must become time not-yet-readable, the boundary being not a barrier but a promissory notation of the next. For Bakhtin, the virgule itself is also the undefinable, the unnameable, the uncanny, the unconscious, because it is the dialogic marking of the intersection of the social and the individual as it moves into meaning, and the chronotope does not demand a definition because it too is like the dialogic, a marker for a defining function.

In Pierre Bourdieu's *Outline of a Theory of Practice*, the binary that occupies a central focus is the theory/practice relationship. It is in the theory/practice ratio that we encounter Bourdieu's version of the linguistic/extralinguistic configuration. During the course of Bourdieu's argument a panoply of binaries such as synchrony/diachrony, objectivism/subjectivism, structure/history, culture/personality, model/performance, and rule/improvisation become the target of analysis, but the initial move in Bourdieu's text that seeks to give visibility to the "theorization effect" does so by giving voice to practice.

For Bourdieu, practice is a process and as such is governed by a "dialectic of strategies" rather than a "mechanics of the model." Whereas the semiformalized "repertoire of rules" is supposed to represent practice, it, in fact, Bourdieu argues, guarantees distortion, a distortion built in by the model's dependence upon the artifice of the subject/object binary:

> The "knowing subject" as the idealist tradition rightly calls him, inflicts on practice a much more fundamental and pernicious alteration which, being a constitutive condition of cognitive operation, is bound to pass unnoticed. In taking up a point of view of the action, withdrawing from it in order to observe it from above and from a distance, he constitutes practical activity as an object of observation and analysis, a representation.[4]

In effect, the nest of exclusionary binaries, such as subject/object, theory/practice, and linguistic/extralinguistic, are interdependent members of the same set. For Bourdieu, then, that which cannot become an object of observation and analysis, and thus cannot become a representation without distortion, is the *habitus*, which is a "socially constituted system of cognitive and motivating structures lying outside of articulation." *Doxa*, that which "goes without saying," is a manifestation of the habitus, and while the habitus itself is a theoretical construct, it refers to those nonarticulated learned strategies that are supplementary to the articulated rules:

> [The habitus is composed of] systems of durable, transposable, dispositions, structured structures, predisposed to function as structuring structures, that is as principles of the generation and structuring of practices and representations, which can be objectively "regulated," and "regular" without in any way being the product of obedience to rules, objectively adapted to their goals without presupposing a conscious aiming at ends or an express master of the operations necessary to attain them and, being all this, collectively orchestrated without being the product of a conductor.[5]

For Bourdieu, the name of the virgule is the habitus, and characteristically the virgule functions both as the separator of the terms adjacent to the virgule, the site of the juncture, and as the name of the right-hand term, the opposition that constitutes the left-hand term. The habitus serves as both the matrix of the body, and the action that is inscribed on the body as the body inscribes itself on the performance. The habitus presses against the articulated to establish constantly boundary conditions. In Bourdieu's analysis, the nature/culture binary becomes hyphenated. Nature and culture are so intertwined, and so interdependent that the artifice of binary representation becomes itself a conglomerative product of the very bilateralism of the body and the virgule as habitus marks the strain of discursive efforts to maintain the separate status of either nature or culture. Of course, the linguistic and the extralinguistic binary is thoroughly implicated in the artifice of the discursive practice.

With Cornelius Castoriadis, the formulation of the linguistic/extralinguistic is reformulated into the symbolic/nonsymbolic. Not surprisingly, he can speak of the "institutional" symbolic. Castoriadis situates the symbolic/nonsymbolic binary in the relation between what he calls "identitarian ensemblist thought" or symbolic organization—those modes that demand that everything must respond to logical or rational completeness as differentiated from that which for such ensemblist modes of signification would be designated as noise or as irrelevance.

Castoriadis, who operates within the ambience of the nature/culture binary, differs from those theorists who would place "language" in the initial space of the binary. Castoriadis relates the extralinguistic to "first-order natural facts." It is not that he would deny that first-order "natural" facts—birth, death, pain, for example—do constitute dikes, barriers, embankments, or limits on human movement. It is, however, that reflection on these limits produces only trivia. In the symbolic/nonsymbolic binary, the symbolic is neither demonstrably generated by, governed by, nor caused by the natural strata. What exists for society need not correspond to any specific organization (rational, identitarian, or otherwise) to become functional or meaningful. For Castoriadis the binary signification/first-order natural stratum is exclusive and exhaustive. Inasmuch as, however, human beings occupy both sides of the binary, an important place must always be found for the first natural stratum, whose being is, both generally and concretely, the very foundation of human existence. But this stratum cannot become foundational or an original text by which translations can be checked or verified. It must cross the boundary, the virgule, the magma, which itself is without discernible features, indeterminate and whose definition can only be connoted. For Castoriadis, then, the virgule is the "magma," a sort of inchoate arena whose moments (one can hardly speak of elements) are indistinct and indeterminate, and whose definition can only be connoted. Magmas belong primarily to the "logic of signification" as opposed to an "identitarian-ensemblist" logic.[6] Castoriadis's virgule is the border marker between nature and culture as well as the arena of the process wherein translations are generated. This virgule is the intertextual vortex(t) between the unreadable text of nature and the readable text of culture.

Frederic Jameson's *The Political Unconscious* does not immediately suggest itself as a text in which the linguistic/extralinguistic binary would play an important role. However, in the concluding paragraphs of the tour de force chapter "On Interpretation," Jameson introduces a somewhat aggressive interplay among key terms such as "History," "Language," and "Necessity." The capitalization of the terms may well be seen as a strategic move of decontextualization, elevating them, by removing them from "ordinary" language. Jameson reminds us that "nothing is to be gained by opposing one reified theme—History—by another—Language—in a polemical debate as to the ultimate authority of one over the other."[7] The critical move Jameson wishes to make here, in order to be able to conceive of "History as a ground and absent cause (so) as to resist . . . thematization and reification," is to place History outside and only indirectly accessible to Language. Jameson wishes to remove History from textuality and language so that it *cannot* be transformed "into one optional code among others."[8]

Such "protective custody" of History is gained by placing History and Necessity within the extralinguistic domain. History, then, implicating the "inexorable logic" of Necessity, can forestall its thematization or reification as a mere object of representation or as one master code among others." "History", he adds, "is what hurts." "History can only be apprehended through its effects, and never directly as some reified force."[9]

In Jameson, then, the virgule of the linguistic/extralinguistic binary has been newly named the "political unconscious," locating itself in the space that lies between Necessity-History, on the one hand, and the Great Story, on the other. History, we learn, is indeed accessible as the *experience* of Necessity, but "experience" is in a radical sense unthematizable. Necessity is not in that sense a type of content, but rather an inexorable form of events. "History is an absent cause which is inaccessible to us except in textual form."[10] History in a sense is the unthematizable Real, which passes through its prior textualiztion, its narrativation, in the political unconscious. What, one can ask, are the rites of passage of the Real through the political unconscious? The Jamesonian revision finds the problematic not on the boundaries between the linguistic and extralinguistic but rather on the boundary marked by the virgule named the "political unconscious," which lies between History and the great collective story. The story, of course, is generated by the alternating polarities of ideological unmasking and utopian promise, which provide for us the vital episodes in a vast unfinished plot. For Jameson, then, the name of the virgule is the political unconscious, which, as a figure in a magic carpet woven of the warp of inexorable necessity and the woof of utopian hope, permits the careful reader to discern the outlines of the master, master narrative.[11]

With Baudrillard, in texts like *Simulations*, the Jamesonian gap between the Great Story and History is unbridgeable simply because there is no Great Story and no History, and the presumptive bridge of the *political unconscious* can, at best, be only a fictional reservoir for decaying fictions. Neither the dialectical gesturing of utopian hope nor that of ideological unmasking are of any consequence, for discourses bearing eulogistic or dyslogistic imprints are but the detached and disembodied voices of the simulacra. The ironic stance, the pejorative thrust and the satiric bite that enliven and eventually disappoint in Baudrillard's discourse depend almost entirely for their power upon an evoked nostalgia, despite his own recognition of the pathetic import of such a response.

The operative nostalgia in Baudrillard depends upon the evocation of a sense of universal loss, an awareness of the implications of our failure to conceal from ourselves the very nature of our symbol-generating systems. Baudrillard's nostalgia is self-reflexive and infinitely regressive. It is a nostalgia for nostalgia, for nostalgia, and so forth. . . . It can exist only within a theoretical discursive project, within symbolic articulation. Such a vision, then, seems to be a most exemplary product of what Bourdieu, in *An Outline of a Theory of Practice*, called the "theorization effect."

To locate the functioning separation between the linguistic and the extralinguistic, Baudrillard asks his interpreter to place a virgule between a past and a present, to observe, in short, the historical processes in which the virgule became an impenetrable vertical bar (Sheffer's stroke?), signifying the total incommensurability of two terms. The simulacra, then, are the product of a historically generated isolation of symbolization from all else in the universe.

Whether Baudrillard's virgule is viewed as an unbreachable wall, as an immutable *fact*, so that the linguistic/extralinguistic binary (word/thing) becomes the exclusive binary of all binaries, or whether the virgule marks only the space of nostalgia, it seems clear that his project is embedded in a *hypernostalgia*, a concept necessary to the development of the threatening notion of the *hyperreal*.

The contrastives, the oppositions of past and present, the marking off of "stages," are crucial to his discourse, and in that sense he must fall back upon his representation of the past and the present. Baudrillard explains:

> Representation starts from the principle that the sign and the real are equivalent (even if this equivalence is utopian, it is a fundamental axiom). Conversely, simulation starts from the *utopia* of this principle of equivalence, from the radical of the sign as value, from the sign as reversion and death sentence of every reference. Whereas representation tries to absorb simulation by treating it as false representation, simulation envelops the whole edifice of representation as itself a simulacrum.
> This would be the successive phases of the image:

—it is the reflection of a basic reality
—it masks and perverts a basic reality
—it masks the absence of a basic reality
—it bears no relation to any reality whatsoever, it is its own
pure simulacrum.[12]

Pursuing Baudrillard along the "fault-line" of his own strategic separation of the linguistic and the extralinguistic illustrates his own dependencies; such a revelation does not, however, neutralize or erase his troubling portrait of contemporary society. Baudrillard can, of course, like the rest of us, rely, perhaps a bit uncomfortably, on the functionally operative freight of referentiality that is continually reborn in us through the pressures and demands of everyday practice in our lives.

Perhaps the most efficient way to bring to a close this economy excursion into the domain of the virgule is to postulate a linear scale running from left to right on which the imagined "left" taxonomically projects the radically unstructured, the unsystematic, the aleatory, the unpredictable, and the most aggressively processual mode of discourse, while the imagined "right" projects the more systematized, more tightly structured, more teleological, with presumptions of predictive power, each position involving contestable philosophical assumptions.

At this point in my story, it would be possible to reiterate the well-known differentials in the Derrida/Lacan discourse. I prefer, however, to use two candidates, Jacques Lacan only briefly and Niklas Luhmann more extensively, as illustrative exemplars who despite the wide rhetorical spaces they leave open for the unsystematizable, embody an energizing drive toward the placing of much higher premiums upon system, structure, and justificatory explanations of the raison d'être of the status quo.

With Lacan, the preception of difference is crucial. It is the perception, the recognition, of sexual differentiaton that is central to our introduction into symbol systems, into language. Castration and the Name-of-the-Father, absence and presence, *Fort!* and *Da!*—desire itself is the product of the ingestion of differentiation. One might say in the aggressively reductive manner of my brief comments that the virgule marks the difference between the me and the I, between the self and the other as well, of course, as the "real" and the "unreal." Difference also marks the boundaries that permit the foundations of "closed" systems, marks the concept of the conscious symbol system and the "unconscious" system. And should one care to speak of ultimacy or penultimacy in the Lacanian system, one could speak of the phallus as the initiatory marker of difference in a system in which the phallus is the virgule.

Thus when one speaks of the linguistic/extralinguistic binary in Lacan, one speaks of the deployment of a system of differentiation, a principle wherein an originary experience of difference becomes determinative of the possibility of symbolic experience itself. The extralinguistic world then seems to exist only as a system of difference always already in place. The closed system of the unconscious and the conscious structures of differentiation, each with its own structural principles, becomes a possibility the moment difference is conceptualized and thereby thematized.

On the basis of the collection of essays in *The Differentiation of Society*, Niklas Luhmann, like Jacques Lacan, differs even more clearly from that loose constellation of *so*-called poststructuralist critics constituted by Derrida, Bakhtin, Bourdieu, Baudrilland, and Deleuze. Both Lacan and Luhmann stabilize their systems around the fundamental concept of difference, but Luhmann pursues a radically different strategy in order to achieve the closures necessary to the very existence of "identifiable" systems. Luhmann's focus is not and probably cannot be upon the linguistic/extralinguistic binary. Luhmann does, however, depend upon a central binary, that is "system" and "environment," and he does deploy a virgule—namely "difference" itself—so his "system/environment—difference" formulation becomes the universal abstract concept of all that constitutes the universe itself. The conflictual relationship between these two linguistically constituted binaries—that is, the linguistic/extralinguistic and the systems/environment one—may serve to illustrate the problematic conceptualization of the nature and function of language in Luhmann's elaborate theoretical construct. The linguistic/extralinguistic binary seems alternately excluded, ignored, evaded, or rhetorically subsumed under the universal umbrella of Luhmann's system/environment—difference, an umbrella, which, most felicitously, has a radius that is always in an indeterminate state of process.

Language constitutes a severe problem for Luhmann. Thus he must find ways of either avoiding the linguistic/extralinguistic binary or reconstituting its problems in alternate ways. Apparently, language does not qualify as a "system" even though it may have a structure, may have an environment, and may be dependent upon processes of differentiation for its development and utility. Why language is not a system in Luhmann's sense or why it does not fulfill his conditions are not fully apparent. What is possible for other systems that are "meaning"-dependent such as economics, politics, law, and communications, is denied language. Language, for Luhman, is sometimes identified as an unanalyzable precondition of communication or, more confidently, as a "code." The various rhetorical moves Luhmann makes in his efforts to maintain that a "code" is not a "system" but a "structure" demand inspection. His argument proceeds almost as if "codes" exist outside symbol systems, as if "codes" themselves were something other than linguistic constructs, something like a precondition. There are, for example, good reasons, if one denies the adequacy of descriptions deriving from sentence-based linguistics, for denying that language is a system, but these same reasons would also deny that language is a "code." Without pressing further into Luhmann's description of language, one can argue that language may very well not constitute a code or be constituted by a code.

Luhmann seems unaware of the kind of objections Bakhtin, for example, raises in his argument that language exists only in discourse and discourse does not reflect but rather organizes, transforms, or resolves a situation. Bakhtin observes:

> Semiotics (in the old sense) prefers to deal with the transmission of a ready-made message by a ready-made code, whereas in living speech messages are, strictly speaking, created for the first time in the process of transmission, and *ultimately there is no code.*[13]

The point of my exploration of Luhmann's theoretical frame is that it illustrates how the attempt to avoid the problems attendant upon theorizing (which can take place only within language) without exploring the implications of the linguistic/extralinguistic binary creates a new set of difficulties. I am suggesting that excessive marginalization or exclusion of the relation between the linguistic and whatever is supplementary to it frequently enough masks a "power" move at the heart of the theoretical discourse. Placing the linguistic/extralinguistic suture in too prominent a position in a given discursive strategy may reveal too transparently the foundational rules and the ideological, self-serving features of any system under too glaring floodlights.

In Luhmann, the juncture of the knowable and the not-yet-known lies along the line of *difference.* Critics of Luhmann are quick to point out that with his systems approach no academic need grow uneasy, much less nervous, for under his theoretical dispensation all the traditional generic disciplinary divisions into faculties can be reconstituted, as it were. All the embedded taxonomic conventions of sociological analysis are recoverable, and in the process, strategies for the proper appreciation of the status quo are reinstated as understandable features of system/environment—difference. Supporters of Luhmann see in his theory another perspective that subverts, deconstructs, offers a more attractive alternative to the grammar-based model of the communication triangle. Furthermore, such supporters would add that Luhmann's approach permits a far more sophisticated grasp of the constitutive and deconstitutive functioning of systems themselves.

Viewed, however, from a Derridean or a Deleuzian stance, Luhmann, in his choice of *difference*, reinstates, reifies, and ontologizes all the problematics of the concepts of system itself. The moment difference is deployed as a concept and difference becomes the very idea around which self-referentiality gyres on its autopoetic imperializing way, engulfing and transforming its environment into *system*, all that seemed lost to the possibilities of writing a satisfactory, functional, and universal formula (totally functional, totally abstract) for the universe itself is restored unto us. All, in Luhmann, depends upon the thematization of *difference*, and if thematization is available, who needs *unity?* Here lies a fundamental difference between Luhmann and Derrida. With Derrida, *différance* cannot be thematized, *différance* is not a concept. Once difference is always deferrence, *différance* is as unthematizable as "supplement," "margin," or, in my translation, "virgule."[14]

In *Anti-Oedipus, A Thousand Plateaus*, and in other works by Deleuze and Guattari, the linguistic/extralinguistic binary comes into focus as the project of a strongly centered, binary-ridden plane of organization. It is only one among the innumerable host of segmentations that mark the rational/irrational, appearance/reality, presence/absence, order/disorder binaries. From the side of the arborescent, Deleuze and Guattari's metaphor for the treelike endless bifurcation of binariness—from this left-hand of the binary comes the dark light that illumines our majoritarian and sedentary habits of thought. Against this mode, Deleuze & Guattari pose the rhizome, a tuberous metaphor that invokes an uncentered plane of embracing multiplicities, open–ended adjacencies, and utterly impermanent connections. Such terms and phrases as "body without organs," "machine assemblages," "collectivities of heterogenous elements which function together," clusters whose "sole unity is that of co-function," provide a sense of that immanence or "plane of consistence" that marks the rhizome. At each turn in the Deleuze and

Guattari oeuvre, the concepts of representation, hierarchy, unity, and identity are brought under inspection. It is not as if they propose abandoning the binary for a new mode of rhizomatic thinking—for they point out that one cannot think without drawing distinctions.

The answer, then, is not to presume to supplant the dyadic mode, but rather to deauthorize specific deeply entrenched dyadic structures by generating alternate dyads, again and again through guerilla tactics. In the Deleuze-Guattari configuration then, the virgule functions doubly. From the arborescent side, it functions as the universal dichotomizing machine. It segmentalizes, dichotomizes, formalizes, establishes ratios, introduces hierarchies, and invites patrimony by legitimizing origins. We dichotomize to bless and damn, authorize and deauthorize. The virgule, viewed from the arborescent side, demythologizes and decontextualizes; it is, in effect, the master antinarrative stroke, serving in its "eitherorness" as a generic marker, differentiating philosophical discourse from all other lesser discursive practices. The alternative rhizomatic function of the virgule in this (arborescent/rhizomatic) configuration is to invoke an alternative— the logic of seduction, to make of the virgule a line of flight, of escape, of movement, flow, and flux.

The problem in representing Deleuze-Guattari has been deliberately rendered extraordinarily complex in the sense that "lines," including the virgule, are themselves so variable in their functions. Deleuze and Guattari insist that we must learn not only about the lines that fix but also about other kinds as well. First, there are rigidly segmented molar lines, the more visible ones, and, second, there are molecular lines with thresholds and quanta, becomings and micro-becomings that do not have the same rhythm as our so-called history. There is, furthermore, the third kind of line, which carries us away through segments, thresholds—toward unknown destinations neither forseeable nor preexistent.[15] The three lines and their intertwining make for a pluridimensionality that renders them inaccessible to the bidimensionality of writing, of inscription, so that the virgule under this dispensation loses its linearity, its directionality, its function of differentiating and distinguishing, becoming complicated, tortuously simple, and abstract.

It is the study of these lines that constitutes Deleuze and Guattari's project of schizoanalysis, micropolitics, pragmatism, diagrammatics, cartography in groups and individuals.[16] For Deleuze and Guattari, it seems, the virgule, the marker that we make and unmake, is the marker that partakes not simply of the redistribution of desire, not only the line that marks the rigidly segmented and the molar flow, but also the line that is the most complicated, the line of celerity or gravity, the line of flight of the steepest gradient, on the edge, rim, margin, signaling that which is about to begin, on the brink, or finally "on the verge." Placing the virgule "on the verge," does not, however, for Deleuze and Guattari, place it in any ordinary sense of placing. There are, strictly speaking, no space-time coordinates for being "on the verge." Furthermore, such a marking does not imply the possibility of some wondrous escape into a utopia of heterogeneity, some naive anarchistic vision of the utterly free. Rather, the virgule functions here as a reminder, as an invitation to a description of the arena in which the speculative notions of the bounded and the unbounded energize each other. The "space" of the virgule between the *either* and the *or* constitutes the interplay of the problematics of systems of whatever kind, be they political, economic, sociological, linguistic, aesthetic, psychological, or philosophical—foregrounding for us the residuals of nonconcurrence and resistance to those systems that at any given moment seem to be operating in the absence of authority sufficient to match their pretensions.

To end, with Deleuze and Guattari, on the verge, is not, however, to assume that one has reached an "end." I have only tentatively sketched the functions of the virgule in the linguistic/extralinguistic binary as it manifests itself in the discourses of a few "poststructuralist" figures, arguing that the placement, deployment, and status attributed to the virgule signals the presence of political and ethical commitments that otherwise might remain obscured. Furthermore, it seems that those discourses that seek to explore, identify, describe, and explain the nature of the space between that which has been named language and that which is not yet language, or that which can never become language have provided us with some of the most important speculative problems of our time.

Notes

1. Bakhtin's comment that all utterances are ideological can be seen as an insistence that all utterances are rooted in a social context, that a disinterested and "objective" utterance is unthinkable, and that the discriminations made between legal, economic, educational, and political elements of the superstructure are themselves inescapably embedded in the conflictual interplay of the multiplicity of heterogeneous and polyvalent voices that populate every utterance. Bakhtin's stance is not, I believe, a "uniquely" Marxist position with its structuring of the base and superstructure, and its postulating of a "scientific" or nonideological alternative. Rather, it seems that Bakhtin's notion of ideology is quite compatible with Deleuze and Guat-

tari's contention in *A Thousand Plateaus* that there is no such thing as ideology, meaning, it seems, that there is no systemlike structure, or ideological paradigm, that governs in any rule-bound way our discursive practices. Both Bakhtin and Deleuze have, I believe, an antistructuralist perspective on the role of ideology. See Deleuze and Guattari's comments that note that to misconstrue ideology as a paradigmatic structure, or as false consciousness, is to fail to understand the nature of language. In brief, "ideology is a most execrable concept, obscuring all the effectively operative social machines" (Gilles Deleuze and Félix Guattari, *A Thousand Plateaus* [Minneapolis: University of Minnesota Press, 1981], p. 68).

2. Jacques Derrida, *Speech and Phenomena* (Evanston: Northwestern University Press, 1973), p. 130.

3. V.N. Voloshinov, *Marxism and the Philosophy of Language* (Cambridge: Harvard University Press, 1966), p. 13. Some attribute partial or even basic authorship to Bakhtin.

4. Pierre Bourdieu, *An Outline of a Theory of Practice* (Cambridge and New York: Cambridge University Press, 1977), p. 2.

5. Ibid., p. 72.

6. John Fekete, *The Structural Allegory* (Minneapolis: University of Minnesota Press, 1984), p. 5.

7. Frederic Jameson, *The Political Unconscious* (Ithaca: Cornell University Press, 1981), p. 100.

8. Ibid., p. 101.

9. Ibid.

10. Ibid.

11. Such decontextualizing moves by Jameson suggest a possible reading of his initial essay "On Interpretation" as a latter-day example of Abrams's *Natural Supernaturalism* in which Northrop Frye's hermeneutic model is seen as an inadequately sanitized medieval Christian hermeneutic. Frye's model of a hierarchically structured interpretive triangle is truncated by Jameson through the collapse of its transcendental layer. Cleansed thereby of its supernatural onus, the kerygmatic voice speaks more comfortably in such key terms as "History," "Necessity," "absent cause," the "great story," and the "political unconscious."

12. Jean Baudrillard, *Simulations* (New York: Semiotext(e), 1983), p. 11.

13. Tzvetan Tzvetan, *Mikhail Bakhtin: The Dialogical Principle* (Minneapolis: University of Minnesota Press, 1984), p. 57.

14. The reading of the difference between *différance* and "difference," which I employ, is, of course, at least a problematic discrimination serving to

reflect a perspective that implicates for me what might be termed an "ontological" difference between a Derridean and Lacanian position, hinging on the way one reads the Lacanian proposition that without the "subject" a physics is possible.

15. Gilles Deleuze and Félix Guattari, *A Thousand Plateaus*. The description here of the rhizomatic/arborescent contrast depends upon the introductory chapter of *A Thousand Plateaus* entitled "Rhizomes" and upon the commentary that introduces an earlier translation of the rhizome section by Paul Patton in *Ideology and Consciousness*, 8 (Spring 1981): 41–71.

16. Interesting parallels, particularly in the speculations on iconicity, between the analysis of the functioning of the diagrammatic, the pragmatic, and the cartographic in C. S. Peirce might prove helpful in elaborating the significance of Deleuze's arguments.

About "Postmodern": a Bibliography

Essentially, two principles of selection shape this bibliography. First, books are included that try to define *postmodern*, *postmodernism*, or *postmodernity*, or the application of these terms in some specific field (such as *postmodern art*). Second, books are included that relate to one or more of the basic themes of postmodern discourse, such as alterity; the death, absence, or radical reconfiguration of the subject; "post-Marxism"; the disruption of received categories such as "philosophy" or "literature"; the present as the crossing of contradictory codes; antifoundationalism; the "crisis of reason"; the end or exhaustion of modernity; the political margins of the West; and so forth. In application, this second principle obviously reflects some degree of subjectivity and discrimination on the bibliographer's part. In that respect, the following list is best considered a perhaps large but nonetheless shrinking part (inscribed as it is in a field experiencing accelerated growth, with no natural bounds) of a discourse which reaches not only into the future, but ever more into the past as well.

Adorno, Theodor W., and Max Horkheimer. *Dialectic of Enlightenment*. Trans. John Cumming. New York: Seabury Press, 1972.

Agacinski, Sylviane. *Aparte: Conceptions and Deaths of Kierkegaard*. Trans. Kevin Newmark. Tallahassee: State University Press, 1988.

Agger, Ben. *Socio(onto)logy: A Disciplinary Reading*. Urbana: University of Illinois Press, 1989.

Allen, Jeffner, and Iris Marion Young. *The Thinking Muse: Feminism and Modern French Philosophy*. Bloomington: Indiana University Press, 1989.

Allison, David B., ed. *The New Nietzsche*. Cambridge, Mass.: MIT Press, 1985.

Altizer, Thomas J. J., et al. *Deconstruction and Theology*. New York: Crossroad, 1982.

Arac, Jonathan, ed. *Postmodernism and Politics*. Minneapolis: University of Minnesota Press, 1986.

Arac, Jonathan. *Critical Genealogies: Historical Situations for Postmodern Literary Studies*. New York: Columbia University Press, 1987.

Aronowitz, Stanley. *Science as Power: Discourse and Ideology in Modern Society*. Minneapolis: University of Minnesota Press, 1988.

Attridge, Derek. *Peculiar Language: Literature as Difference from the Renaissance to James Joyce.* Ithaca, N.Y.: Cornell University Press, 1988.

Attridge, Derek, Geoff Bennington, and Robert Young, eds. *Post-Structuralism and the Question of History.* Cambridge: Cambridge University Press, 1987.

Baker, Houston A., Jr. *Blues, Ideology, and Afro-American Literature: A Vernacular Theory.* Chicago: University of Chicago Press, 1984.

Bannett, Eve Tavor. *Structuralism and the Logic of Dissent: Barthes, Derrida, Foucault, Lacan.* Urbana: University of Illinois Press, 1989.

Barthes, Roland. *Camera Lucida: Reflections on Photography.* Trans. Richard Howard. New York: Hill and Wang, 1981.

———. *Empire of Signs.* Trans. Richard Howard. New York: Hill and Wang, 1982.

———. *Image, Music, Text.* Trans. Stephen Heath. New York: Hill and Wang, 1977.

———. *Mythologies.* Trans. Annette Lavers. New York: Hill and Wang, 1972.

———. *The Pleasure of the Text.* Trans. Richard Miller. New York: Hill and Wang, 1974.

———. *S/Z.* Trans. Richard Miller. New York: Hill and Wang, 1974.

Bataille, Georges. *The Accursed Share.* Vol. 1. Trans. Robert Hurley. New York: Zone Books, 1988.

———. *Inner Experience.* Trans. Leslie Anne Boldt. Albany, N.Y.: State University of New York Press, 1988.

———. *Theory of Religion.* Trans. Robert Hurley. New York: Zone Books, 1989.

———. *Visions of Excess: Selected Writings, 1927–1939.* Ed. Allan Stoekl. Trans. Allan Stoekl, with Carl R. Lovitt and Donald M. Leslie, Jr. Minneapolis: University of Minnesota Press, 1985.

Baynes, Kenneth, James Bohman, and Thomas McCarthy, eds. *After Philosophy: End or Transformation?* Cambridge, Mass.: MIT Press, 1987.

Baudrillard, Jean. *America.* Trans. Chris Turner. London: Verso Press, 1988.

———. *For a Critique of the Political Economy of the Sign.* Trans. Charles Levin. St. Louis: Telos Press, 1981.

———. *The Mirror of Production.* Trans. Mark Poster. St. Louis: Telos Press, 1975.

———. *Simulations*. Trans. Paul Foss, Paul Patton, and Philip Beitchman. New York: Semiotext(e), 1983.

———. *Selected Writings*. Ed. Mark Poster. Stanford: Stanford University Press, 1988.

Bennington, Geoffrey. *Lyotard: Writing the Event*. New York: Columbia University Press, 1988.

Berman, Marshall. *All That Is Sold Melts Into Air: The Experience of Modernity*. New York: Simon and Schuster, 1982.

Bernasconi, Robert. *The Question of Language in Heidegger's History of Being*. Atlantic Highlands: Humanities Press, 1985.

Bernasconi, Robert, and David Wood, eds. *The Provocation of Levinas: Rethinking the Other*. London: Routledge, 1989.

Bernstein, Richard J. *Beyond Objectivism and Relativism: Science, Hermeneutics, and Praxis*. Philadelphia: University of Pennsylvania Press, 1983.

———, ed. *Habermas and Modernity*. Cambridge, Mass.: MIT Press, 1985.

Bigelow, Pat. *Kierkegaard and the Problem of Writing*. Tallahassee: Florida State University Press, 1987.

Blau, Herbert. *The Eye of Prey: Subversions of the Postmodern*. Bloomington: Indiana University Press, 1987.

Bloom, Harold. *A Map of Misreading*. Oxford: Oxford University Press, 1975.

Borradori, Giovanna, ed. *Recoding Metaphysics: The New Italian Philosophy*. Evanston, Ill.: Northwestern University Press, 1988.

Bratosevich, Nicolas. *Postmodernismo y vanguardia*. Madrid: La Muralla D.L., 1979.

Burger, Peter and Christa, eds. *Postmoderne: Alltag, Allegorie, und Avantgarde*. Frankfurt am Main: Suhrkamp, 1987.

Burgin, Victor. *The End of Art Theory: Criticism and Postmodernity*. New York: Macmillan, 1986.

Caputo, John D. *Radical Hermeneutics: Repetition, Deconstruction, and the Hermeneutic Project*. Bloomington: Indiana University Press, 1987.

Cascardi, Anthony, ed. *Literature and the Question of Philosophy*. Baltimore: Johns Hopkins University Press, 1987.

Castoriadis, Cornelius. *The Imaginary Institution of Society*. Trans. Kathleen Blamey. Cambridge, Mass.: MIT Press, 1987.

Carroll, David. *Paraesthetics: Foucault, Lyotard, Derrida*. New York: Methuen, 1987.

Certeau, Michel de. *Heterologies: Discourse on the Other.* Trans. Brian Massumi. Minneapolis: University of Minnesota Press, 1986.

Cixous, Helene, and Catherine Clement. *The Newly Born Woman.* Trans. Betsy Wing. Minneapolis: University of Minnesota Press, 1986.

Connolly, William. *Political Theory and Modernity.* London: Basil Blackwell, 1989.

Corlett, William. *Community Without Unity: A Politics of Derridian Extravagance.* Durham: Duke University Press, 1989.

Coward, Rosalind, and John Ellis. *Language and Materialism: Developments in Semiology and the Theory of the Subject.* London: Routledge, 1977.

Culler, Jonathan. *On Deconstruction: Theory and Criticism after Structuralism.* Ithaca, N.Y.: Cornell University Press, 1982.

Dasenbrock, Reed W., ed. *Redrawing the Lines: Analytic Philosophy, Deconstruction, and Literary Theory.* Minneapolis: University of Minnesota Press, 1989.

Dallmayr, Fred R. *Twilight of Subjectivity: Contributions to a Post-Individualist Theory.* Amherst: University of Massachusetts Press, 1981.

Debord, Guy. *Society of the Spectacle.* Detroit: Black and Red, 1983.

De Lauretis, Teresa. *Alice Doesn't: Feminism, Semiotics, Cinema.* Bloomington: Indiana University Press, 1984.

———. *Technologies of Gender: Essays on Theory, Film, and Fiction.* Bloomington: Indiana University Press, 1987.

Deleuze, Gilles. *Foucault.* Trans. Sean Hand. Minneapolis: University of Minnesota Press, 1988.

Deleuze, Gilles, and Claire Parnet. *Dialogues.* Trans. Hugh Tomlinson and Barbara Habberjam. New York: Columbia University Press, 1987.

Deleuze, Gilles, and Felix Guattari. *Anti-Oedipus: Capitalism and Schizophrenia.* Trans. Robert Hurley, Mark Seem, and Helen R. Lane. Minneapolis: University of Minnesota Press, 1983.

———. *A Thousand Plateaus: Capitalism and Schizophrenia.* Trans. Brian Massumi. Minneapolis: University of Minnesota Press, 1987.

De Man, Paul. *Allegories of Reading: Figural Language in Rousseau, Nietzsche, Rilke, and Proust.* New Haven: Yale University Press, 1979.

———. *Blindness and Insight: Essays in the Rhetoric of Contemporary Criticism.* 2d ed., rev. Minneapolis: University of Minnesota Press, 1983.

———. *The Rhetoric of Romanticism.* New York: Columbia University Press, 1984.

Derrida, Jacques. *Glas.* Trans. John P. Leavey, Jr. and Richard Rand. Lincoln: University of Nebraska Press, 1986.

———. *Margins of Philosophy.* Trans. Alan Bass. Chicago: University of Chicago Press, 1982.

———. *Of Grammatology.* Trans. Gayatri Chakravorty Spivak. Baltimore: Johns Hopkins University Press, 1976.

———. *Positions.* Trans. Alan Bass. Chicago: University of Chicago Press, 1981.

———. *The Postcard: From Socrates to Freud and Beyond.* Trans. Alan Bass. Chicago: University of Chicago Press, 1987.

———. *Speech and Phenomena, and Other Essays on Husserl's Theory of Signs.* Trans. David B. Allison. Evanston, Ill.: Northwestern University Press, 1973.

———. *Truth in Painting.* Trans. Geoff Bennington and Ian McLeod. Chicago: University of Chicago Press, 1987.

———. *Writing and Difference.* Trans. Alan Bass. Chicago: University of Chicago Press, 1978.

Descombes, Vincent. *Modern French Philosophy.* Trans. L. Scott-Fox and J. M. Harding. Cambridge: Cambridge University Press, 1980.

Dews, Peter. *Logics of Disintegration: Post-Structuralist Thought and the Claims of Critical Theory.* London: Verso, 1987.

Dowling, William C. *Jameson, Althusser, Marx: An Introduction to* The Political Unconscious. Ithaca, N.Y.: Cornell University Press, 1984.

Dreyfus, Hubert L., and Paul Rabinow. *Michel Foucault: Beyond Structuralism and Hermeneutics.* 2d. ed. Chicago: University of Chicago Press, 1983.

Eco, Umberto. *Travels in Hyperreality.* Trans. William Weaver. New York: Harcourt Brace Jovanovich, 1986.

Falk, Colin. *Myth, Truth, and Literature: Towards a True Post-Modernism.* Cambridge: Cambridge University Press, 1989.

Fekete, John, ed. *Life After Postmodernism: Essays on Value and Culture.* Montreal: New World Perspectives, 1987.

Feyerabend, Paul. *Against Method: Outline of an Anarchistic Theory of Knowledge.* London: Verso Press, 1978.

Fish, Stanley. *Doing What Comes Naturally: Change, Rhetoric, and the Practice of Theory in Literary and Legal Studies.* Durham, N.C.: Duke University Press, 1989.

————. *Is There A Text In This Class? The Authority of Interpretive Communities.* Cambridge, Mass.: Harvard University Press, 1980.

Fogel, Stanley. *The Postmodern University.* Toronto: ECW Press, 1988.

Forester, John, ed. *Critical Theory and Public Life.* Cambridge, Mass.: MIT Press, 1985.

Foster, Hal. *Recodings: Art, Spectacle, Cultural Politics.* Port Townsend: Bay Press, 1985.

————. ed. *The Anti-Aesthetic: Essays on Postmodern Culture.* Port Townsend: Bay Press, 1983.

Foucault, Michel. *The Archeology of Knowledge.* Trans. A. M. Sheridan Smith. New York: Pantheon Books, 1977.

————. *Discipline and Punish.* Trans. Alan Sheridan. New York: Pantheon Books, 1977.

————. *The History of Sexuality.* Vol. 1., *An Introduction.* Trans. Robert Hurley. New York: Pantheon Books, 1978.

————. *The Use of Pleasure.* Vol. 2 of *The History of Sexuality.* Trans. Robert Hurley. New York: Pantheon Books, 1985.

————. *The Care of the Self.* Vol. 3 of *The History of Sexuality.* Trans. Robert Hurley. New York: Pantheon Books, 1986.

————. *The Order of Things: An Archaeology of the Human Sciences.* New York: Vintage Books, 1973.

————. *Power/Knowledge.* Ed. Colin Gordon. New York: Pantheon Books, 1980.

Frampton, Kenneth. *Modern Architecture: A Critical History.* New York: Thames and Hudson, 1985.

Frankel, Boris. *The Post-Industrial Utopians.* Madison: University of Wisconsin Press, 1987.

Fuller, Steve. *Social Epistemology.* Bloomington: Indiana University Press, 1988.

Gadamer, Hans-Georg. *Reason in the Age of Science.* Trans. Frederick G. Lawrence. Cambridge, Mass.: MIT Press, 1981.

Garvin, Harry R., ed. *Romanticism, Modernism, Postmodernism.* Lewisburg, Pa.: Bucknell University Press, 1980.

Gasche, Rodolphe. *The Tain of the Mirror: Derrida and the Philosophy of Reflection.* Cambridge, Mass.: Harvard University Press, 1986.

Gates, Henry Louis, Jr., ed. *Black Literature and Literary Theory.* New York: Methuen, 1986.

———. *The Signifying Monkey: A Theory of Afro-American Literary Criticism.* Oxford: Oxford University Press, 1988.

Geertz, Clifford. *Local Knowledge.* New York: Basic Books, 1983.

Gibbons, Michael T., ed. *Interpreting Politics.* New York: New York University Press, 1987.

Gilligan, Carol. *In a Different Voice: Psychological Theory and Women's Development.* Cambridge, Mass.: Harvard University Press, 1982.

Goldberg, Jonathan. *Voice Terminal Echo: Postmodernism and English Renaissance Texts.* New York: Methuen, 1986.

Goodman, Nelson. *Ways of Worldmaking.* Indianapolis: Hackett Publishers, 1978.

Gorz, Andre. *Farewell to the Working Class: An Essay on Post-Industrial Socialism.* Trans. Michael Sonenscher. London: Pluto Press, 1982.

Graff, Gerald. *Literature Against Itself: Literary Ideas in Modern Society.* Chicago: University of Chicago Press, 1979.

Griffiths, A. Phillips, ed. *Contemporary French Philosophy.* Cambridge: Cambridge University Press, 1987.

Habermas, Jurgen. *The Philosophical Discourse of Modernity.* Trans. Frederick Lawrence. Cambridge, Mass.: MIT Press, 1987.

———. *The Theory of Communicative Action.* Vol. 1, *Reason and the Rationalization of Society.* Trans. Thomas McCarthy. Boston: Beacon Press, 1984.

———. *The Theory of Communicative Action.* Vol. 2, *Lifeworld and System: A Critique of Functionalist Reason.* Trans. Thomas McCarthy. Boston: Beacon Press, 1987.

Handelman, Susan. *The Slayers of Moses: The Emergence of Rabbinic Interpretation in Modern Literary Theory.* Albany, N.Y.: State University of New York Press, 1982.

Hartman, Geoffrey. *Saving the Text: Literature, Derrida, Philosophy.* Baltimore: Johns Hopkins University Press, 1981.

Harvey, David. *The Condition of Postmodernity.* London: Basil Blackwell, forthcoming.

Harvey, Irene. *Derrida and the Economy of Différance.* Bloomington, Indiana University Press, 1986.

Hassan, Ihab. *The Postmodern Turn: Essays in Postmodern Theory and Culture.* Columbus: Ohio State University Press, 1987.

Heidegger, Martin. *Being and Time.* Trans. John Macquarrie and Edward Robinson. New York: Harper and Row, 1962.

———. *Early Greek Thinking.* Trans. David Farrell Krell and Frank A. Capuzzi. New York: Harper and Row, 1975.

———. *On the Way to Language.* Trans. Peter D. Hertz. New York: Harper and Row, 1971.

———. *Poetry, Language, Thought.* Trans. Albert Hofstadter. New York: Harper and Row, 1971.

———. *The Question Concerning Technology.* Trans. William Lovitt. New York: Harper and Row, 1977.

Hirsh, Arthur. *The French New Left: An Intellectual History from Sartre to Gorz.* Boston: South End Press, 1981.

Holt, Nancy, ed. *The Writings of Robert Smithson: Essays and Illustrations.* New York: New York University Press, 1979.

Horkheimer, Max. *Critical Theory: Selected Essays.* Trans. Matthew J. O'Connell et al. New York: Continuum, 1972.

Husserl, Edmund. *The Crisis of European Sciences and Transcendental Phenomenology.* Trans. David Carr. Evanston, Ill.: Northwestern University Press, 1970.

Hutcheon, Linda. *A Poetics of Postmodernism: History, Theory, Fiction.* London: Routledge, 1988.

Huyssen, Andreas. *After the Great Divide: Modernism, Mass Culture, Postmodernism.* Bloomington: Indiana University Press, 1986.

Ingram, David. *Habermas and the Dialectic of Reason.* New Haven: Yale University Press, 1987.

Irigaray, Luce. *Speculum of the Other Woman.* Trans. Gillian C. Gill. Ithaca, N.Y.: Cornell University Press, 1985.

———. *This Sex Which Is Not One.* Trans. Catherine Porter. Ithaca, N.Y.: Cornell University Press, 1985.

Jameson, Fredrick. *The Concept of Postmodernism.* Durham, N.C.: Duke University Press, forthcoming.

———. *The Ideologies of Theory.* Vol. 1, *Situations of Theory.* Minneapolis: University of Minnesota Press, 1988.

———. *The Ideologies of Theory.* Vol. 2, *The Syntax of History.* Minneapolis: University of Minnesota Press, 1988.

―――. *The Political Unconscious: Narrative as a Socially Symbolic Act.* Ithaca, N.Y.: Cornell University Press, 1981.

Jay, Gregory S., and David L. Miller, eds. *After Strange Texts: The Role of Theory in the Study of Literature.* Tuscaloosa, University of Alabama Press, 1985.

Jay, Martin. *Marxism and Totality: The Adventures of a Concept from Lukacs to Habermas.* Berkeley: University of California Press, 1984.

Jencks, Charles. *The Language of Post-Modern Architecture.* New York: Rizolli, 1977.

―――. *What is Post-Modernism?* New York: St. Martin's Press, 1986.

Johnson, Michael L. *Mind, Language, Machine: Artificial Intelligence in the Poststructuralist Age.* New York: St. Martin's Press, 1988.

Kaplan, E. Ann. *Rocking Around the Clock: Music Television, Postmodernism, and Consumer Culture.* New York: Methuen, 1987.

―――, ed. *Postmodernism and its Discontents.* London: Verso, 1988.

Kaplan, Cora. *Sea Changes: Essays on Culture and Feminism.* London: Verso, 1986.

Kariel, Henry. *The Desperate Politics of Postmodernism.* Amherst: University of Massachusetts Press, 1989.

Kearney, Richard. *The Wake of Imagination: Toward a Postmodern Culture.* Minneapolis: University of Minnesota Press, 1988.

Kellner, Douglas R., ed. *Postmodernism/Jameson/Critique.* Washington, D.C.: Maisonneuve Press, 1989.

Klinkowitz, Jerome. *Rosenberg, Barthes, Hassan: The Postmodern Habit of Thought.* Athens, Ga.: University of Georgia Press, 1988.

Klotz, Heinrich, ed. *Postmodern Visions: Drawings, Paintings, and Models by Contemporary Architects.* New York: Abbeville Press, 1985.

Knabb, Ken, ed. and trans. *Situationist International Anthology.* Berkeley: Bureau of Public Secrets, 1981.

Koelb, Clayton. *Nietzsche and Postmodernism.* Albany, N.Y.: State University of New York Press, forthcoming.

Kolb, David. *Critique of Pure Modernity: Hegel, Heidegger, and After.* Chicago: University of Chicago Press, 1986.

Koslowski, Peter. *Die Postmoderne Kultur: gesellschaftliche-kulturelle Konsequenzen der technischen Entwicklung.* Munich: C.H. Beck, 1987.

Krauss, Rosalind. *The Originality of the Avant-Garde and Other Modernist Myths.* Cambridge, Mass.: MIT Press, 1985.

Krell, David Farrell, and David Wood, eds. *Exceedingly Nietzsche: Aspects of Contemporary Nietzsche Interpretation.* London: Routledge, 1988.

Kroker, Arthur, and David Cook. *The Postmodern Scene: Excremental Culture and Hyper-Aesthetics.* New York: St. Martin's Press, 1986.

Krupnick, Mark, ed. *Displacement: Derrida and After.* Bloomington: Indiana University Press, 1983.

Kuhn, Thomas S. *The Structure of Scientific Revolutions.* Chicago: University of Chicago Press, 1962.

Lacan, Jacques. *Ecrits: A Selection.* Trans. Alan Sheridan. New York: Norton, 1977.

———. *The Four Fundamental Concepts of Psycho-Analysis.* Ed. Jacques-Alain Miller. Trans. Alan Sheridan. New York: Norton, 1981.

Lacan, Jacques, et al. *Feminine Sexuality.* Ed. Juliet Mitchell and Jacqueline Rose. Trans. Jacqueline Rose. London: Mcmillan, 1982.

LaCapra, Dominick. *Rethinking Intellectual History: Texts, Contexts, Language.* Ithaca, N.Y.: Cornell University Press, 1983.

Laclau, Ernesto, and Chantal Mouffe. *Hegemony and Socialist Strategy: Towards a Radical Democratic Politics.* Trans. Winston Moore and Paul Cammack. London: Verso, 1985.

Lentricchia, Frank. *After the New Criticism.* Chicago: University of Chicago Press, 1980.

———. *Criticism and Social Change.* Chicago: University of Chicago Press, 1983.

Levin, David Michael. *The Opening of Vision: Nihilism and the Postmodern Situation.* New York: Routledge, 1988.

Levinas, Emmanuel. *Time and the Other.* Trans. Richard A. Cohen. Pittsburgh: Duquesne University Press, 1987.

———. *Collected Philosophical Papers.* Trans. Alphonso Lingis. Dordrecht: Nijhoff, 1987.

Lima, Luiz Costa. *Control of the Imaginary: Reason and Imagination in Modern Times.* Trans. Ronald W. Sousa. Minneapolis: University of Minnesota Press, 1988.

Lingis, Alphonso. *Deathbound Subjectivity.* Bloomington: Indiana University Press, 1989.

———. *Excesses: Eros and Culture.* Albany, N.Y.: State University of New York Press, 1983.

———. *Libido: The French Existential Theories.* Bloomington: Indiana University Press, 1985.

Llewelyn, John. *Derrida on the Threshold of Sense.* New York: St. Martin's Press, 1986.

Love, Nancy S. *Marx, Nietzsche, and Modernity.* New York: Columbia University Press, 1986.

Lunn, Eugene. *Marxism and Modernity: An Historical Study of Lukacs, Brecht, Benjamin, and Adorno.* Berkeley: University of California Press, 1982.

Lyotard, Jean-Francois. *The Differend: Phrases in Dispute.* Trans. Georges Van Den Abbeele. Minneapolis: University of Minnesota Press.

———. *Driftworks.* Ed. Richard McKeon. New York: Semiotext(e), 1984.

———. *Peregrinations: Law, Form, Event.* New York: Columbia University Press, 1988.

———. *The Postmodern Condition: A Report on Knowledge.* Trans. Geoff Bennington and Brian Massumi. Minneapolis: University of Minnesota Press, 1984.

———. *Le Postmoderne explique aux infants: correspondence 1982–1985.* Paris: Editions Galilee, 1986.

MacCannell, Juliet Flower. *Figuring Lacan: Criticism and the Cultural Unconscious.* Lincoln: University of Nebraska Press, 1986.

Macherey, Pierre. *A Theory of Literary Production.* Trans. Geoffrey Wall. London: Routledge, 1978.

Mackey, Louis. *Points of View: Readings of Kierkegaard.* Tallahassee: Florida State University Press, 1986.

Macksey, Richard, and Eugene Donato, eds. *The Structuralist Controversy: The Languages of Criticism and the Sciences of Man.* Baltimore: Johns Hopkins University Press, 1972.

Madison, G. B. *The Hermeneutics of Postmodernity: Figures and Themes.* Bloomington: Indiana University Press, 1988.

Mandel, Ernest. *Late Capitalism.* Trans. Joris De Bres. London: Verso, 1978.

Margolis, Joseph. *Pragmatism without Foundations: Reconciling Realism and Relativism.* London: Basil Blackwell, 1986.

———. *Science without Unity: Reconciling the Human and Natural Sciences.* London: Basil Blackwell, 1987.

————. *Texts without Referents: Reconciling Science and Narrative*. London: Basil Blackwell, 1989.

Marks, Elaine, and Isabelle de Courtivron, eds. *New French Feminisms*. New York: Schocken Books, 1981.

MacCabe, Colin. *Tracking the Signifier: Theoretical Essays on Film, Linguistics, and Literature*. Minneapolis: University of Minnesota Press, 1985.

McCumber, John. *Poetic Interaction: Language, Freedom, Reason*. Chicago: University of Chicago Press, 1989.

McHale, Brian. *Postmodernist Fiction*. London: Methuen, 1987.

McLuhan, Marshall. *Understanding Media: The Extensions of Man*. New York: McGraw-Hill, 1964.

Megill, Allan. *Prophets of Extremity: Nietzsche, Heidegger, Foucault, Derrida*. Berkeley: University of California Press, 1987.

Melville, Stephen. *Philosophy Beside Itself: On Deconstruction and Modernism*. Minneapolis: University of Minnesota Press, 1986.

Merleau-Ponty, Maurice. *The Prose of the World*. Ed. Claude Lefort. Trans. John O'Neill. Evanston, Ill.: Northwestern University Press, 1973.

Merrill, Robert, ed. *Ethics/Aesthetics: Postmodern Positions*. Washington, D.C.: Maisonneuve Press, 1988.

Michaels, Walter Benn. *The Gold Standard and the Logic of Naturalism: American Literature at the Turn of the Century*. Berkeley: University of California Press, 1987.

Miller, Mark Crispin. *Boxed In: The Culture of TV*. Evanston, Ill.: Northwestern University Press, 1988.

Miyoshi, Masao, ed. *Postmodernism and Japan*. Durham, N.C.: Duke University Press, 1989.

Modleski, Tania, ed. *Studies in Entertainment: Critical Approaches to Mass Culture*. Bloomington: Indiana University Press, 1986.

Moi, Toril. *Sexual/Textual Politics: Feminist Literary Theory*. London: Methuen, 1985.

Montefiore, Alan. *Philosophy in France Today*. Cambridge: Cambridge University Press, 1983.

Mudimbe, V. Y. *The Invention of Africa: Gnosis, Philosophy, and the Order of Knowledge*. Bloomington: Indiana University Press, 1988.

Murphy, John W. *Postmodern Social Analysis and Criticism*. New York: Greenwood Press, 1989.

Nelson, Cary, and Lawrence Grossberg, eds. *Marxism and the Interpretation of Culture.* Urbana: University of Illinois Press, 1988.

Newman, Charles Hamilton. *The Post-Modern Aura: The Act of Fiction in an Age of Inflation.* Evanston, Ill.: Northwestern University Press, 1985.

Norberg-Schulz, Christian. *The Concept of Dwelling: On the Way to Figurative Architecture.* New York: Rizolli, 1985.

Norris, Christopher. *The Contest of the Faculties: Philosophy and Theory After Deconstruction.* London: Methuen, 1985.

————. *Paul de Man: Deconstruction and the Critique of Aesthetic Ideology.* London: Routledge, 1988.

Olsen, Lance. *Ellipse of Uncertainty: An Introduction to Postmodern Fantasy.* New York: Greenwood Press, 1987.

Perloff, Marjorie. *The Poetics of Indeterminacy: Rimbaud to Cage.* Evanston, Ill.: Northwestern University Press, 1983.

Peukert, Helmut. *Science, Action, and Fundamental Theology: Toward a Theology of Communicative Action.* Trans. James Bohman. Cambridge, Mass.: MIT Press, 1984.

Portoghesi, Paulo. *Postmodern, the Architecture of the Postmodern Society.* Trans. Ellen Shapiro. New York: Rizolli, 1983.

Poster, Mark. *Foucault, Marxism, and History: Mode of Production Versus Mode of Information.* Cambridge, U. K.: Polity Press, 1984.

Ragland-Sullivan, Ellie. *Jacques Lacan and the Philosophy of Psychoanalysis.* Urbana: University of Illinois Press, 1987.

Rajchman, John. *Michel Foucault: The Freedom of Philosophy.* New York: Columbia University Press, 1985.

Rappaport, Herman. *Milton and the Postmodern.* Lincoln: University of Nebraska Press, 1983.

Relph, E. *Place and placelessness.* London: Pion Limited, 1976.

Ricoeur, Paul. *The Conflict of Interpretations.* Ed. Don Ihde. Evanston, Ill.: Northwestern University Press, 1974.

————. *Hermeneutics and the Human Sciences.* Ed. and Trans. John B. Thomson. Cambridge: Cambridge University Press, 1981.

Rochberg-Halton, Eugene. *Meaning and Modernity: Social Theory in the Pragmatic Mode.* Chicago: University of Chicago Press, 1986.

Rorty, Richard. *Consequences of Pragmatism.* Minneapolis: University of Minnesota Press, 1982.

————. *Contingency, Irony, and Solidarity.* Cambridge: Cambridge University Press, 1989.

————. *Philosophy and the Mirror of Nature.* Princeton: Princeton University Press, 1979.

Rosen, Stanley. *Hermeneutics as Politics.* Oxford: Oxford University Press, 1987.

Rosenfeld, Alvin H. *A Double Dying: Reflections on Holocaust Literature.* Bloomington: Indiana University Press, 1988.

Ross, Andrew, ed. *Universal Abandon? The Politics of Postmodernism.* Minneapolis: University of Minnesota Press, 1988.

Ross, Kristin. *The Emergence of Social Space: Rimbaud and the Paris Commune.* Minneapolis: University of Minnesota Press, 1988.

Rose, Gillian. *Dialectic of Nihilism: Post-Structuralism and Law.* London: Basil Blackwell, 1984.

Ryan, Michael. *Marxism and Deconstruction: A Critical Articulation.* Baltimore: Johns Hopkins University Press, 1982.

Said, Edward. *Orientalism.* New York: Pantheon Books, 1978.

————. *The World, The Text, and The Critic.* Cambridge, Mass.: Harvard University Press, 1983.

Sallis, John. *Spacings: Of Reason and Imagination.* Chicago: University of Chicago Press, 1987.

Sallis, John, ed. *Deconstruction and Philosophy: The Texts of Jacques Derrida.* Chicago: University of Chicago Press, 1987.

Schmidt, Burghardt. *Postmoderne, Stratagien der Vergessens: ein kritischer Bericht.* Darmstadt: Luchterhand, 1986.

Schmidt, Dennis J. *The Ubiquity of the Finite: Hegel, Heidegger, and the Entitlements of Philosophy.* Cambridge, Mass.: MIT Press, 1988.

Scott, Charles. *The Language of Difference.* Atlantic Highlands: Humanities Press, 1989.

Serres, Michel. *The Parasite.* Trans. Lawrence R. Schehr. Baltimore: Johns Hopkins University Press, 1982.

Shapiro, Gary. *Nietzschean Narratives.* Bloomington: Indiana University Press, 1989.

Shapiro, Gary, and Alan Sica, eds. *Hermeneutics: Questions and Prospects.* Amherst: University of Massachusetts Press, 1984.

Shapiro, Michael, ed. *Language and Politics.* New York: New York University, 1984.

Sharrett, Bernard. *Reading Relations: Structures of Literary Production.* Atlantic Highlands: Humanities Press, 1982.

Silliman, Ron. *The New Sentence.* New York: Roof Books, 1987.

Silverman, Hugh J. *Inscriptions: Between Phenomenology and Structuralism.* New York: Routledge, 1987.

———. ed. *Philosophy and Non-Philosophy Since Merleau-Ponty.* New York: Routledge, 1988.

Silverman, Hugh J., and Don Ihde, eds. *Hermeneutics and Deconstruction.* Albany, N.Y.: State University of New York Press, 1985.

Silverman, Hugh J., John Sallis, Thomas M. Seebohm, eds. *Continental Philosophy in America.* Pittsburgh: Duquesne University Press, 1983.

Silverman, Hugh J., and Don Welton, eds. *Postmodernism and Continental Philosophy.* Albany, N.Y.: State University of New York Press, 1985.

Silverman, Kaja. *The Subject of Semiotics.* Oxford: Oxford University Press, 1983.

Sloterdijk, Peter. *Critique of Cynical Reason.* Trans. Michael Eldred. Minneapolis: University of Minnesota Press, 1987.

Smith, Paul. *Discerning the Subject.* Minneapolis: University of Minnesota Press, 1988.

Smyth, John Vignaux. *A Question of Eros: Irony in Sterne, Kierkegaard, and Barthes.* Tallahassee: Florida State University Press, 1986.

Soja, Edward W. *Postmodern Geographies: The Reassertion of Space in Critical Social Theory.* London: Verso, 1989.

Spanos, William. *Martin Heidegger and the Question of Literature: Toward a Postmodern Literary Hermeneutics.* Bloomington: Indiana University Press, 1979.

———. *Repititions: The Postmodern Occasion in Literature and Culture.* Baton Rouge: Louisiana State University Press, 1987.

Spivak, Gayatri Chakravorty. *In Other Worlds: Essays in Cultural Criticism.* London: Methuen, 1987.

Sprinker, Michael. *Imaginary Relations: Aesthetics and Ideology in the Theory of Historical Materialism.* London: Verso, 1987.

Stauth, Georg. *Nietzsche's Dance.* Oxford: Basil Blackwell, 1988.

Strong, Tracy B. *Friedrich Nietzsche and the Politics of Transfiguration*. Berkeley: University of California Press, 1988.

Tafuri, Manfredo. *Architecture and Utopia: Design and Capitalist Development*. Cambridge, Mass.: MIT Press, 1987.

Taylor, Brandon. *Modernism, Postmodernism, Realism: A Critical Perspective for Art*. Winchester: Winchester School of Art Press, 1987.

Taylor, Mark. *Altarity*. Chicago: University of Chicago Press, 1987.

———. *Erring: A Postmodern A/Theology*. Chicago: University of Chicago Press, 1984.

Thiher, Allen. *Words in Reflection: Modern Language Theory and Postmodern Fiction*. Chicago: University of Chicago Press, 1984.

Trachtenberg, Stanley, ed. *The Postmodern Moment: A Handbook of Contemporary Innovation in the Arts*. Westport: Greenwood Press, 1985.

Tyler, Stephen A. *The Unspeakable: Discourse, Dialogue, and Rhetoric in the Postmodern World*. Madison: University of Wisconsin Press, 1987.

Ulmer, Gregory L. *Applied Grammatology: Post(e)-Pedagogy from Jacques Derrida to Joseph Beuys*. Baltimore: Johns Hopkins University Press, 1985.

Unger, Roberto Mangabeira. *The Critical Legal Studies Movement*. Cambridge, Mass.: Harvard University Press, 1983.

Vaneigem, Raoul. *The Revolution of Everyday Life*. Trans. Donald Nicholson-Smith. London: Left Bank Books, 1983.

Vattimo, Gianni. *The End of Modernity: Nihilism and Hermeneutics in Postmodern Culture*. Trans. Jon R. Snyder. Baltimore: Johns Hopkins University Press, 1989.

Virilio, Paul. *Speed and Politics: An Essay on Dromology*. Trans. Mark Polizzotti. New York: Semiotext(e), 1986.

Wachterhauser, Brice R., ed. *Hermeneutics and Modern Philosophy*. Albany, N.Y.: State University of New York Press, 1986.

Wallis, Brian. *Art After Modernism: rethinking representation*. New York: New York Museum of Modern Art, 1984.

Warren, Michael. *Nietzsche and Political Thought*. Cambridge, Mass.: MIT Press, 1988.

Wellmer, Albrecht. *Zur Dialektik von Moderne und Postmoderne: Vernunftkritik nach Adorno*. Frankfurt am Main: Suhrkamp, 1985.

West, Cornell, and John Rajchman, eds. *Post-Analytic Philosophy*. New York: Columbia University Press, 1985.

White, Hayden. *Tropics of Discourse*. Baltimore: Johns Hopkins University Press, 1978.

Wiseman, Mary. *The Ecstasies of Roland Barthes*. London: Routledge, 1989.

Wright, Elizabeth. *Postmodern Brecht: A Re-Presentation*. London: Routledge, 1989.

Notes on Contributors

PHILIP AUSLANDER teaches in the English Department of the Georgia Institute of Technology. He is the author of *The New York School Poets as Playwrights: Ashbery, O'Hara, Koch, Schuyler and the Visual Arts* (1989) and of articles on performance and theory in *Theatre Journal, The Drama Review,* and elsewhere. He is currently working on a book on the politics of postmodern performance.

ROGER BELL has worked as a designer and is a lecturer in the Department of Philosophy at Sonoma State University, California. He is currently completing a collection of essays on postmodernism drawn from philosophy, literature, film, art, and architecture, and is working on a book about Derrida and the problem of writing.

CAROL BERNSTEIN is Associate Professor of English at Bryn Mawr College. Her publications include *Precarious Enchantment: A Reading of Meredith's Poetry.* She has recently completed a book on the representation of the city in the nineteenth century English novel.

GERALD BRUNS is the William and Hazel White Professor of English at the University of Notre Dame. He is the author of *Modern Poetry and the Idea of Language: A Critical and Historical Study* (1974); *Inventions: Writing, Textuality, and Understanding in Literary History* (1982); and *Heidegger's Estrangements: Language, Truth and Poetry in the Later Writings* (1989). He is currently completing a study of *Hermeneutics Ancient and Modern.*

ANTHONY J. CASCARDI is Associate Professor of Comparative Literature at the University of California, Berkeley. His most recent books are *The Bounds of Reason: Cervantes, Dostoevsky, Flaubert* and (as editor) *Literature and the Question of Philosophy.* He is at work on a study of modernity.

EDWARD CASEY is a Professor of Philosophy at the State University of New York at Stony Brook. He is the author of *Imagining* (1979) and *Remembering* (1987) and is at work on a book to be titled *Getting Back into Place.*

ANTONY EASTHOPE teaches Literature and Culture Studies at Manchester Polytechnic. His books include *Poetry as Discourse* (1983), *The Masculine Myth in Popular Culture* (1986), *British Post-Structuralism* (1988), and *Poetry*

351

and Phantasy (1989). He is working on a book on cultural studies and plans another to be called *Englishness Today: Studies in a Decadent Culture.*

STEVE FULLER is Assistant Professor in the Center for the Study of Science in Society, Virginia Polytechnic Institute. He is the executive editor of *Social Epistemology: A Journal of Knowledge, Culture, and Policy.* He has written *Social Epistemology* (Indiana, 1988) and *Philosophy of Science and Its Discontents* (Westview, 1989).

DIANE GHIRARDO teaches in the School of Architecture at the University of Southern California. She has written several articles on Italian architecture and postmodernism, and has translated Aldo Rossi's *The Architecture of the City* (1982). Professor Ghirardo is at work on a book, *Italian and American New Towns Between the Wars.*

JOHN C. GILMOUR is Professor of Philosophy at Alfred University. His publications include *Picturing the World* (1986) and a number of articles in the philosophy of art. His book *Fire on the Earth: Anselm Kiefer and the Postmodern World* will appear in 1990.

TIMOTHY GOULD teaches philosophy at Metropolitan State College in Denver. He has written about issues of aesthetics and action in Kant, Wordsworth, Nietzsche, and Freud. His essay "Where the Action Is" recently appeared in *The Senses of Stanley Cavell,* a special issue of the *Bucknell Review.*

JOHN JOHNSTON is Assistant Professor of English at Emory University. He has translated works by Foucault and Baudrillard and is the author of several essays on contemporary literature and literary theory.

VIRGIL LOKKE is Professor Emeritus of Comparative Literature at Purdue University. His recent publications include "Narratology, Obsolescent Paradigms and 'Scientific' Poetics" in *Modern Fiction Studies* (1987). He is a co-editor of two collections to which he has also contributed: *Ruined Eden of the Present: Hawthorne, Melville and Poe* (1980) and *The Current in Criticism* (1987). Professor Lokke is at work on a series of studies concerning the linguistic/extra-linguistic binary.

BILL MARTIN is completing a dissertation in philosophy at the University of Kansas; it is entitled "Matrix and Line: Derrida and the Possibilities of Post-secular Social Theory." He has recently published a number of papers including "The Feminist Path to Postmodernity: *To the Lighthouse*" (*Philosophy and Literature,* 1989), "Politics of Irony in Paul de Man" (*Canadian Journal of Political and Social Theory,* 1989) and "How Marxism Became Analytic" (*Journal of Philosophy,* 1989).

STEPHEN MELVILLE is Associate Professor of English at Syracuse University. He has published *Philosophy Beside Itself* (1986) as well as a number of essays on literary theory and contemporary art. He is now completing a book that deals with these subjects.

JOHH O'NEILL is a Distinguished Research Professor of Sociology at York University and an Affiliate of the Centre for Comparative Literature at the University of Toronto. He is the author of *Sociology as a Skin Trade* (1972), *Making Sense Together* (1974), *For Marx Against Althusser* (1982), *Essaying Montaigne* (1982), *Five Bodies* (1985), and *The Communicative Body: Studies in Communicative Philosophy, Politics and Psychology* (1989). He is Co-editor of the international quarterly, *Philosophy of the Social Sciences*.

STEPHEN DAVID ROSS is Professor of Philosophy and Comparative Literature at the State University of New York at Binghamton. He is the author of several books, including *Literature and Philosophy* (1969), *Transition to an Ordinal Metaphysics* (1980), *A Theory of Art: Inexhaustibility by Contrast* (1982), *Metaphysical Aporia and Philosophical Heresy* (1989), and *Inexhaustibility and Human Being: An Essay on Locality*, the first volume of a trilogy.

ALAN D. SCHRIFT is Assistant Professor of Philosophy at Grinnell College. In addition to publishing a number of articles on Nietzsche and contemporary French and German philosophy, he is co-editor of *The Hermeneutic Tradition: From Ast to Ricoeur*, and *Transforming the Hermeneutic Context: From Nietzsche to Nancy* (both SUNY Press, 1989). He has recently completed a manuscript on *Nietzsche and the Question of Interpretation: Between Hermeneutics and Deconstruction*.

RICHARD SHUSTERMAN, Associate Professor of Philosophy at Temple University, has published numerous articles in literary criticism, literary theory, and hermeneutics. He wrote *The Object of Literary Criticism* (1984), and *T. S. Eliot and the Philosophy of Criticism* (1988). He has edited *Analytic Aesthetics* (1989) and is currently at work on a book to be titled *Art, Theory, Praxis: Pragmatist Aesthetics for Postmodern Conditions*.

MARY BITTNER WISEMAN is Professor of Philosophy and Comparative Literature at the Graduate School of the City University of New York and at Brooklyn College. She is the author of many articles in aesthetics and of *The Ecstasies of Roland Barthes* (1989).

About the Editor

Gary Shapiro is Professor of Philosophy at the University of Kansas. He is the author of *Nietzschean Narratives* (1989) and the co-editor of *Hermeneutics: Questions and Prospects*. He has published a number of essays on aesthetics, continental philosophy, and the history of philosophy that have appeared in *New Literary History, Arts Magazine, History and Theory* and elsewhere; he is completing a book on philosophy as text.

Index